lock Bones 6

Miki & Sherdog & Takeru

Story: Yuma Ando **Art: Yuki Sato**

CHARACTERS

Takeru Wajima

A nineteen-year-old rookie police officer. He is Sherdog's owner and the one person who can understand him. He realized he wanted to be a police officer while solving difficult cases with Sherdog. He has a crush on his childhood friend Miki.

Sherdog

The mixed-breed puppy that Takeru adopted. His true identity is that of the world-famous detective, Sherlock Holmes. When he has the Wajima family's heirloom pipe in his mouth, he can speak to Takeru. He solves crimes with Takeru, learning about the modern world in the process.

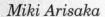

Miki Arisaka

Takeru's friend since childhood, and currently a freshman in college. An aspiring journalist, she works part-time at a newspaper company.

Miki Arisaka

Takeru and Miki's classmate from high school. Her reputation was once saved by Takeru. She became a police officer, possibly to be with Takeru.

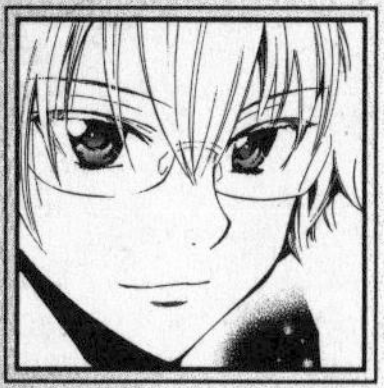

Kento Munakata

A career detective at the London Police Department the same age as Takeru. An elite freshly back from New York, he boasts of his experience whenever he gets the chance.

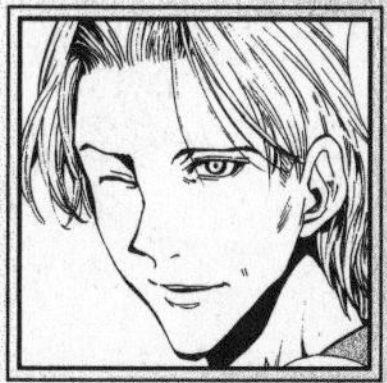

Muneo Tsuzuki

A popular newscaster, famous for charming older women. He killed his wife in a fight about an affair he was having, and in a burst of inspiration, he plotted to disguise the murder and get away with the perfect crime. He is also a wine enthusiast.

Members of the Wajima Family

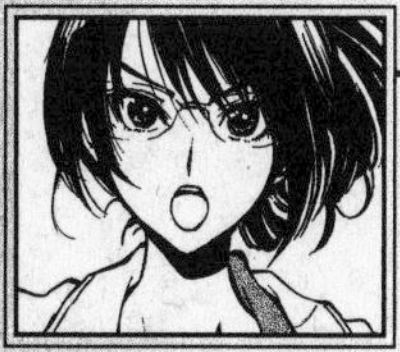

Airin Wajima

Takeru's sister, an inspector in the Violent Crimes Division, and a rather sexy woman. Sherdog calls her Irene.

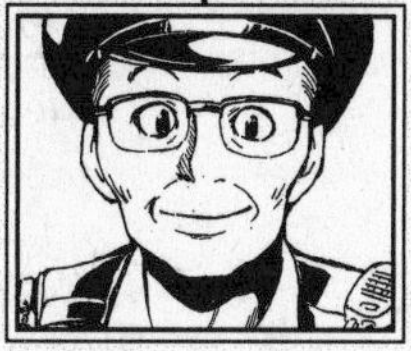

Kōsuke Wajima

Takeru's father. A sergeant in the police force.

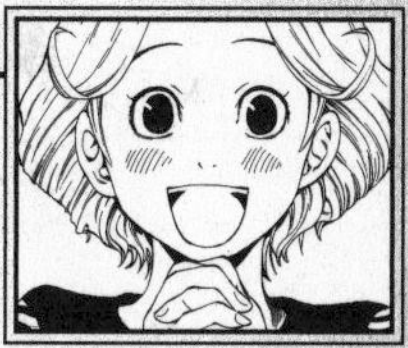

Satoko Wajima

Takeru's mother. She really hates it when Sherdog sits in her favorite rocking chair.

THE STORY SO FAR

The puppy Sherdog—reincarnation of Sherlock Holmes—and his owner Takeru Wajima team up to solve tough cases!! Soon after graduating police academy and becoming a police officer, Takeru is faced with his very first case. The popular anchorman Muneo Tsuzuki has killed his wife and is trying to play it off as someone else's murder!

STORY

CONTENTS

Case 8: ⚜ Requiem for a New Beginning, Part 3

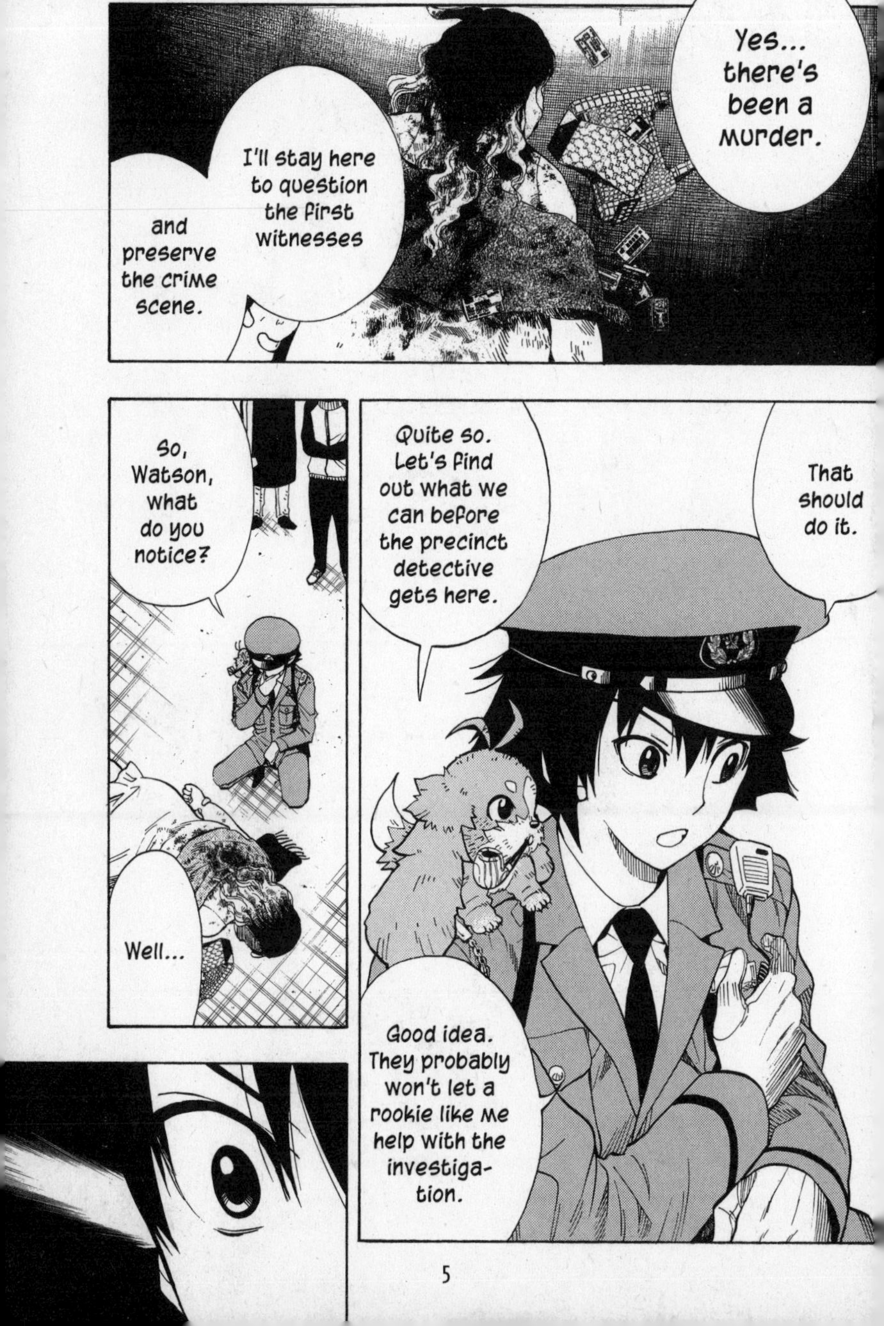

Yes... there's been a murder.
I'll stay here to question the first witnesses
and preserve the crime scene.
That should do it.
Quite so. Let's find out what we can before the precinct detective gets here.
Good idea. They probably won't let a rookie like me help with the investiga-tion.
So, Watson, what do you notice?
Well...

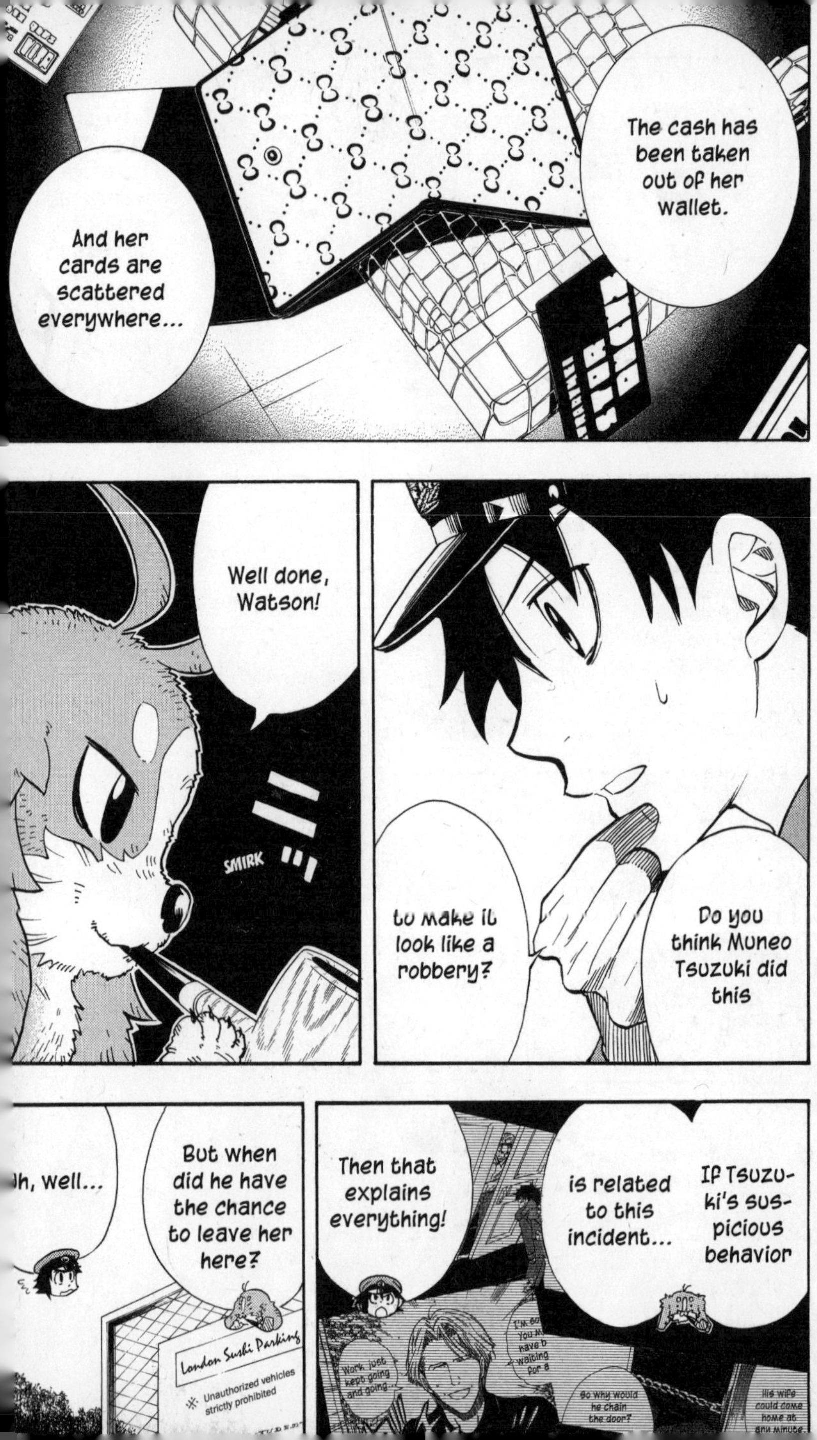
The cash has been taken out of her wallet.
And her cards are scattered everywhere...
Do you think Muneo Tsuzuki did this
to make it look like a robbery?
Well done, Watson!
SMIRK
If Tsuzuki's suspicious behavior
is related to this incident...
Then that explains everything!
His wife could come home at any minute...
So why would he chain the door?
Work just kept going and going...
But when did he have the chance to leave her here?
h, well...
London Sushi Parking
※ Unauthorized vehicles strictly prohibited

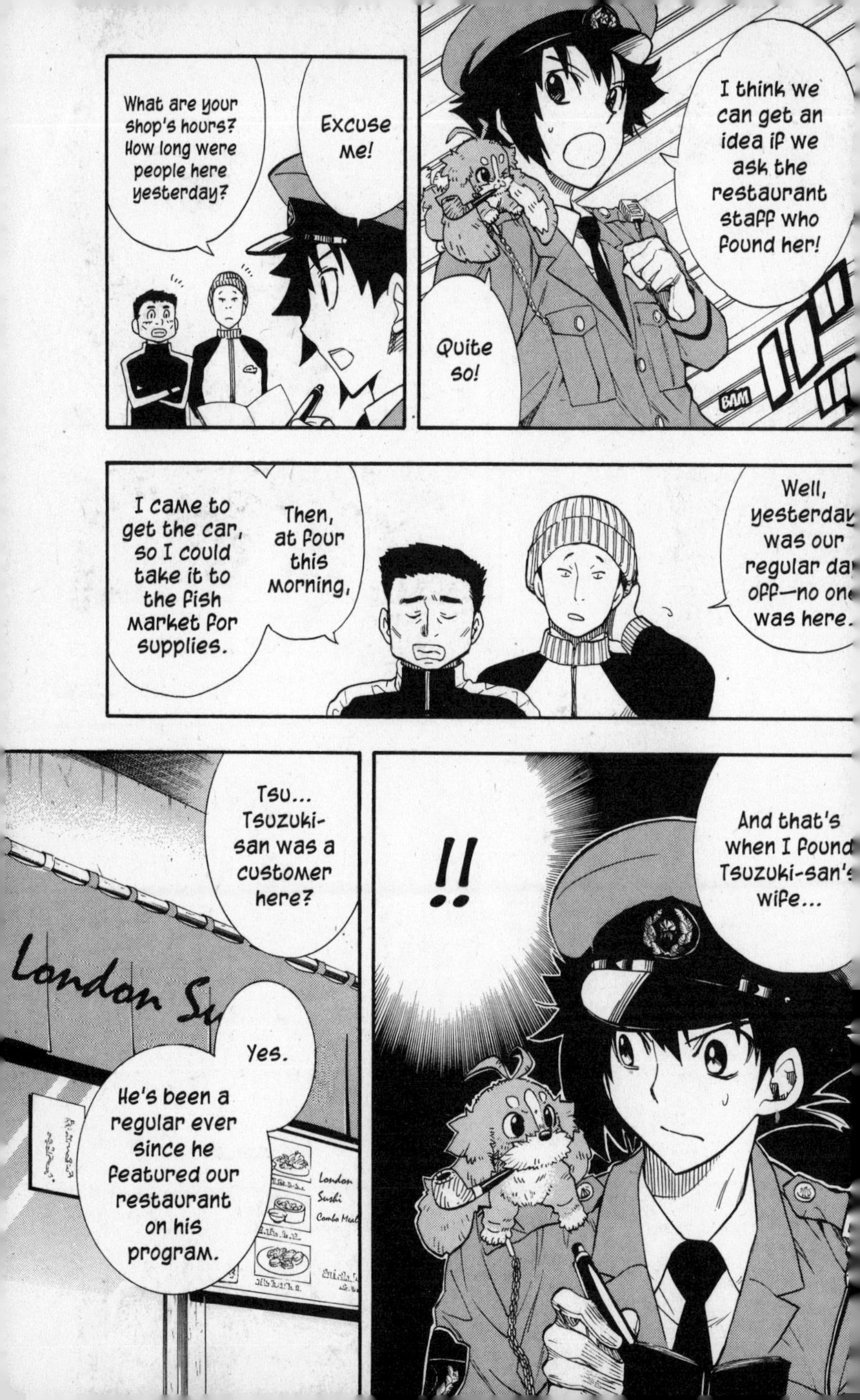
I think we can get an idea if we ask the restaurant staff who found her!
BAM
Quite so!
Excuse me!
What are your shop's hours? How long were people here yesterday?
Well, yesterda was our regular da off—no on was here.
Then, at four this morning,
I came to get the car, so I could take it to the fish market for supplies.
And that's when I found Tsuzuki-san's wife...
!!
Tsu... Tsuzuki-san was a customer here?
London Su
Yes.
He's been a regular ever since he featured our restaurant on his program.
London Sushi Combo Meal

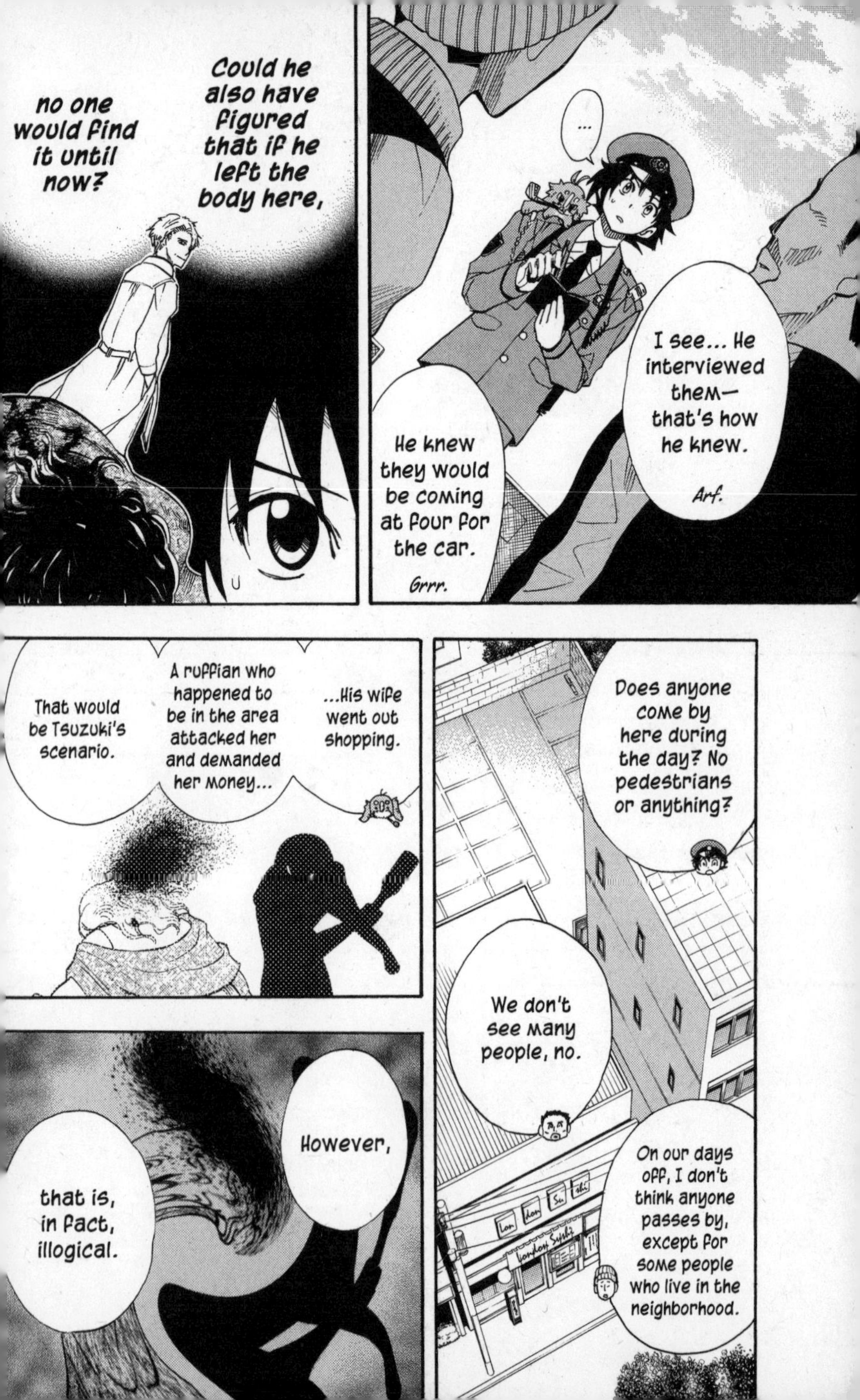
...
I see... He interviewed them—that's how he knew.
Arf.
He knew they would be coming at four for the car.
Grrr.
Could he also have figured that if he left the body here,
no one would find it until now?
Does anyone come by here during the day? No pedestrians or anything?
Lon don Su shi
We don't see many people, no.
On our days off, I don't think anyone passes by, except for some people who live in the neighborhood.
...His wife went out shopping.
A ruffian who happened to be in the area attacked her and demanded her money...
That would be Tsuzuki's scenario.
However,
that is, in fact, illogical.

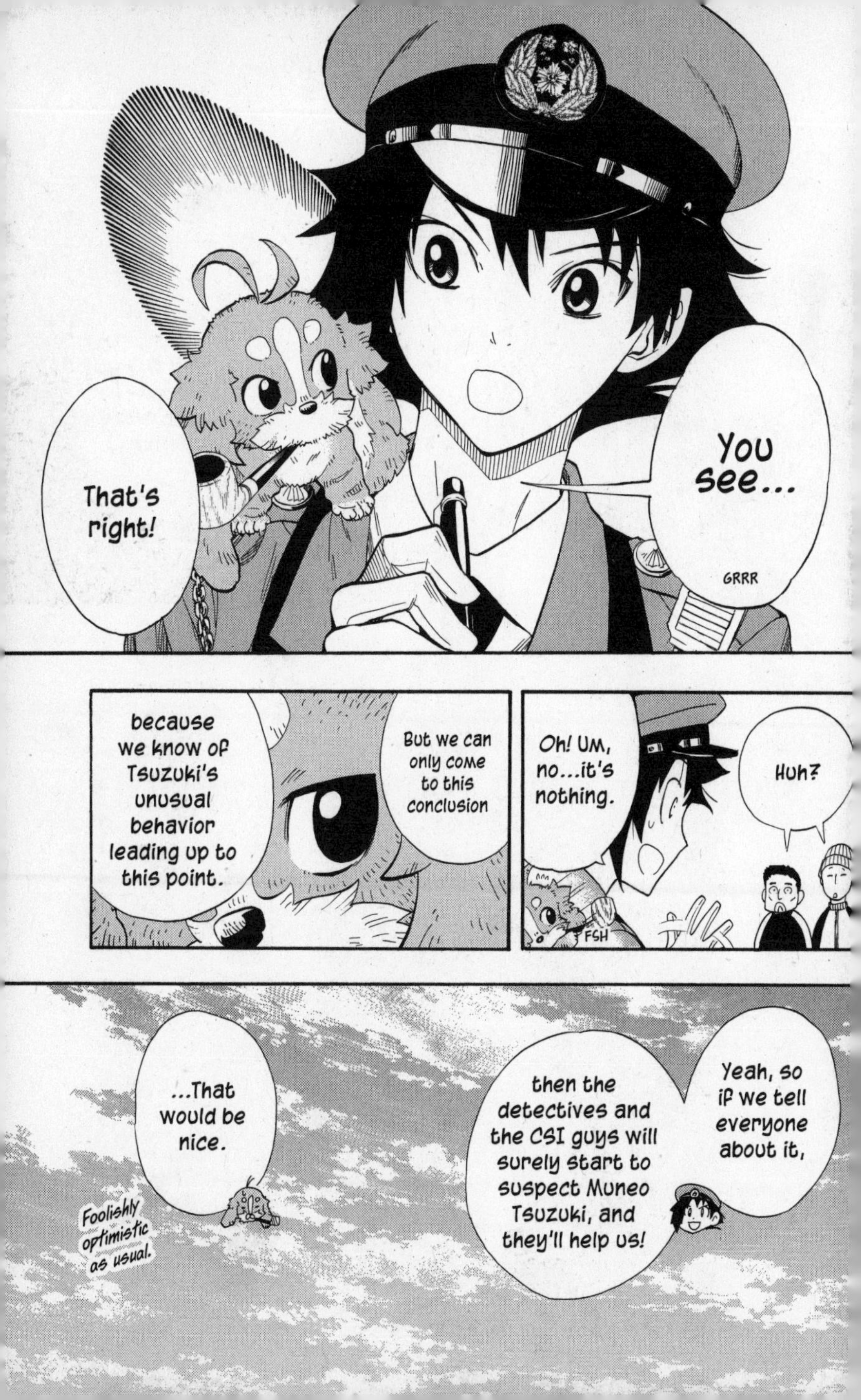

You see...
GRRR
That's right!
Huh?
Oh! Um, no...it's nothing.
FSH
But we can only come to this conclusion
because we know of Tsuzuki's unusual behavior leading up to this point.
Yeah, so if we tell everyone about it,
then the detectives and the CSI guys will surely start to suspect Muneo Tsuzuki, and they'll help us!
...That would be nice.
Foolishly optimistic as usual.

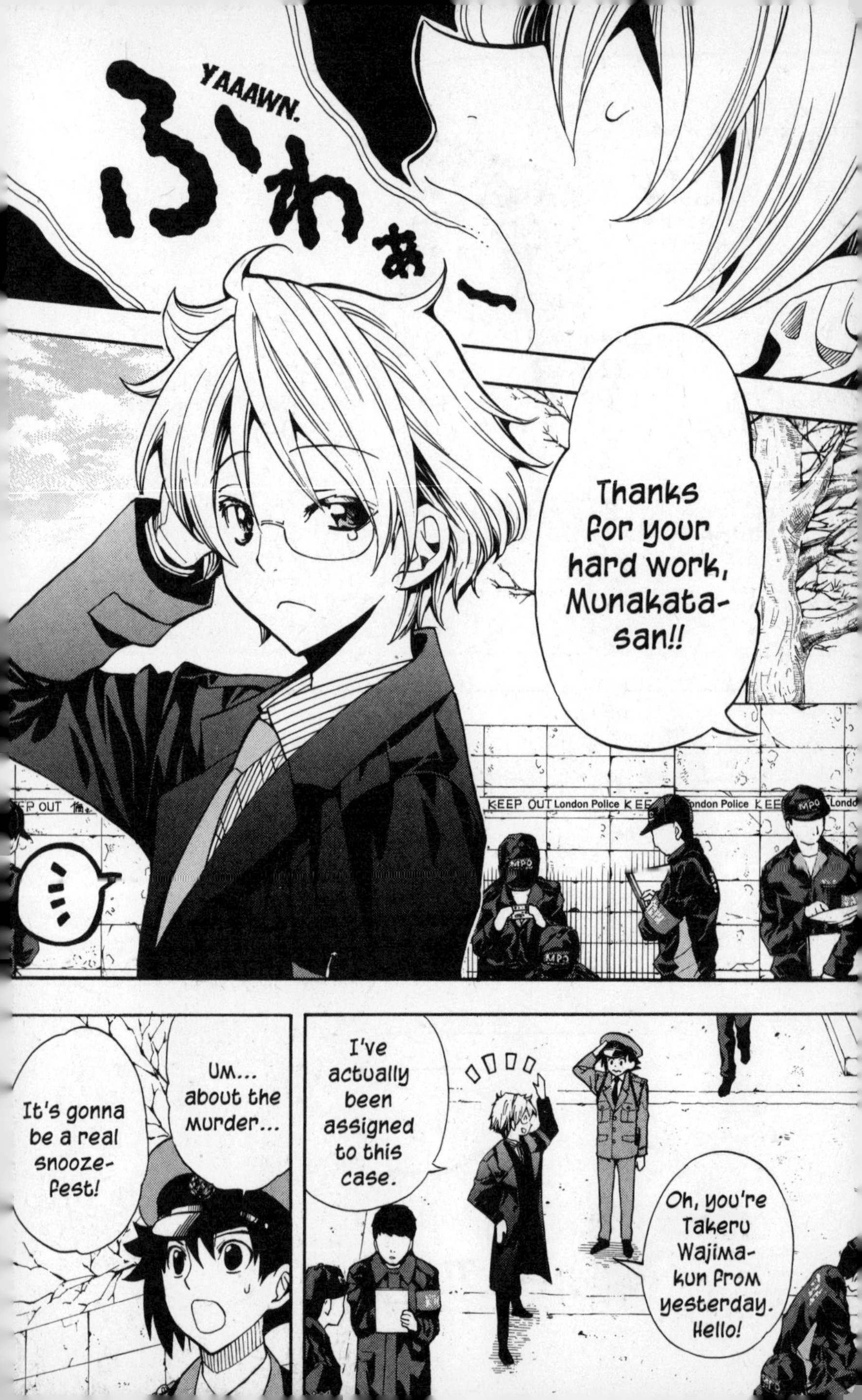
YAAAWN.
ふわぁ～
Thanks for your hard work, Munakata-san!!
KEEP OUT London Police KEEP OUT London Police
Oh, you're Takeru Wajima-kun from yesterday. Hello!
I've actually been assigned to this case.
Um... about the murder...
It's gonna be a real snooze-fest!

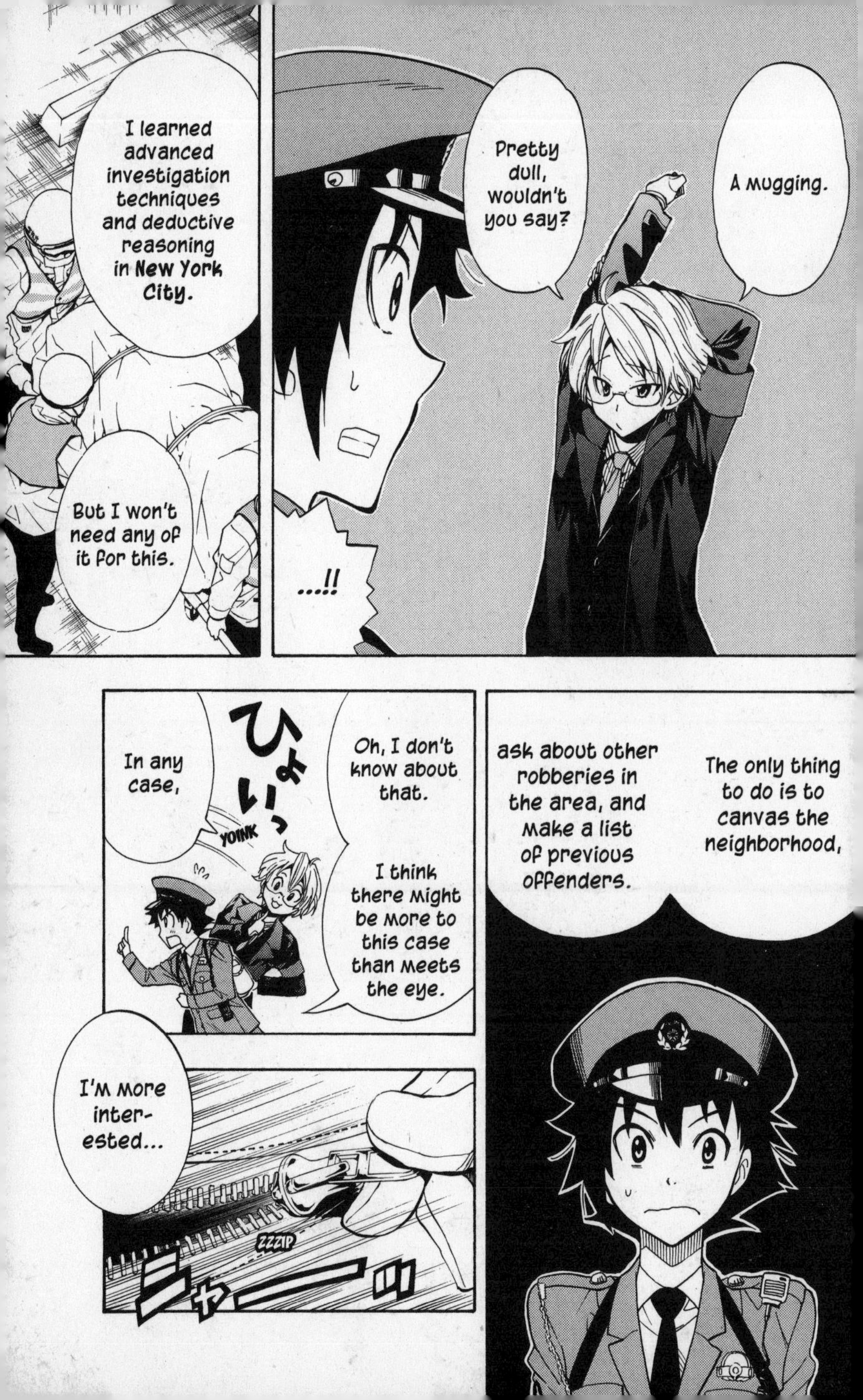

A mugging.
Pretty dull, wouldn't you say?
...!!
I learned advanced investigation techniques and deductive reasoning in New York City.
But I won't need any of it for this.
The only thing to do is to canvas the neighborhood,
ask about other robberies in the area, and make a list of previous offenders.
Oh, I don't know about that.
I think there might be more to this case than meets the eye.
ひょいっ
YOINK
In any case,
I'm more interested...
ZZZIP

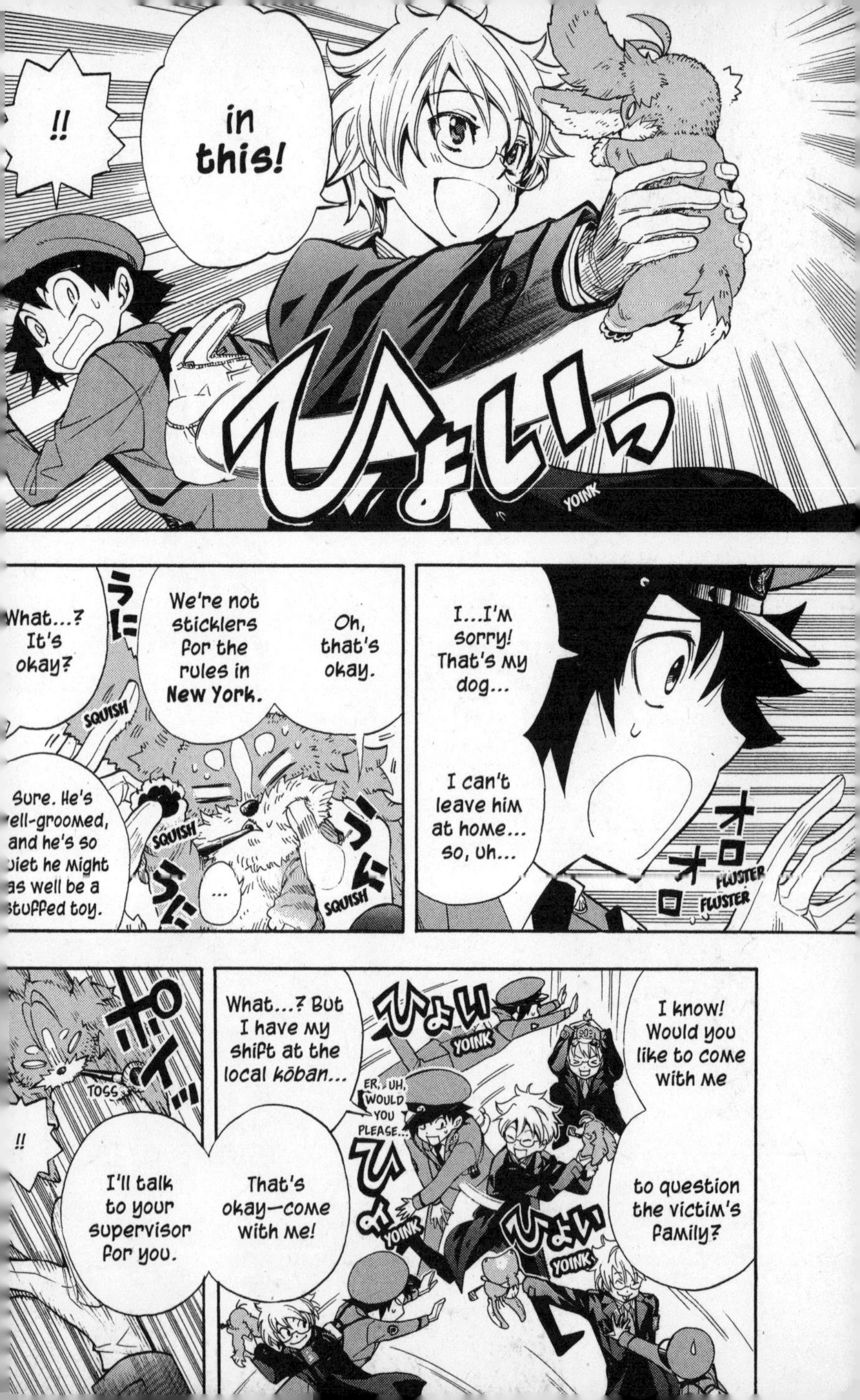
in this!
ひょいっ
YOINK
!!
I...I'm sorry! That's my dog...
I can't leave him at home... so, uh...
オロオロ
FLUSTER FLUSTER
Oh, that's okay.
We're not sticklers for the rules in New York.
What...? It's okay?
うに
SQUISH
うに
SQUISH
うに
SQUISH
...
Sure. He's ell-groomed, and he's so uiet he might as well be a stuffed toy.
I know! Would you like to come with me
to question the victim's family?
ひょい
YOINK
What...? But I have my shift at the local kōban...
ER, UH, WOULD YOU PLEASE...
ひょい
YOINK
ひょい
YOINK
That's okay—come with me!
I'll talk to your supervisor for you.
ポイッ
TOSS
!!

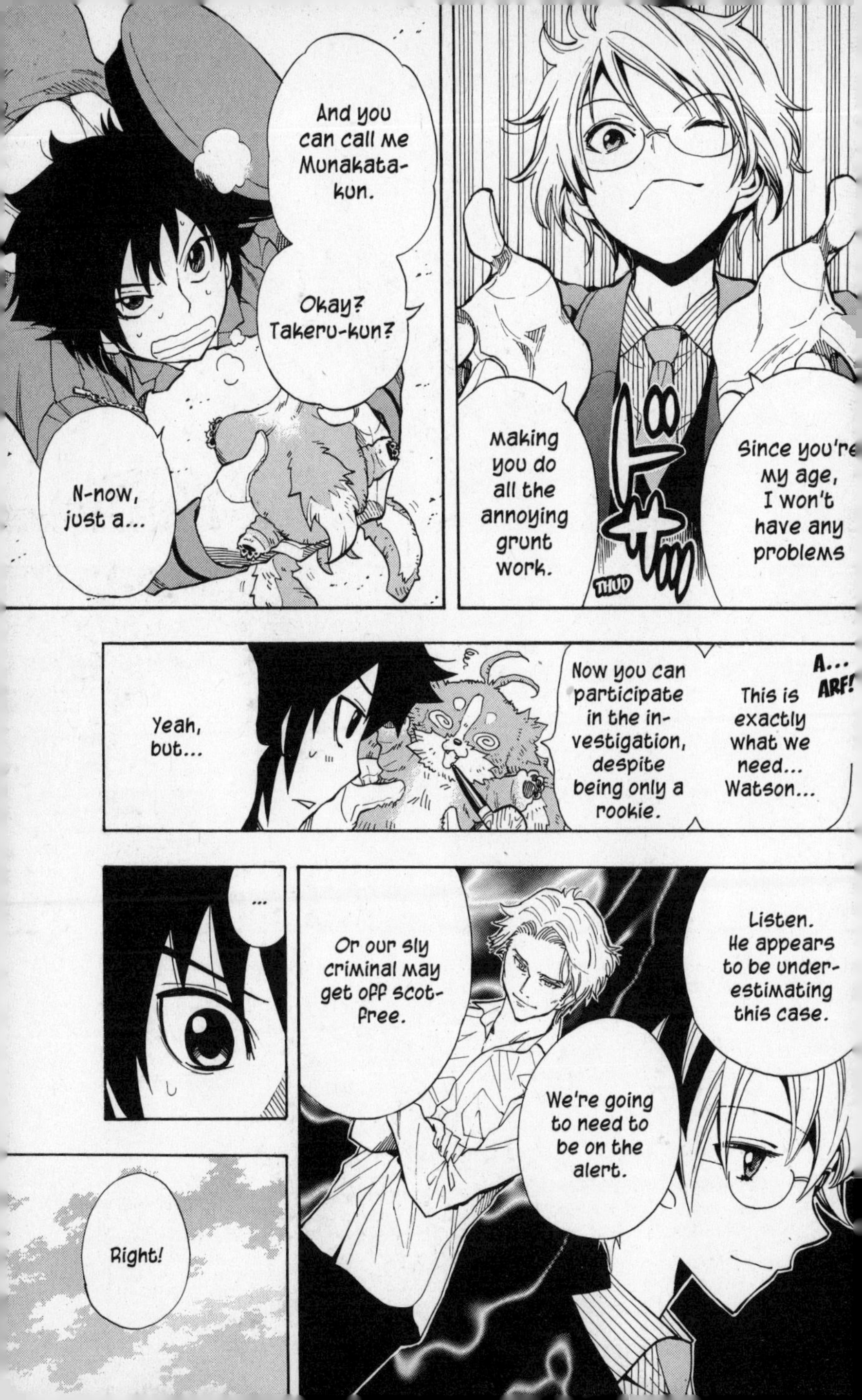
Since you're my age, I won't have any problems
Making you do all the annoying grunt work.
THUD
And you can call me Munakata-kun.
Okay? Takeru-kun?
N-now, just a...
This is exactly what we need... Watson...
A... ARF!
Now you can participate in the investigation, despite being only a rookie.
Yeah, but...
Listen. He appears to be under-estimating this case.
We're going to need to be on the alert.
Or our sly criminal may get off scot-free.
...
Right!

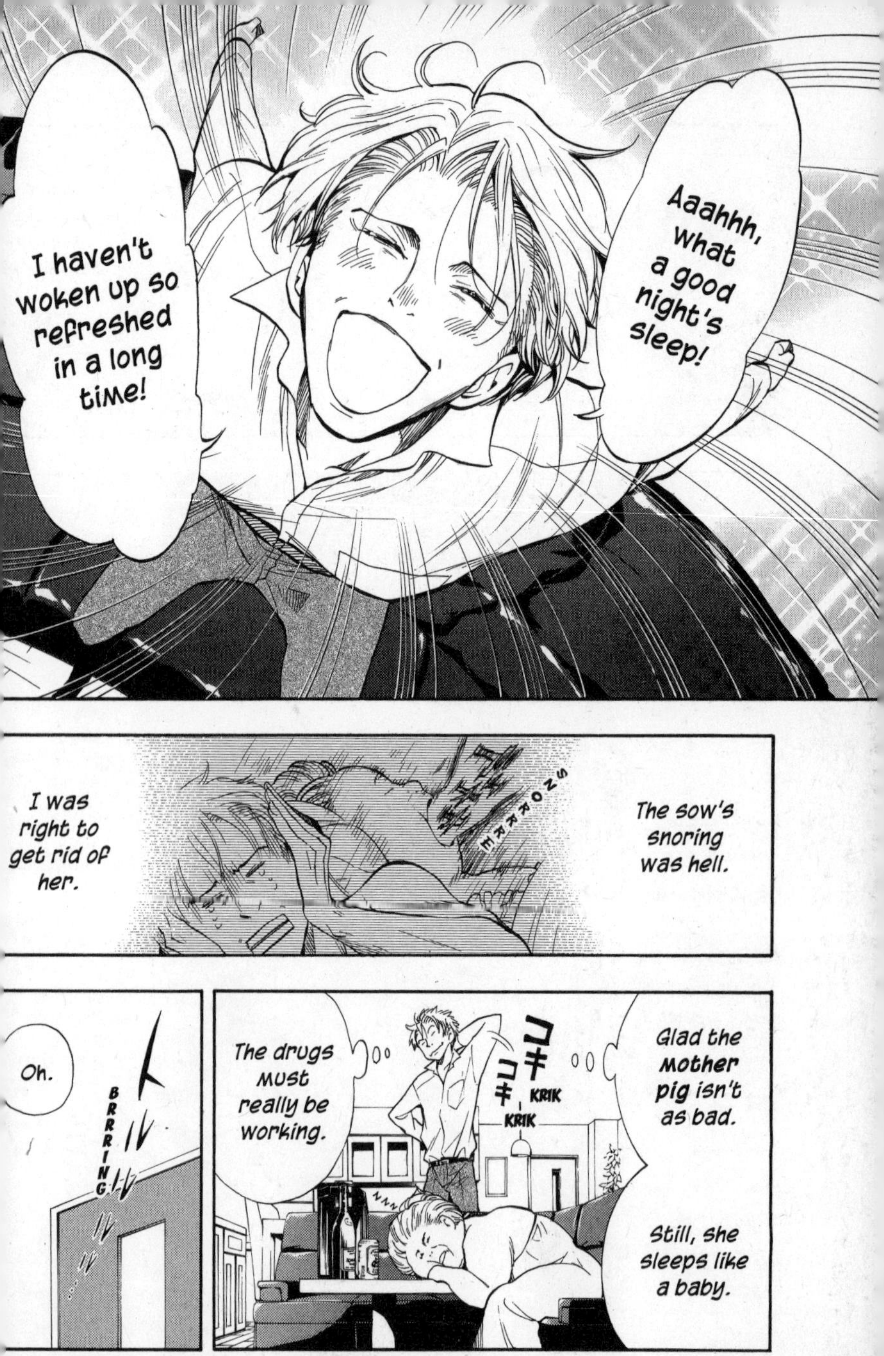
Aaahhh, what a good night's sleep!
I haven't woken up so refreshed in a long time!
The sow's snoring was hell.
SNORRRE
I was right to get rid of her.
Glad the mother pig isn't as bad.
KRIK
KRIK
The drugs must really be working.
Still, she sleeps like a baby.
NNN
BRRRING
Oh.

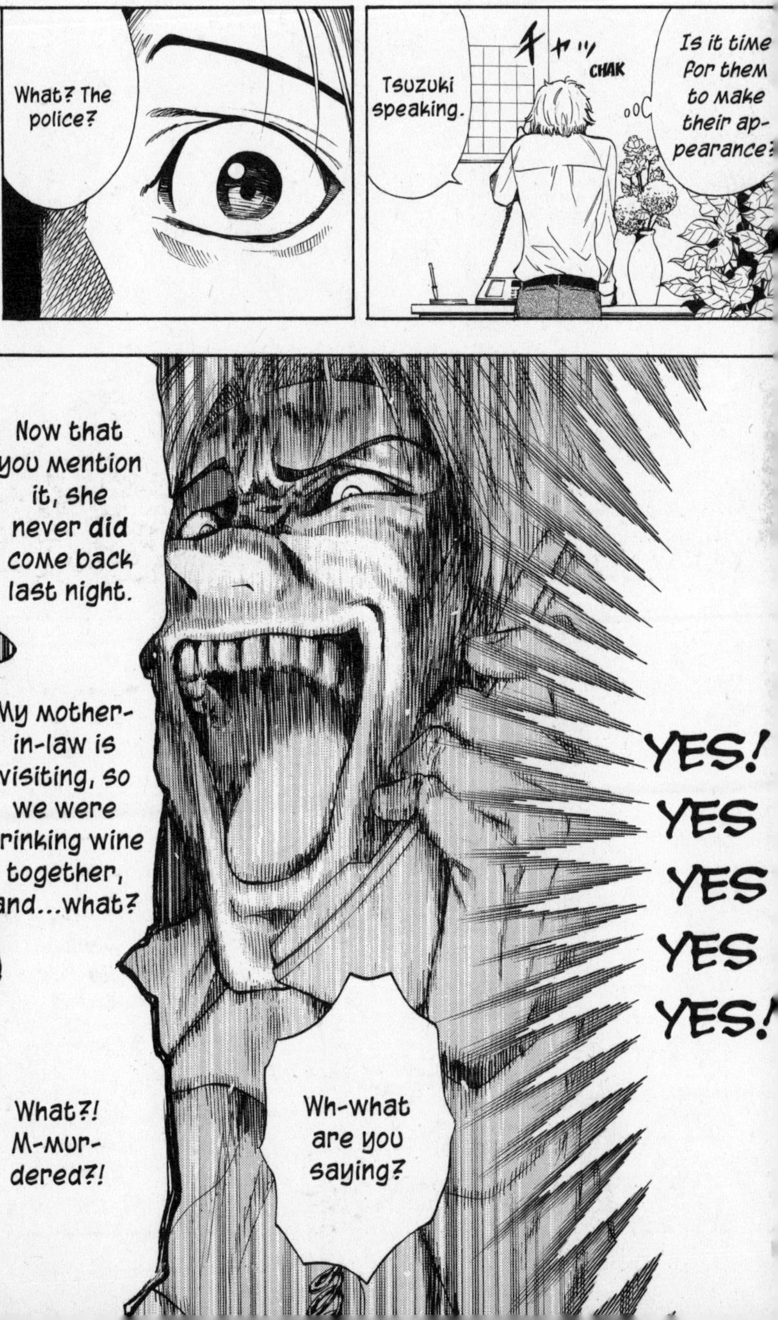
Is it time for them to make their appearance?
チャッ
CHAK
Tsuzuki speaking.
What? The police?
YES! YES YES YES YES!
Now that you mention it, she never did come back last night.
My mother-in-law is visiting, so we were drinking wine together, and...what?
Wh-what are you saying?
What?! M-murdered?!

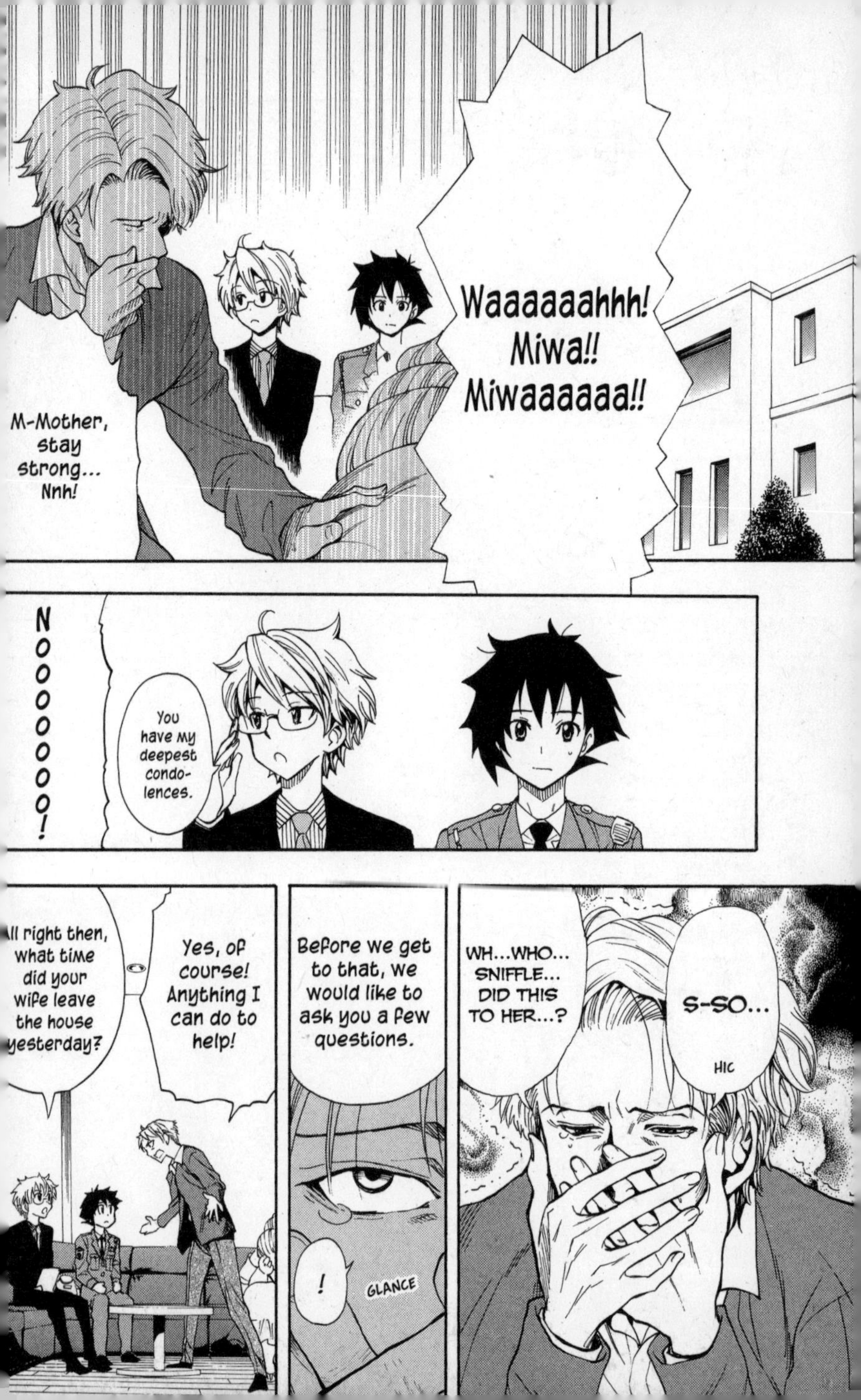
Waaaaaaahhh! Miwa!! Miwaaaaaaa!!
M-Mother, stay strong... Nnh!
You have my deepest condo-lences.
NOOOOOOOOO!
S-SO...
HIC
WH...WHO... SNIFFLE... DID THIS TO HER...?
Before we get to that, we would like to ask you a few questions.
!
GLANCE
Yes, of course! Anything I can do to help!
ll right then, what time did your wife leave the house yesterday?

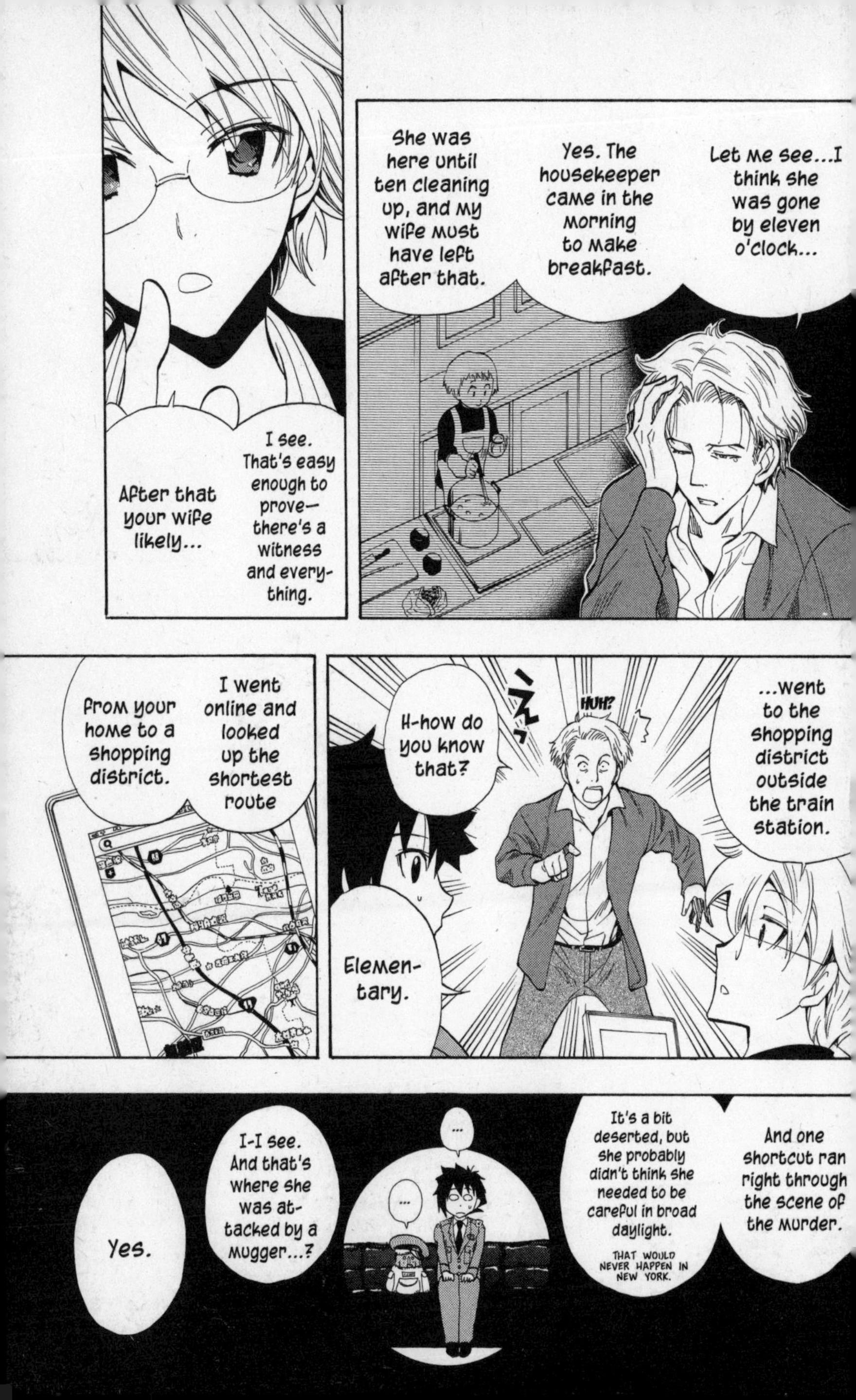
Let me see...I think she was gone by eleven o'clock...
Yes. The housekeeper came in the morning to make breakfast.
She was here until ten cleaning up, and my wife must have left after that.
I see. That's easy enough to prove—there's a witness and everything.
After that your wife likely...
...went to the shopping district outside the train station.
HUH?
H-how do you know that?
Elementary.
I went online and looked up the shortest route
from your home to a shopping district.
And one shortcut ran right through the scene of the murder.
It's a bit deserted, but she probably didn't think she needed to be careful in broad daylight.
THAT WOULD NEVER HAPPEN IN NEW YORK.
...
...
I-I see. And that's where she was attacked by a mugger...?
Yes.

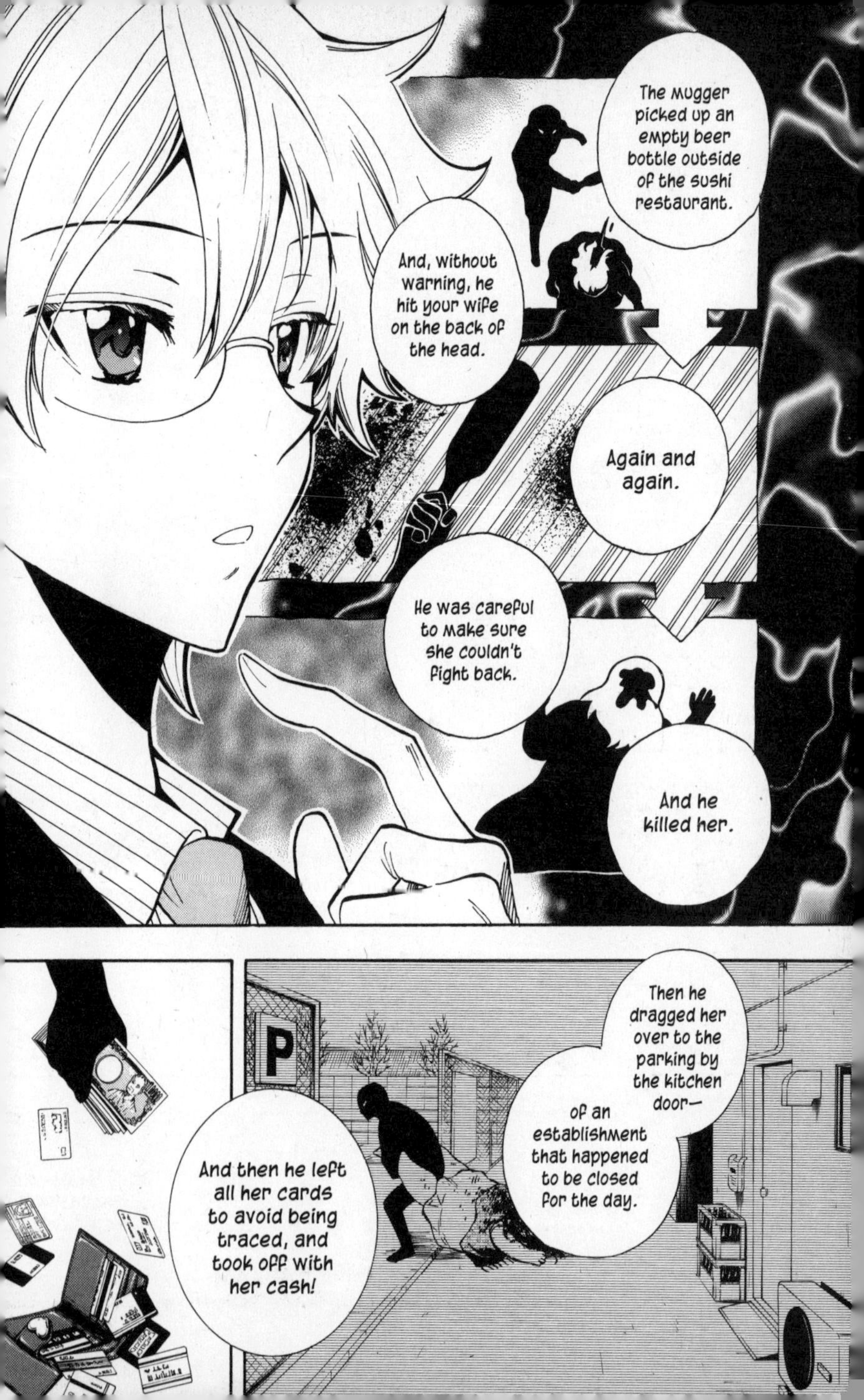
The mugger picked up an empty beer bottle outside of the sushi restaurant.
And, without warning, he hit your wife on the back of the head.
Again and again.
He was careful to make sure she couldn't fight back.
And he killed her.
Then he dragged her over to the parking by the kitchen door—
of an establishment that happened to be closed for the day.
P
And then he left all her cards to avoid being traced, and took off with her cash!

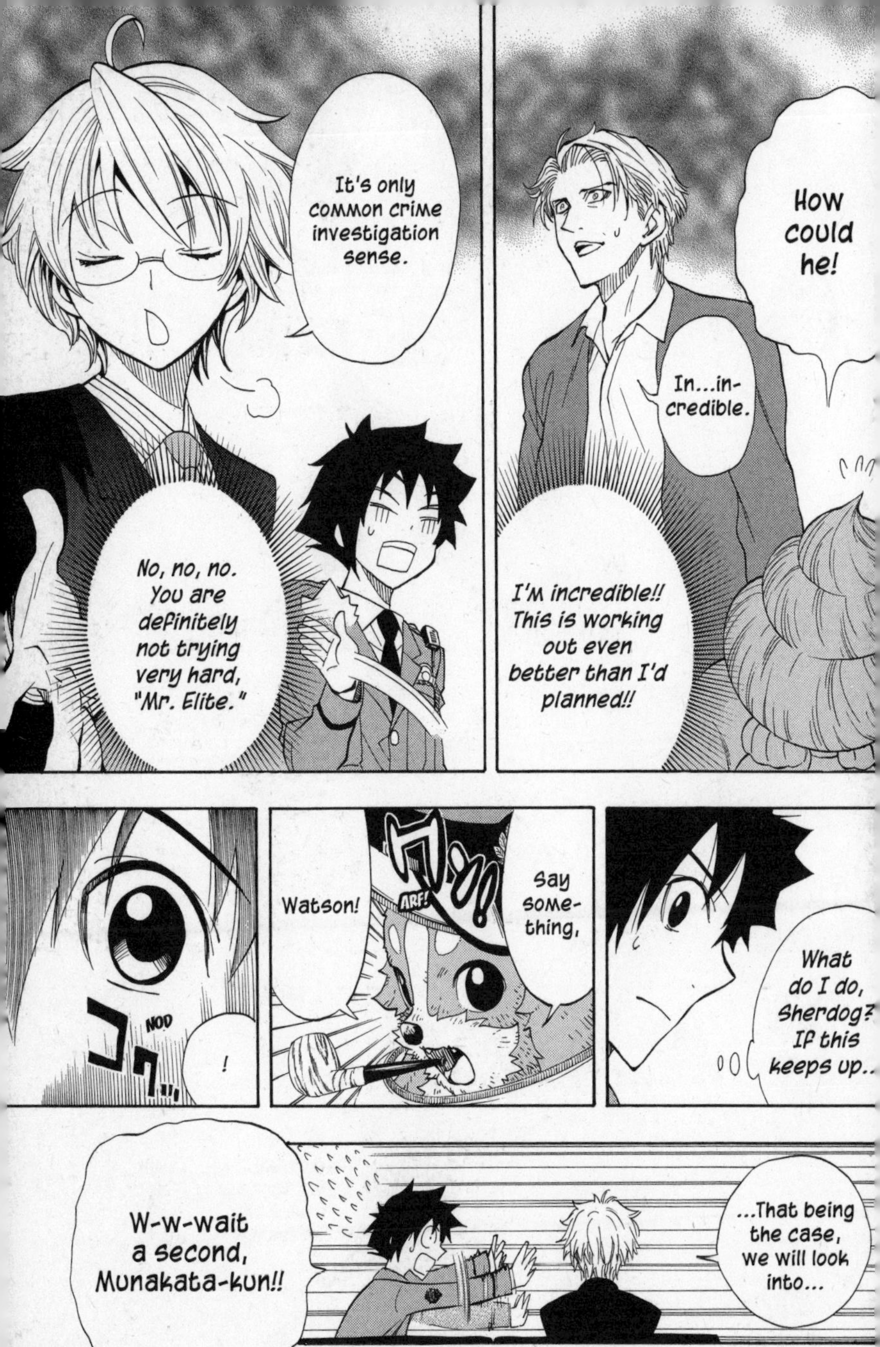
How could he!
In...in-credible.
I'm incredible!! This is working out even better than I'd planned!!
It's only common crime investigation sense.
No, no, no. You are definitely not trying very hard, "Mr. Elite."
What do I do, Sherdog? If this keeps up...
Say some-thing,
ARF!
Watson!
!
NOD
...That being the case, we will look into...
W-w-wait a second, Munakata-kun!!

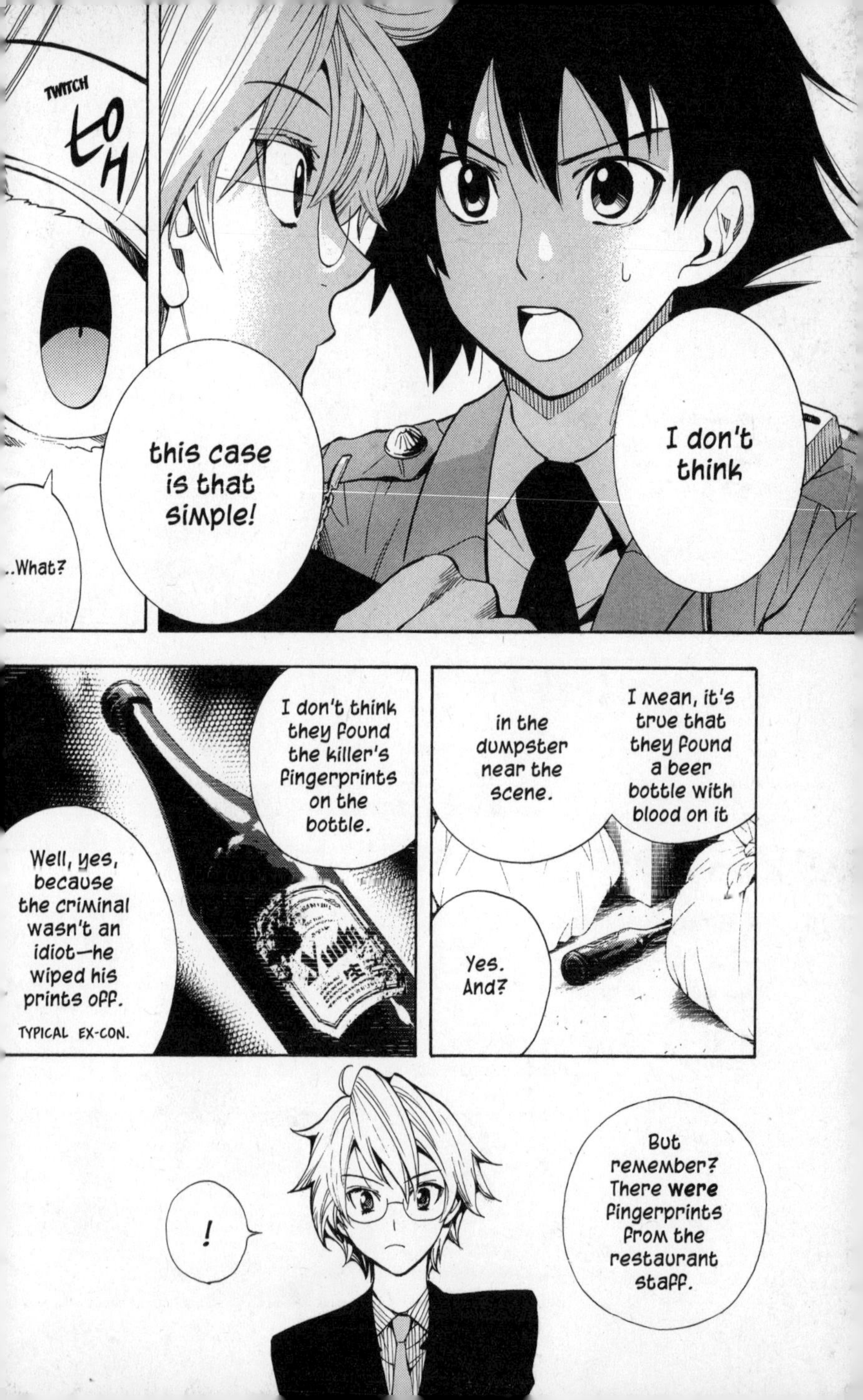
I don't think
this case is that simple!
TWITCH
..What?
I mean, it's true that they found a beer bottle with blood on it
in the dumpster near the scene.
Yes. And?
I don't think they found the killer's fingerprints on the bottle.
Well, yes, because the criminal wasn't an idiot—he wiped his prints off.
TYPICAL EX-CON.
But remember? There **were** fingerprints from the restaurant staff.
!

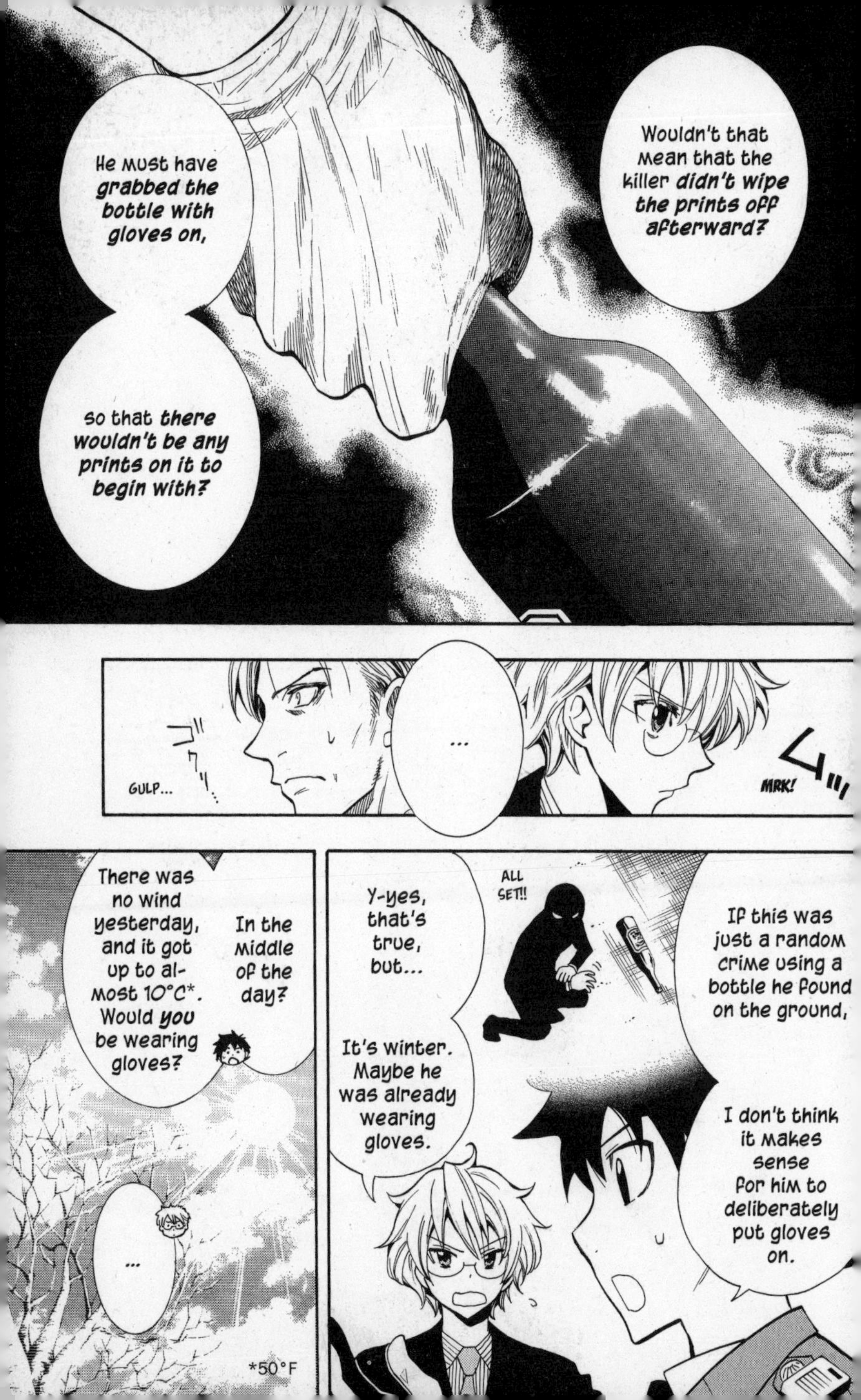
Wouldn't that mean that the killer didn't wipe the prints off afterward?
He must have grabbed the bottle with gloves on,
so that there wouldn't be any prints on it to begin with?
MRK!
...
GULP...
If this was just a random crime using a bottle he found on the ground,
I don't think it makes sense for him to deliberately put gloves on.
ALL SET!!
Y-yes, that's true, but...
It's winter. Maybe he was already wearing gloves.
In the middle of the day?
There was no wind yesterday, and it got up to almost 10°C*. Would you be wearing gloves?
...
*50°F

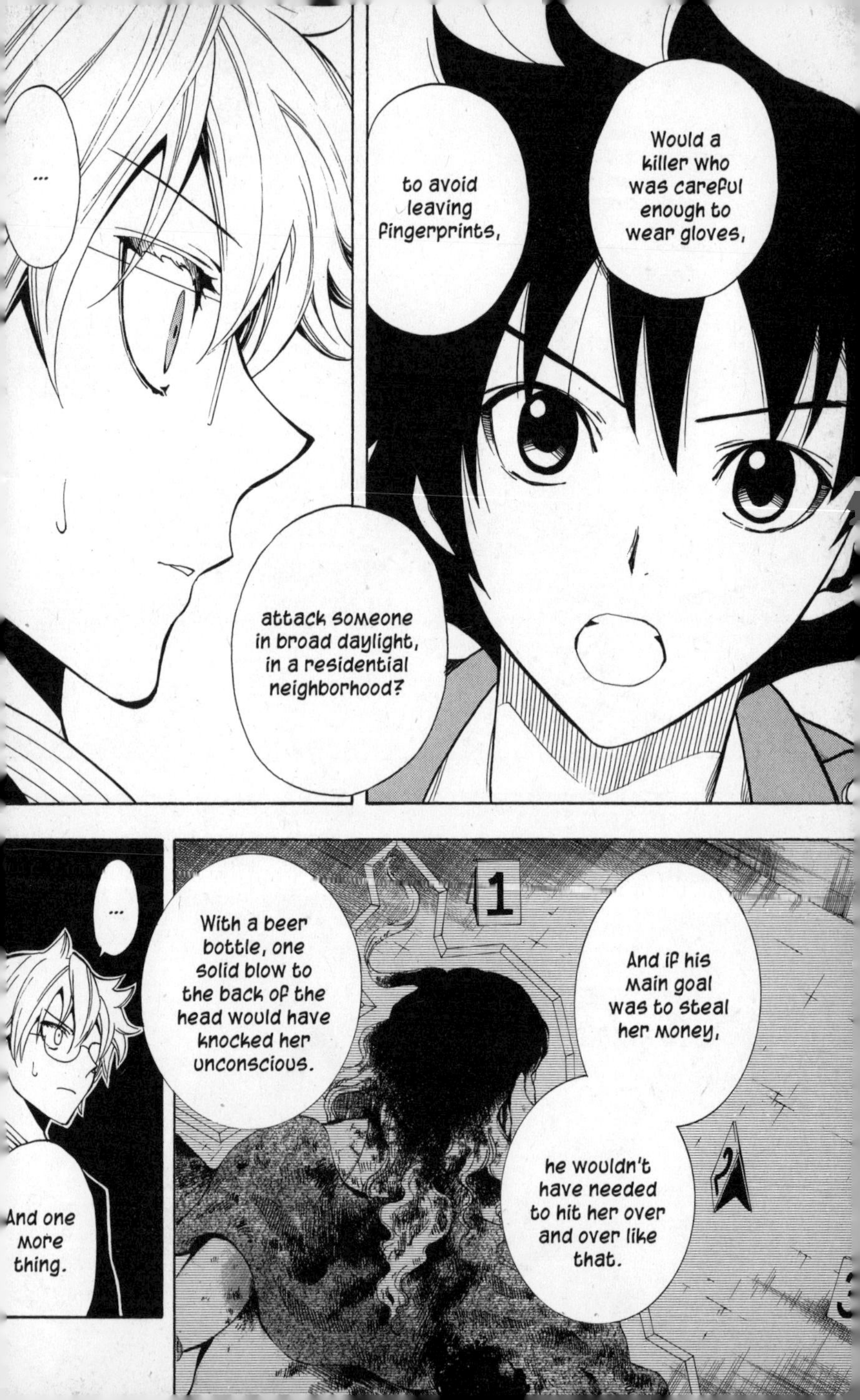
Would a killer who was careful enough to wear gloves,
to avoid leaving fingerprints,
attack someone in broad daylight, in a residential neighborhood?
...
And if his main goal was to steal her money,
he wouldn't have needed to hit her over and over like that.
With a beer bottle, one solid blow to the back of the head would have knocked her unconscious.
...
And one more thing.

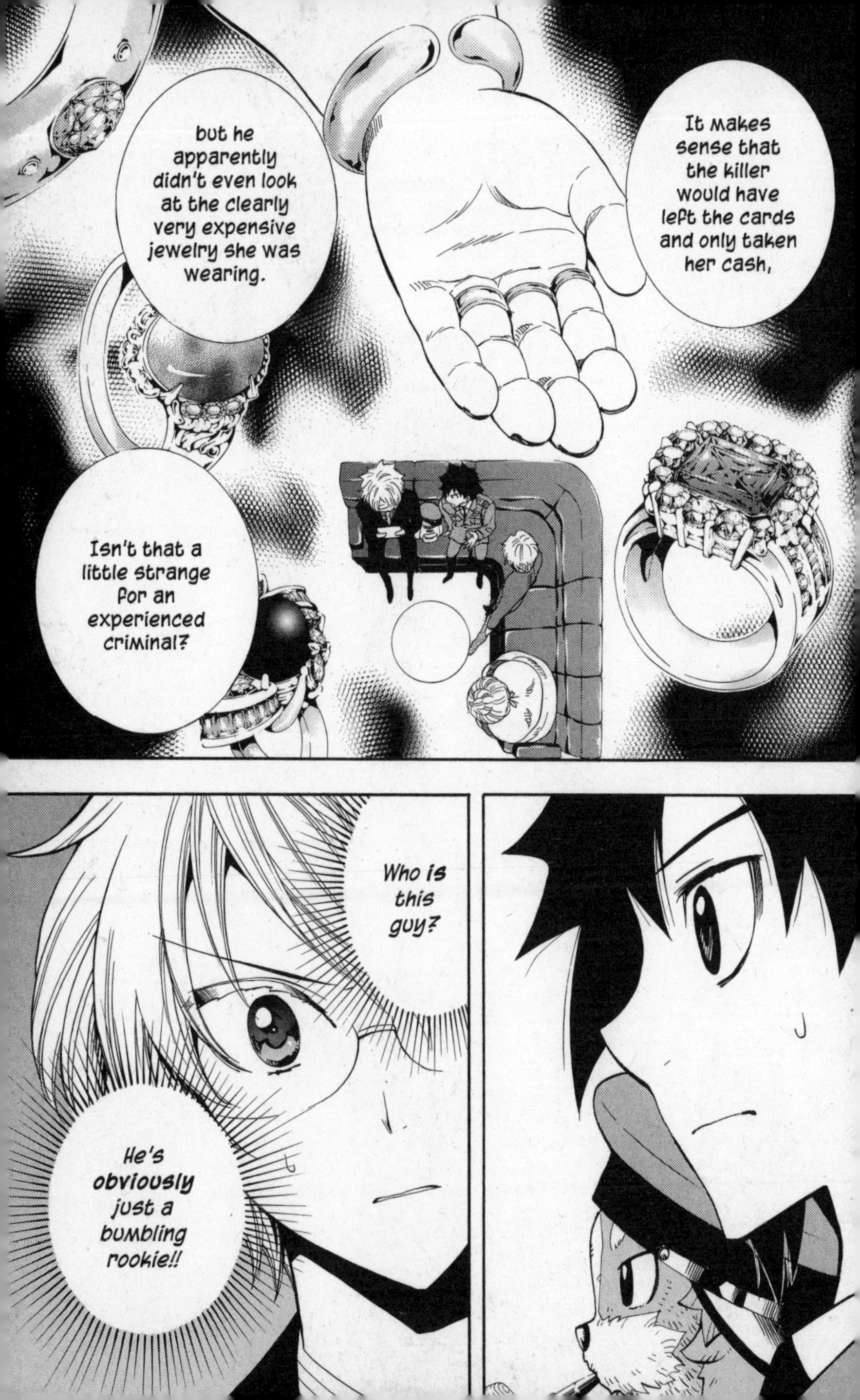
It makes sense that the killer would have left the cards and only taken her cash,
but he apparently didn't even look at the clearly very expensive jewelry she was wearing.
Isn't that a little strange for an experienced criminal?
Who *is* this guy?
He's **obviously** just a bumbling rookie!!

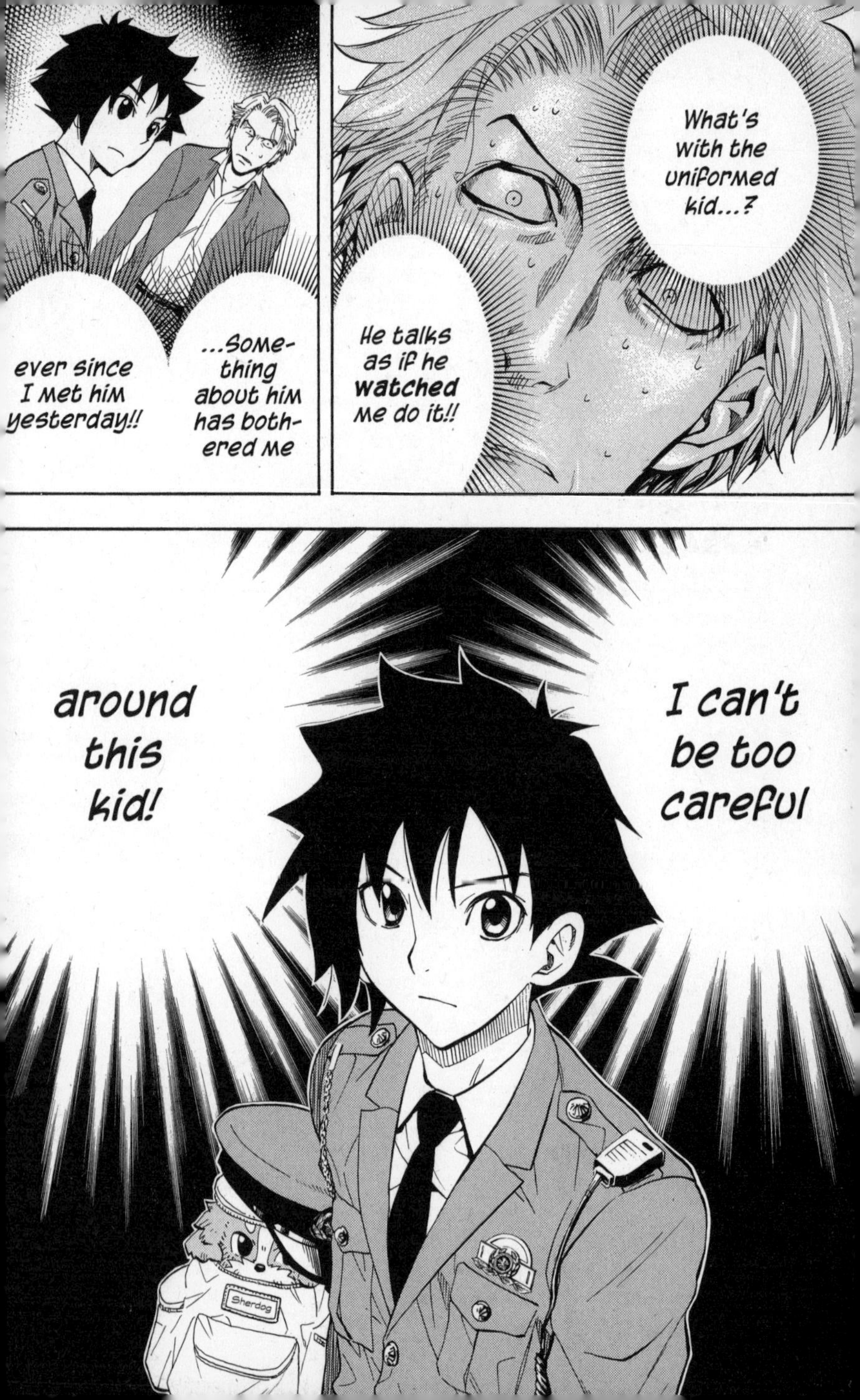
What's with the uniformed kid...?
He talks as if he watched me do it!!
...Some-thing about him has both-ered me
ever since I met him yesterday!!
I can't be too careful
around this kid!
Sherdog

Case 8: ⚜ Requiem for a New Beginning, Part 4

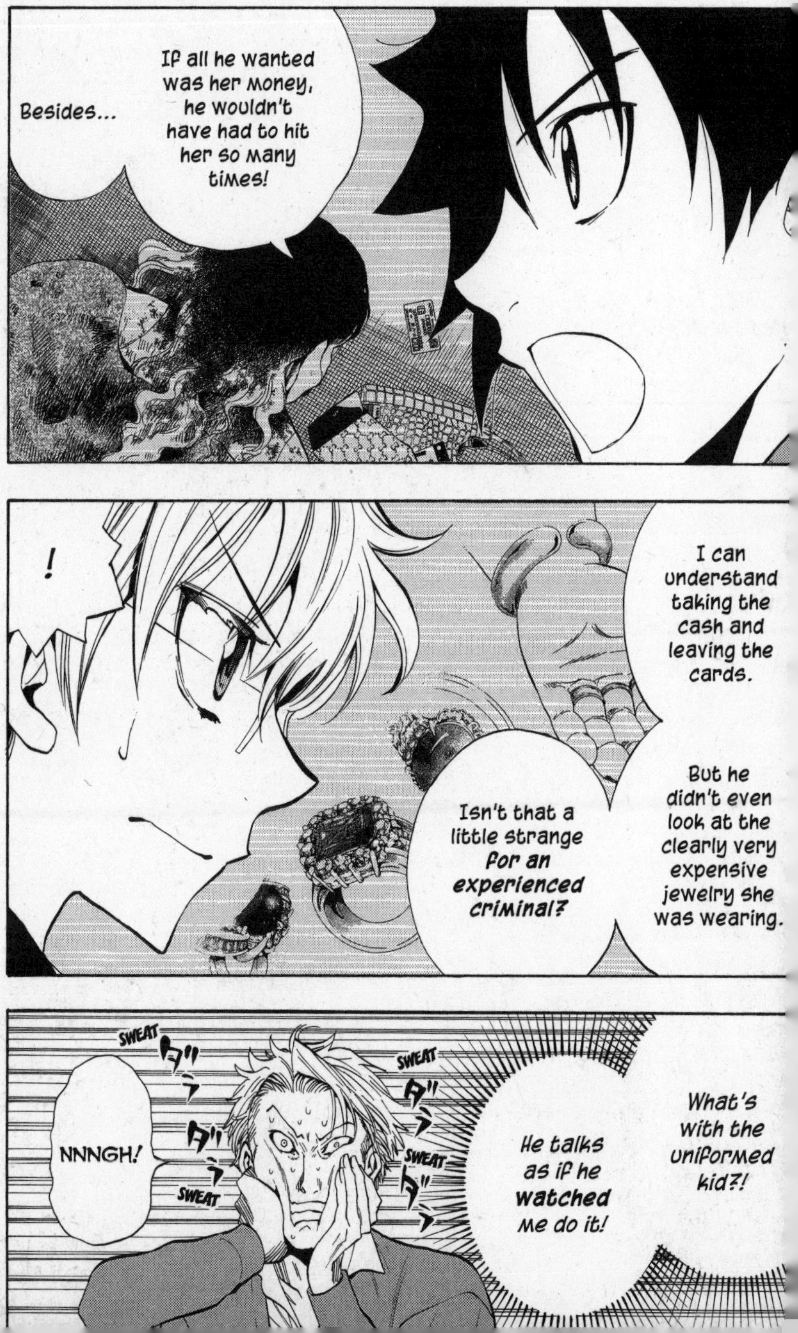

If all he wanted was her money, he wouldn't have had to hit her so many times!
Besides...
I can understand taking the cash and leaving the cards.
But he didn't even look at the clearly very expensive jewelry she was wearing.
Isn't that a little strange *for an experienced criminal?*
!
What's with the uniformed kid?!
He talks as if he **watched** me do it!
SWEAT
SWEAT
SWEAT
SWEAT
NNNGH!

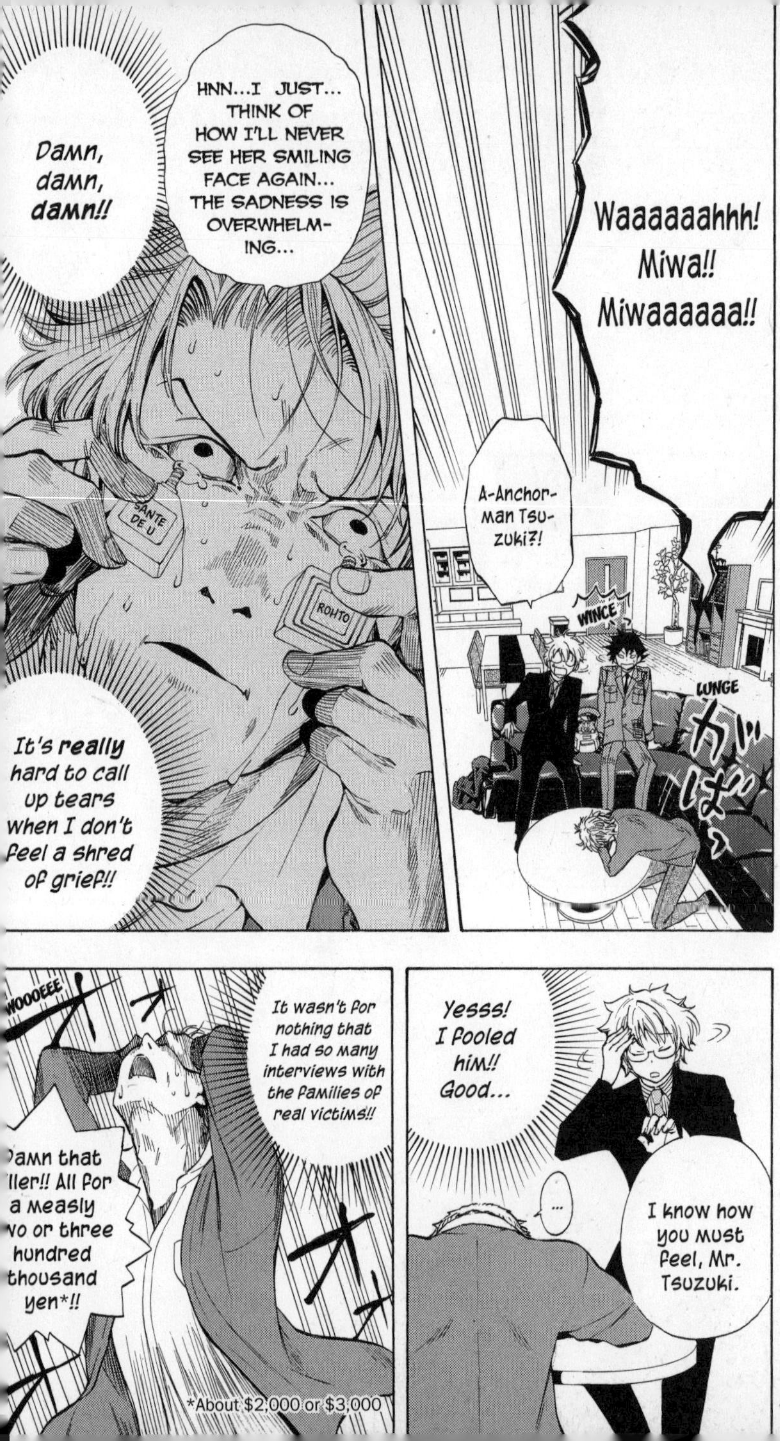
Waaaaaahhh! Miwa!! Miwaaaaaa!!
A-Anchor-man Tsuzuki?!
WINCE
LUNGE
HNN...I JUST... THINK OF HOW I'LL NEVER SEE HER SMILING FACE AGAIN... THE SADNESS IS OVERWHELM-ING...
Damn, damn, damn!!
SANTE DE U
ROHTO
It's really hard to call up tears when I don't feel a shred of grief!!
Yesss! I fooled him!! Good...
...
I know how you must feel, Mr. Tsuzuki.
WOOOEEE
It wasn't for nothing that I had so many interviews with the families of real victims!!
amn that ller!! All for a measly wo or three hundred thousand yen*!!

*About $2,000 or $3,000

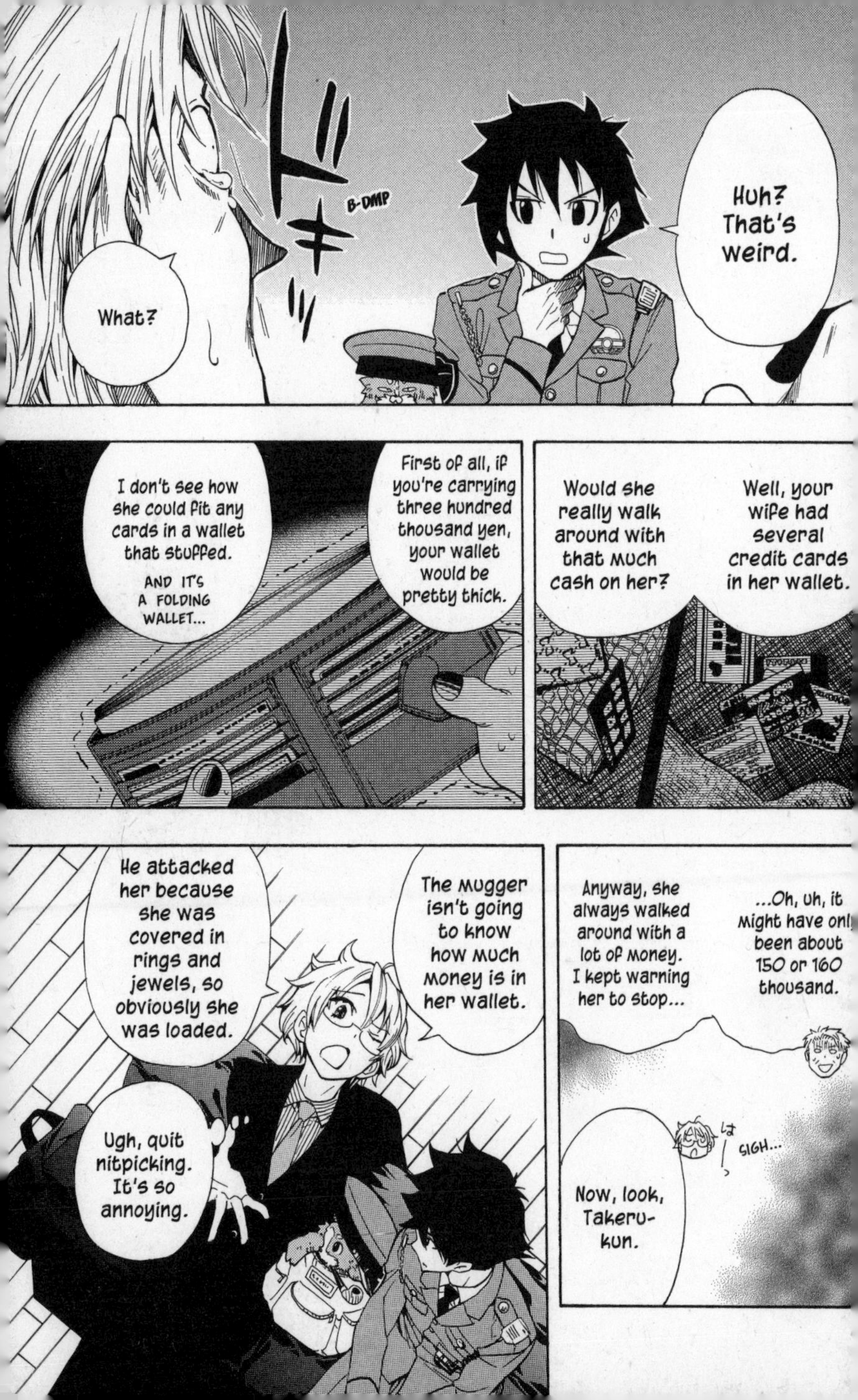
Huh? That's weird.
B-DMP
What?
Well, your wife had several credit cards in her wallet.
Would she really walk around with that much cash on her?
First of all, if you're carrying three hundred thousand yen, your wallet would be pretty thick.
I don't see how she could fit any cards in a wallet that stuffed.
AND IT'S A FOLDING WALLET...
...Oh, uh, it might have onl been about 150 or 160 thousand.
Anyway, she always walked around with a lot of money. I kept warning her to stop...
SIGH...
Now, look, Takeru-kun.
The mugger isn't going to know how much money is in her wallet.
He attacked her because she was covered in rings and jewels, so obviously she was loaded.
Ugh, quit nitpicking. It's so annoying.

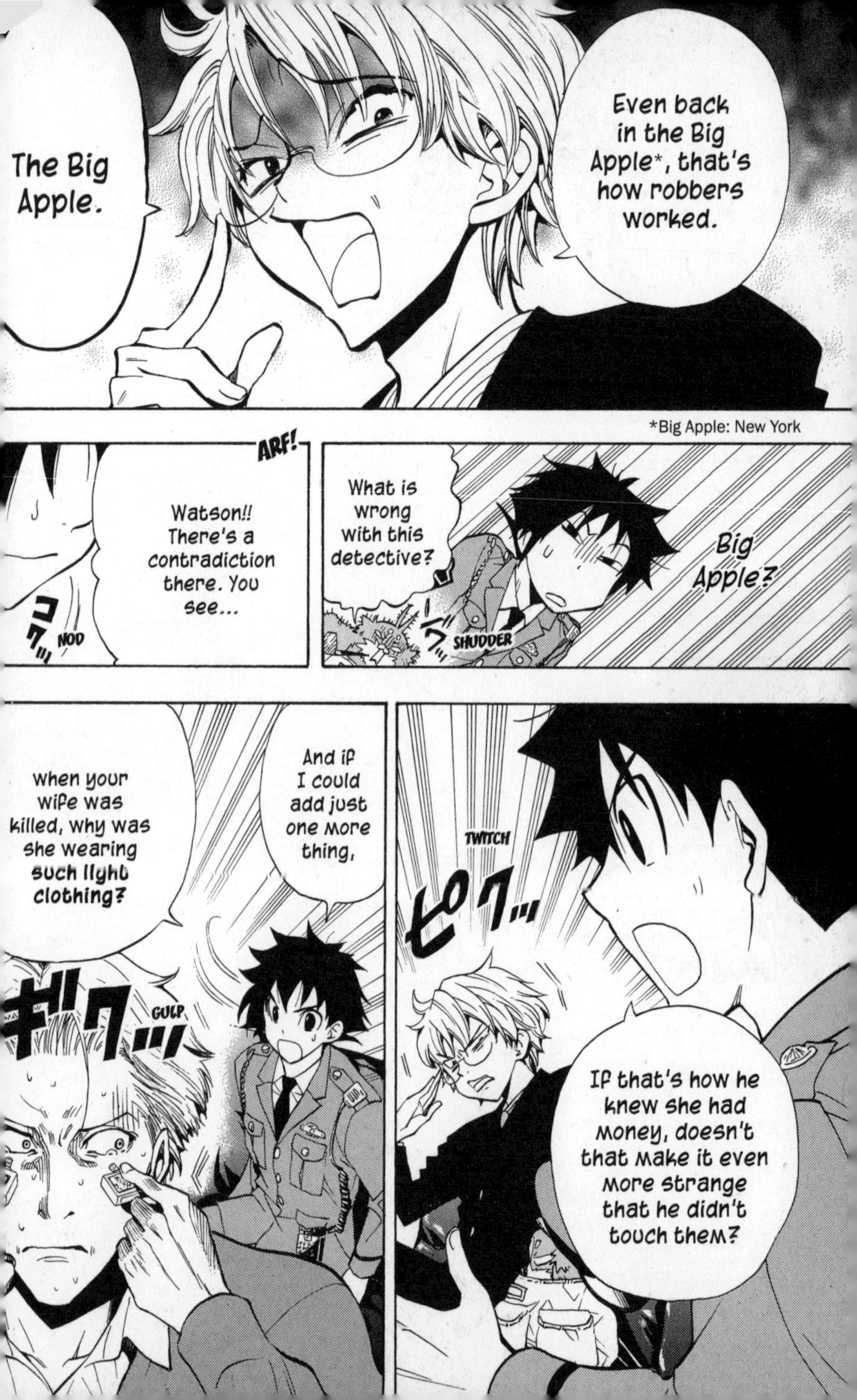
Even back in the Big Apple*, that's how robbers worked.
The Big Apple.
*Big Apple: New York
Big Apple?
What is wrong with this detective?
SHUDDER
ARF!
Watson!! There's a contradiction there. You see...
NOD
TWITCH
If that's how he knew she had money, doesn't that make it even more strange that he didn't touch them?
And if I could add just one more thing,
when your wife was killed, why was she wearing such light clothing?
GULP

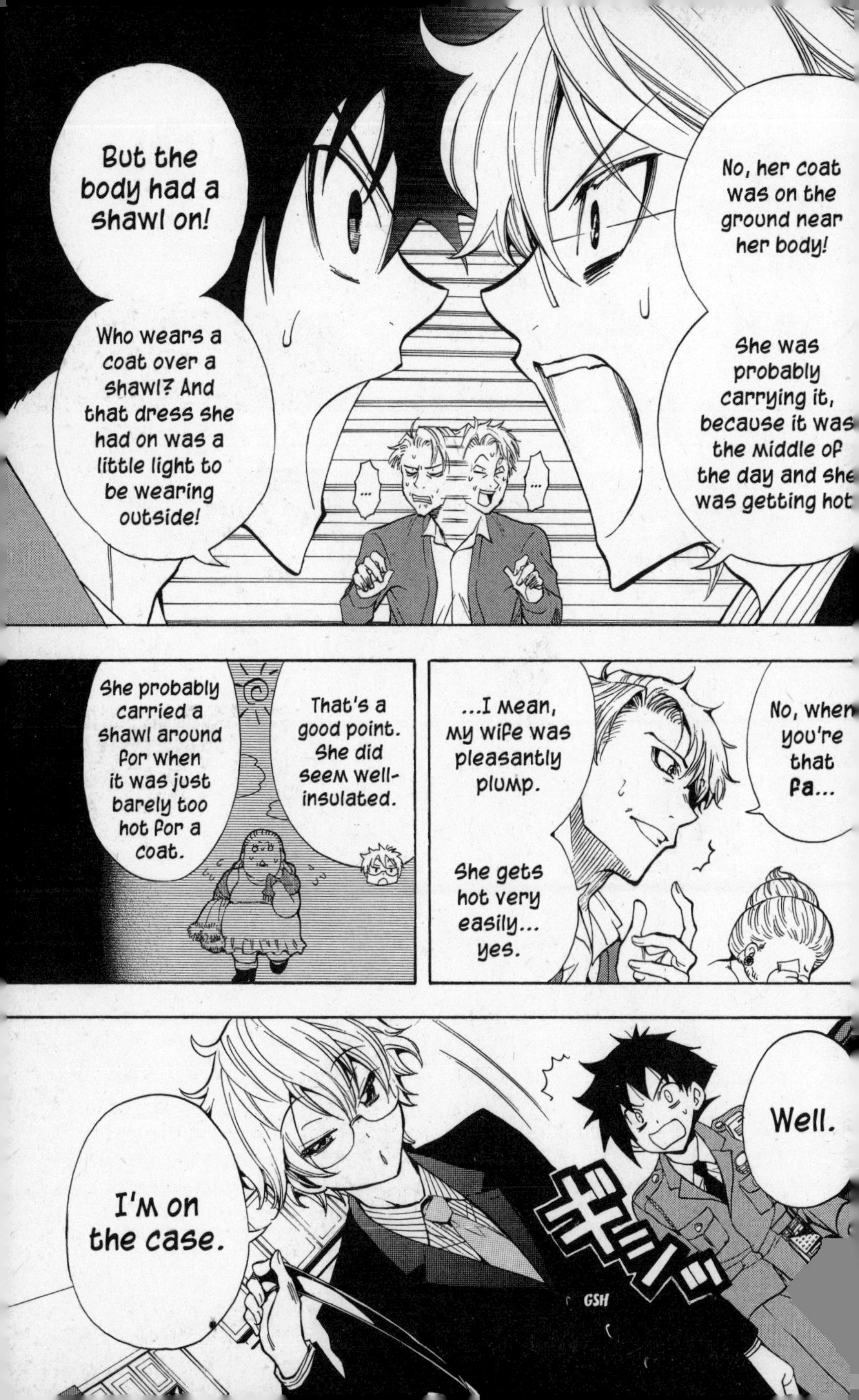
No, her coat was on the ground near her body!
She was probably carrying it, because it was the middle of the day and she was getting hot
But the body had a shawl on!
Who wears a coat over a shawl? And that dress she had on was a little light to be wearing outside!
...
...
No, when you're that fa...
...I mean, my wife was pleasantly plump.
She gets hot very easily... yes.
That's a good point. She did seem well-insulated.
She probably carried a shawl around for when it was just barely too hot for a coat.
Well.
I'm on the case.
GSH

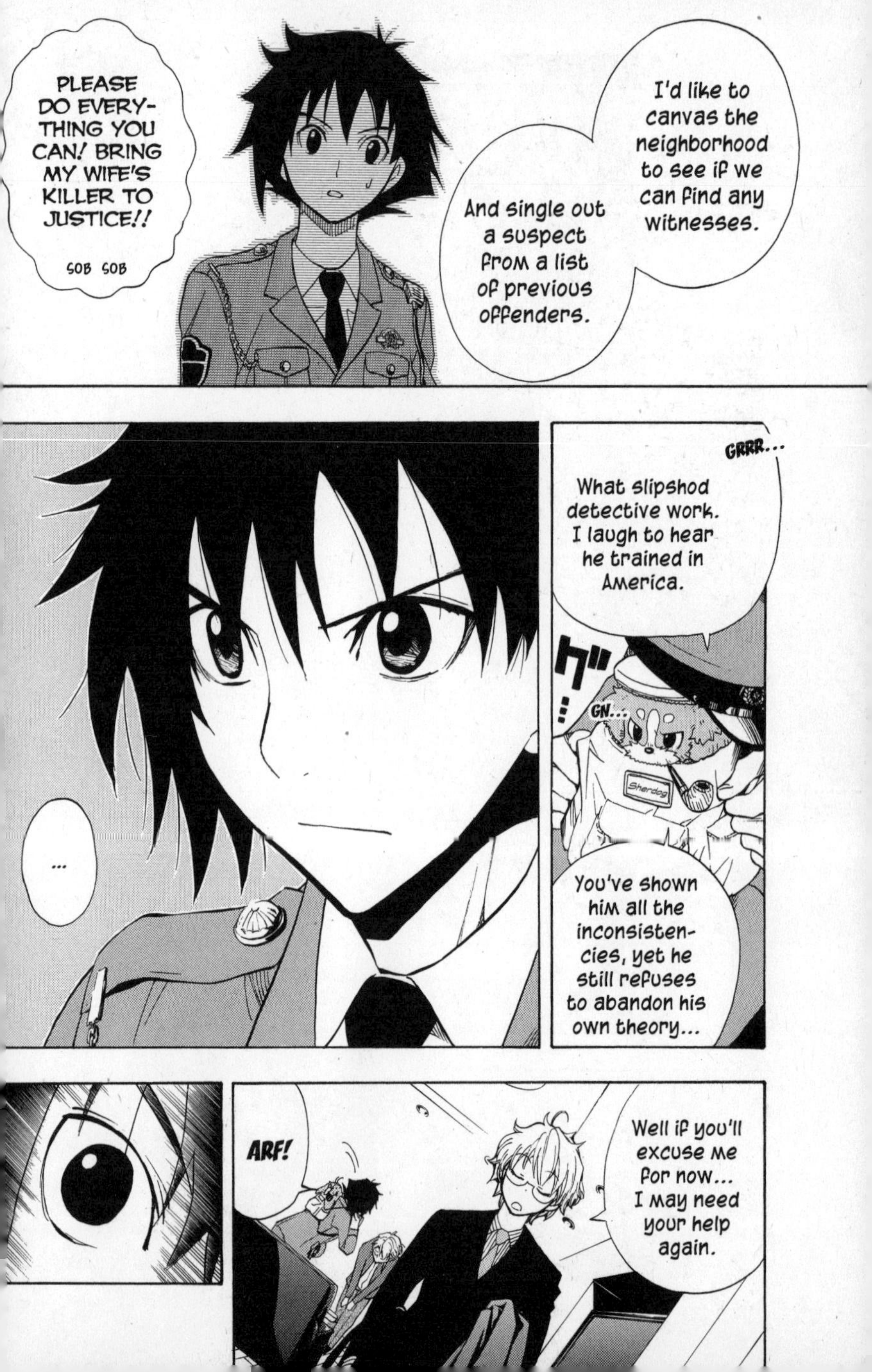
I'd like to canvas the neighborhood to see if we can find any witnesses.
And single out a suspect from a list of previous offenders.
PLEASE DO EVERY-THING YOU CAN! BRING MY WIFE'S KILLER TO JUSTICE!!
SOB SOB
GRRR...
What slipshod detective work. I laugh to hear he trained in America.
ガ
GN...
You've shown him all the inconsisten-cies, yet he still refuses to abandon his own theory...
...
Well if you'll excuse me for now... I may need your help again.
ARF!

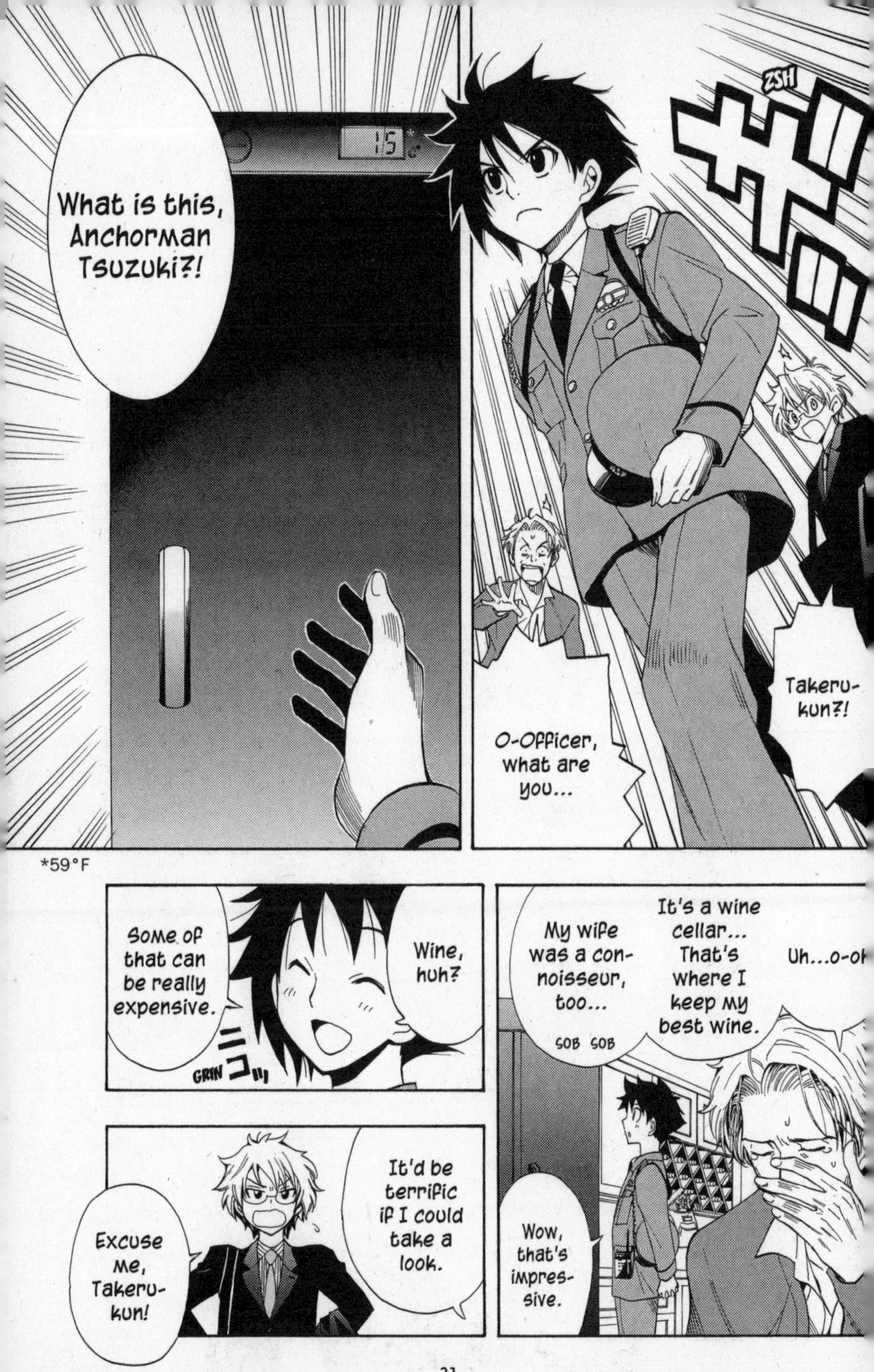
ZSH
Takeru-kun?!
O-Officer, what are you...
What is this, Anchorman Tsuzuki?!
15*
*59°F
Uh...o-oh
It's a wine cellar... That's where I keep my best wine.
My wife was a connoisseur, too...
SOB SOB
Wow, that's impressive.
Wine, huh?
Some of that can be really expensive.
GRIN
It'd be terrific if I could take a look.
Excuse me, Takeru-kun!

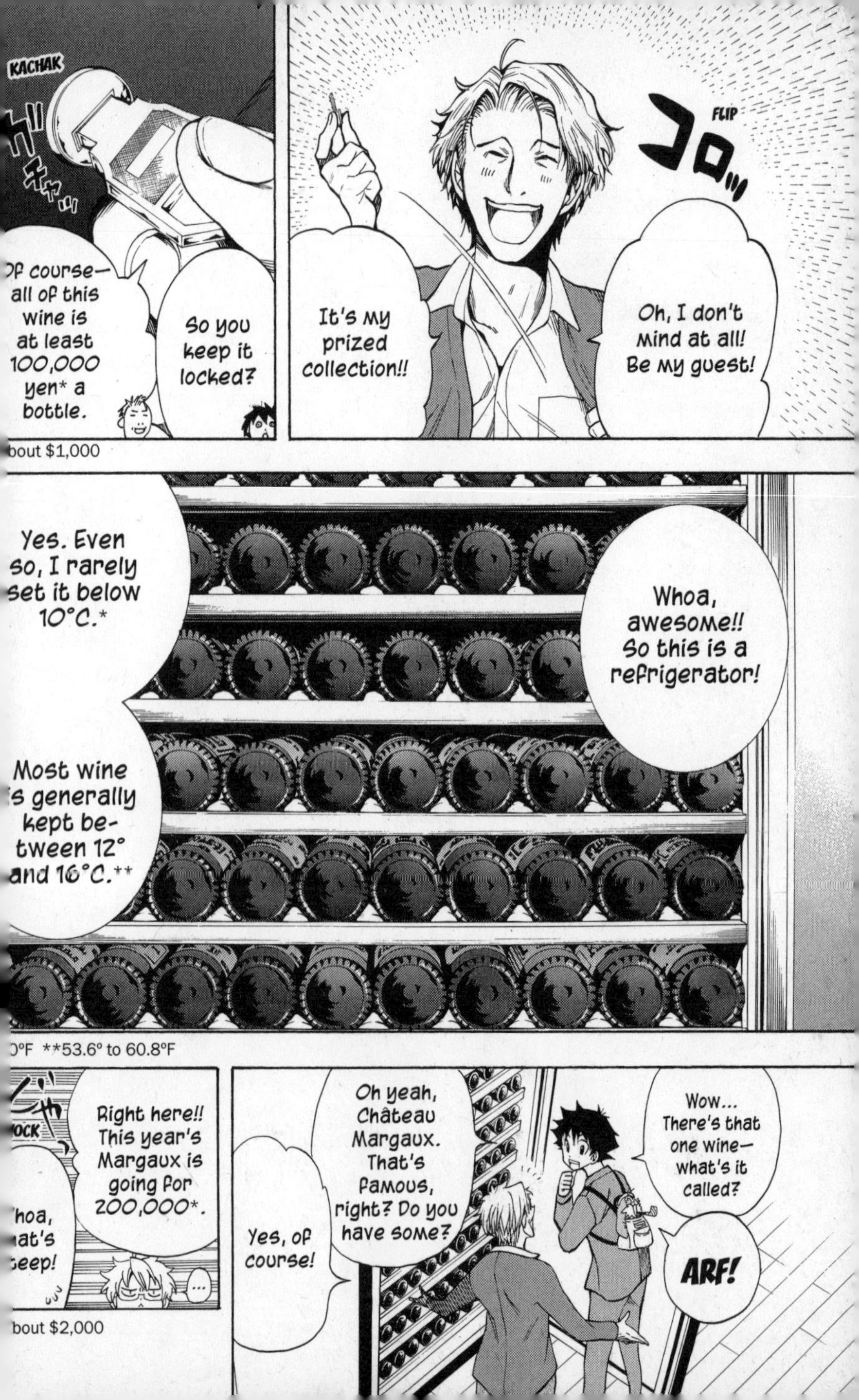
FLIP
Oh, I don't mind at all! Be my guest!
It's my prized collection!!
KACHAK
So you keep it locked?
Of course—all of this wine is at least 100,000 yen* a bottle.
Whoa, awesome!! So this is a refrigerator!
Yes. Even so, I rarely set it below 10°C.*
Most wine s generally kept be-tween 12° and 16°C.**
Wow... There's that one wine—what's it called?
ARF!
Oh yeah, Château Margaux. That's famous, right? Do you have some?
Yes, of course!
OCK
Right here!! This year's Margaux is going for 200,000*.
hoa, at's eep!
...

bout $1,000

0°F **53.6° to 60.8°F

bout $2,000

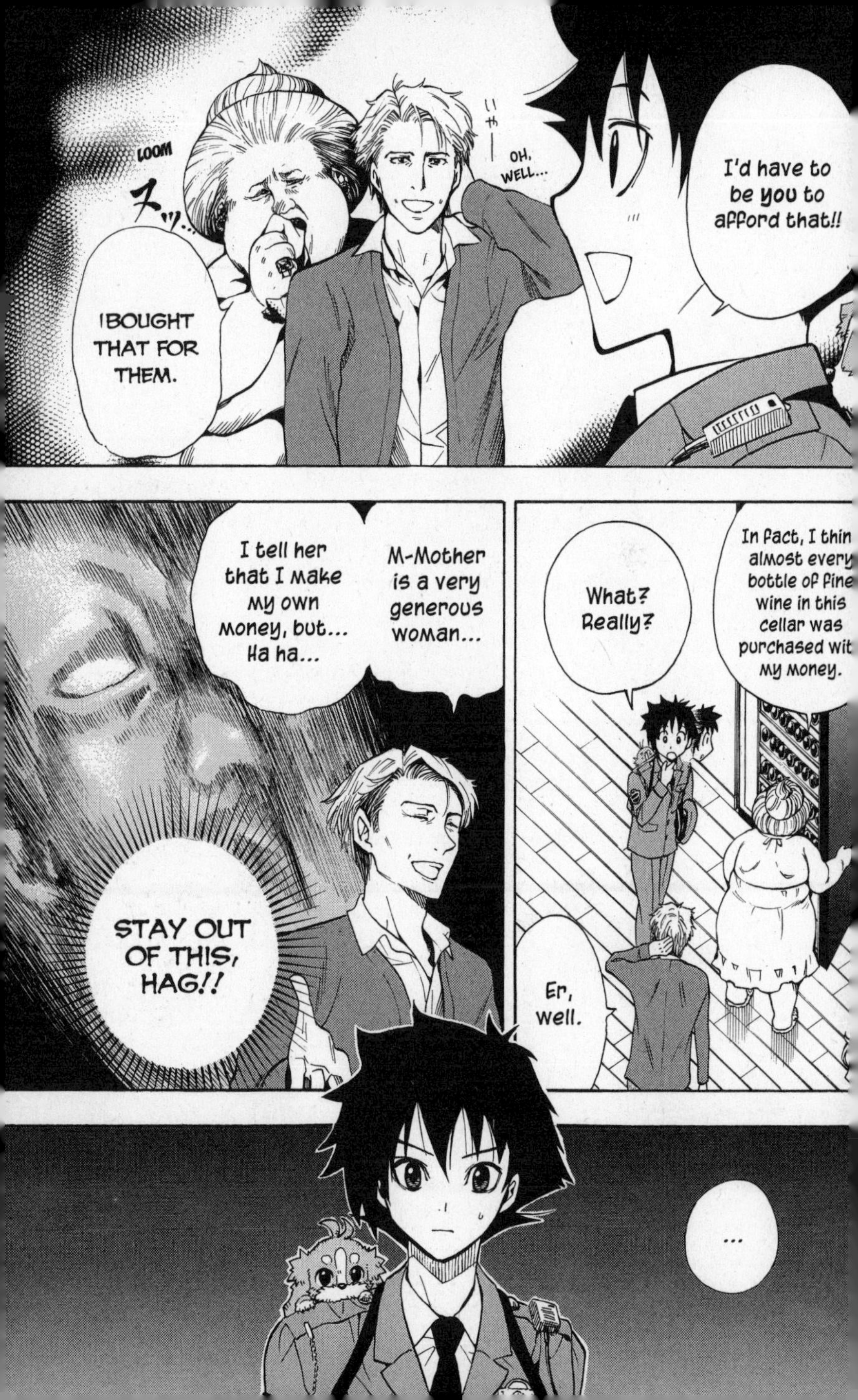
I'd have to be you to afford that!!
いやー
OH, WELL...
LOOM
ヌッ...
I BOUGHT THAT FOR THEM.
In fact, I thin almost every bottle of fine wine in this cellar was purchased wit my money.
What? Really?
Er, well.
M-Mother is a very generous woman...
I tell her that I make my own money, but... Ha ha...
STAY OUT OF THIS, HAG!!
...

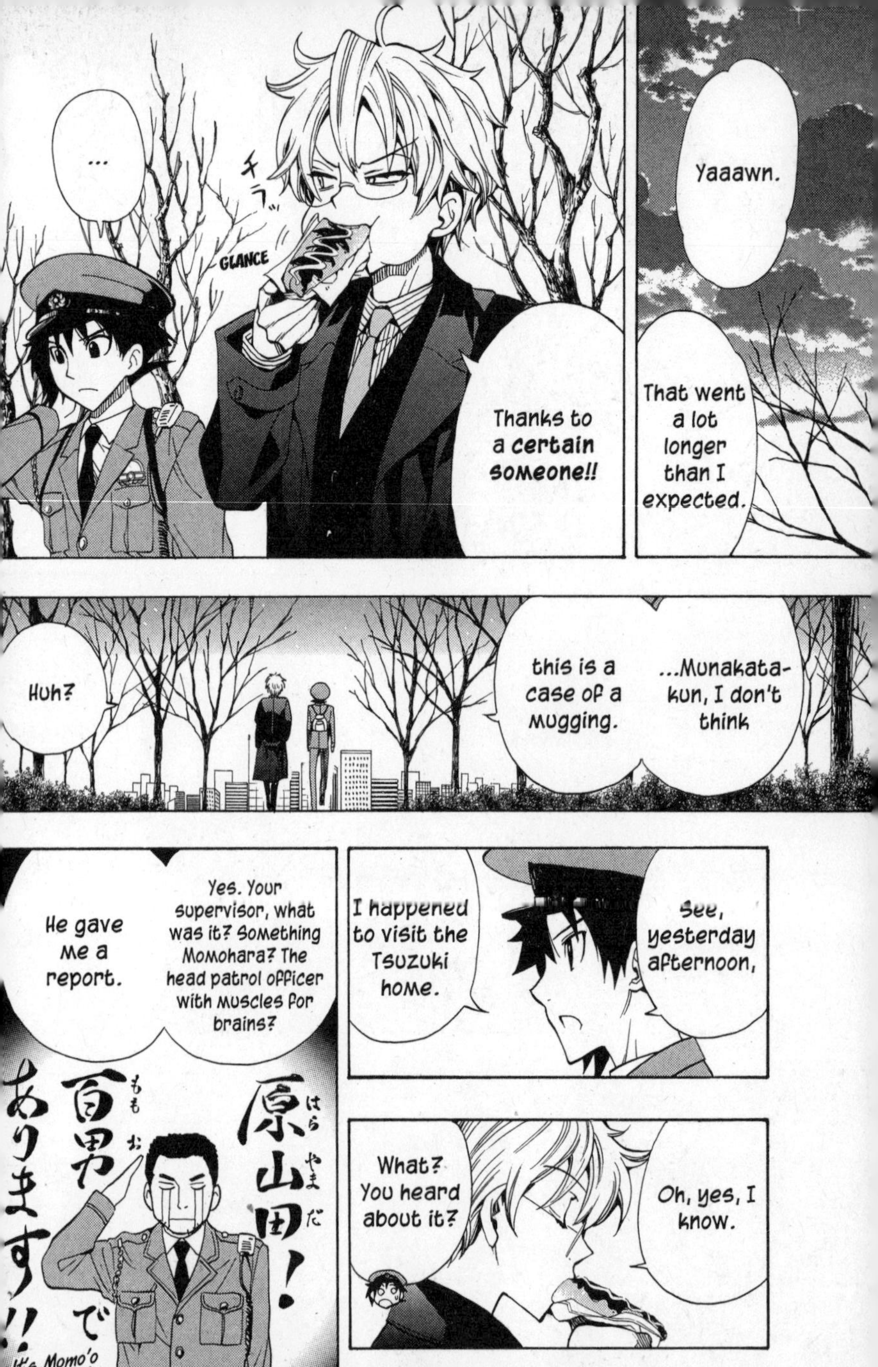
Yaaawn.
That went a lot longer than I expected.
Thanks to a certain someone!!
チラッ
GLANCE
...
...Munakata-kun, I don't think
this is a case of a mugging.
Huh?
See, yesterday afternoon,
I happened to visit the Tsuzuki home.
Oh, yes, I know.
What? You heard about it?
Yes. Your supervisor, what was it? Something Momohara? The head patrol officer with muscles for brains?
He gave me a report.
原山田！百男であります!!
It's Momo'o Harayamada, sir!!

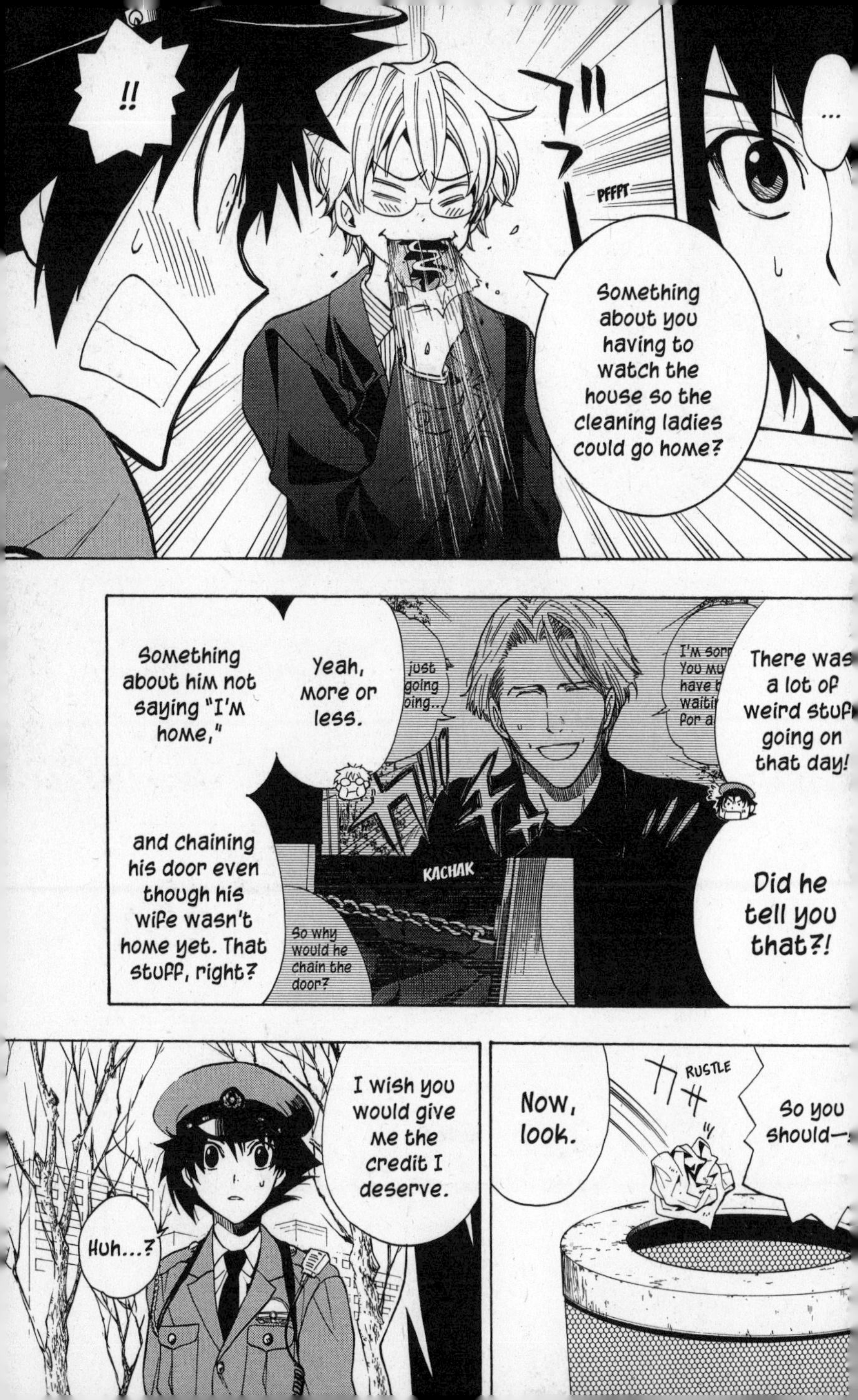
...
PFFFT
Something about you having to watch the house so the cleaning ladies could go home?
!!
There was a lot of weird stuff going on that day!
Did he tell you that?!
Yeah, more or less.
Something about him not saying "I'm home,"
and chaining his door even though his wife wasn't home yet. That stuff, right?
KACHAK
So why would he chain the door?
So you should—
RUSTLE
Now, look.
I wish you would give me the credit I deserve.
Huh...?

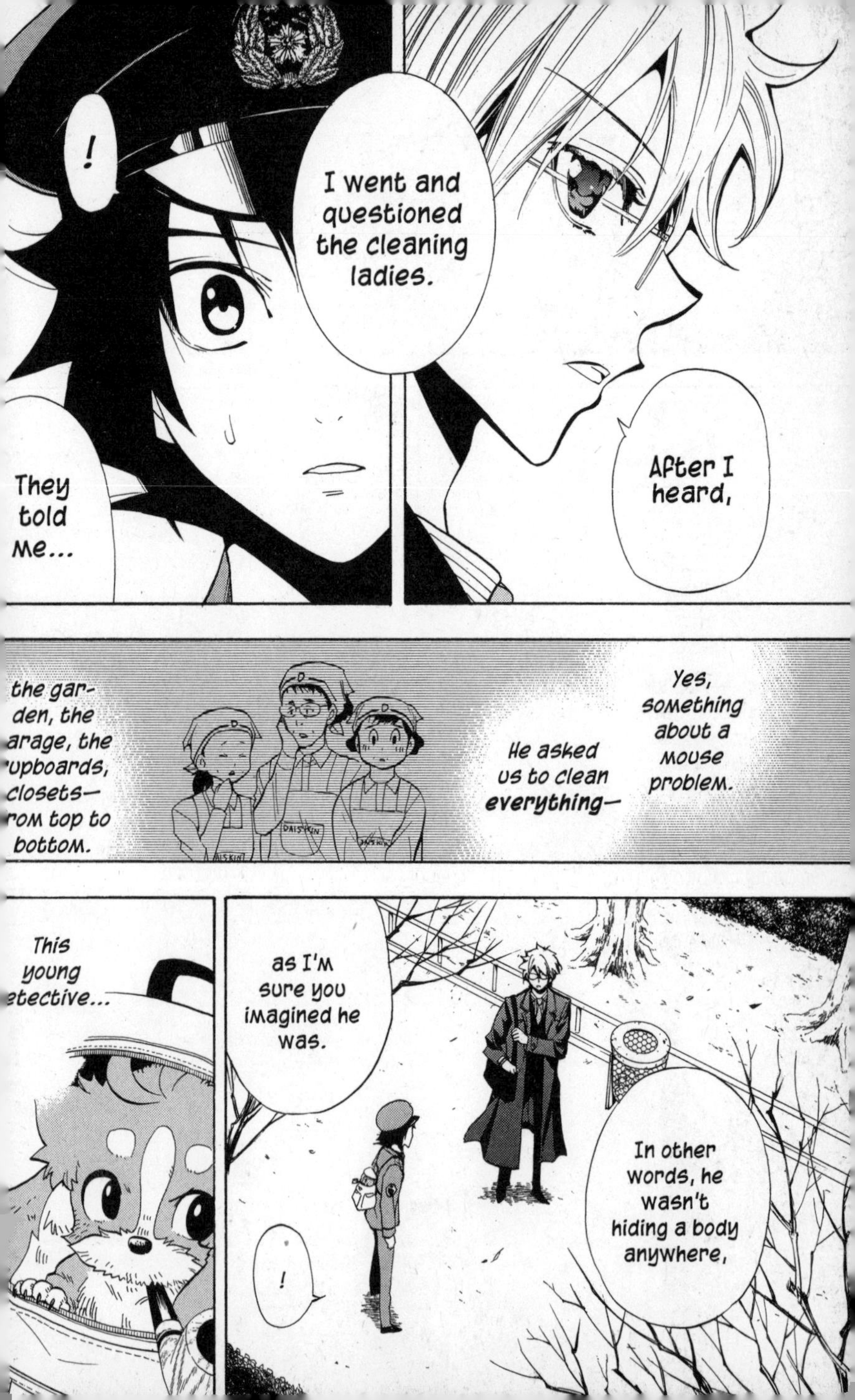

I went and questioned the cleaning ladies.
After I heard,
!
They told me...
Yes, something about a mouse problem.
He asked us to clean everything—
the gar- den, the arage, the upboards, closets— rom top to bottom.
DAISKIN
In other words, he wasn't hiding a body anywhere,
as I'm sure you imagined he was.
!
This young etective...

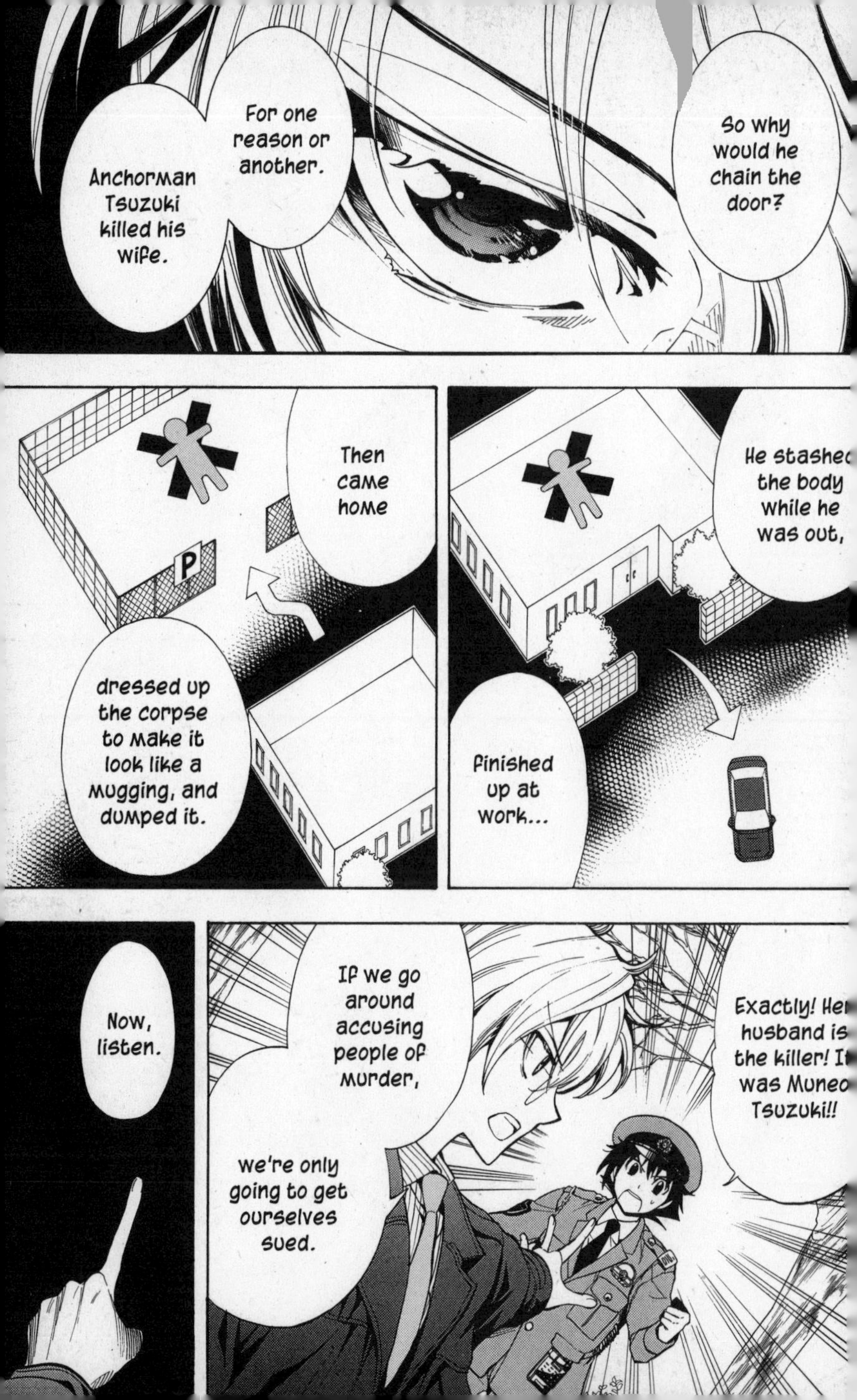
So why would he chain the door?
For one reason or another.
Anchorman Tsuzuki killed his wife.
He stashed the body while he was out,
finished up at work...
Then came home
dressed up the corpse to make it look like a mugging, and dumped it.
Exactly! Her husband is the killer! It was Muneo Tsuzuki!!
If we go around accusing people of murder,
we're only going to get ourselves sued.
Now, listen.

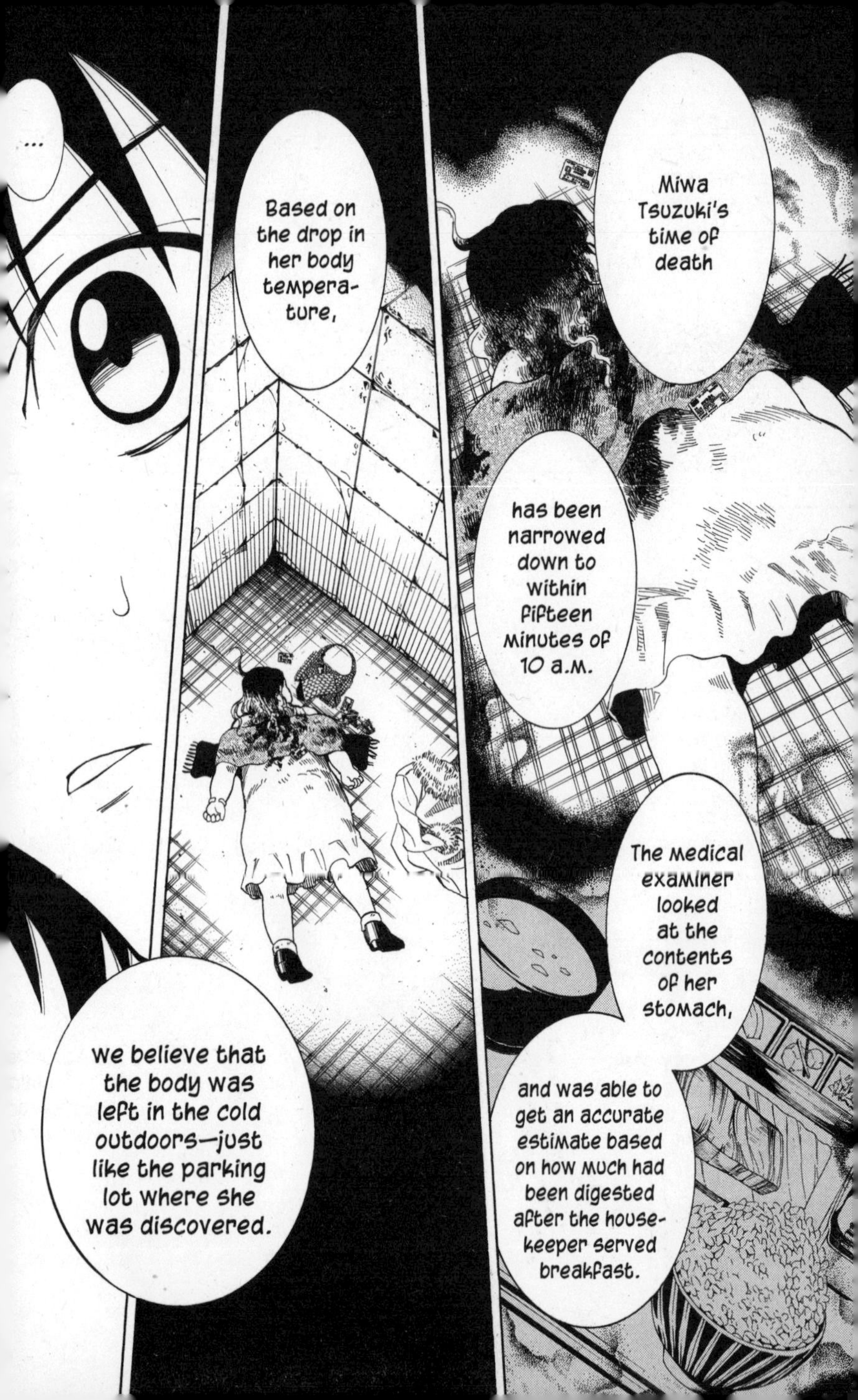
Miwa Tsuzuki's time of death
has been narrowed down to within fifteen minutes of 10 a.m.
The medical examiner looked at the contents of her stomach,
and was able to get an accurate estimate based on how much had been digested after the house-keeper served breakfast.
Based on the drop in her body tempera-ture,
we believe that the body was left in the cold outdoors—just like the parking lot where she was discovered.
...

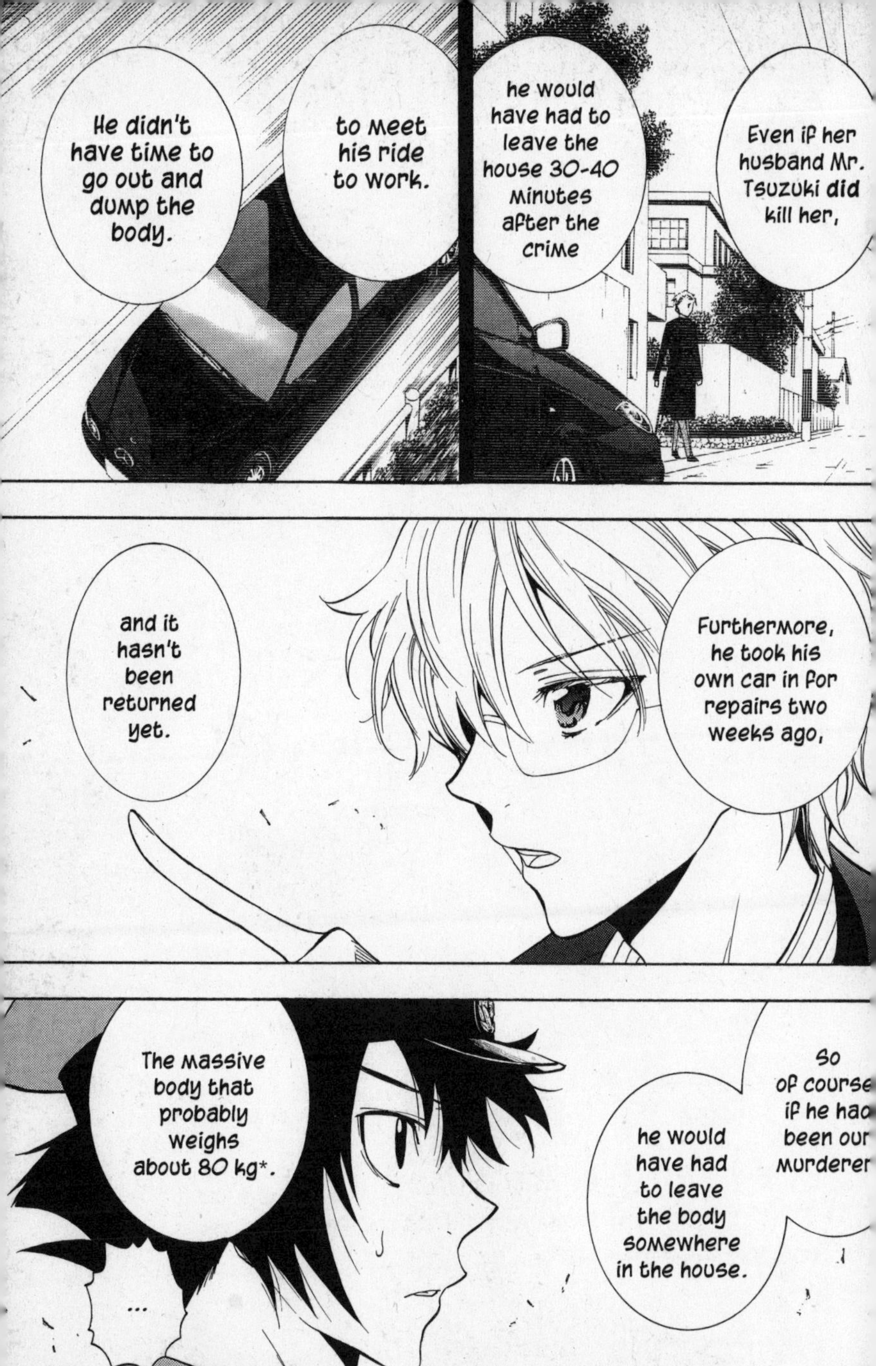

Even if her husband Mr. Tsuzuki did kill her,
he would have had to leave the house 30-40 minutes after the crime
to meet his ride to work.
He didn't have time to go out and dump the body.
Furthermore, he took his own car in for repairs two weeks ago,
and it hasn't been returned yet.
So of course if he had been our murderer
he would have had to leave the body somewhere in the house.
The massive body that probably weighs about 80 kg*.
...

*About 176 lbs.

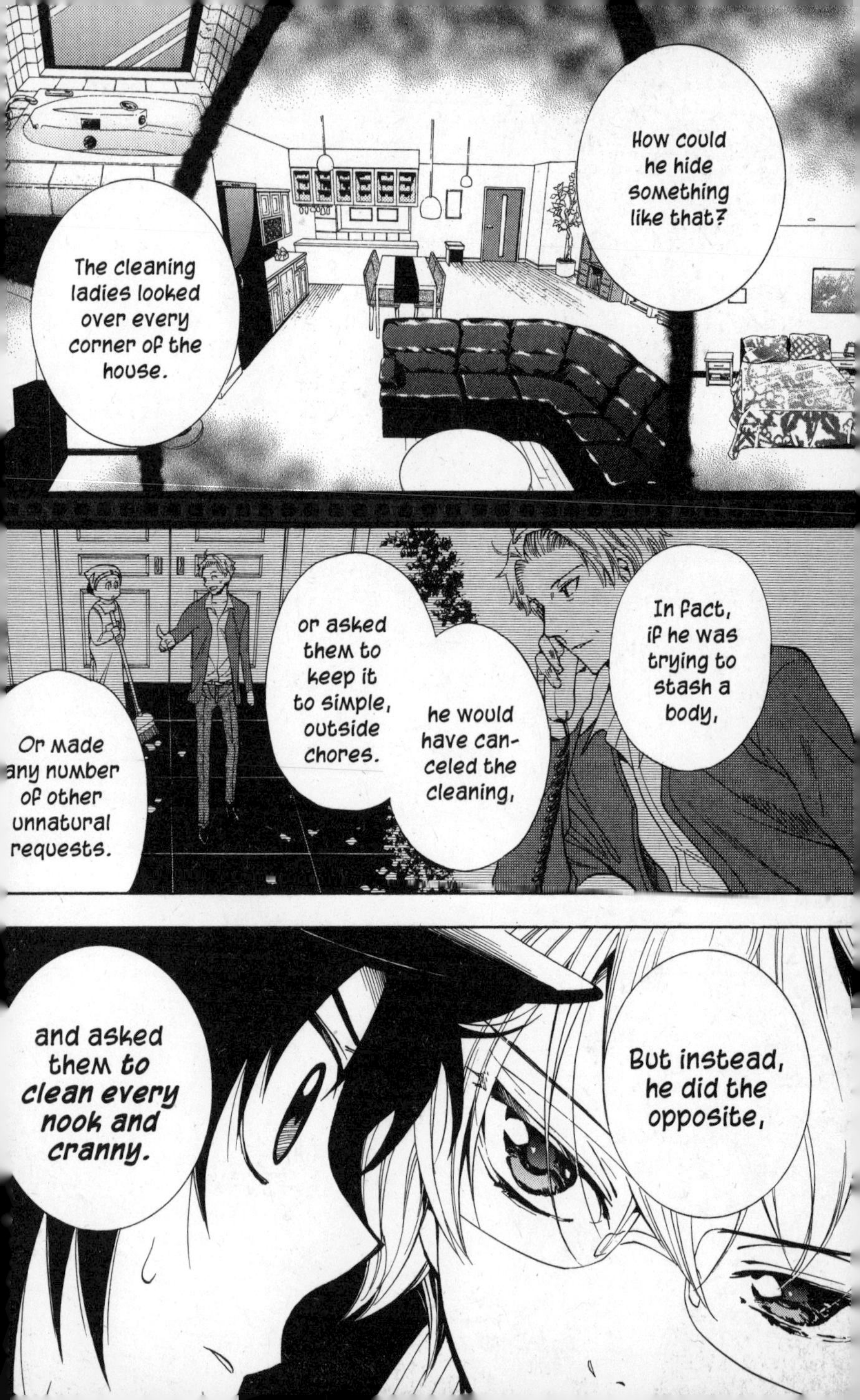
How could he hide something like that?
The cleaning ladies looked over every corner of the house.
In fact, if he was trying to stash a body,
he would have canceled the cleaning,
or asked them to keep it to simple, outside chores.
Or made any number of other unnatural requests.
But instead, he did the opposite,
and asked them to clean every nook and cranny.

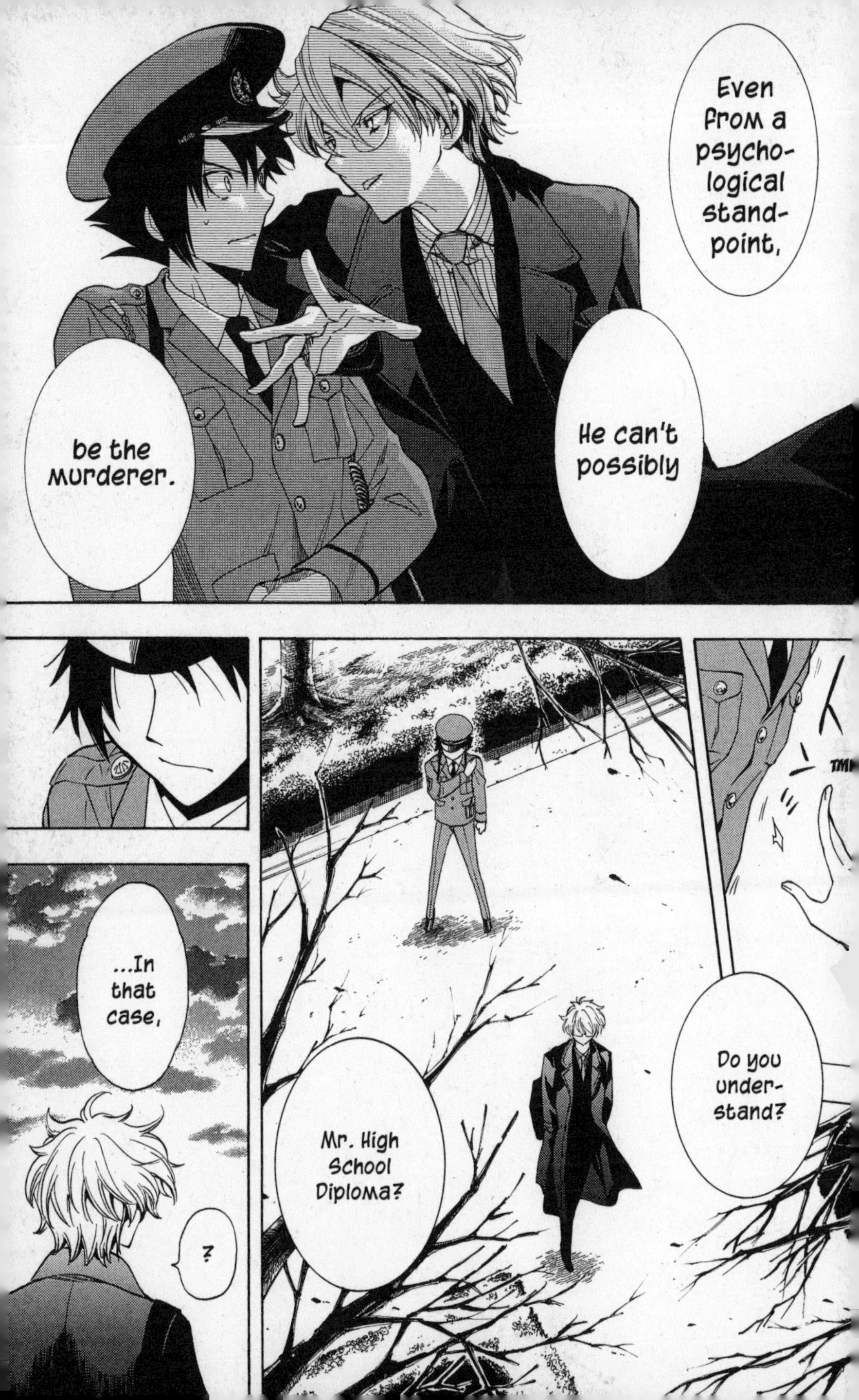
Even from a psychological standpoint,
He can't possibly
be the murderer.
Do you understand?
Mr. High School Diploma?
...In that case,
?

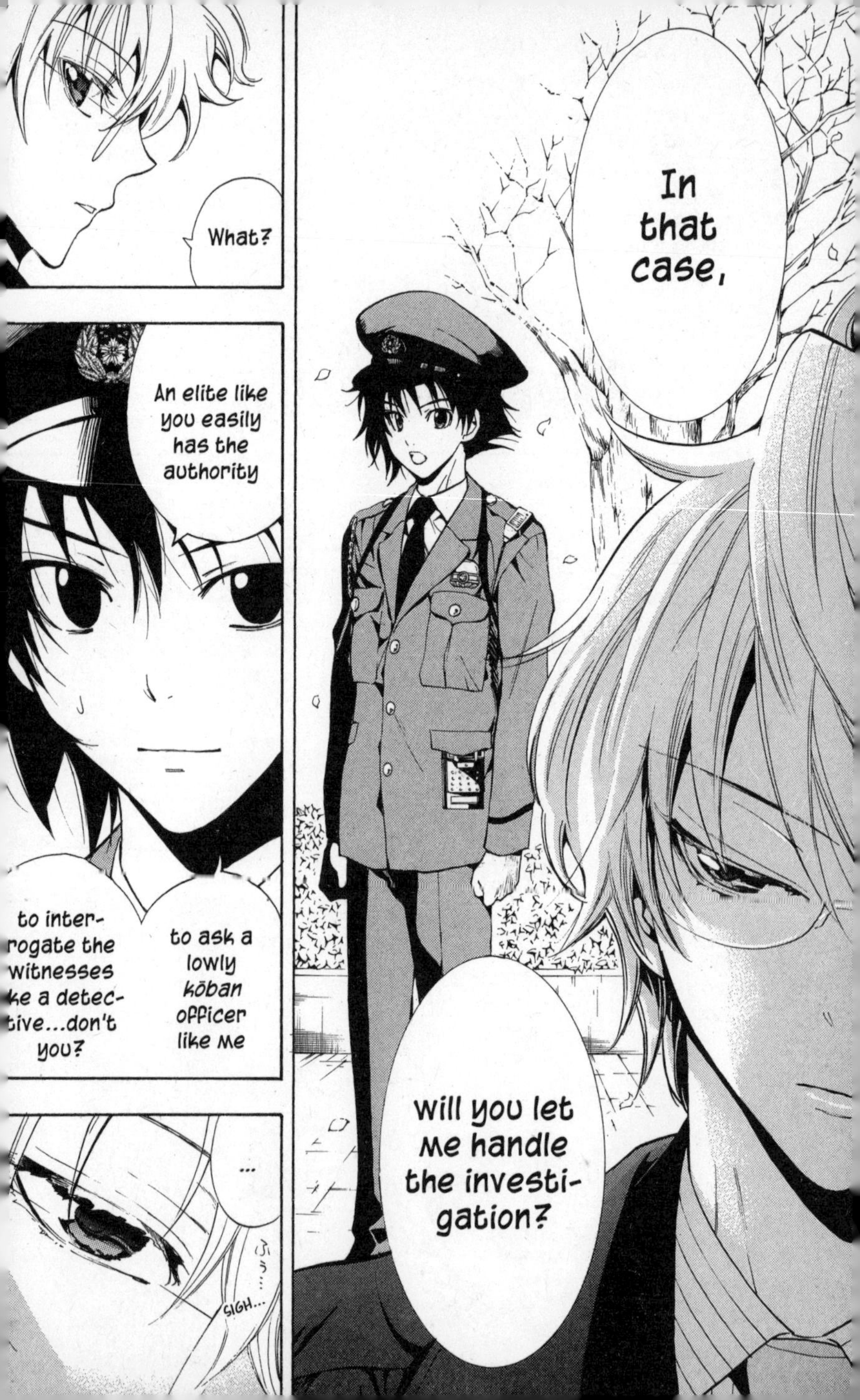

In that case,
Will you let me handle the investi-gation?
What?
An elite like you easily has the authority
to ask a lowly kōban officer like me
to inter-rogate the witnesses ke a detec-tive...don't you?
...
ふう...
SIGH...

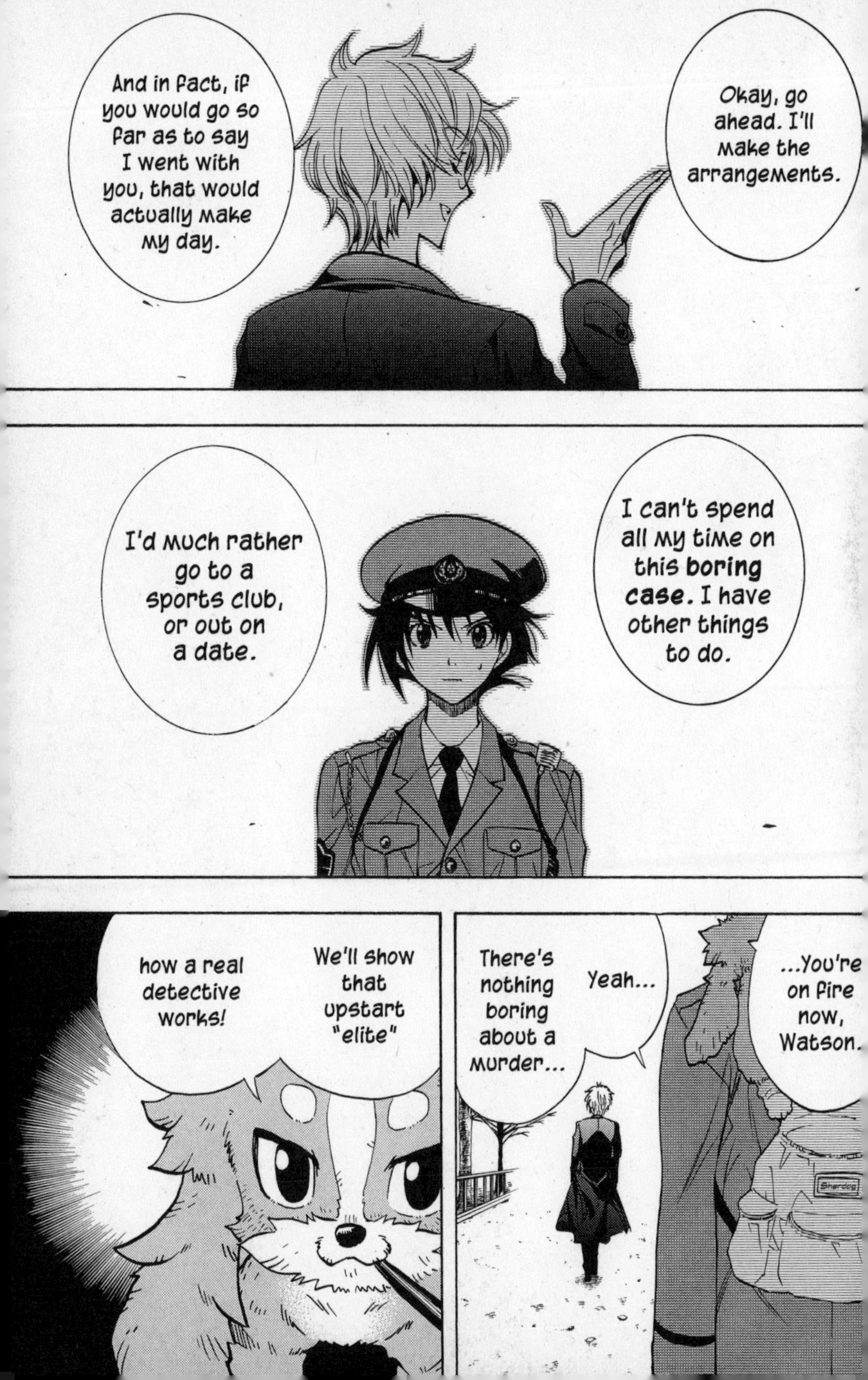
Okay, go ahead. I'll make the arrangements.
And in fact, if you would go so far as to say I went with you, that would actually make my day.
I can't spend all my time on this boring case. I have other things to do.
I'd much rather go to a sports club, or out on a date.
...You're on fire now, Watson.
Yeah...
There's nothing boring about a murder...
We'll show that upstart "elite"
how a real detective works!
Sherdog

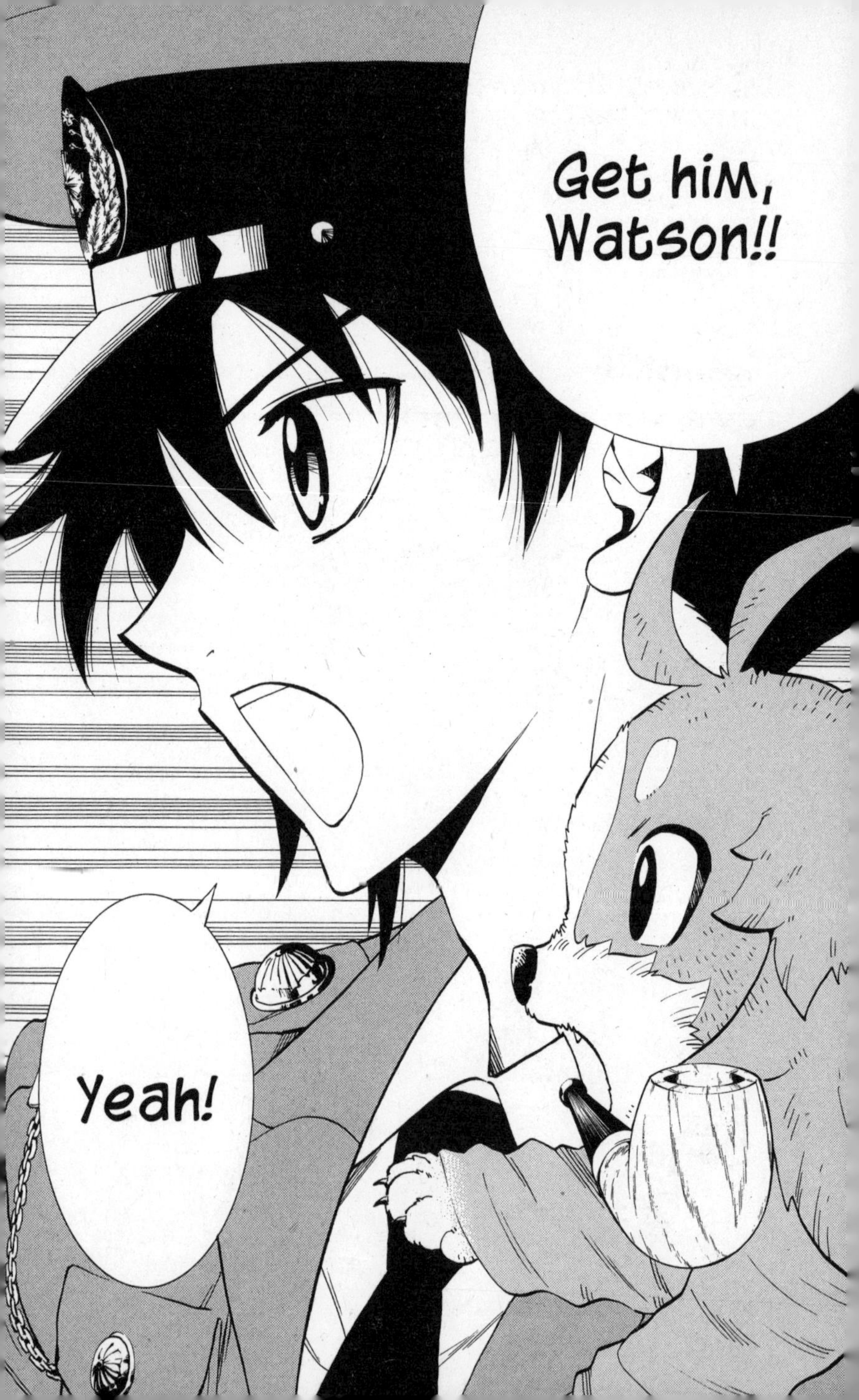
Get him, Watson!!
Yeah!

Case 8: ⚜ Requiem for a New Beginning, Part 5

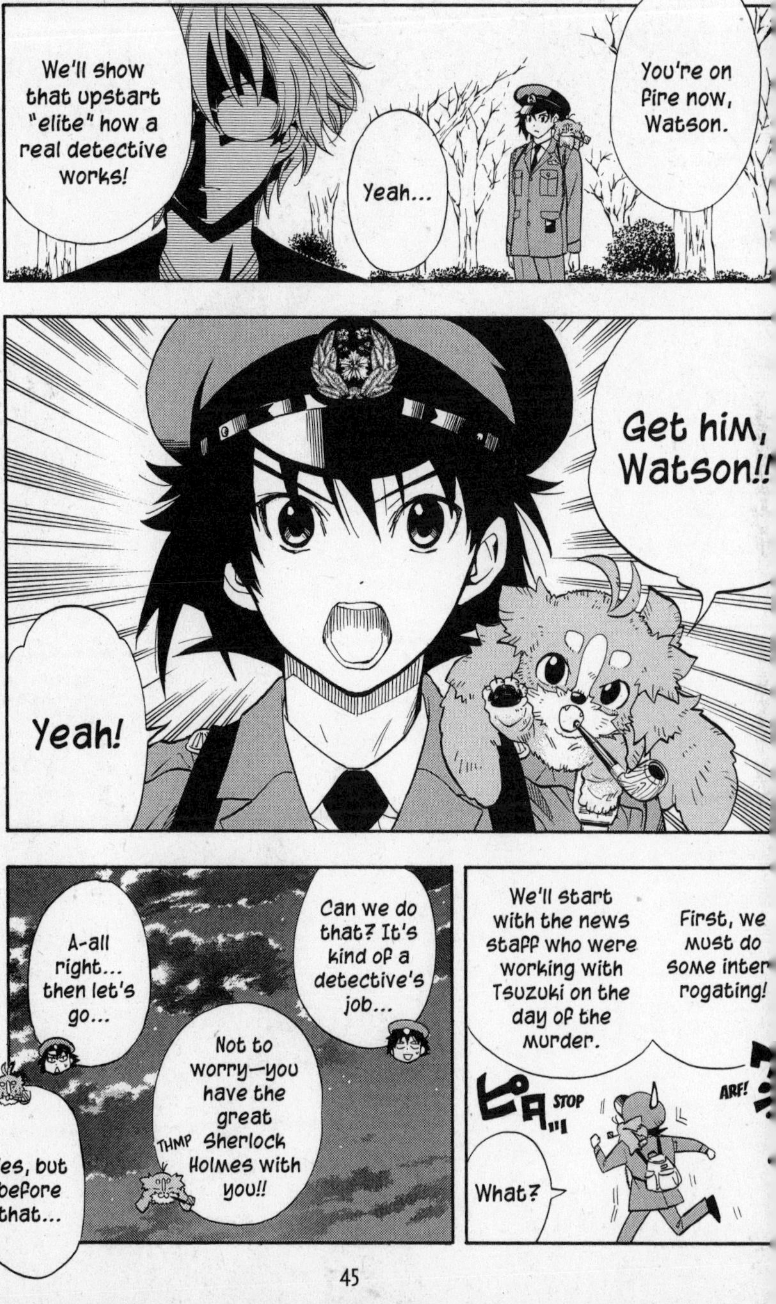
We'll show that upstart "elite" how a real detective works!
Yeah...
You're on fire now, Watson.
Get him, Watson!!
Yeah!
A-all right... then let's go...
Can we do that? It's kind of a detective's job...
Not to worry—you have the great Sherlock Holmes with you!!
THMP
Yes, but before that...
First, we must do some interrogating!
We'll start with the news staff who were working with Tsuzuki on the day of the murder.
STOP
ARF!
What?

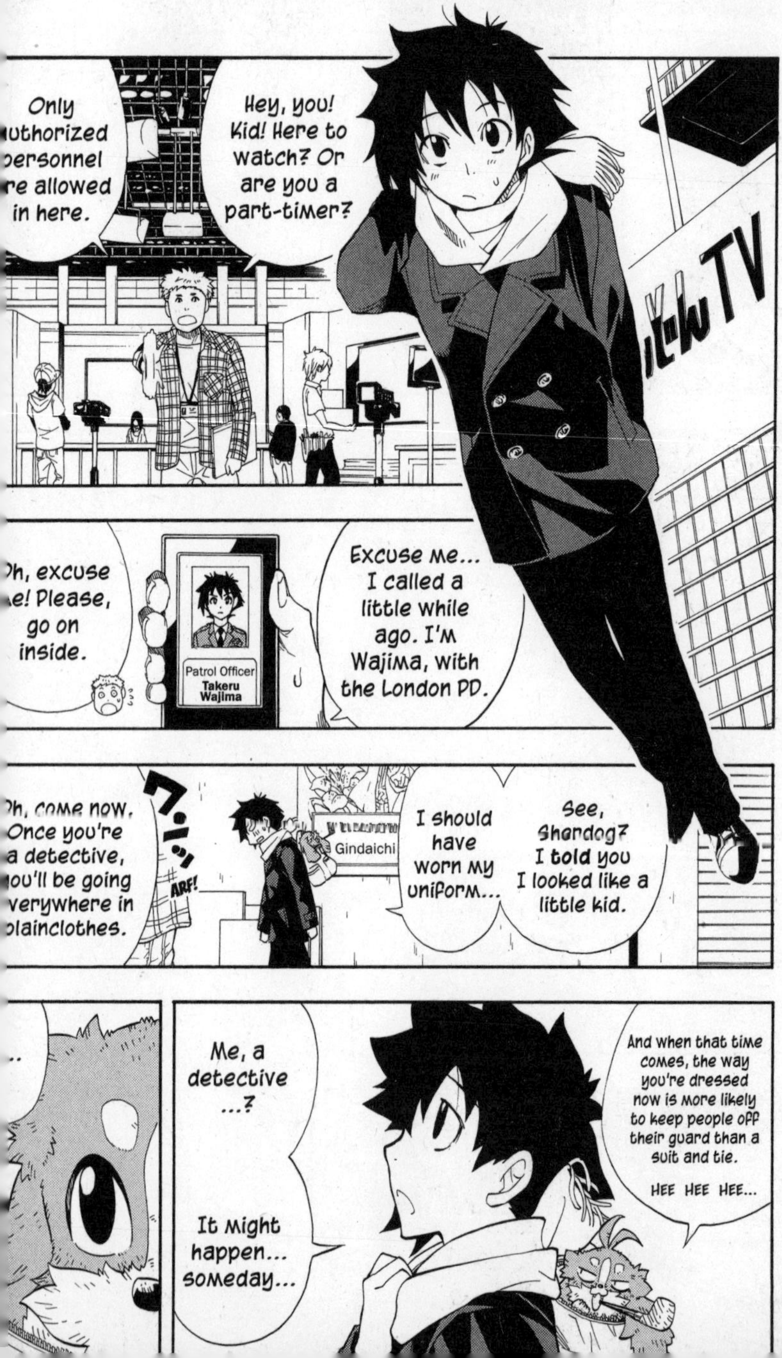

Hey, you! Kid! Here to watch? Or are you a part-timer?
Only uthorized ersonnel re allowed in here.
Excuse me... I called a little while ago. I'm Wajima, with the London PD.
Patrol Officer Takeru Wajima
h, excuse e! Please, go on inside.
See, Shardog? I told you I looked like a little kid.
I should have worn my uniform...
Gindaichi
ARF!
h, come now. Once you're a detective, ou'll be going verywhere in lainclothes.
And when that time comes, the way you're dressed now is more likely to keep people off their guard than a suit and tie.
HEE HEE HEE...
Me, a detective ...?
It might happen... someday...

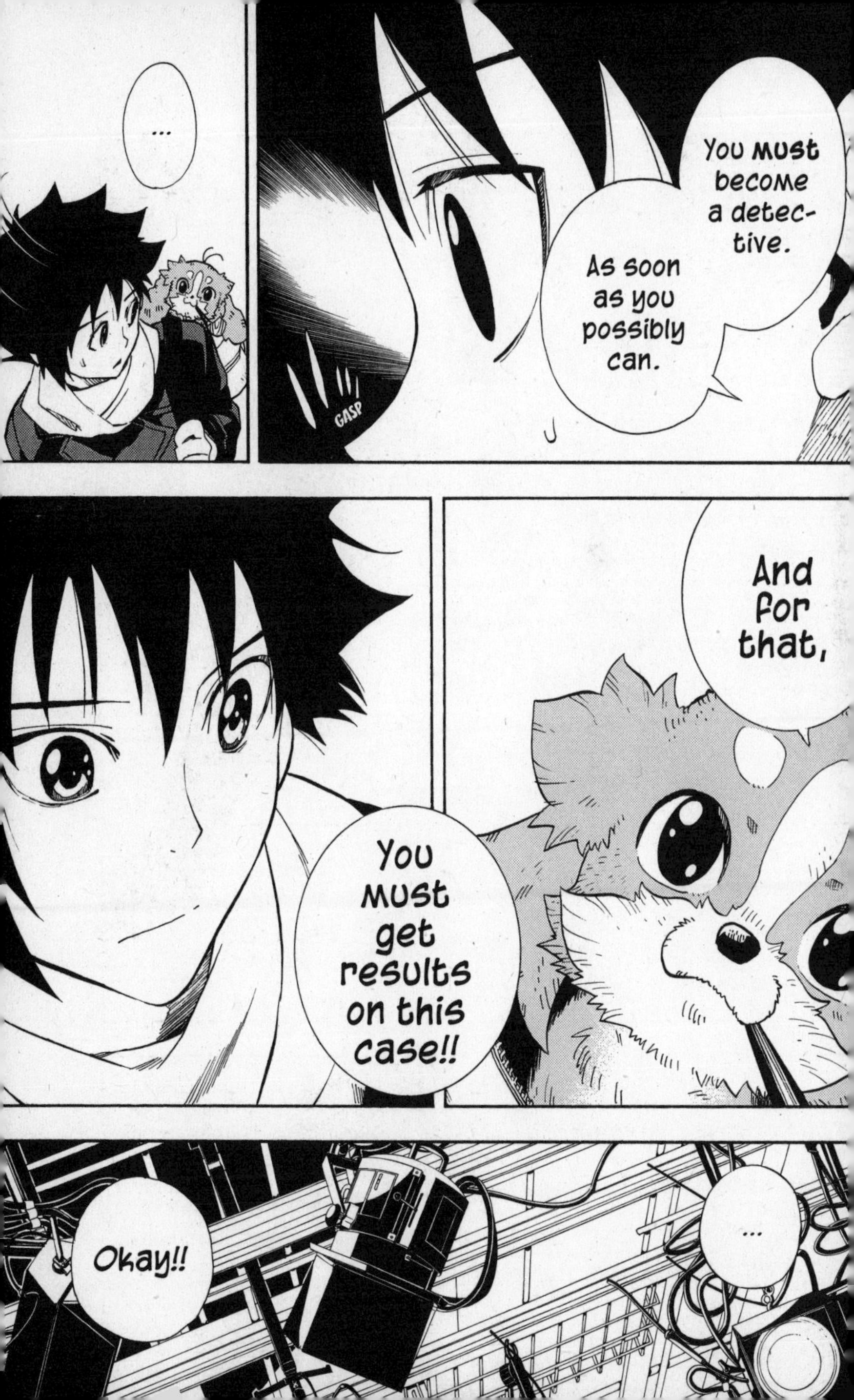
You must become a detective.
As soon as you possibly can.
GASP
...
And for that,
You must get results on this case!!
...
Okay!!

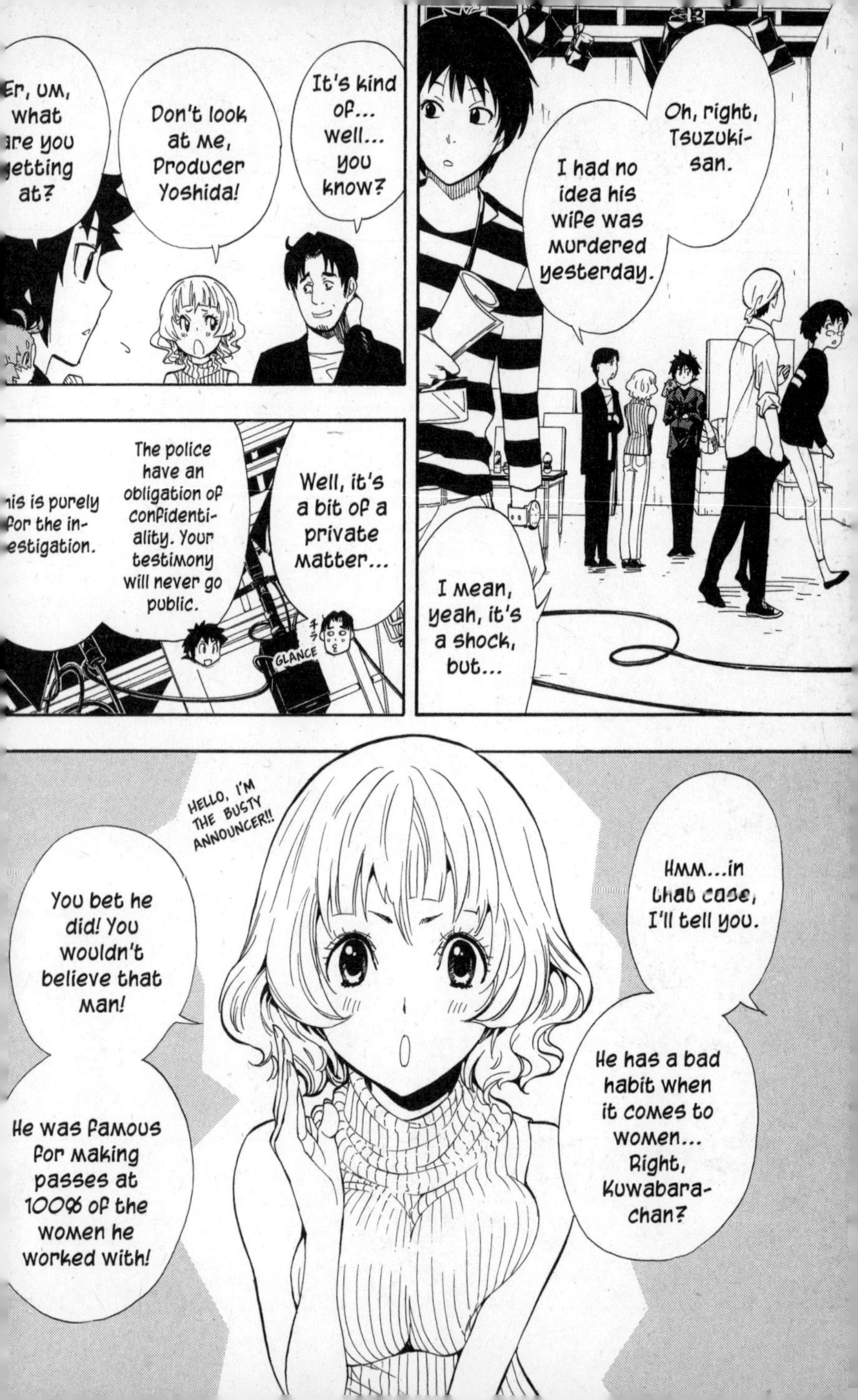
Oh, right, Tsuzuki-san.
I had no idea his wife was murdered yesterday.
I mean, yeah, it's a shock, but...
It's kind of... well... you know?
Don't look at me, Producer Yoshida!
Er, um, what are you getting at?
Well, it's a bit of a private matter...
The police have an obligation of confidenti-ality. Your testimony will never go public.
This is purely for the in-vestigation.
チラ
GLANCE
HELLO, I'M THE BUSTY ANNOUNCER!!
Hmm...in that case, I'll tell you.
He has a bad habit when it comes to women... Right, Kuwabara-chan?
You bet he did! You wouldn't believe that man!
He was famous for making passes at 100% of the women he worked with!

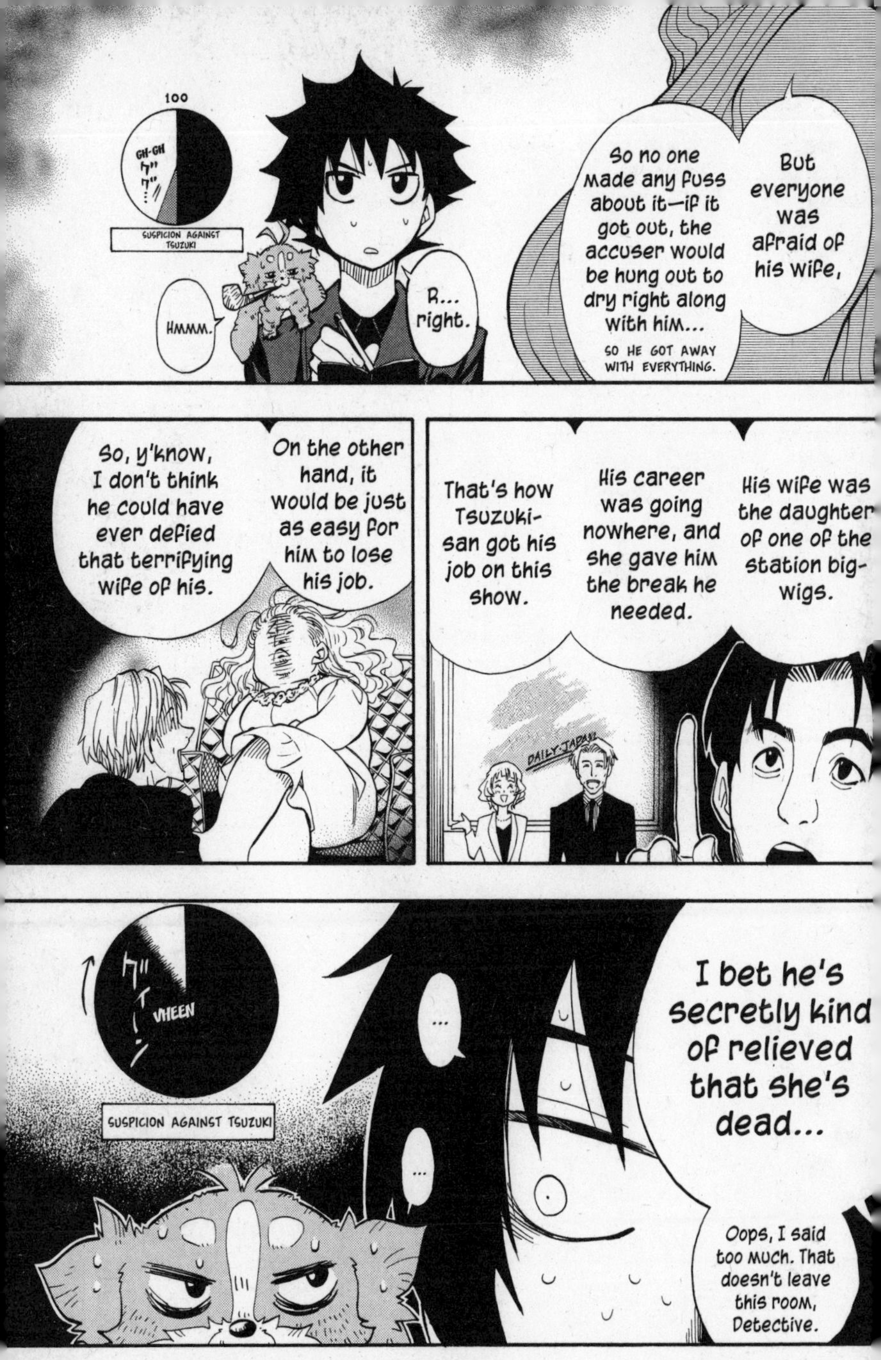
But everyone was afraid of his wife,
So no one made any fuss about it—if it got out, the accuser would be hung out to dry right along with him...
SO HE GOT AWAY WITH EVERYTHING.
R... right.
100
GH-GH
SUSPICION AGAINST TSUZUKI
HMMM.
His wife was the daughter of one of the station big-wigs.
His career was going nowhere, and she gave him the break he needed.
That's how Tsuzuki-san got his job on this show.
DAILY JAPAN
On the other hand, it would be just as easy for him to lose his job.
So, y'know, I don't think he could have ever defied that terrifying wife of his.
I bet he's secretly kind of relieved that she's dead...
Oops, I said too much. That doesn't leave this room, Detective.
...
...
VHEEN
SUSPICION AGAINST TSUZUKI

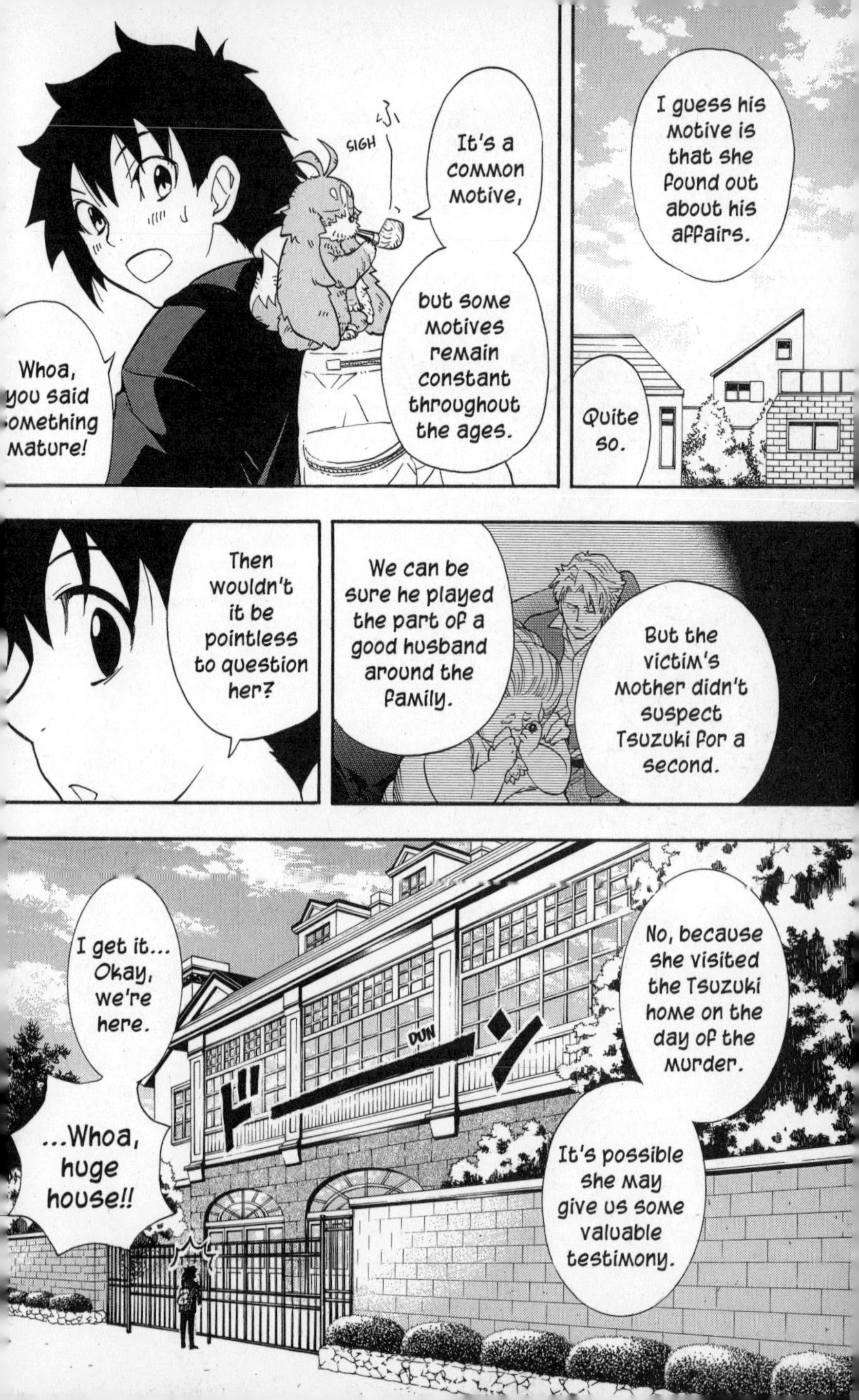
I guess his motive is that she found out about his affairs.
Quite so.
It's a common motive,
SIGH
but some motives remain constant throughout the ages.
Whoa, you said omething mature!
We can be sure he played the part of a good husband around the family.
But the victim's mother didn't suspect Tsuzuki for a second.
Then wouldn't it be pointless to question her?
No, because she visited the Tsuzuki home on the day of the murder.
It's possible she may give us some valuable testimony.
DUN
I get it... Okay, we're here.
...Whoa, huge house!!

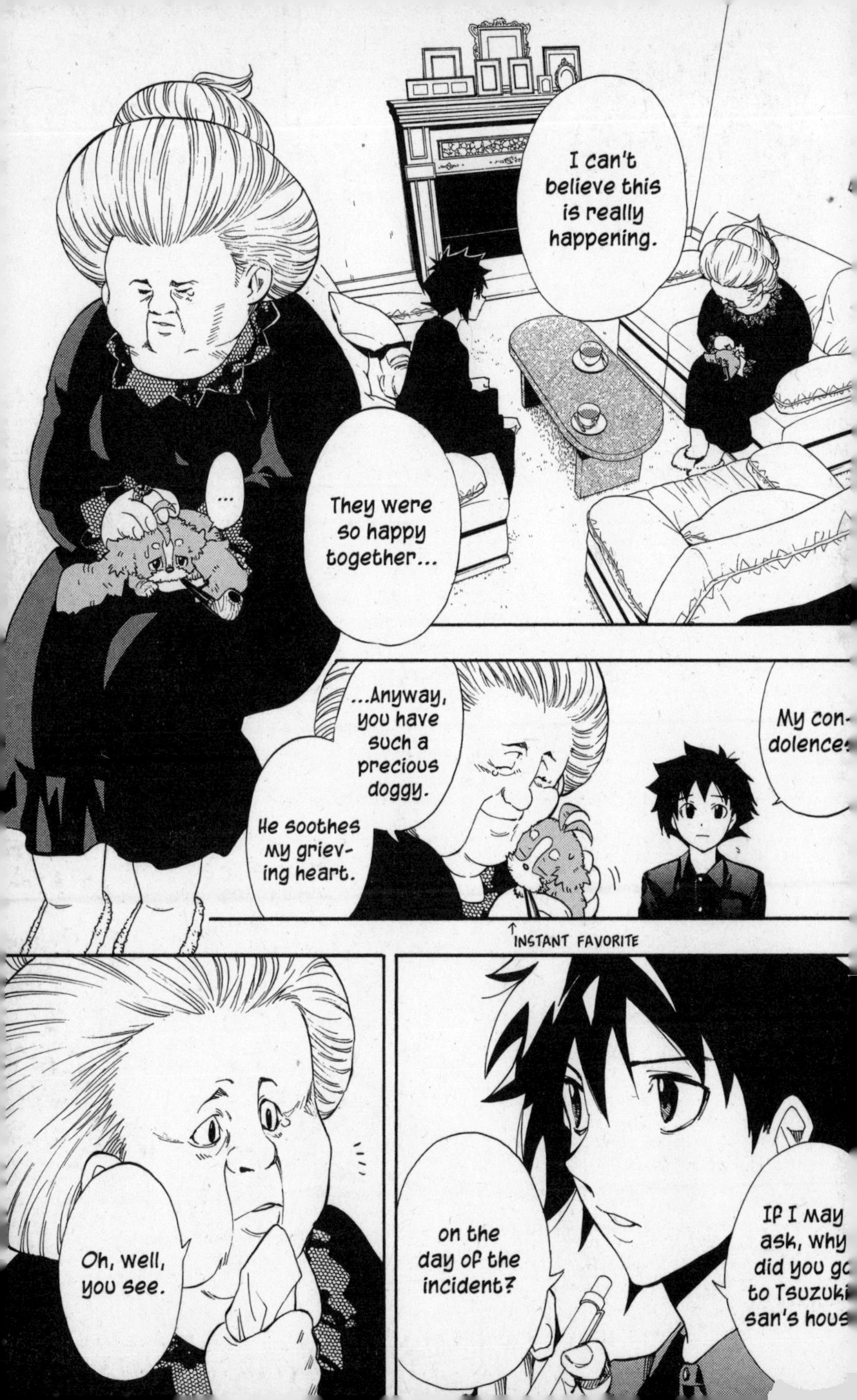
I can't believe this is really happening.
They were so happy together...
My condolences
...Anyway, you have such a precious doggy.
He soothes my grieving heart.
INSTANT FAVORITE
...
If I may ask, why did you go to Tsuzuki-san's house
on the day of the incident?
Oh, well, you see.

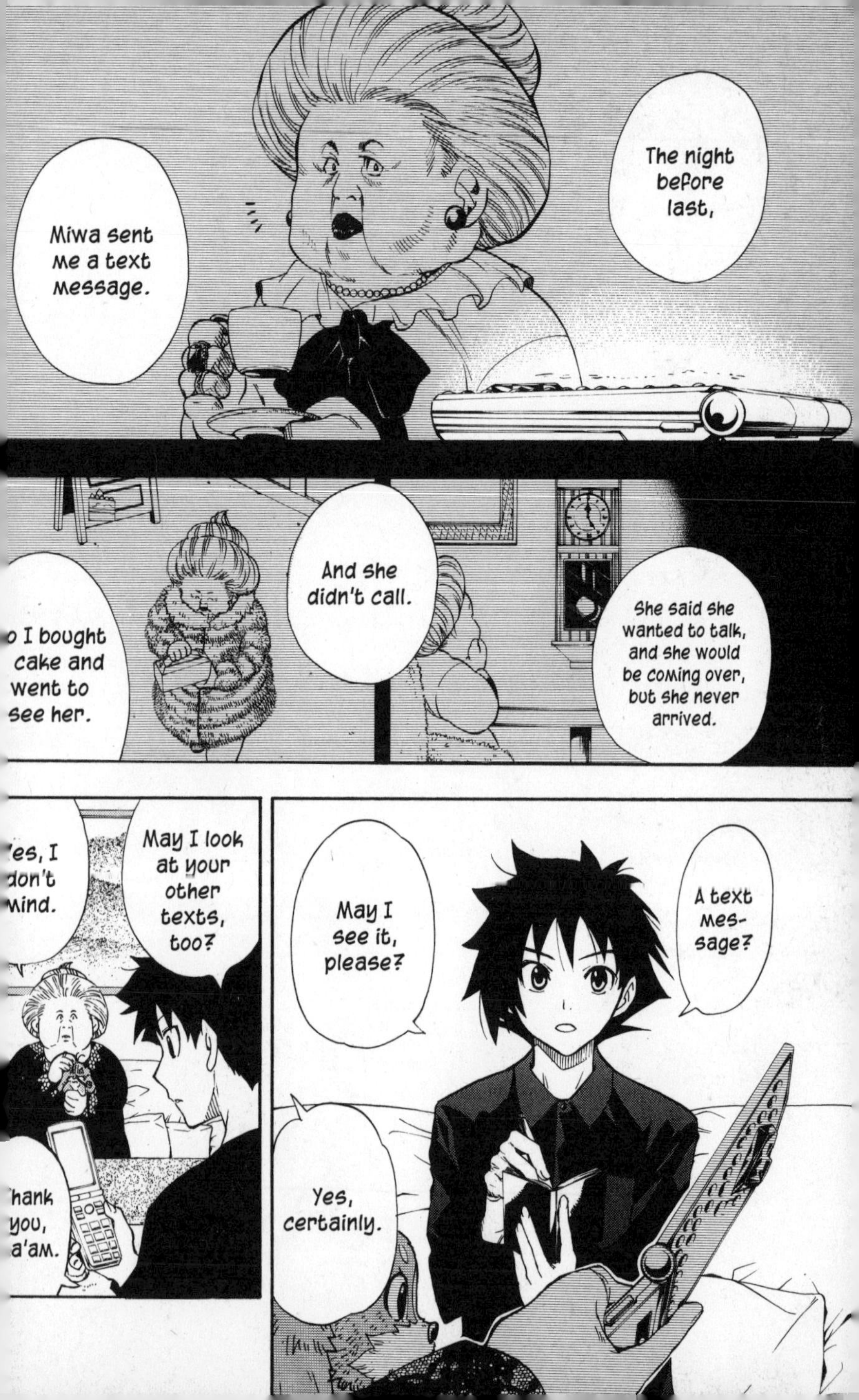

The night before last,
Miwa sent me a text message.
She said she wanted to talk, and she would be coming over, but she never arrived.
And she didn't call.
o I bought cake and went to see her.
A text mes-sage?
May I see it, please?
Yes, certainly.
May I look at your other texts, too?
es, I don't mind.
hank you, a'am.

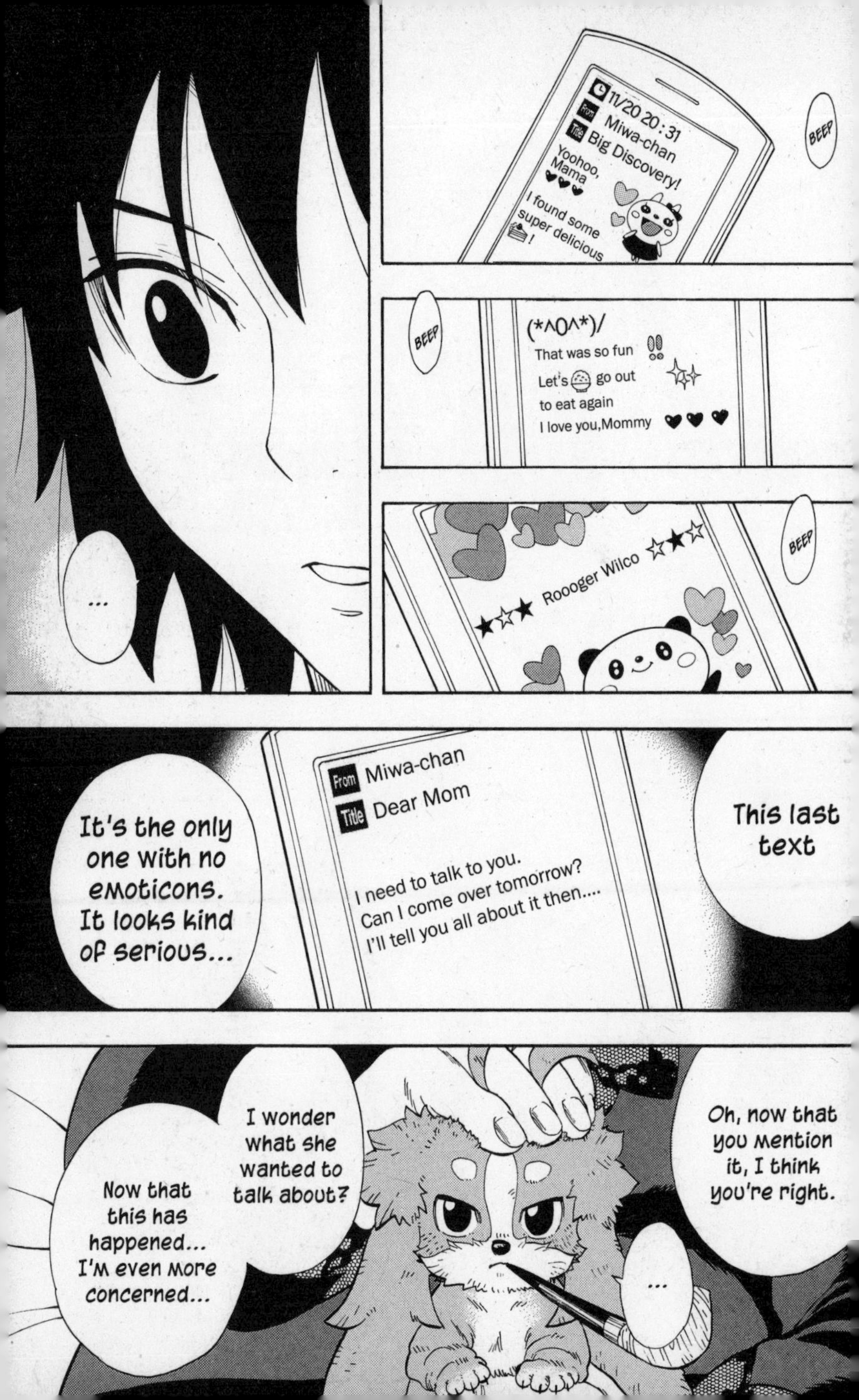
BEEP
11/20 20 : 31
From Miwa-chan
Title Big Discovery!
Yoohoo, Mama
I found some super delicious !
BEEP
(*^O^*)/
That was so fun
Let's go out to eat again
I love you,Mommy
BEEP
Roooger Wilco
...
This last text
From Miwa-chan
Title Dear Mom
I need to talk to you. Can I come over tomorrow? I'll tell you all about it then....
It's the only one with no emoticons. It looks kind of serious...
Oh, now that you mention it, I think you're right.
...
I wonder what she wanted to talk about?
Now that this has happened... I'm even more concerned...

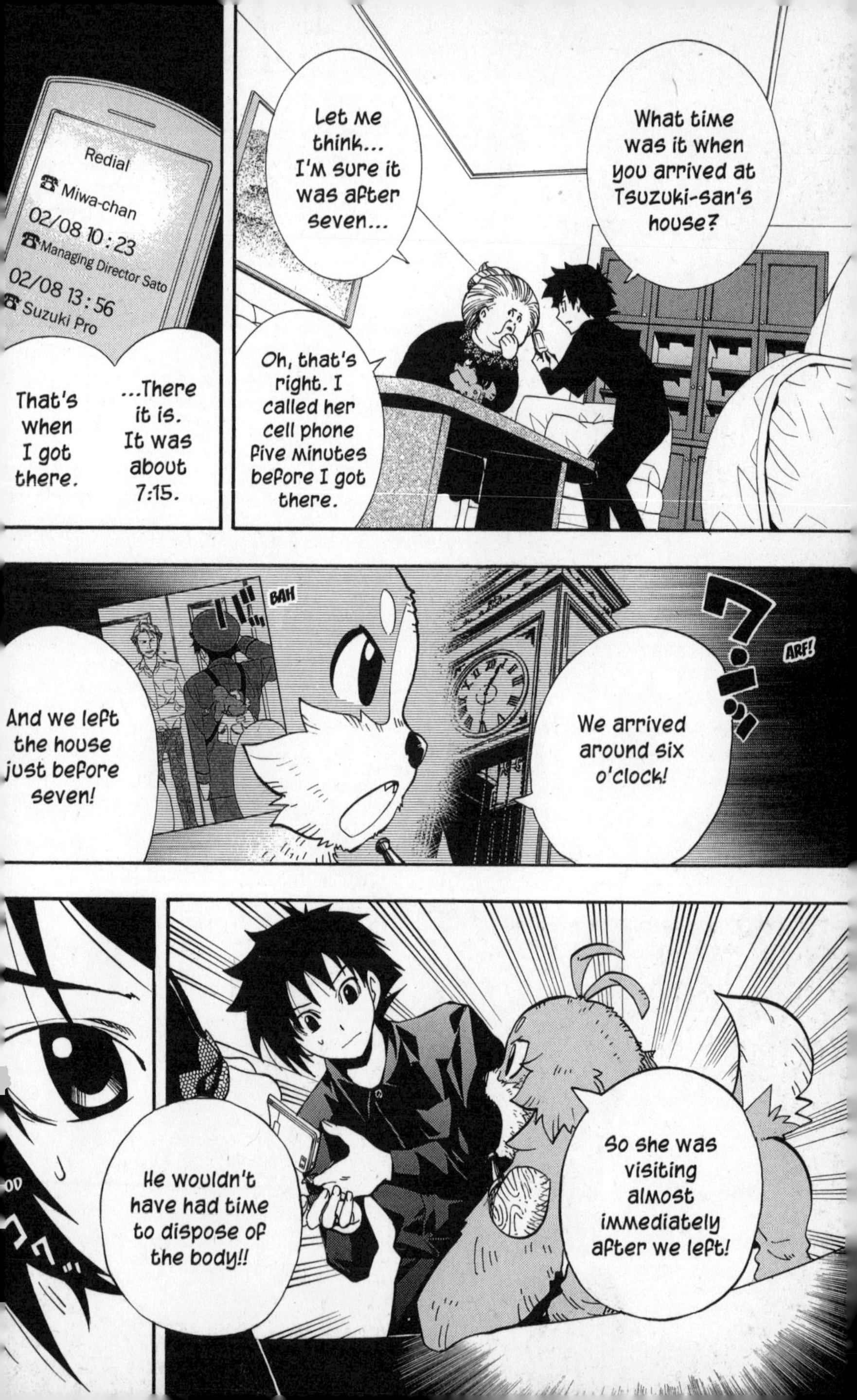
What time was it when you arrived at Tsuzuki-san's house?
Let me think... I'm sure it was after seven...
Oh, that's right. I called her cell phone five minutes before I got there.
Redial
Miwa-chan
02/08 10:23
Managing Director Sato
02/08 13:56
Suzuki Pro
...There it is. It was about 7:15.
That's when I got there.
ARF!
We arrived around six o'clock!
BAH
And we left the house just before seven!
So she was visiting almost immediately after we left!
He wouldn't have had time to dispose of the body!!

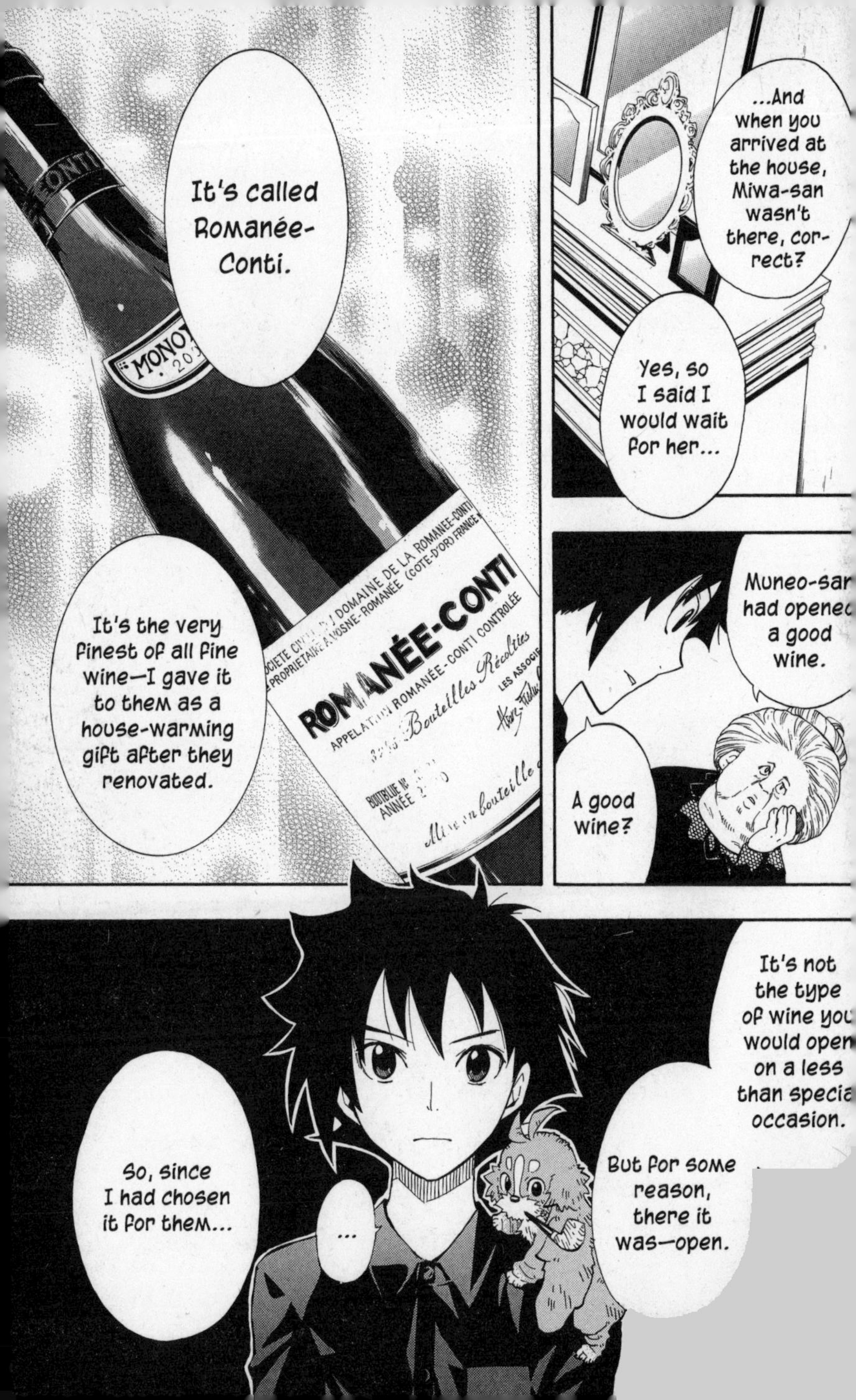
...And when you arrived at the house, Miwa-san wasn't there, correct?
Yes, so I said I would wait for her...
Muneo-sar had openec a good wine.
A good wine?
It's called Romanée-Conti.
ROMANÉE-CONTI
It's the very finest of all fine wine—I gave it to them as a house-warming gift after they renovated.
It's not the type of wine you would open on a less than specia occasion.
But for some reason, there it was—open.
...
So, since I had chosen it for them...

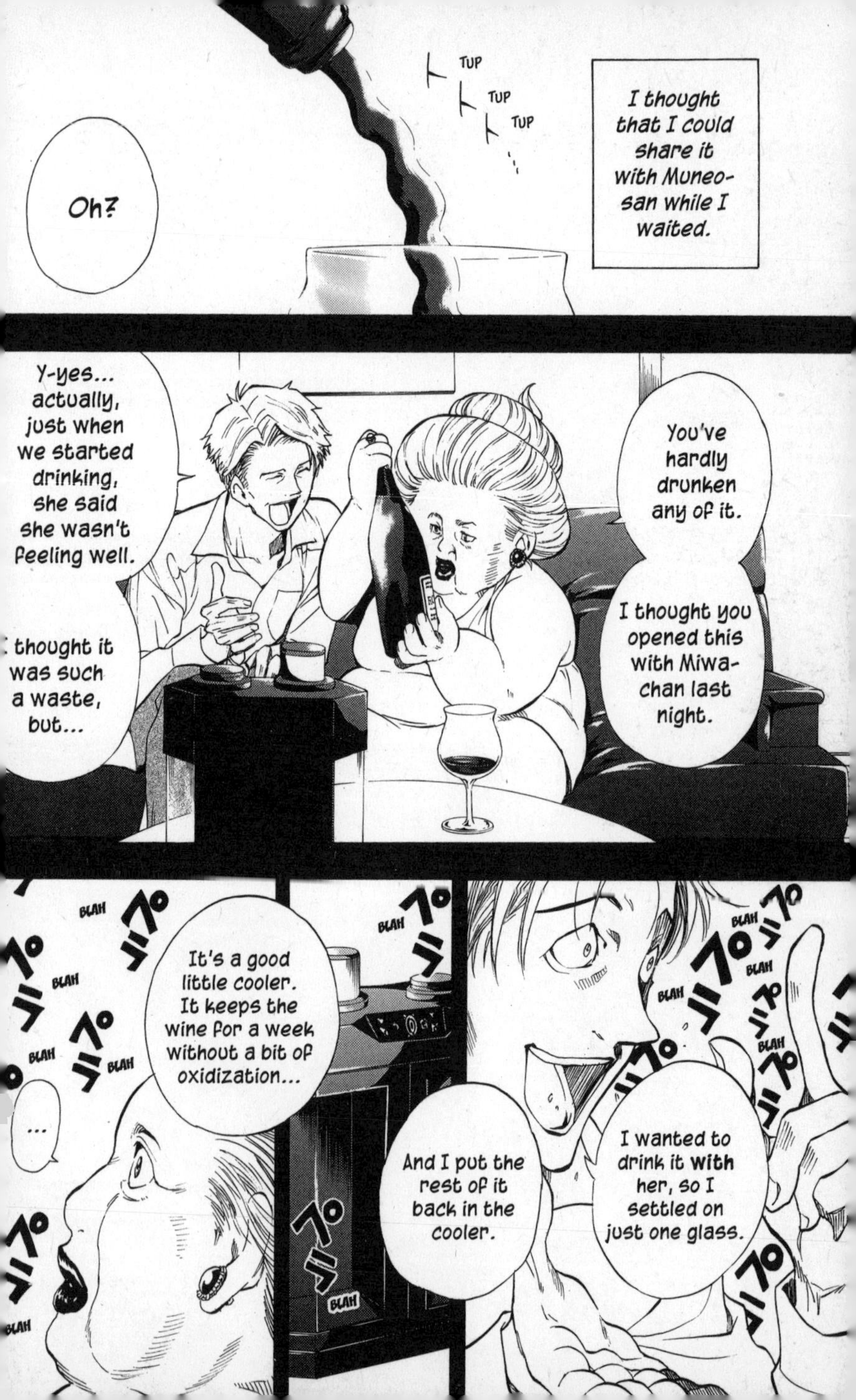
I thought that I could share it with Muneo-san while I waited.
TUP
TUP
TUP
Oh?
You've hardly drunken any of it.
I thought you opened this with Miwa-chan last night.
Y-yes... actually, just when we started drinking, she said she wasn't feeling well.
thought it was such a waste, but...
BLAH
I wanted to drink it with her, so I settled on just one glass.
And I put the rest of it back in the cooler.
BLAH
It's a good little cooler. It keeps the wine for a week without a bit of oxidization...
BLAH
...

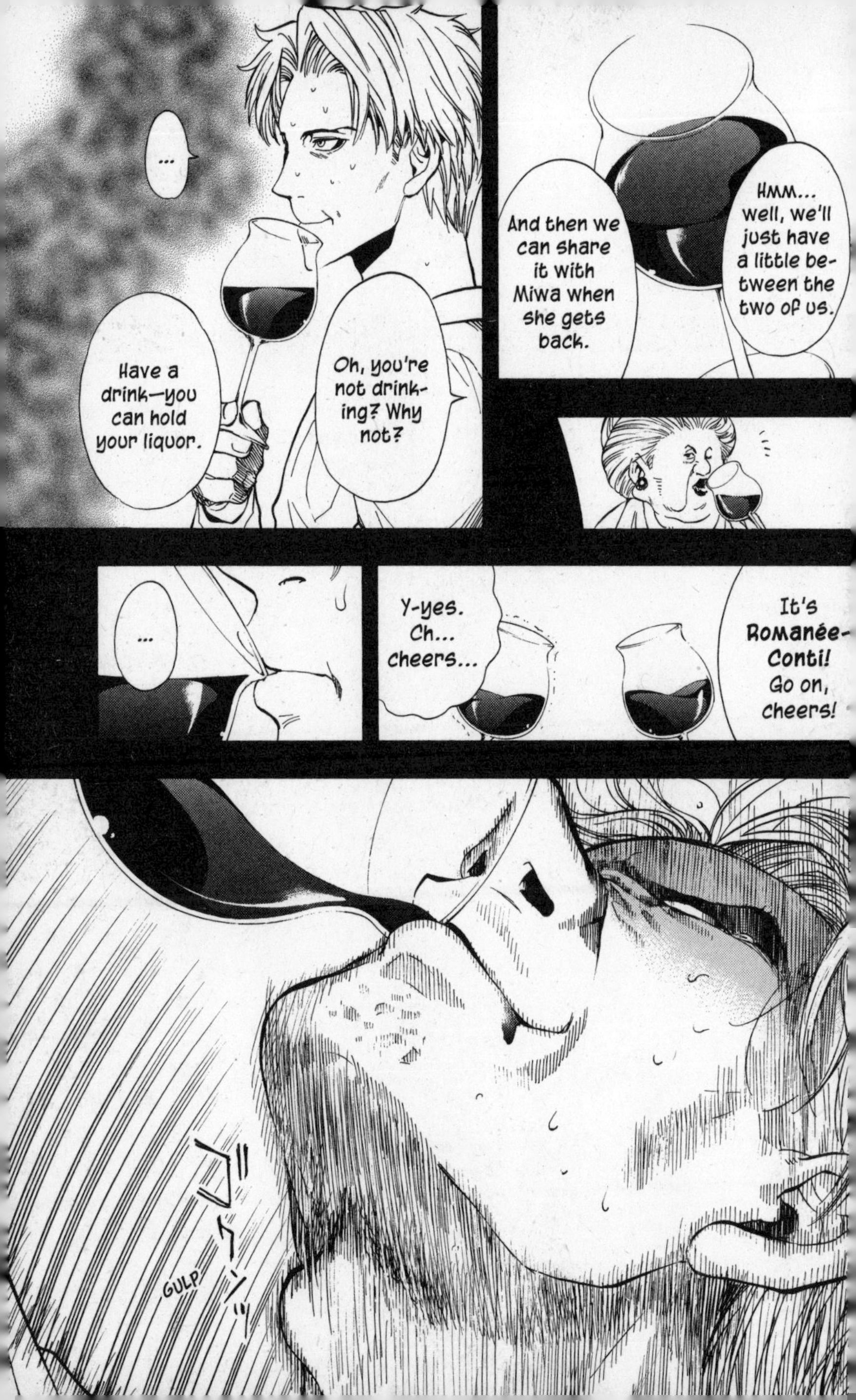
Hmm... well, we'll just have a little between the two of us.
And then we can share it with Miwa when she gets back.
...
Oh, you're not drinking? Why not?
Have a drink—you can hold your liquor.
It's Romanée-Conti! Go on, cheers!
Y-yes. Ch... cheers...
...
GULP

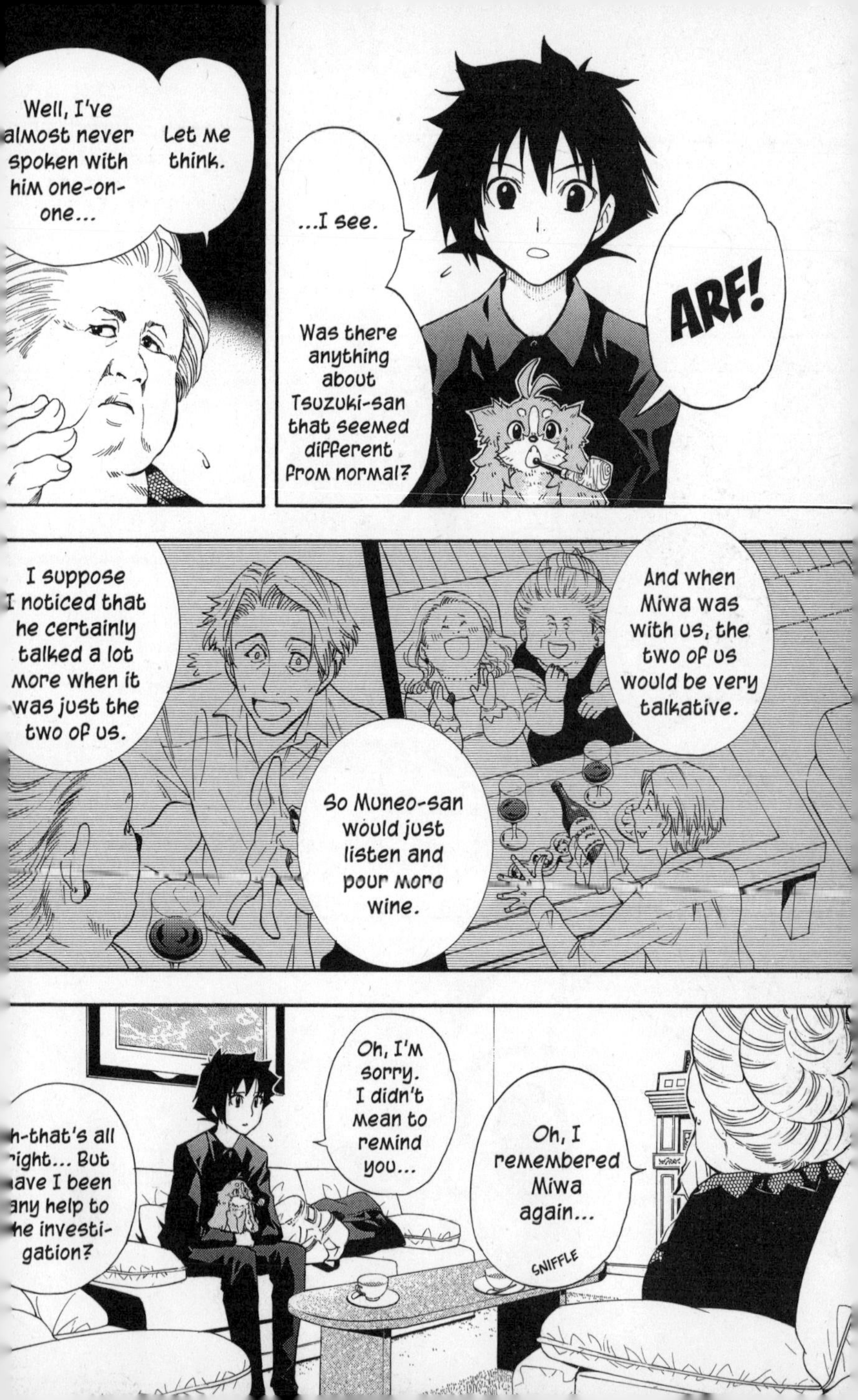
...I see.
Was there anything about Tsuzuki-san that seemed different from normal?
ARF!
Let me think.
Well, I've almost never spoken with him one-on-one...
And when Miwa was with us, the two of us would be very talkative.
So Muneo-san would just listen and pour more wine.
I suppose I noticed that he certainly talked a lot more when it was just the two of us.
Oh, I remembered Miwa again...
SNIFFLE
Oh, I'm sorry. I didn't mean to remind you...
h-that's all ight... But ave I been any help to he investi-gation?

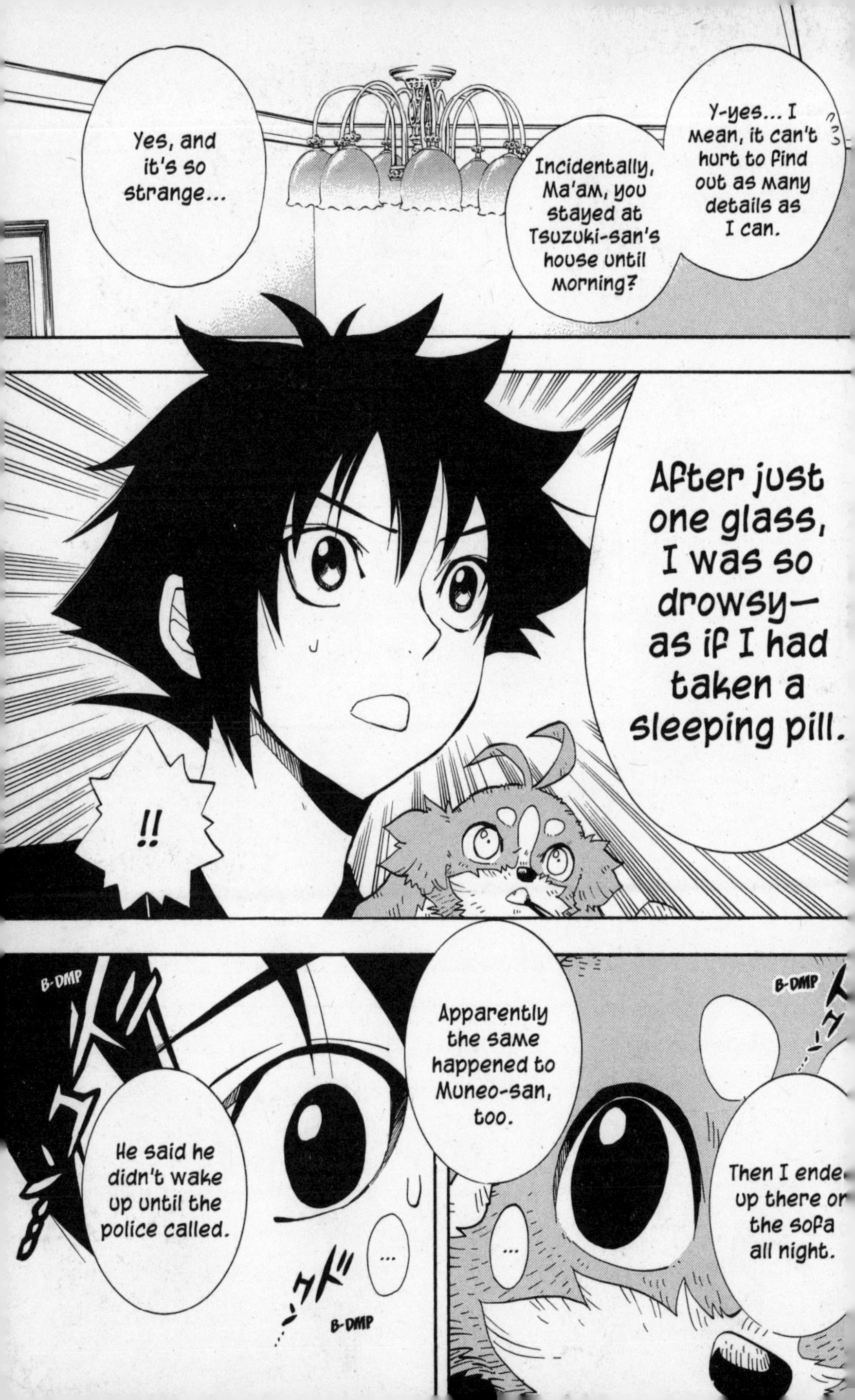
Y-yes... I mean, it can't hurt to find out as many details as I can.
Incidentally, Ma'am, you stayed at Tsuzuki-san's house until morning?
Yes, and it's so strange...
After just one glass, I was so drowsy— as if I had taken a sleeping pill.
!!
B-DMP
Then I ende up there or the sofa all night.
...
Apparently the same happened to Muneo-san, too.
B-DMP
He said he didn't wake up until the police called.
...
B-DMP

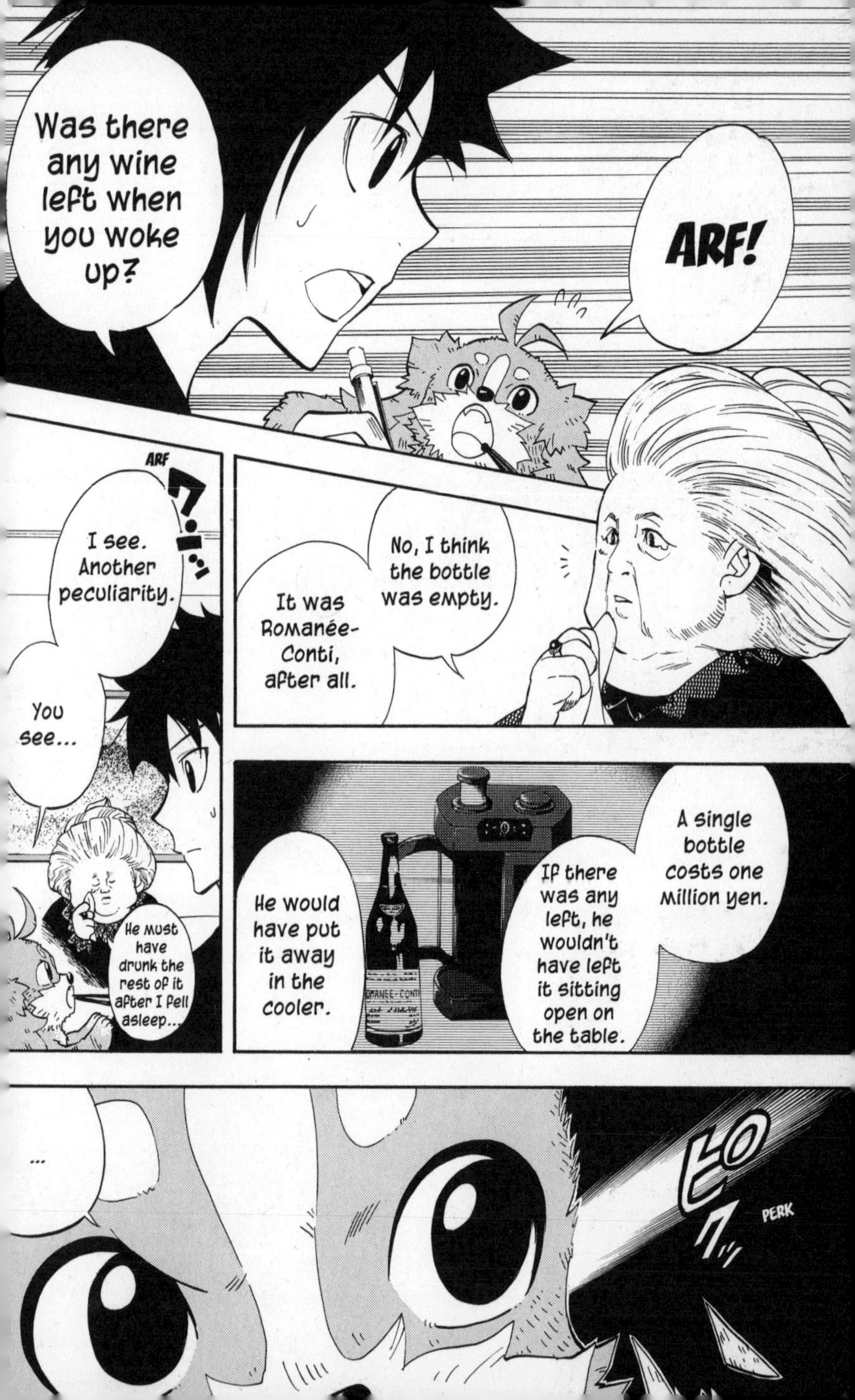

Was there any wine left when you woke up?
ARF!
No, I think the bottle was empty.
It was Romanée-Conti, after all.
A single bottle costs one million yen.
If there was any left, he wouldn't have left it sitting open on the table.
He would have put it away in the cooler.
ARF
I see. Another peculiarity.
You see...
He must have drunk the rest of it after I fell asleep...
PERK
...

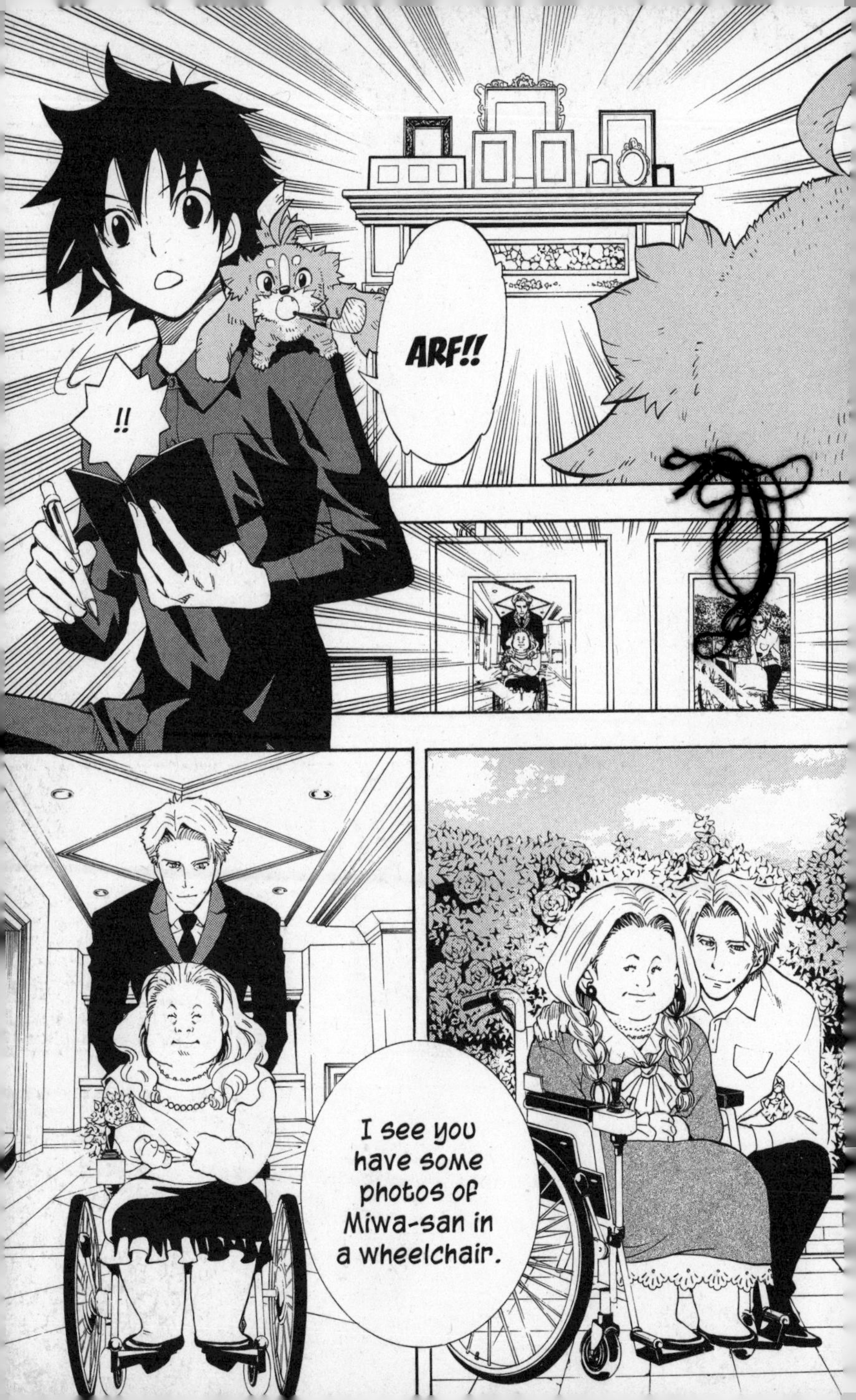
ARF!!
!!
I see you have some photos of Miwa-san in a wheelchair.

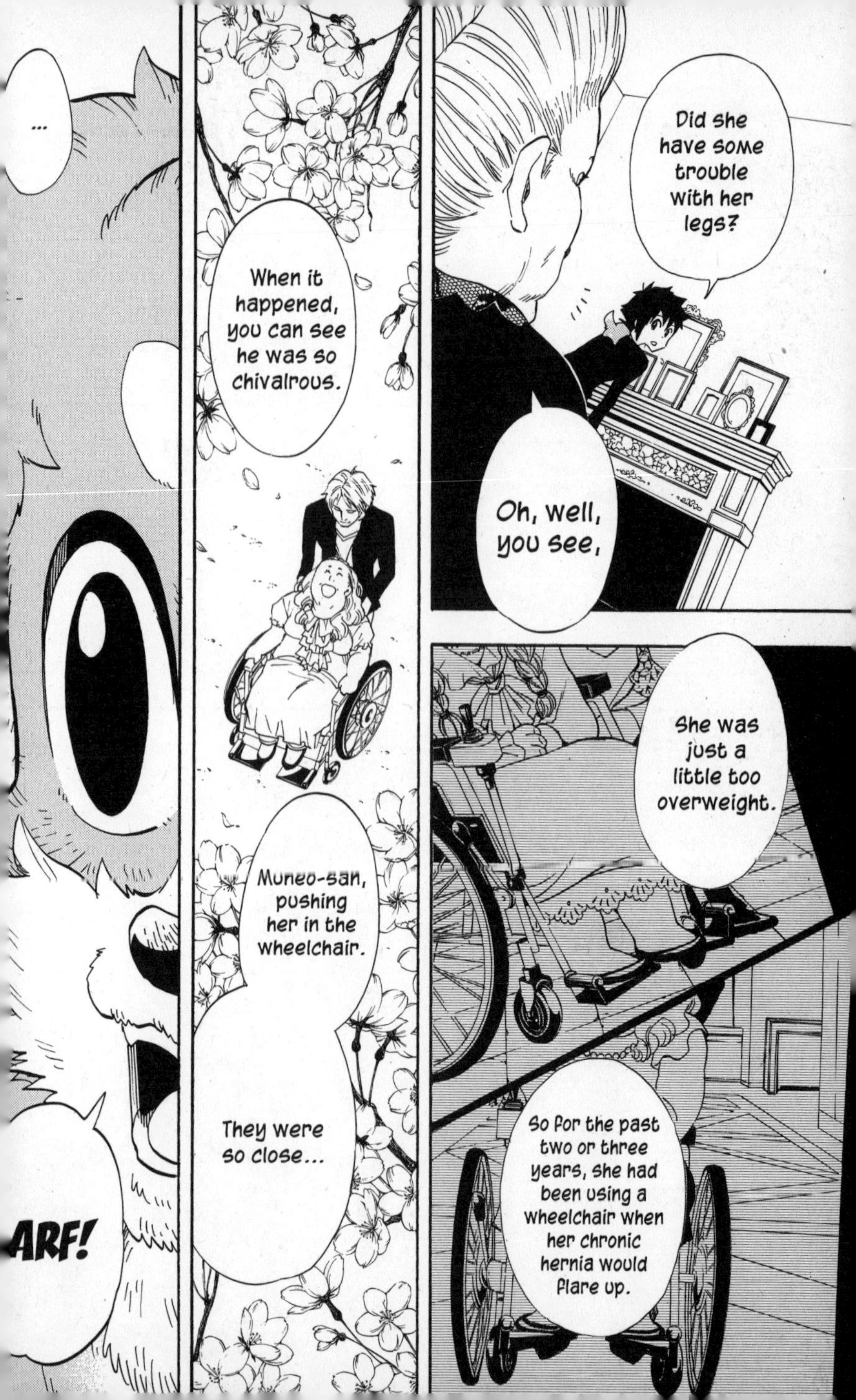
Did she have some trouble with her legs?
Oh, well, you see,
She was just a little too overweight.
So for the past two or three years, she had been using a wheelchair when her chronic hernia would flare up.
When it happened, you can see he was so chivalrous.
Muneo-san, pushing her in the wheelchair.
They were so close...
...
ARF!

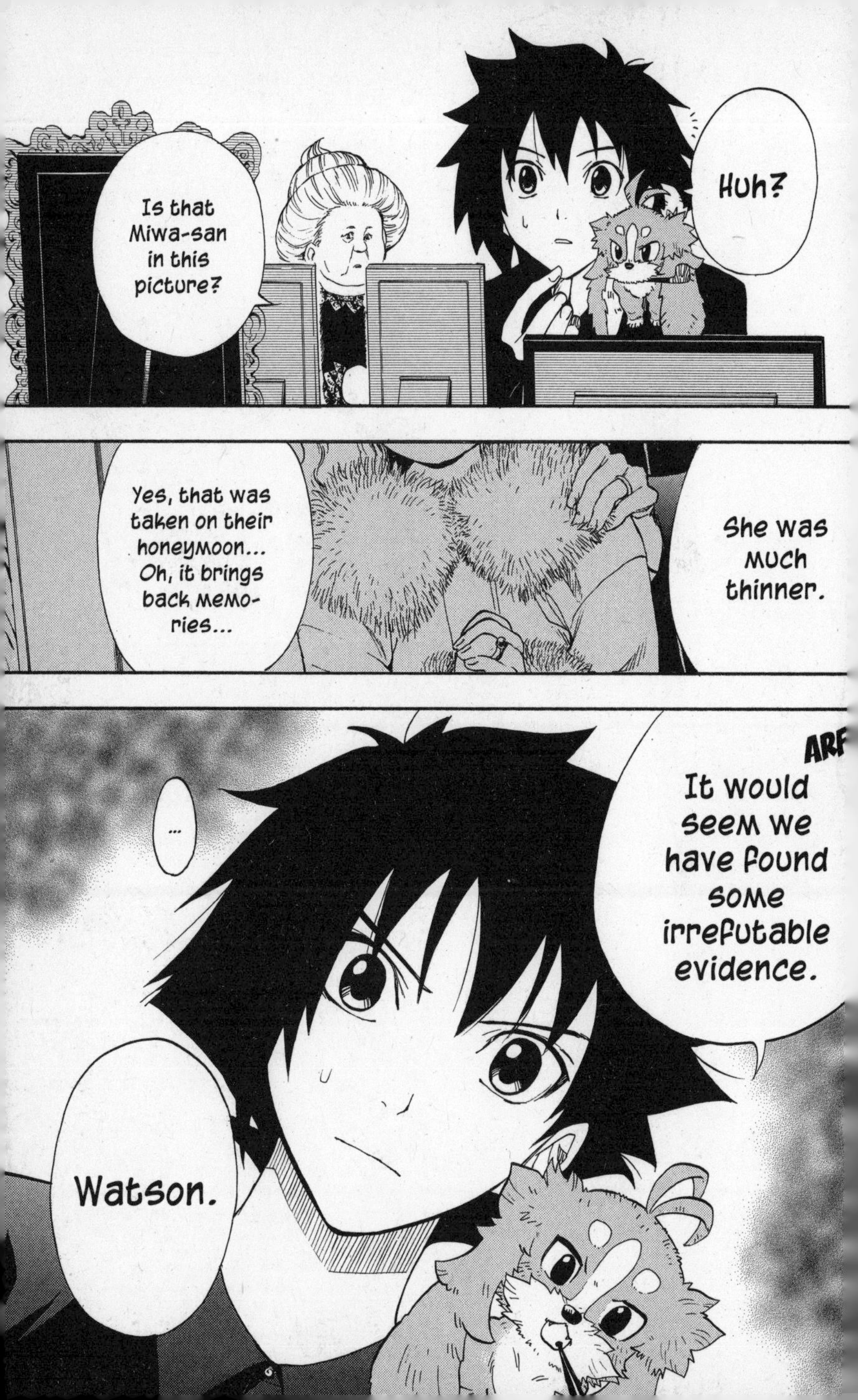

Huh?
Is that Miwa-san in this picture?
She was much thinner.
Yes, that was taken on their honeymoon... Oh, it brings back memo-ries...
ARF
It would seem we have found some irrefutable evidence.
...
Watson.

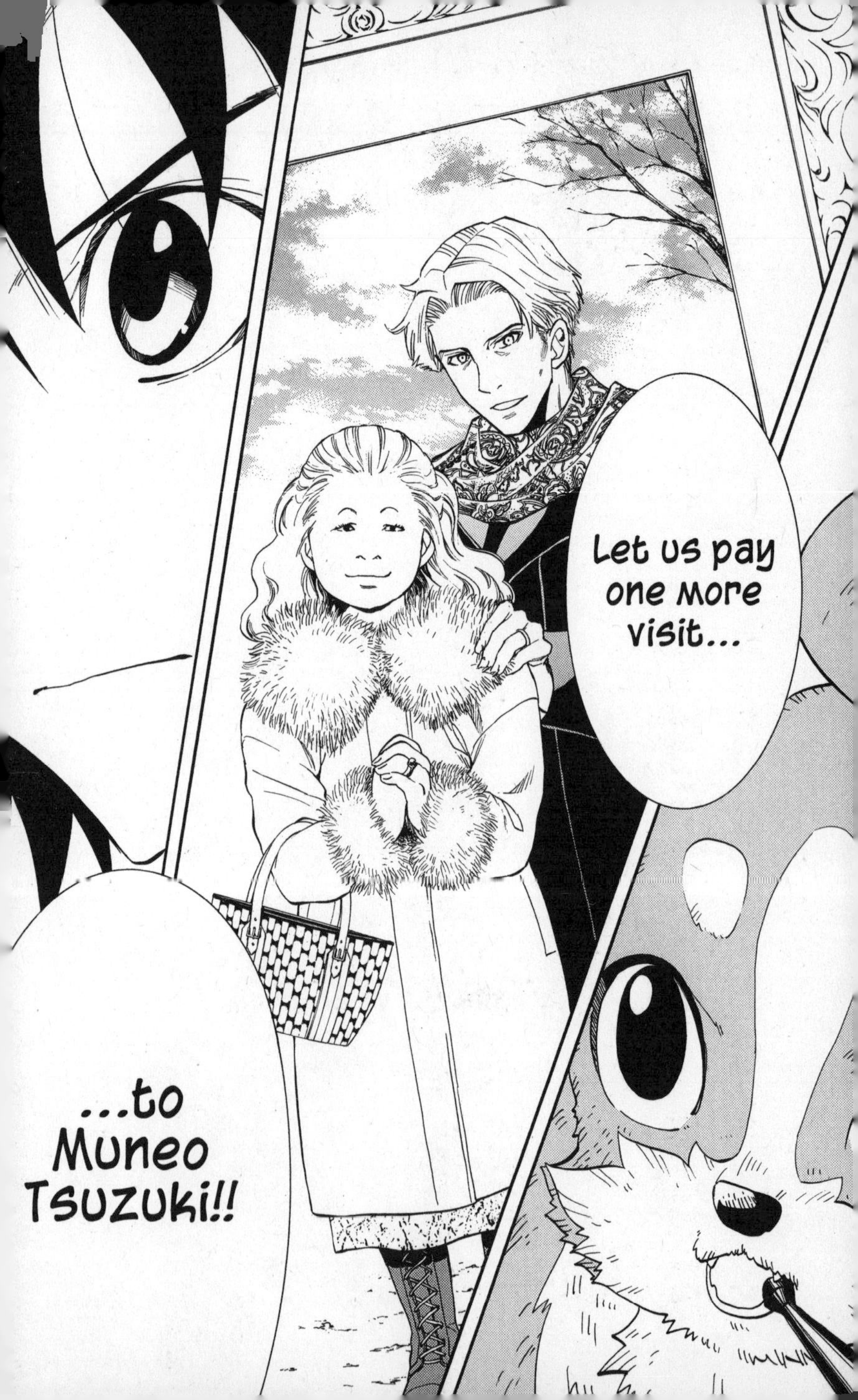
Let us pay one more visit...
...to Muneo TSUZUKi!!

Case 8: ⚜ Requiem for a New Beginning, Part 6

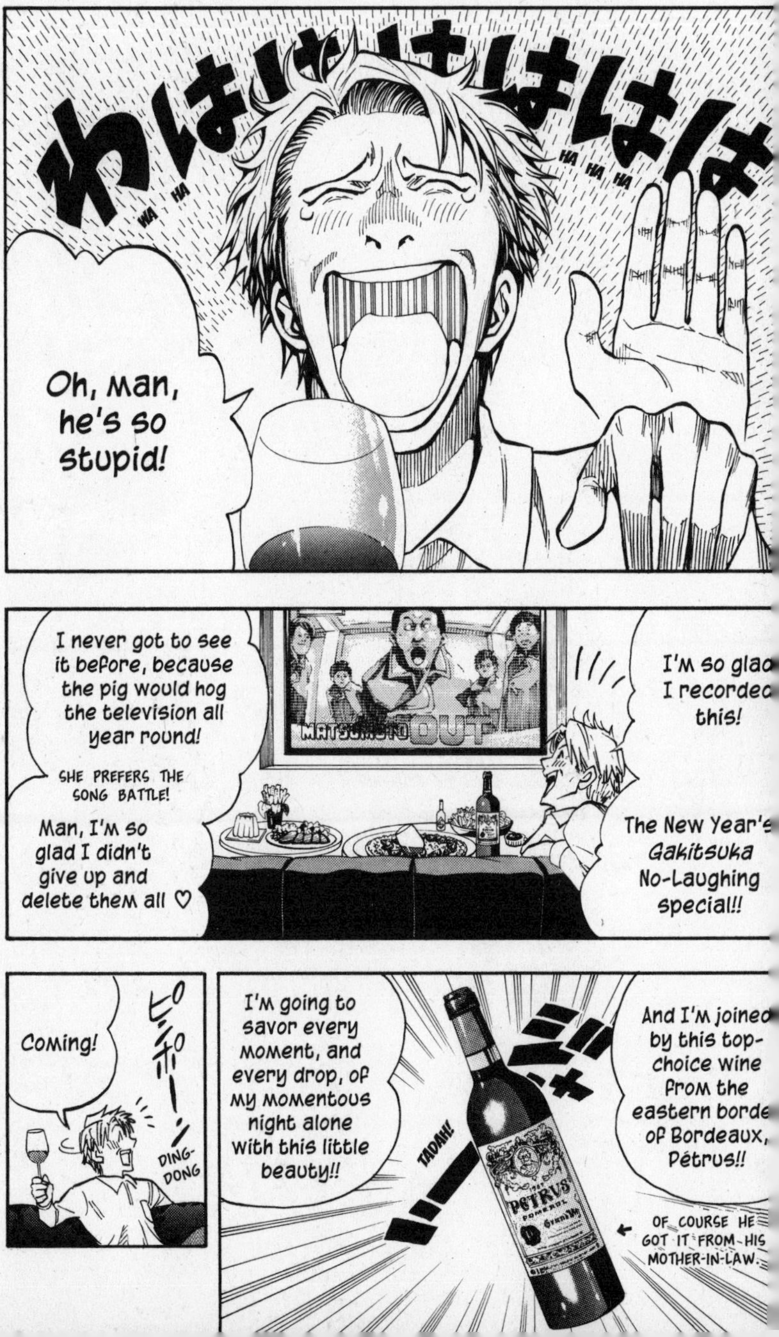

わはははははは
HA HA HA
WA HA
Oh, man, he's so stupid!
I'm so glad I recorded this!
The New Year's Gakitsuka No-Laughing special!!
MATSUMOTO OUT
I never got to see it before, because the pig would hog the television all year round!
SHE PREFERS THE SONG BATTLE!
Man, I'm so glad I didn't give up and delete them all ♡
And I'm joined by this top-choice wine from the eastern border of Bordeaux, Pétrus!!
OF COURSE HE GOT IT FROM HIS MOTHER-IN-LAW.
I'm going to savor every moment, and every drop, of my momentous night alone with this little beauty!!
TADAH!
PETRUS
POMEROL
ピンポーン
DING-DONG
Coming!

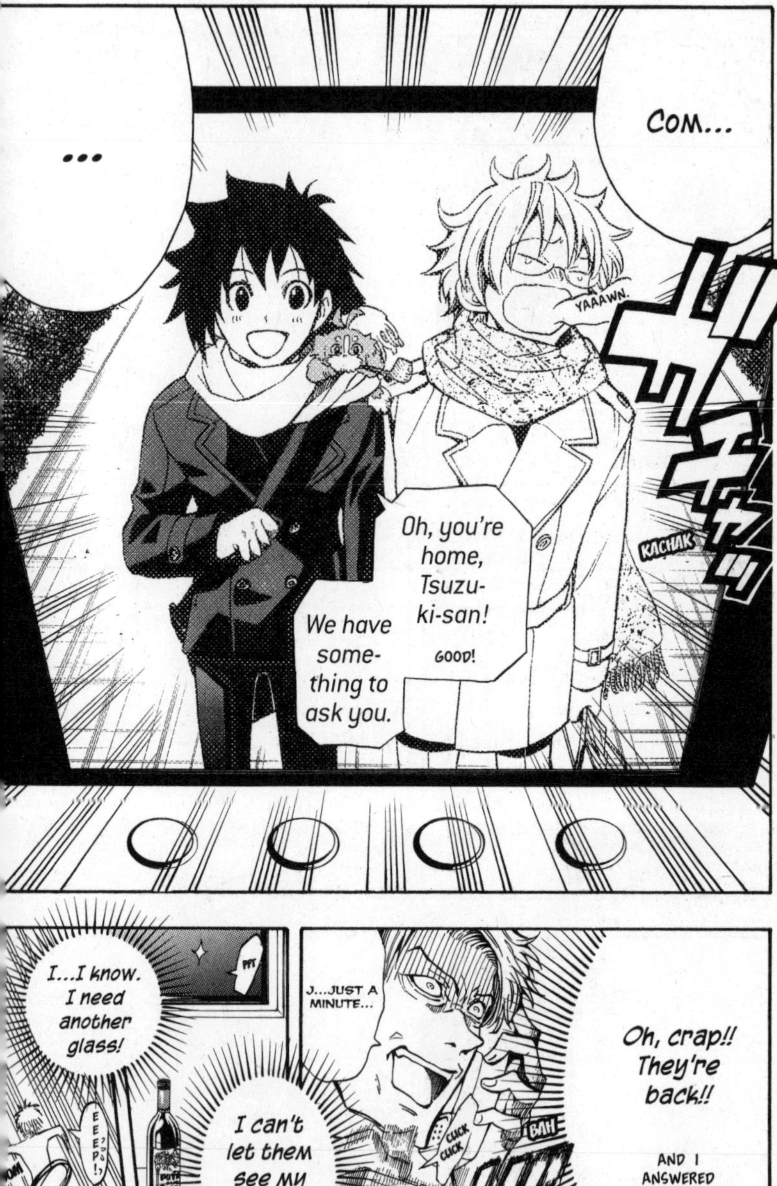
COM...
YAAAWN.
KACHAK
...
Oh, you're home, Tsuzuki-san!
GOOD!
We have something to ask you.
Oh, crap!! They're back!!
AND I ANSWERED THE INTERCOM!
J...JUST A MINUTE...
BAH
CLICK CLICK
I can't let them see my one-man party!!
I...I know. I need another glass!
PPT
EEEP!

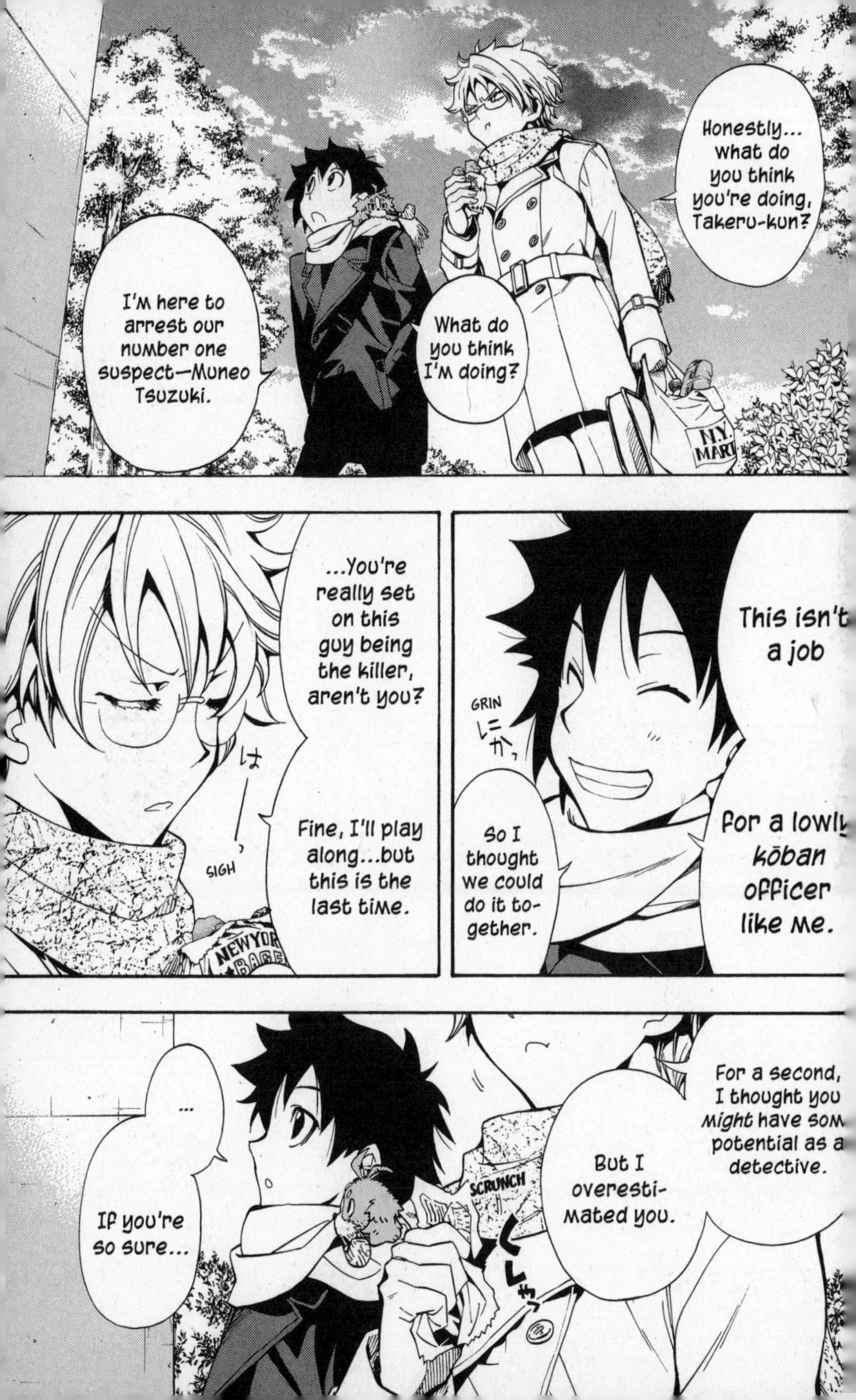
Honestly... what do you think you're doing, Takeru-kun?
What do you think I'm doing?
I'm here to arrest our number one suspect—Muneo Tsuzuki.
This isn't a job for a lowly kōban officer like me.
GRIN
So I thought we could do it together.
...You're really set on this guy being the killer, aren't you?
SIGH
Fine, I'll play along...but this is the last time.
For a second, I thought you might have som potential as a detective.
But I overestimated you.
SCRUNCH
...
If you're so sure...

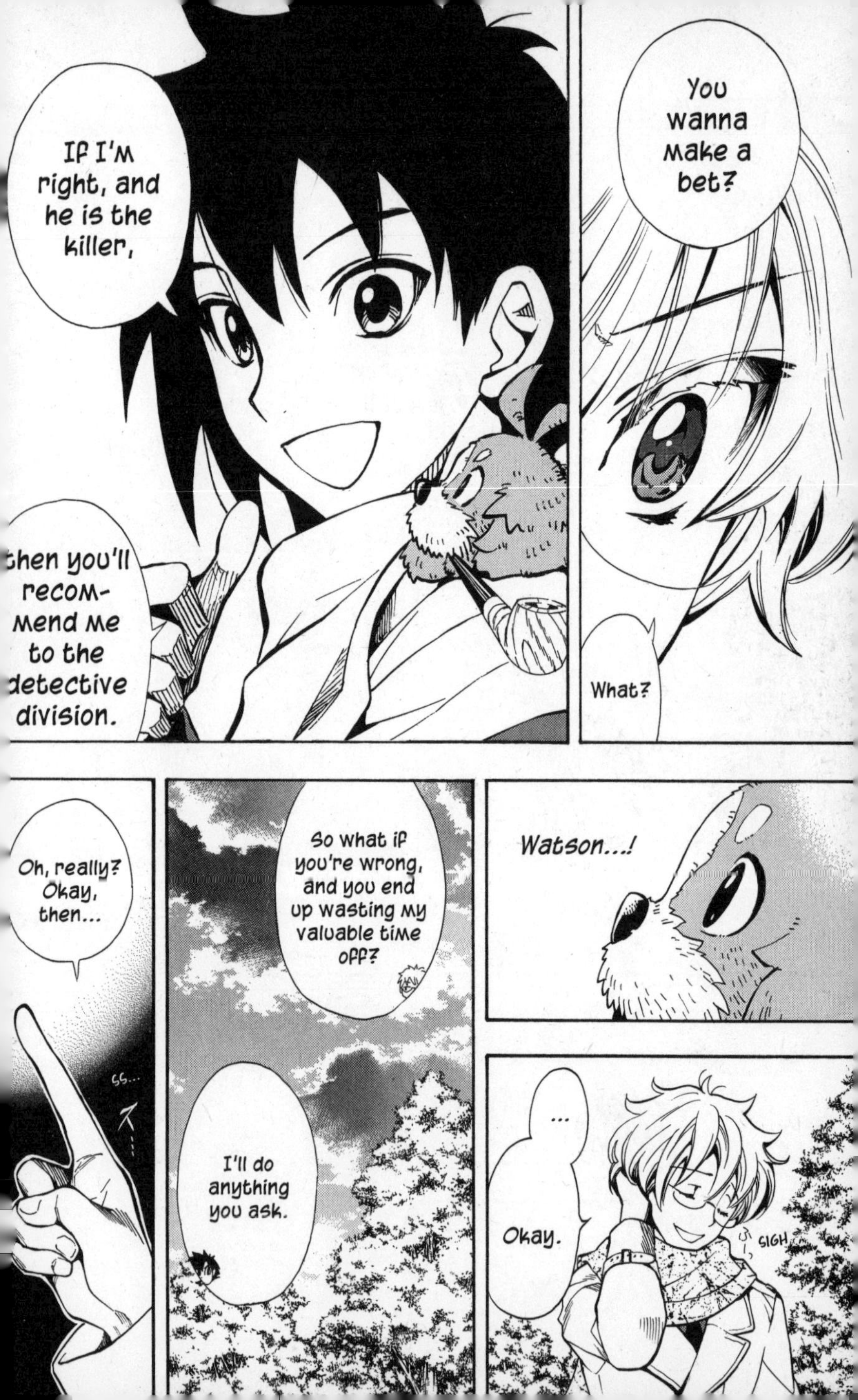
You wanna make a bet?
What?
If I'm right, and he is the killer,
then you'll recommend me to the detective division.
Watson...!
...
Okay.
SIGH
So what if you're wrong, and you end up wasting my valuable time off?
I'll do anything you ask.
Oh, really? Okay, then...
SS...

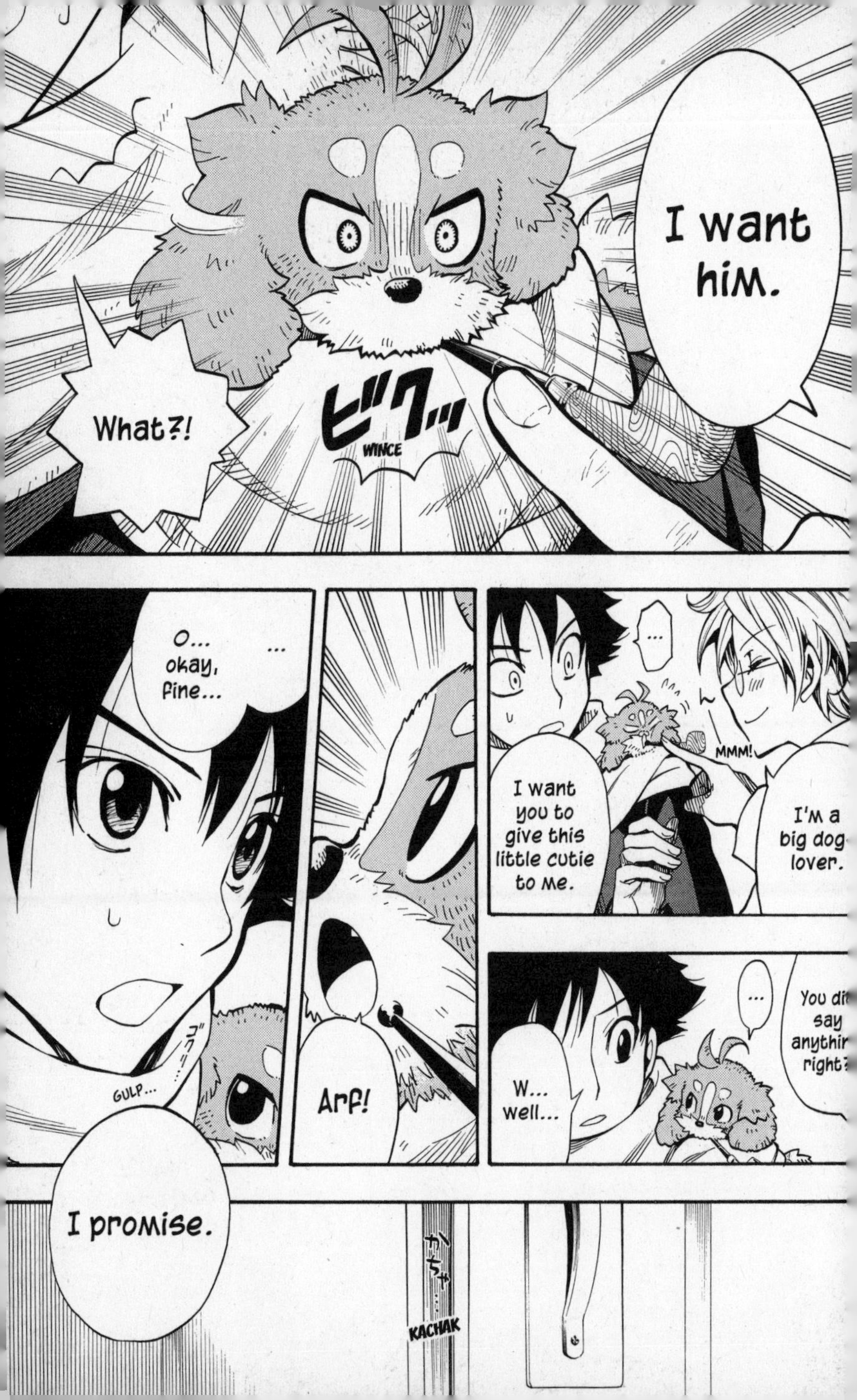
I want him.
WINCE
What?!
...
MMM!
I'm a big dog lover.
I want you to give this little cutie to me.
You di say anythi right?
...
W... well...
Arf!
...
O... okay, fine...
GULP...
I promise.
KACHAK

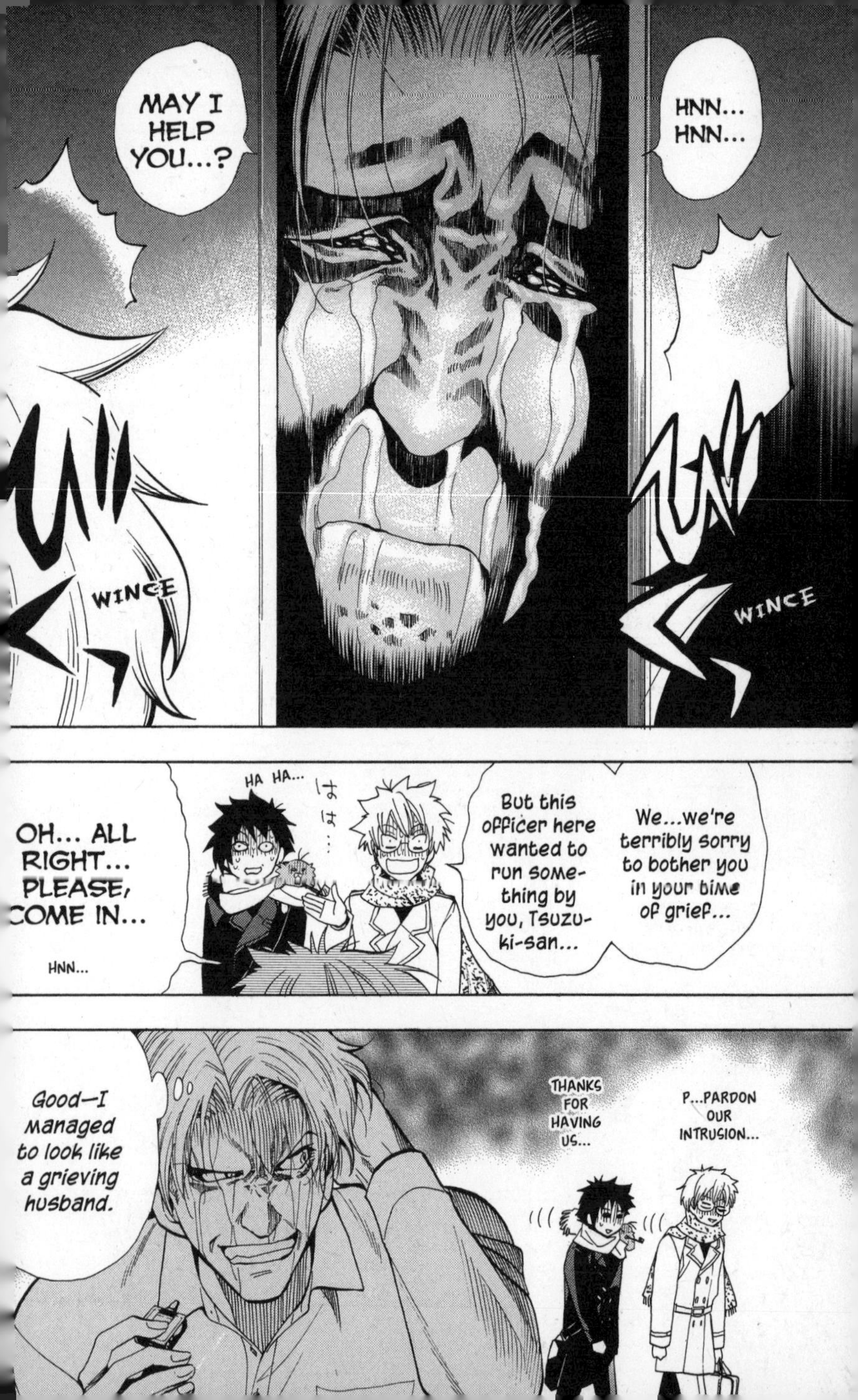
HNN... HNN...
WINCE
MAY I HELP YOU...?
WINCE
We...we're terribly sorry to bother you in your time of grief...
But this officer here wanted to run some-thing by you, Tsuzu-ki-san...
HA HA...
はは…
OH... ALL RIGHT... PLEASE, COME IN...
HNN...
P...PARDON OUR INTRUSION...
THANKS FOR HAVING US...
Good—I managed to look like a grieving husband.

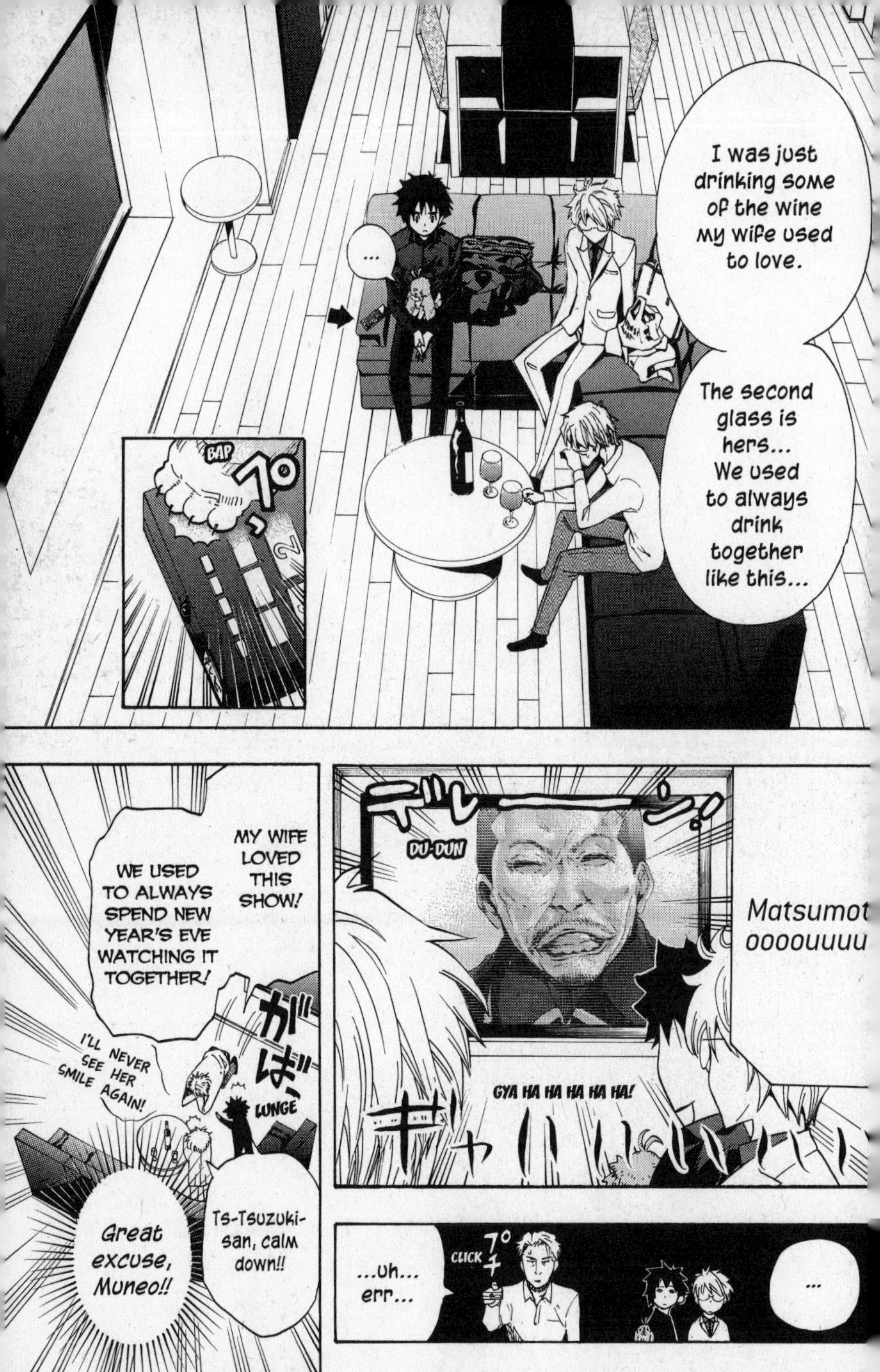
I was just drinking some of the wine my wife used to love.
The second glass is hers... We used to always drink together like this...
...
BAP
Matsumot oooouuuu
DU-DUN
GYA HA HA HA HA HA!
...
CLICK
...uh... err...
MY WIFE LOVED THIS SHOW!
WE USED TO ALWAYS SPEND NEW YEAR'S EVE WATCHING IT TOGETHER!
I'LL NEVER SEE HER SMILE AGAIN!
LUNGE
Ts-Tsuzuki-san, calm down!!
Great excuse, Muneo!!

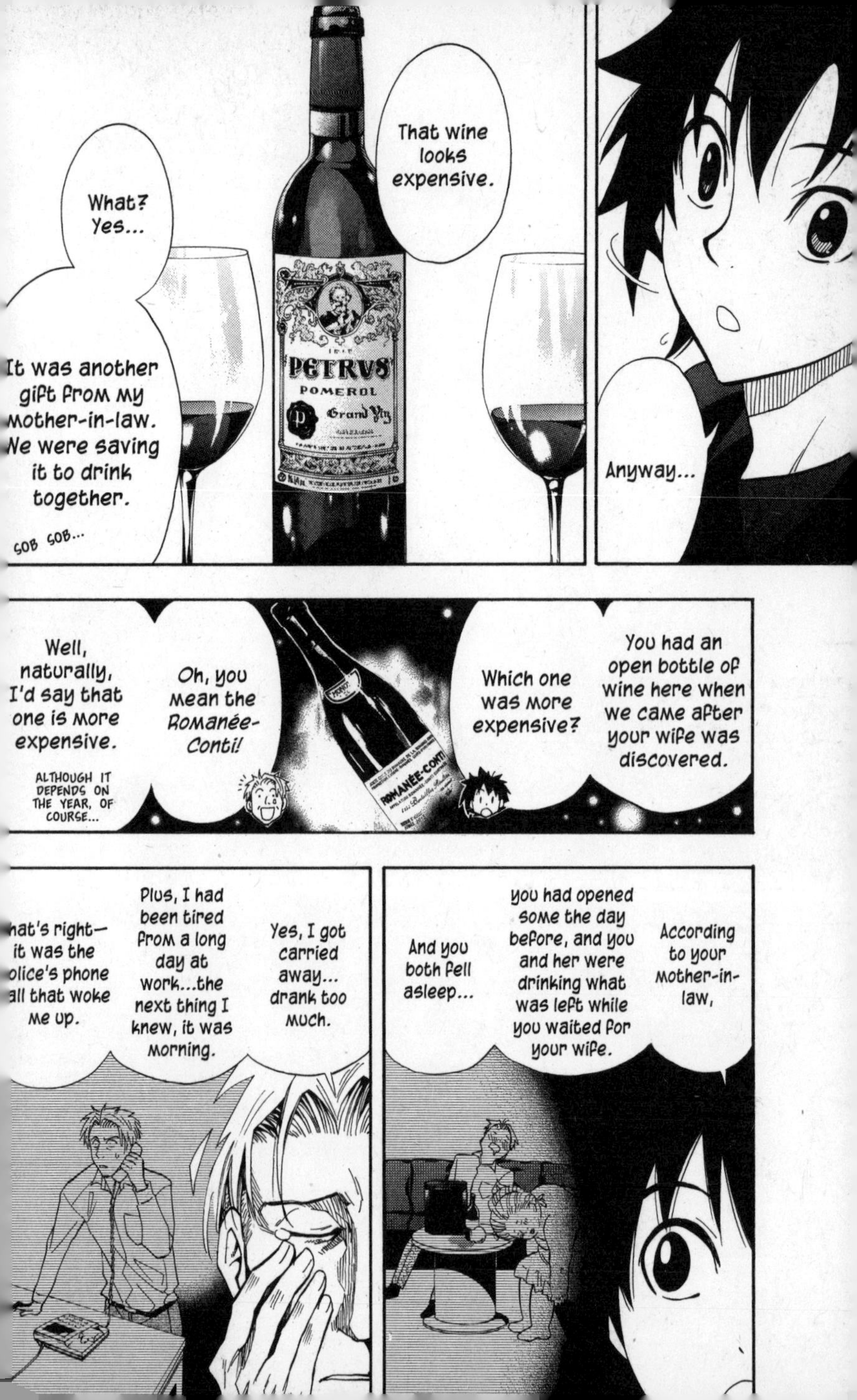
Anyway...
That wine looks expensive.
What? Yes...
PETRUS
POMEROL
It was another gift from my mother-in-law. Ne were saving it to drink together.
SOB SOB...
You had an open bottle of wine here when we came after your wife was discovered.
Which one was more expensive?
ROMANÉE-CONTI
Oh, you mean the Romanée-Conti!
Well, naturally, I'd say that one is more expensive.
ALTHOUGH IT DEPENDS ON THE YEAR, OF COURSE...
According to your mother-in-law,
you had opened some the day before, and you and her were drinking what was left while you waited for your wife.
And you both fell asleep...
Yes, I got carried away... drank too much.
Plus, I had been tired from a long day at work...the next thing I knew, it was morning.
hat's right— it was the olice's phone all that woke me up.

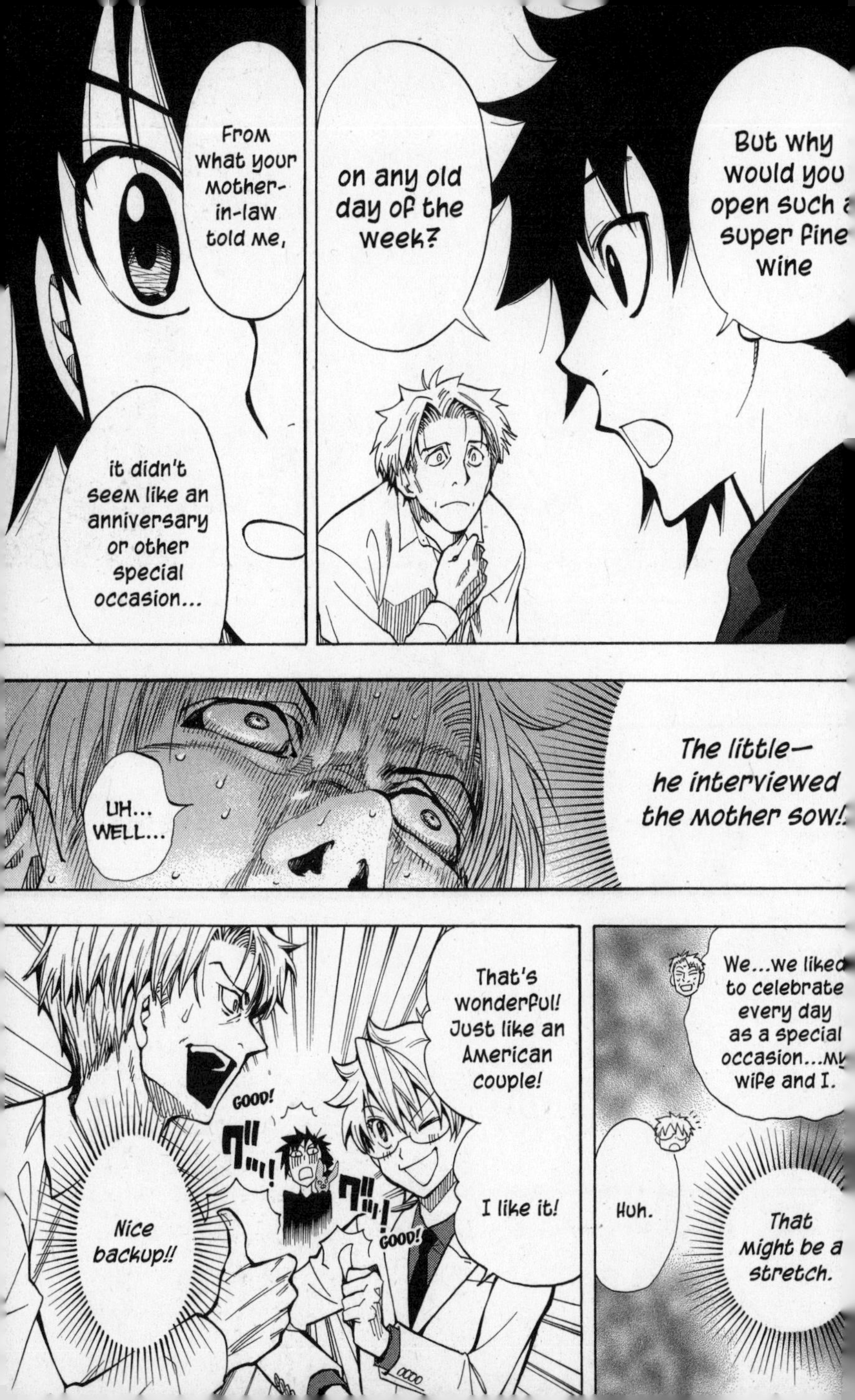
But why would you open such a super fine wine
on any old day of the week?
From what your mother-in-law told me,
it didn't seem like an anniversary or other special occasion...
The little— he interviewed the mother sow!
UH... WELL...
We...we liked to celebrate every day as a special occasion...my wife and I.
Huh.
That might be a stretch.
That's wonderful! Just like an American couple!
I like it!
GOOD!
GOOD!
Nice backup!!

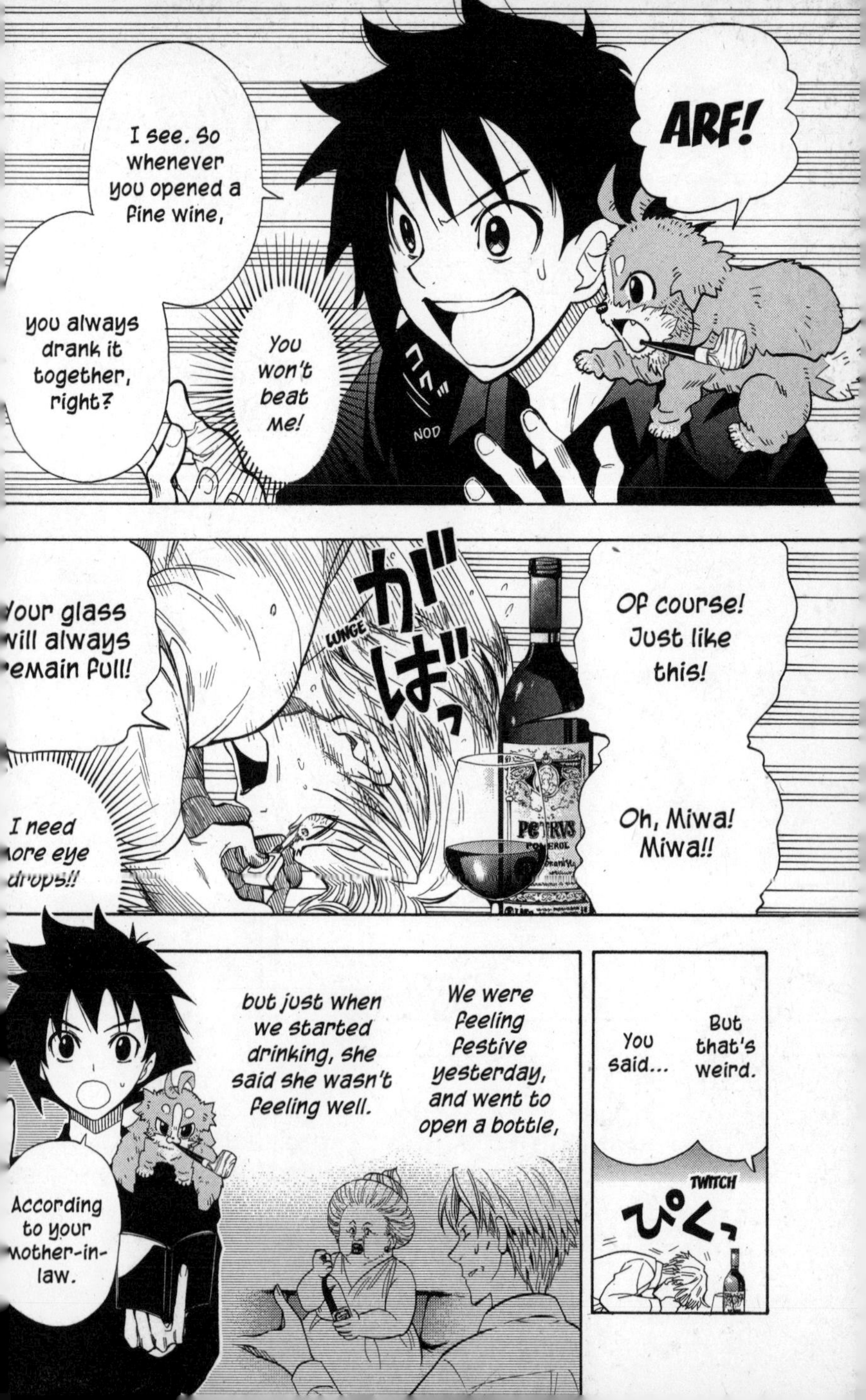
ARF!
I see. So whenever you opened a fine wine,
you always drank it together, right?
NOD
You won't beat me!
Of course! Just like this!
Oh, Miwa! Miwa!!
LUNGE
Your glass will always remain full!
I need more eye drops!!
But that's weird.
You said...
TWITCH
We were feeling festive yesterday, and went to open a bottle,
but just when we started drinking, she said she wasn't feeling well.
According to your mother-in-law.

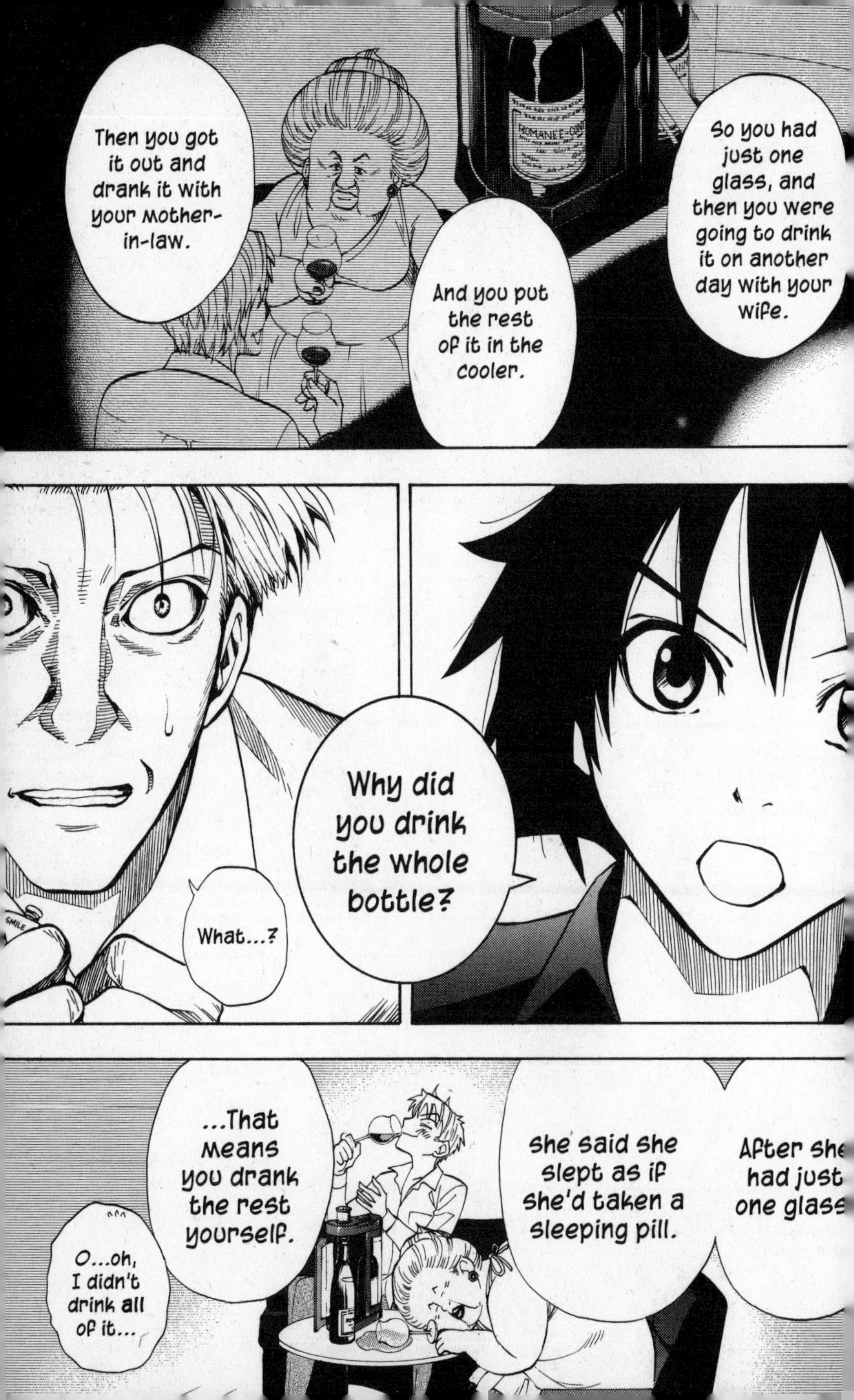
So you had just one glass, and then you were going to drink it on another day with your wife.
And you put the rest of it in the cooler.
Then you got it out and drank it with your mother-in-law.
Why did you drink the whole bottle?
What...?
After she had just one glass
She said she slept as if she'd taken a sleeping pill.
...That means you drank the rest yourself.
O...oh, I didn't drink all of it...

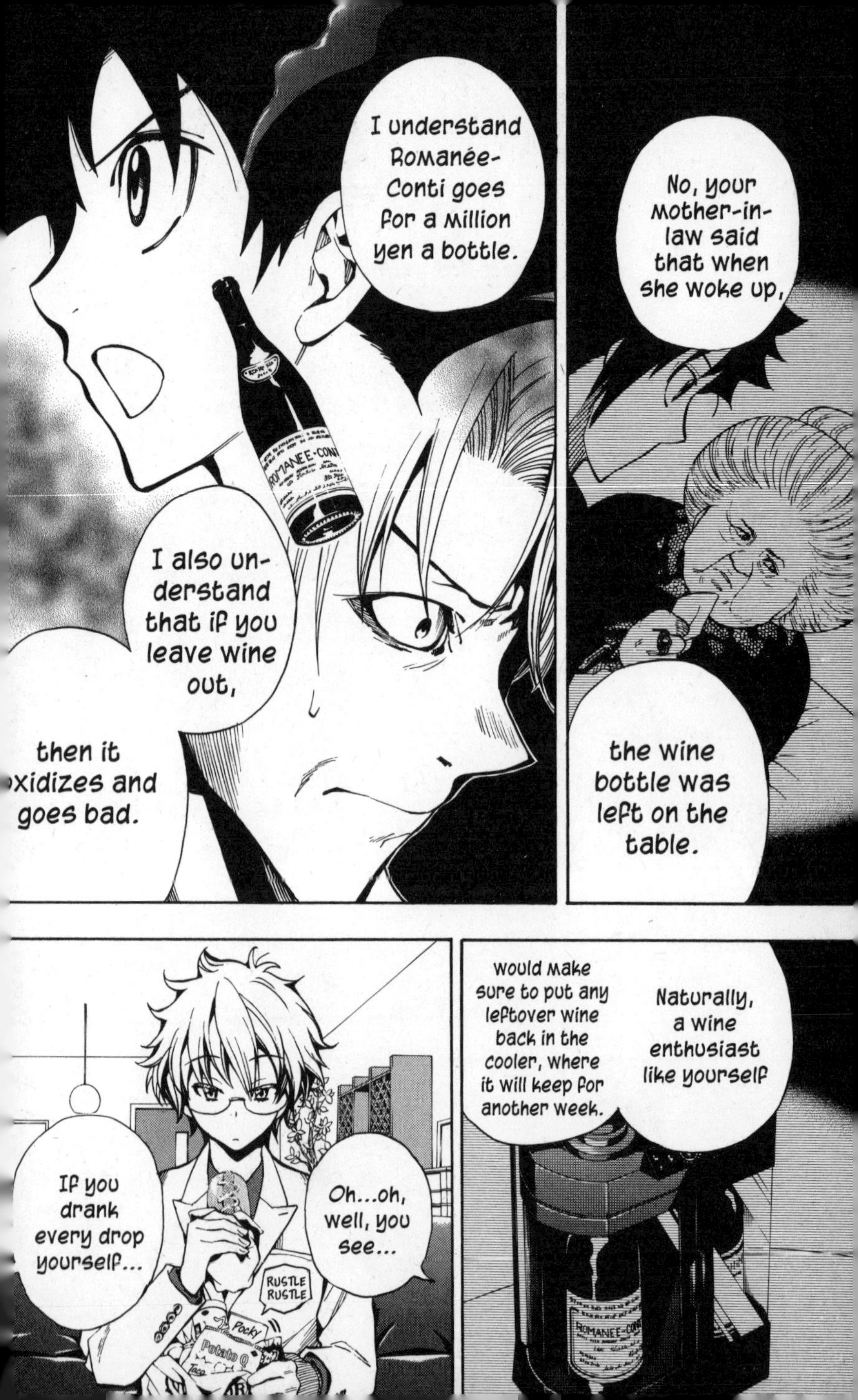

No, your mother-in-law said that when she woke up,
the wine bottle was left on the table.
I understand Romanée-Conti goes for a million yen a bottle.
ROMANEE-CONTI
I also understand that if you leave wine out,
then it oxidizes and goes bad.
Naturally, a wine enthusiast like yourself
would make sure to put any leftover wine back in the cooler, where it will keep for another week.
ROMANEE-CONTI
Oh...oh, well, you see...
If you drank every drop yourself...
RUSTLE RUSTLE
Pocky
Potato Q

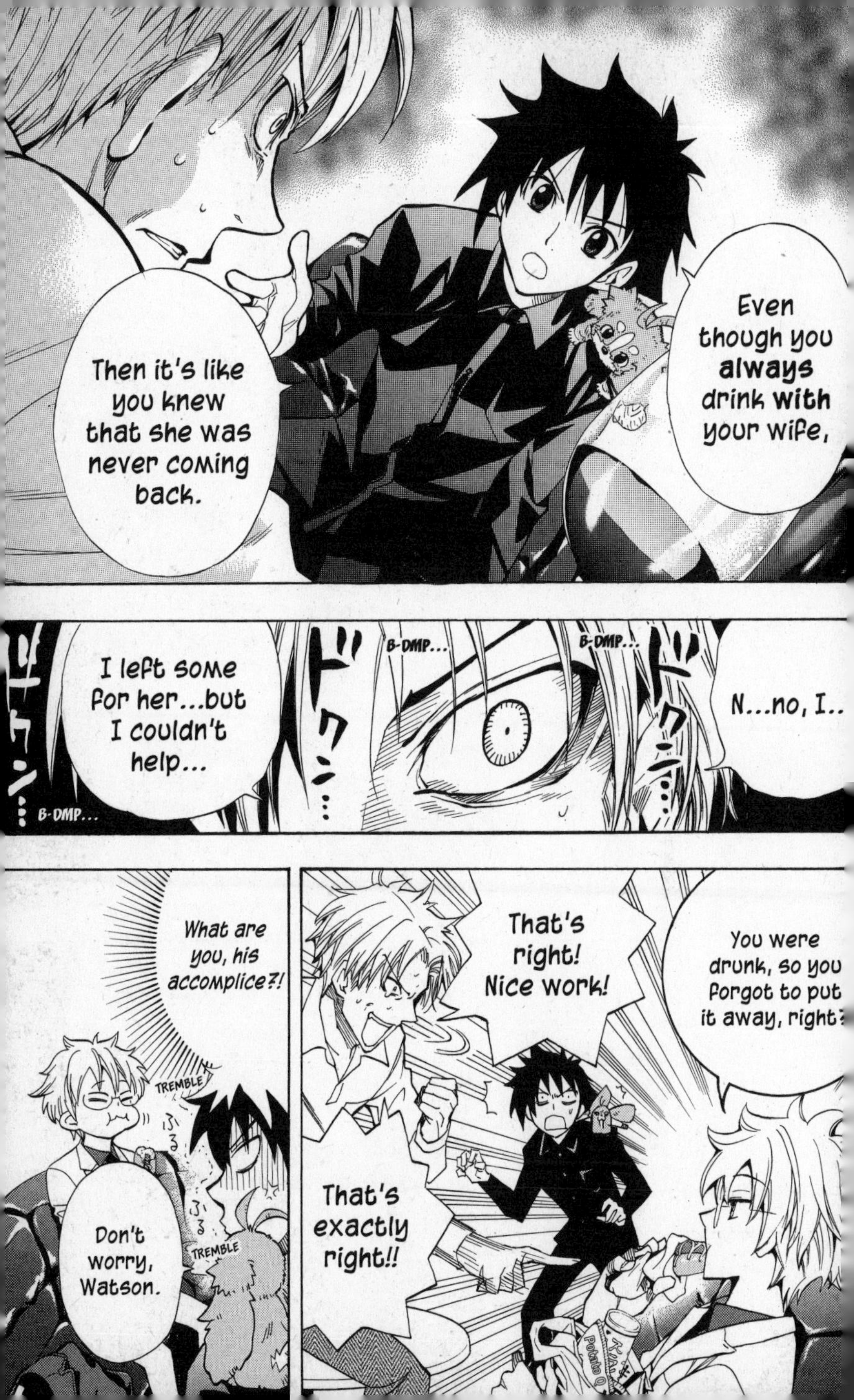
Even though you always drink with your wife,
Then it's like you knew that she was never coming back.
N...no, I..
B-DMP...
ドクン...
B-DMP...
ドクン...
I left some for her...but I couldn't help...
B-DMP...
You were drunk, so you forgot to put it away, right?
That's right! Nice work!
That's exactly right!!
What are you, his accomplice?!
TREMBLE
TREMBLE
Don't worry, Watson.

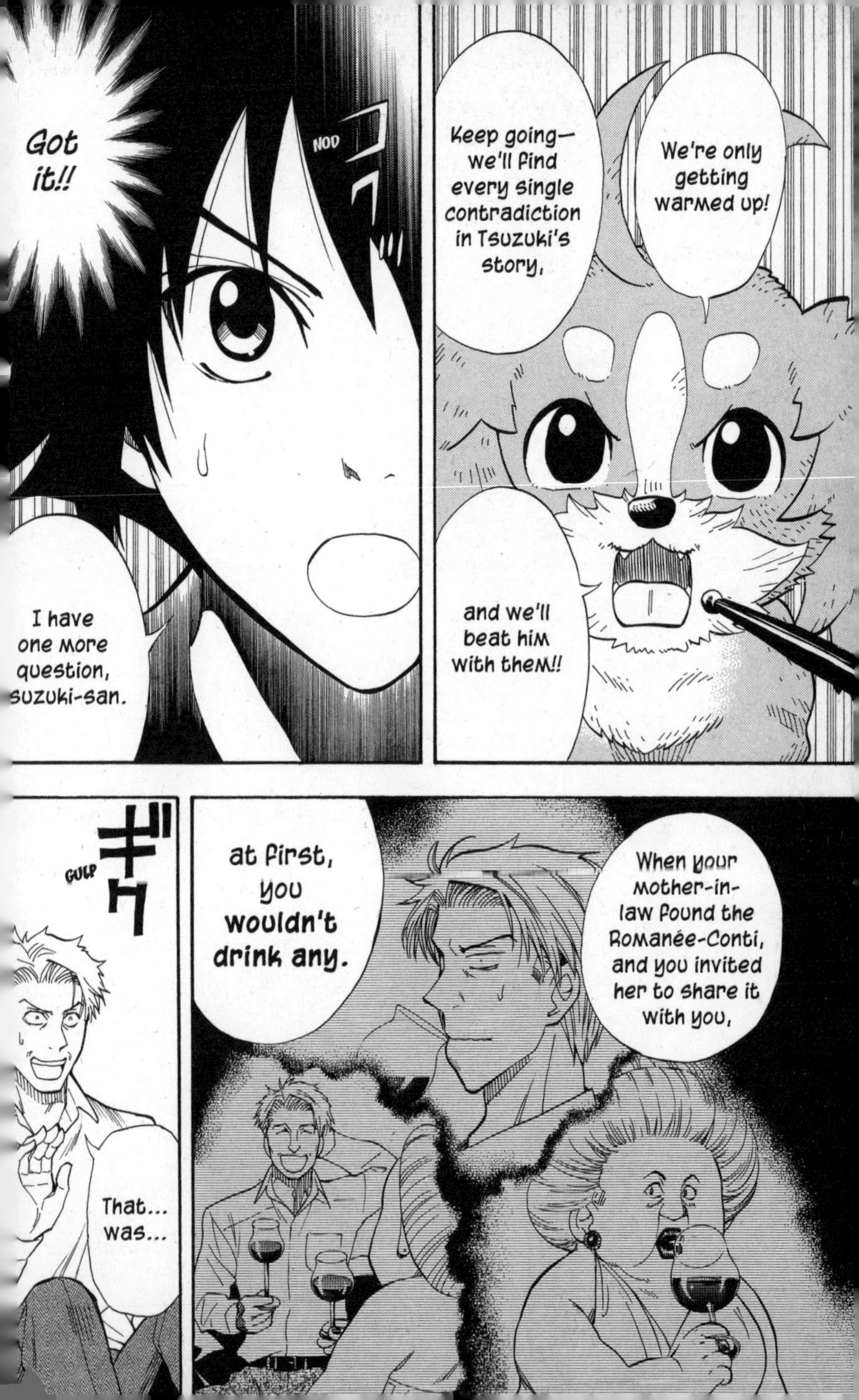
We're only getting warmed up!
Keep going—we'll find every single contradiction in Tsuzuki's story,
and we'll beat him with them!!
Got it!!
NOD
I have one more question, Suzuki-san.
When your mother-in-law found the Romanée-Conti, and you invited her to share it with you,
at first, you wouldn't drink any.
GULP
That... was...

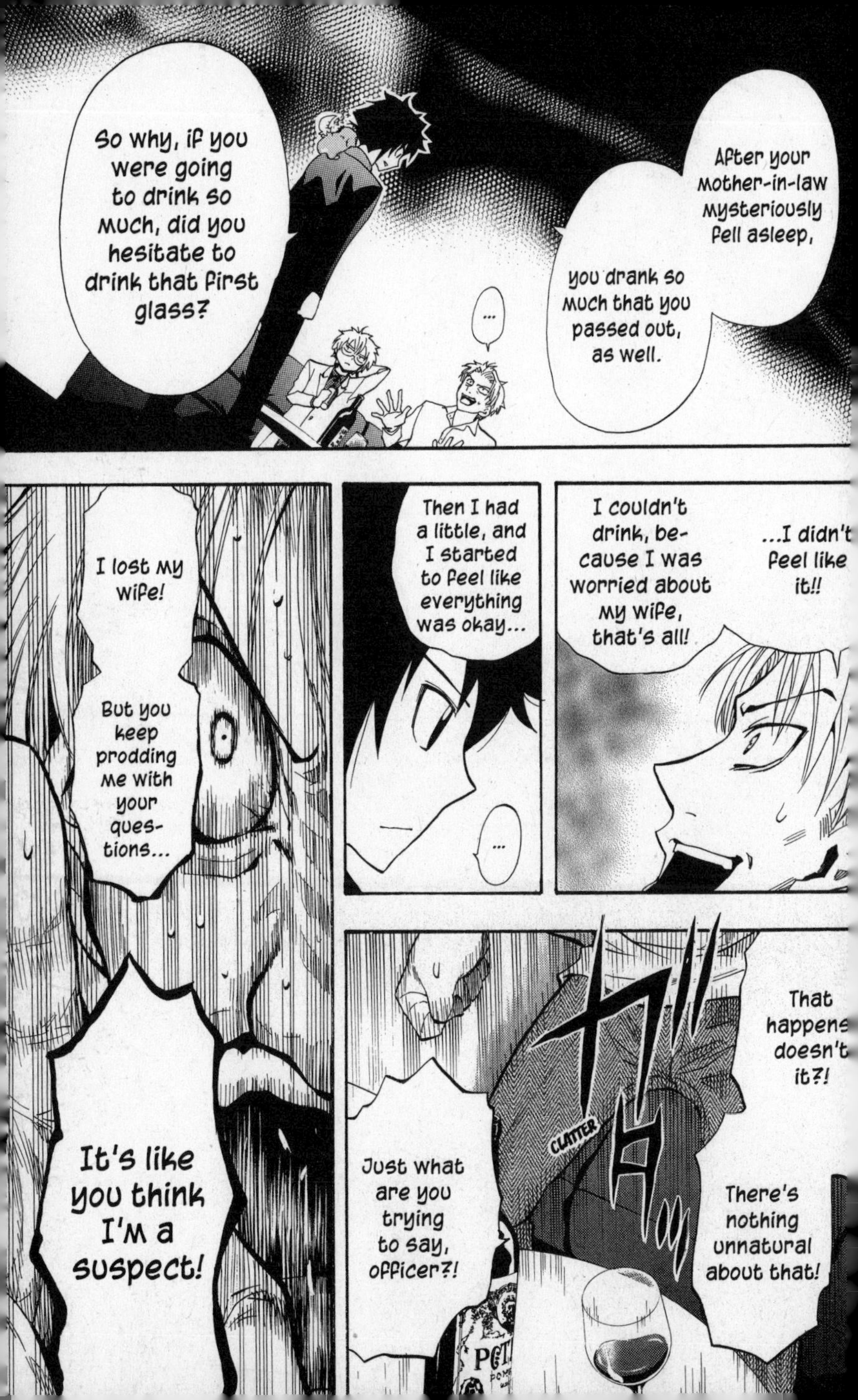
After your mother-in-law mysteriously fell asleep,
you drank so much that you passed out, as well.
...
So why, if you were going to drink so much, did you hesitate to drink that first glass?
...I didn't feel like it!!
I couldn't drink, be-cause I was worried about my wife, that's all!
Then I had a little, and I started to feel like everything was okay...
...
That happens doesn't it?!
CLATTER
There's nothing unnatural about that!
Just what are you trying to say, officer?!
I lost my wife!
But you keep prodding me with your ques-tions...
It's like you think I'm a suspect!

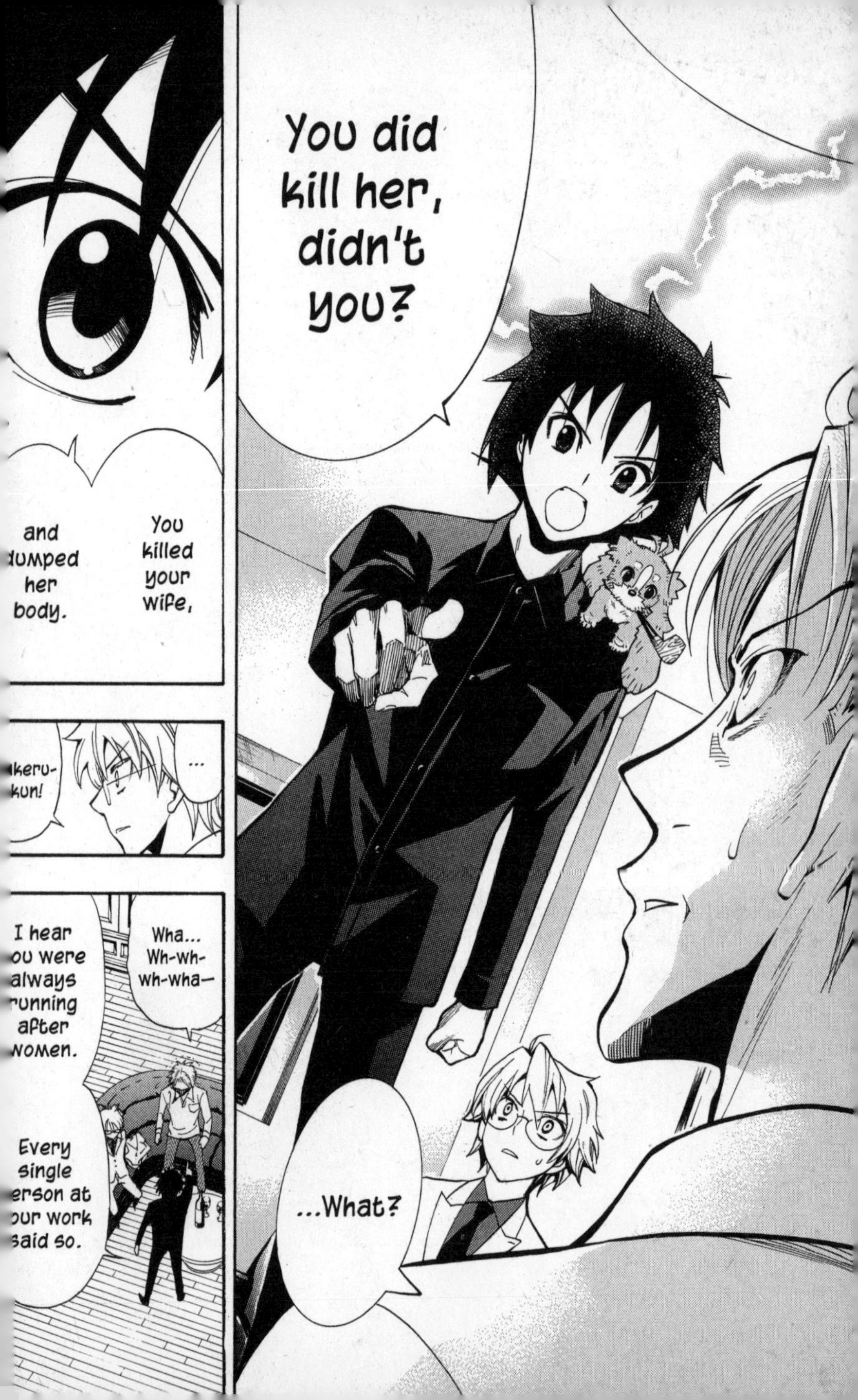
You did kill her, didn't you?
...What?
You killed your wife,
and dumped her body.
...
keru-kun!
Wha... Wh-wh-wh-wha—
I hear ou were always running after women.
Every single erson at our work said so.

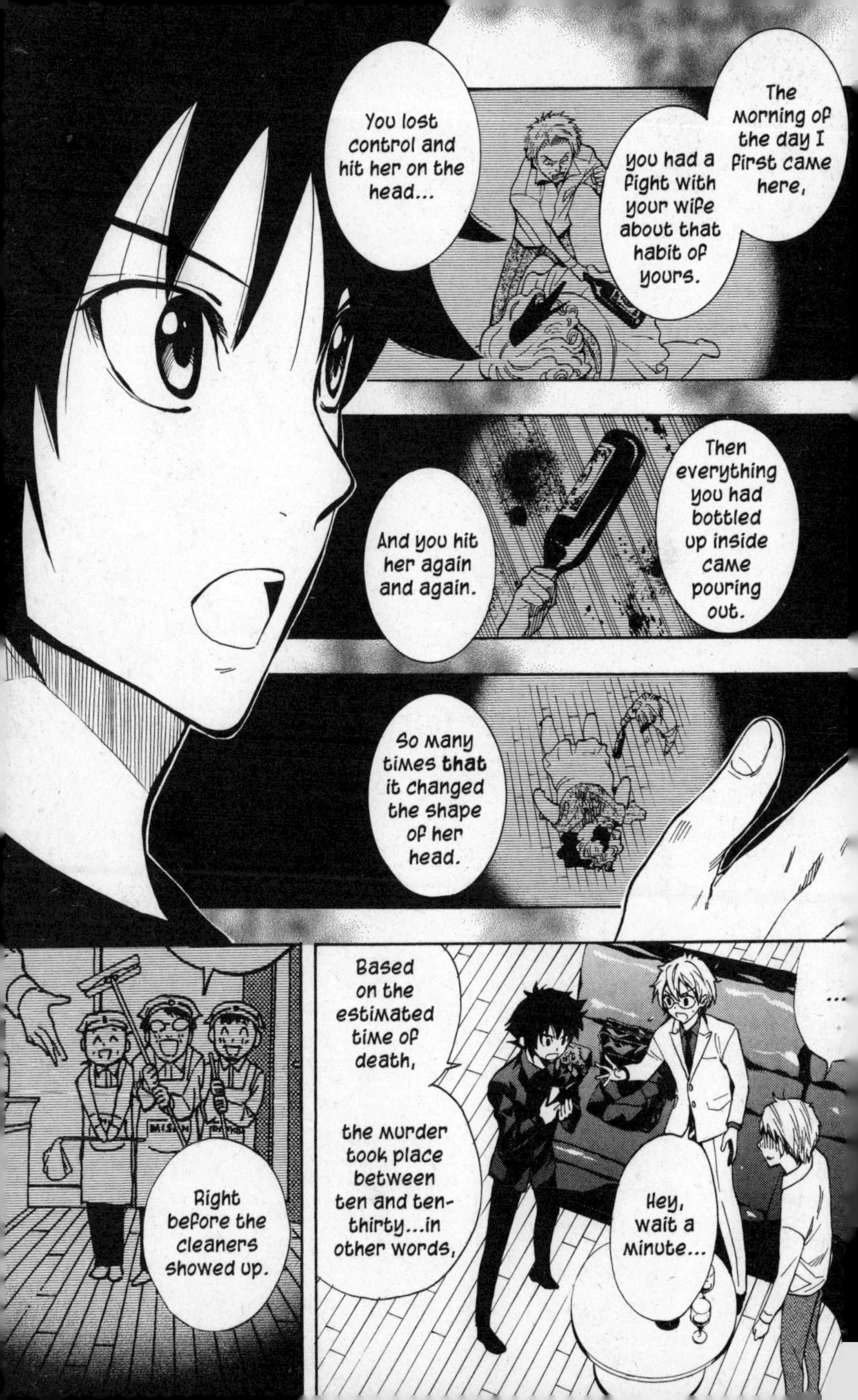

The morning of the day I first came here,
you had a fight with your wife about that habit of yours.
You lost control and hit her on the head...
Then everything you had bottled up inside came pouring out.
And you hit her again and again.
So many times **that** it changed the shape of her head.
...
Based on the estimated time of death,
the murder took place between ten and ten-thirty...in other words,
Hey, wait a minute...
Right before the cleaners showed up.

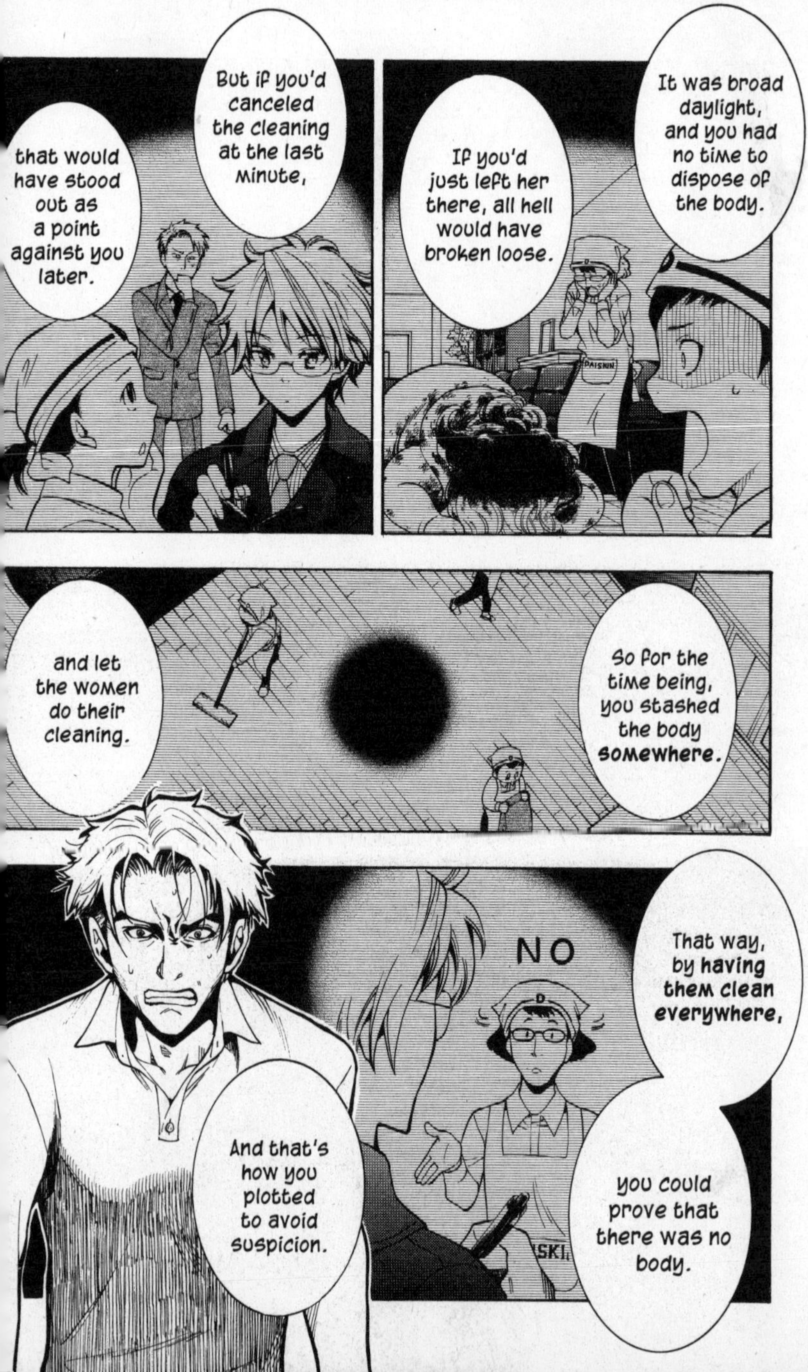
It was broad daylight, and you had no time to dispose of the body.
If you'd just left her there, all hell would have broken loose.
But if you'd canceled the cleaning at the last minute,
that would have stood out as a point against you later.
So for the time being, you stashed the body **somewhere.**
and let the women do their cleaning.
That way, by having them clean everywhere,
NO
you could prove that there was no body.
And that's how you plotted to avoid suspicion.

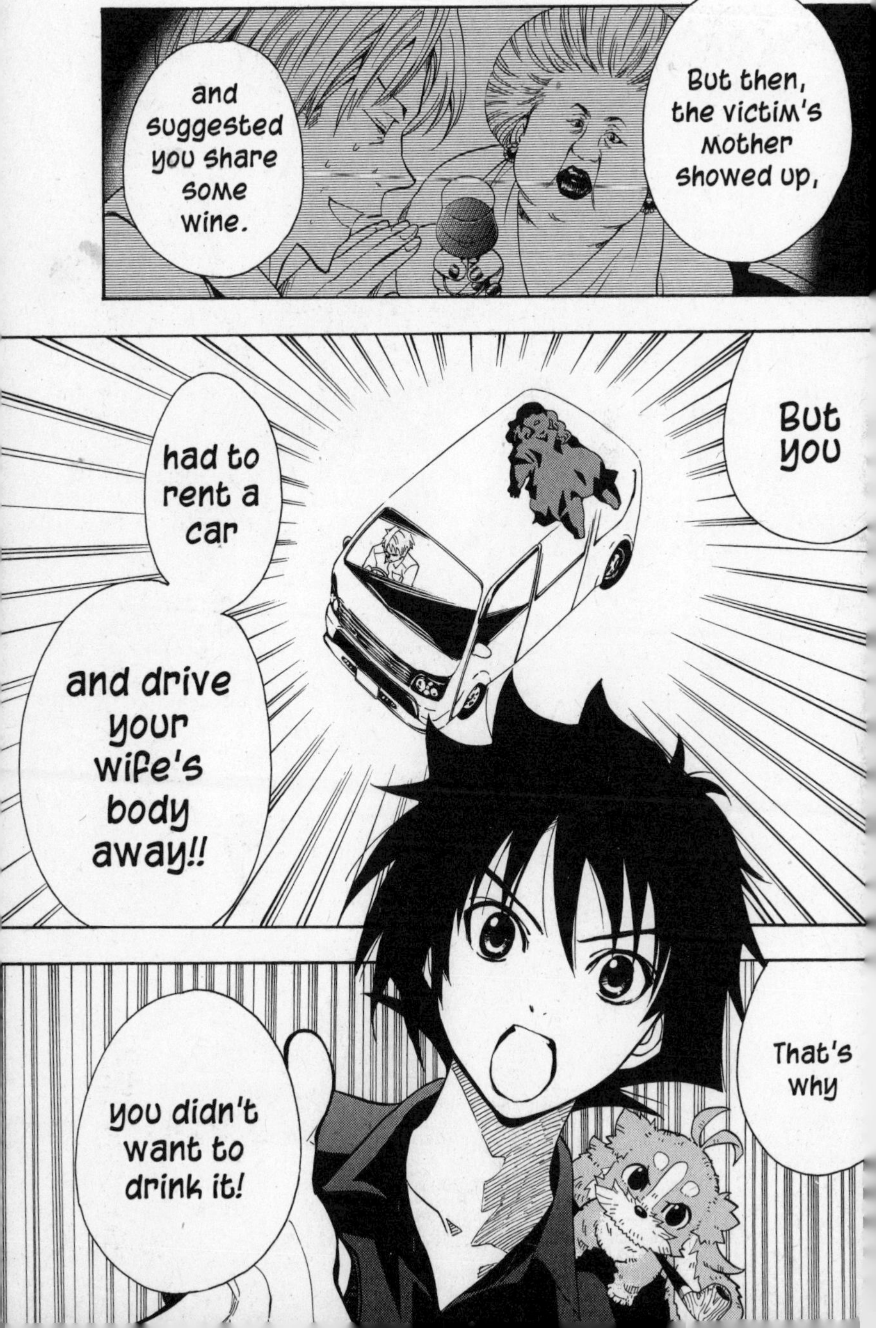
But then, the victim's mother showed up,
and suggested you share some wine.
But you
had to rent a car
and drive your wife's body away!!
That's why
you didn't want to drink it!

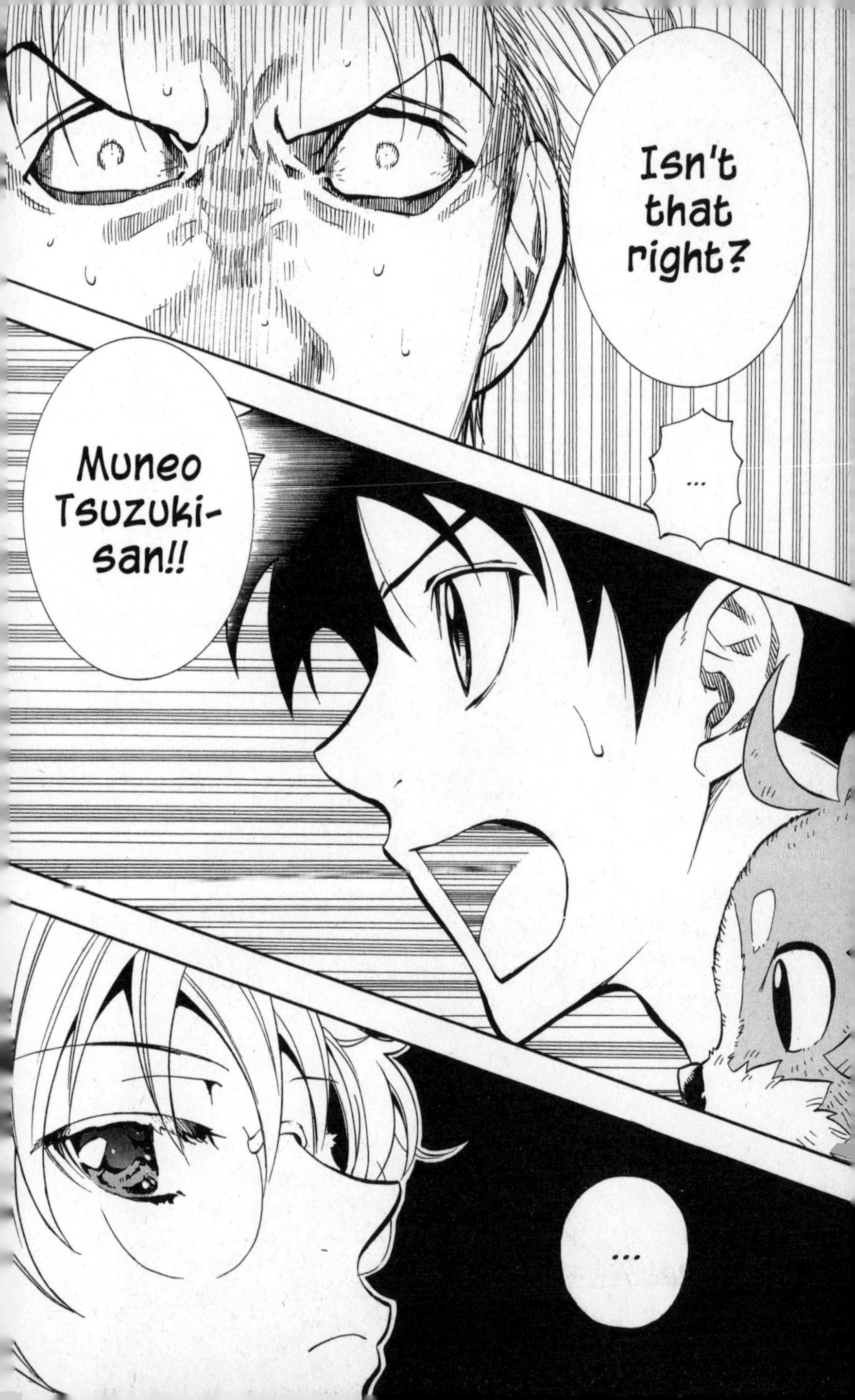
Isn't that right?
...
Muneo Tsuzuki-san!!
...

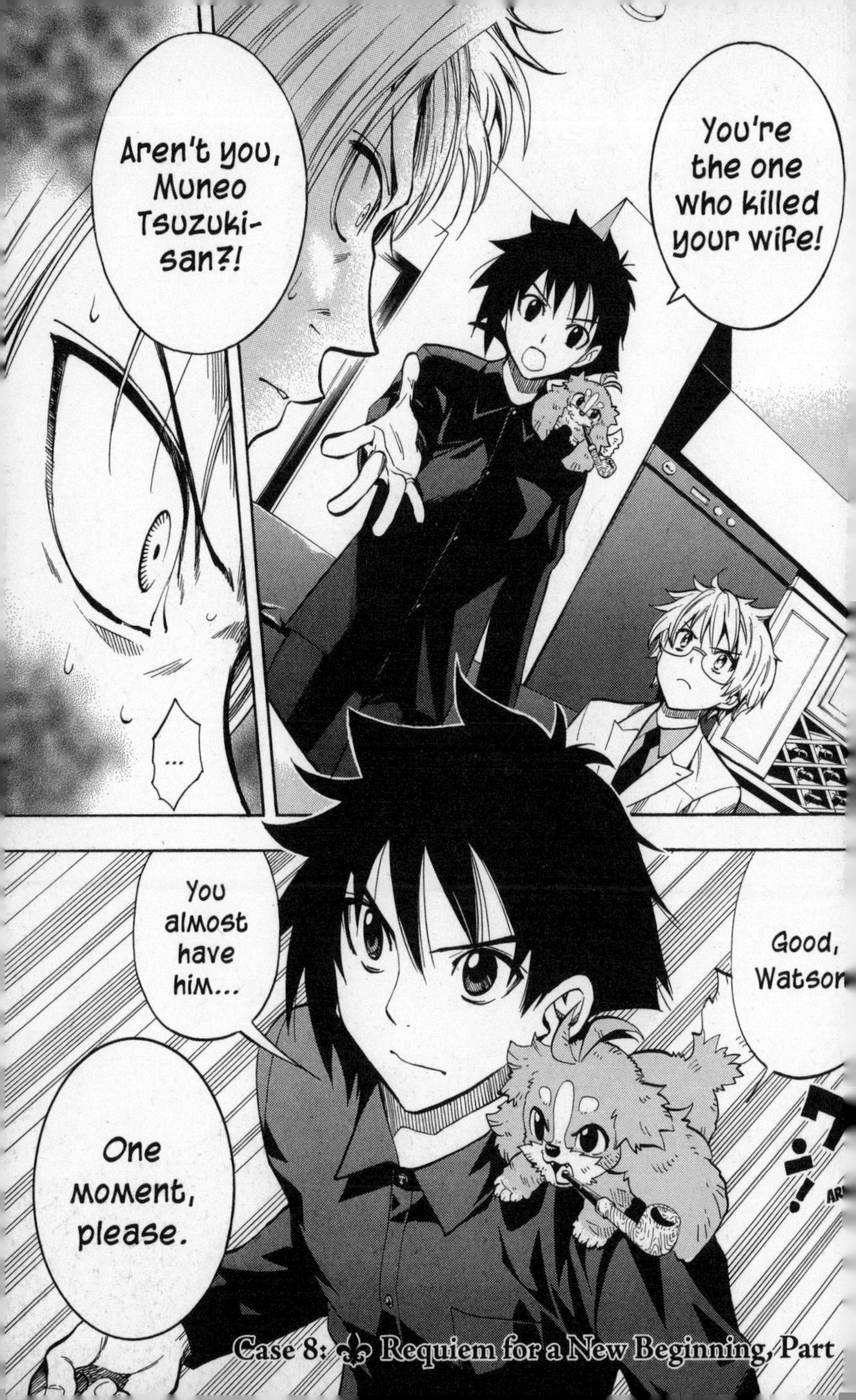
You're the one who killed your wife!
Aren't you, Muneo Tsuzuki-san?!
...
Good, Watson
?!
You almost have him...
One moment, please.
Case 8: Requiem for a New Beginning, Part

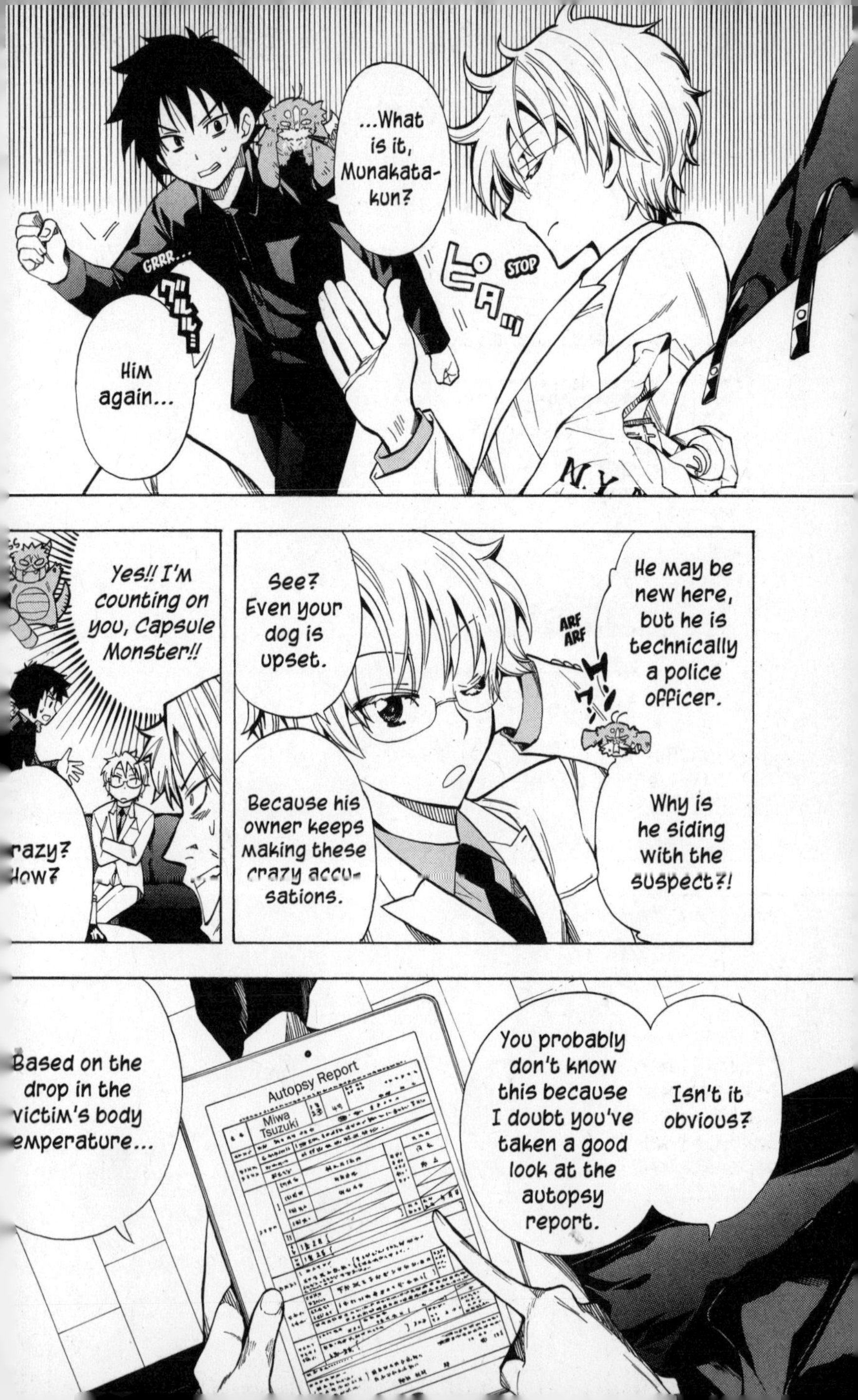
...What is it, Munakata-kun?
STOP
GRRR...
Him again...
He may be new here, but he is technically a police officer.
ARF ARF
See? Even your dog is upset.
Why is he siding with the suspect?!
Because his owner keeps making these crazy accusations.
Yes!! I'm counting on you, Capsule Monster!!
razy? How?
Isn't it obvious?
You probably don't know this because I doubt you've taken a good look at the autopsy report.
Autopsy Report
Miwa Tsuzuki
Based on the drop in the victim's body emperature...

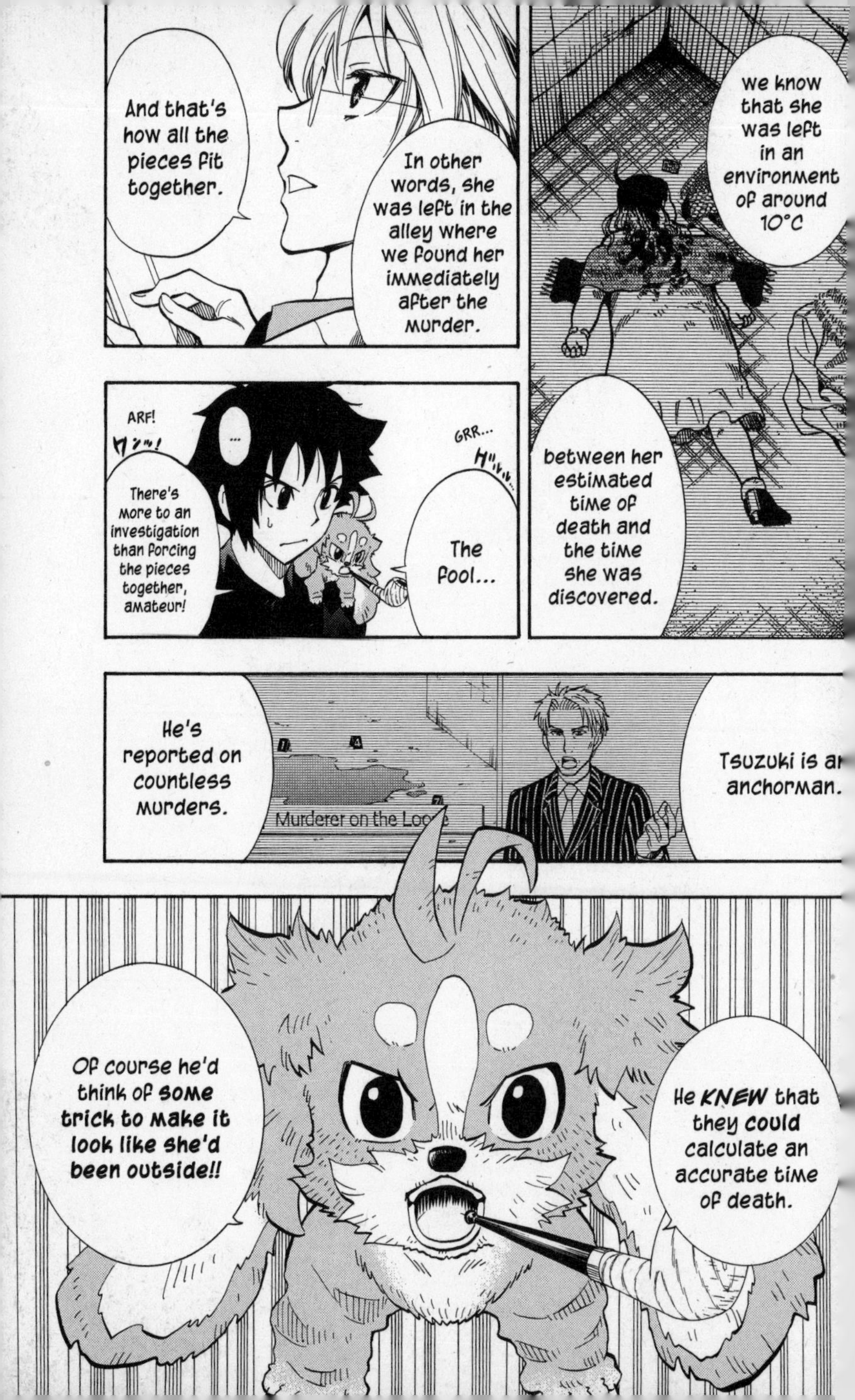

we know that she was left in an environment of around 10°C
between her estimated time of death and the time she was discovered.
In other words, she was left in the alley where we found her immediately after the murder.
And that's how all the pieces fit together.
GRR...
The fool...
ARF!
...
There's more to an investigation than forcing the pieces together, amateur!
Tsuzuki is an anchorman.
Murderer on the Loose
He's reported on countless murders.
He KNEW that they could calculate an accurate time of death.
Of course he'd think of some trick to make it look like she'd been outside!!

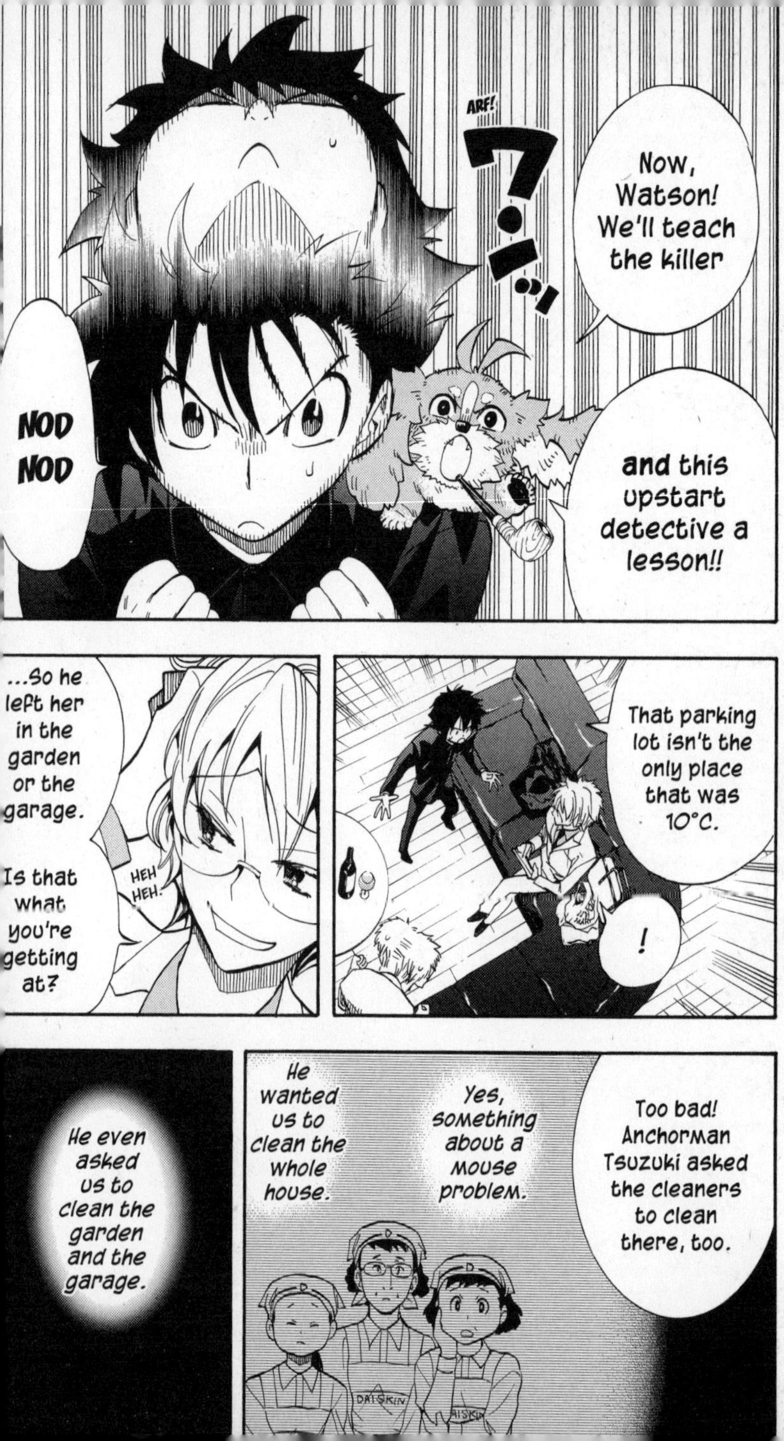
Now, Watson! We'll teach the killer
and this upstart detective a lesson!!
ARF!
NOD NOD
That parking lot isn't the only place that was 10°C.
!
...So he left her in the garden or the garage.
HEH HEH.
Is that what you're getting at?
Too bad! Anchorman Tsuzuki asked the cleaners to clean there, too.
Yes, something about a mouse problem.
He wanted us to clean the whole house.
DAISKIN
He even asked us to clean the garden and the garage.

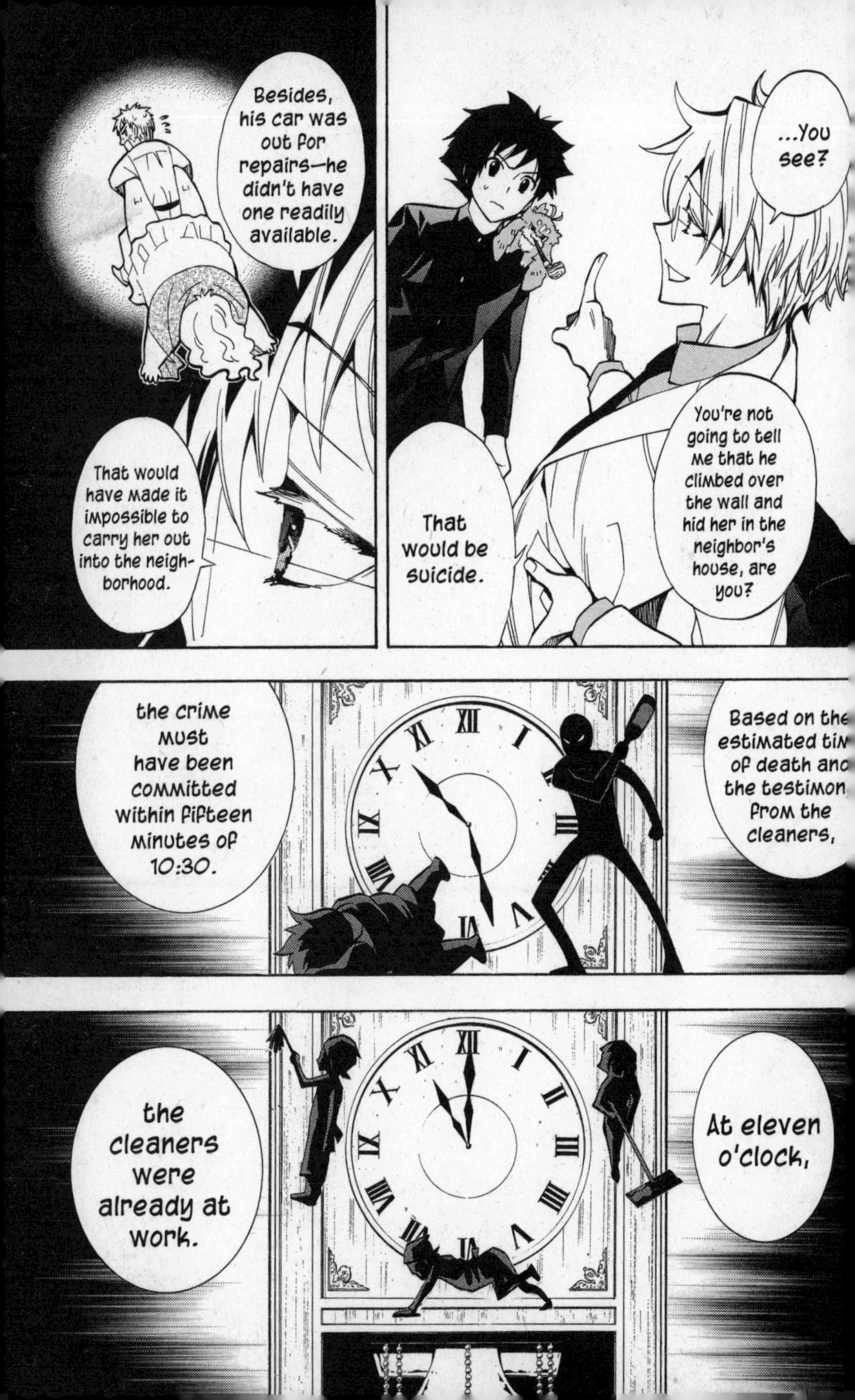
...You see?
You're not going to tell me that he climbed over the wall and hid her in the neighbor's house, are you?
That would be suicide.
Besides, his car was out for repairs—he didn't have one readily available.
That would have made it impossible to carry her out into the neighborhood.
Based on the estimated tim of death and the testimon from the cleaners,
the crime must have been committed within fifteen minutes of 10:30.
At eleven o'clock,
the cleaners were already at work.

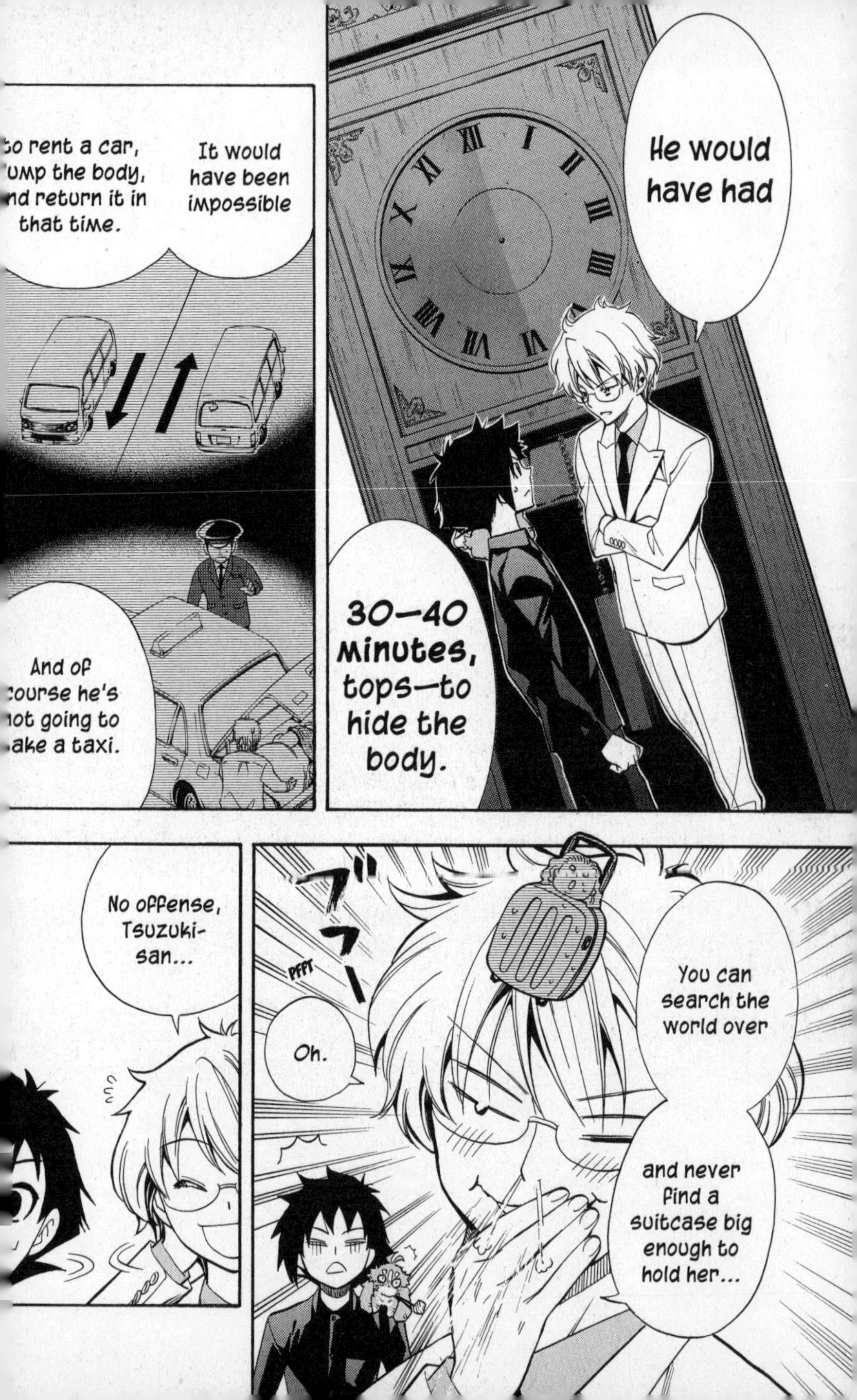
He would have had
30–40 minutes, tops—to hide the body.
It would have been impossible
o rent a car, ump the body, nd return it in that time.
And of ourse he's ot going to ake a taxi.
You can search the world over
and never find a suitcase big enough to hold her...
ブフー
PFFT
Oh.
No offense, Tsuzuki-san...

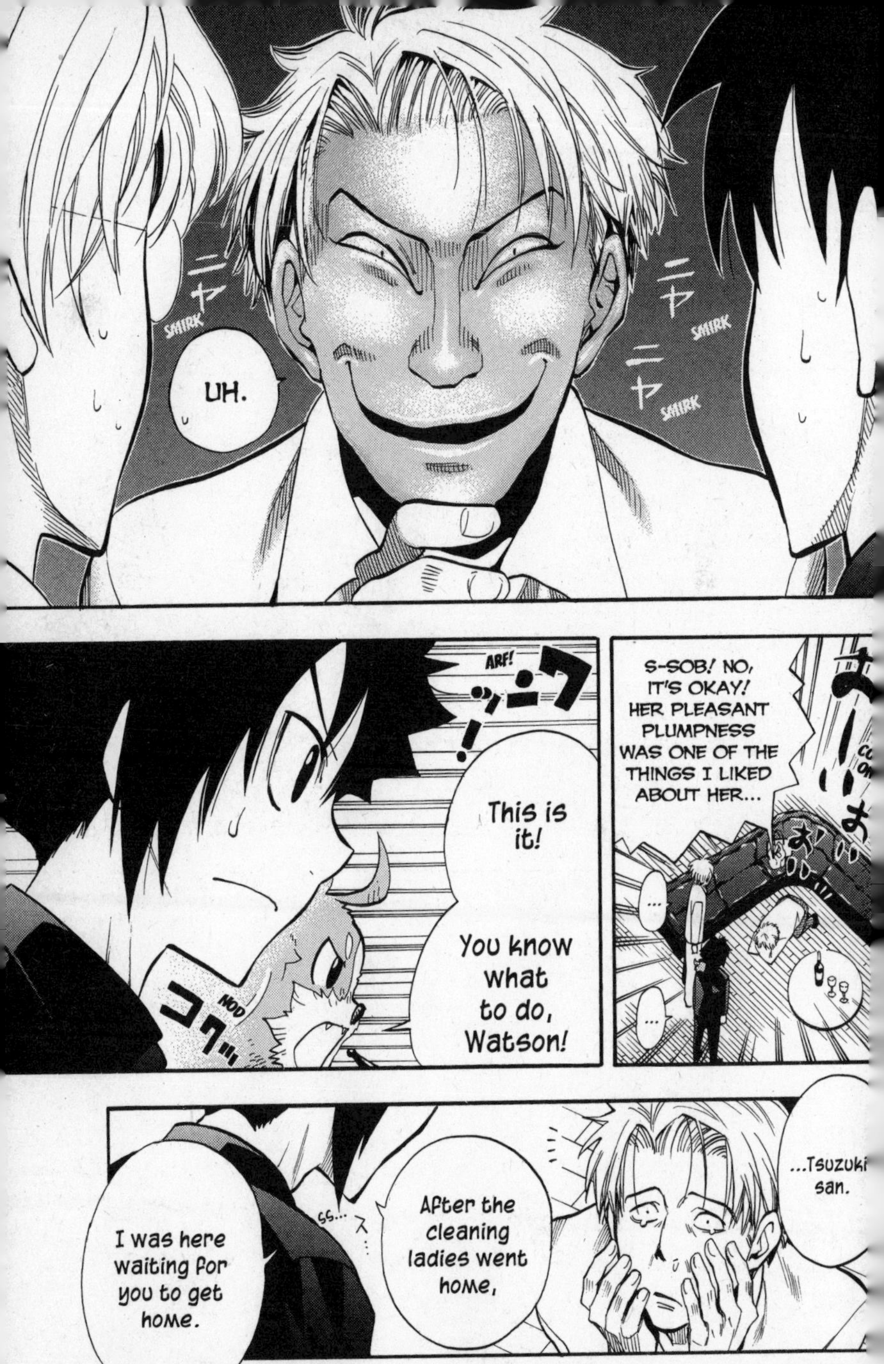
ニヤ
SMIRK
ニヤ
SMIRK
ニヤ
SMIRK
UH.
S-SOB! NO, IT'S OKAY! HER PLEASANT PLUMPNESS WAS ONE OF THE THINGS I LIKED ABOUT HER...
...
...
ARF!
ワンッ!
This is it!
You know what to do, Watson!
NOD
コクッ
...Tsuzuki san.
After the cleaning ladies went home,
SS...
ス...
I was here waiting for you to get home.

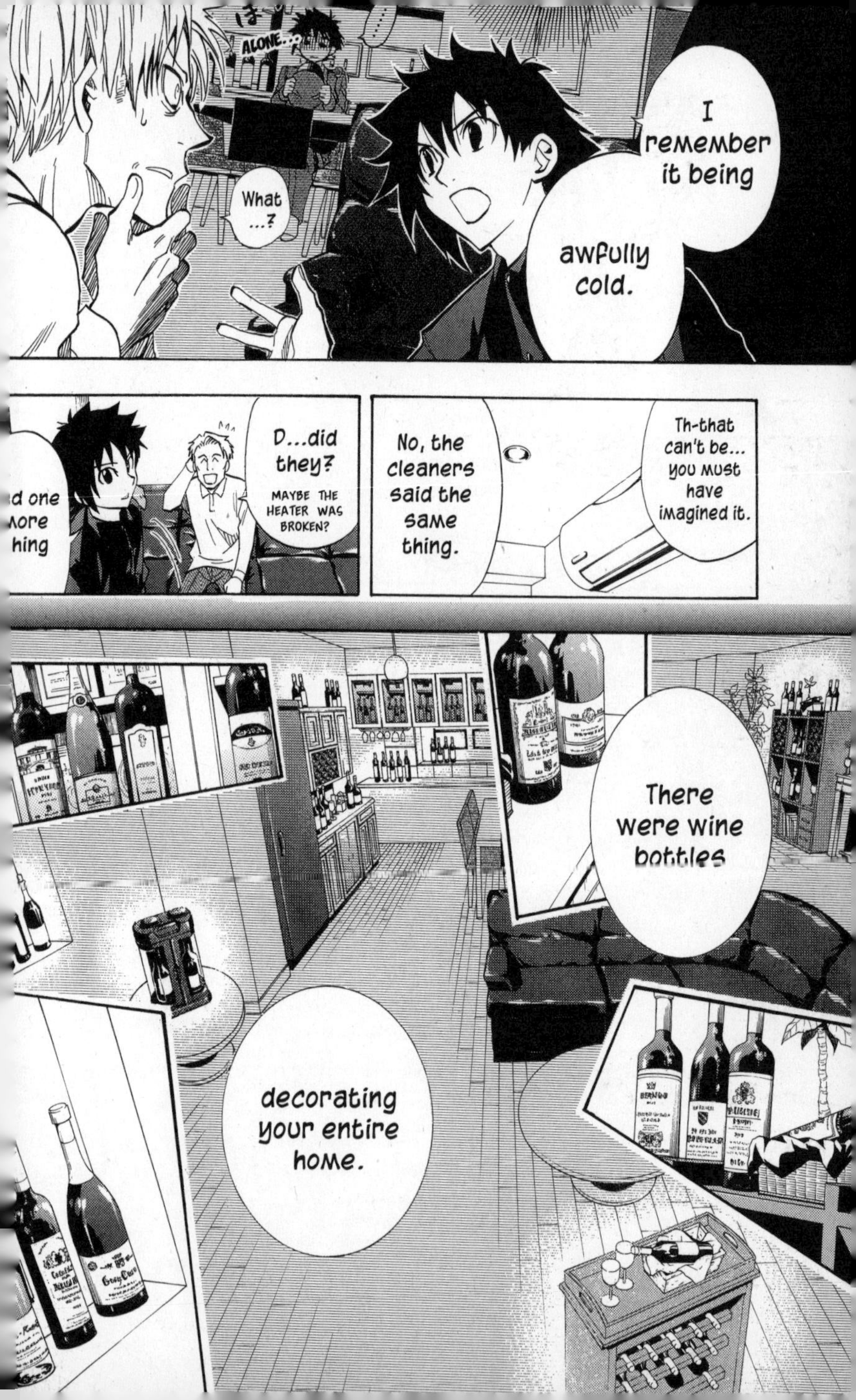

I remember it being
awfully cold.
...
ALONE...
What ...?
Th-that can't be... you must have imagined it.
No, the cleaners said the same thing.
D...did they?
MAYBE THE HEATER WAS BROKEN?
d one more hing
There were wine bottles
decorating your entire home.

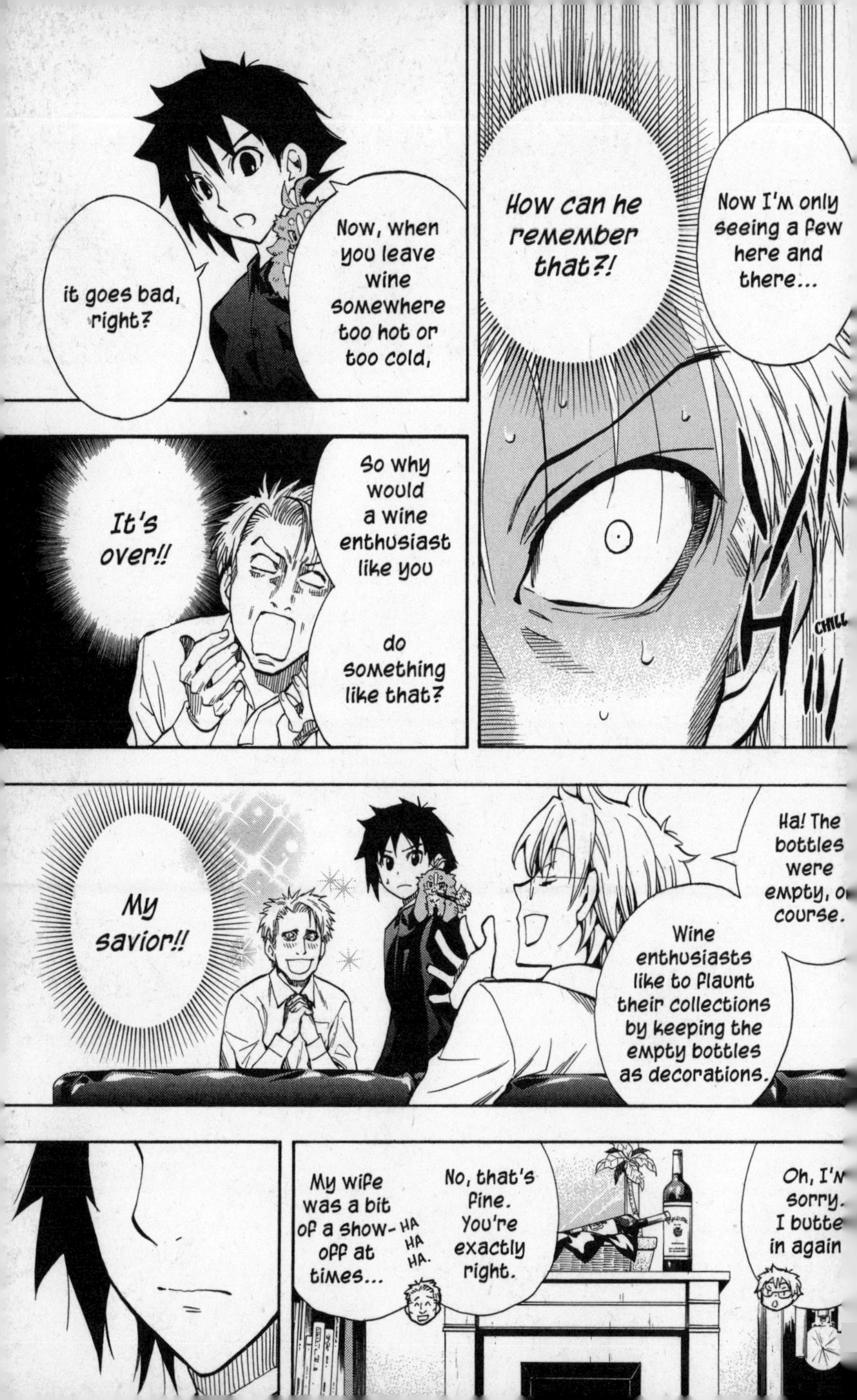
Now I'm only seeing a few here and there...
How can he remember that?!
CHILL
Now, when you leave wine somewhere too hot or too cold,
it goes bad, right?
So why would a wine enthusiast like you do something like that?
It's over!!
Ha! The bottles were empty, o course.
Wine enthusiasts like to flaunt their collections by keeping the empty bottles as decorations.
My savior!!
Oh, I'm sorry. I butte in again
No, that's fine. You're exactly right.
HA HA HA.
My wife was a bit of a show-off at times...

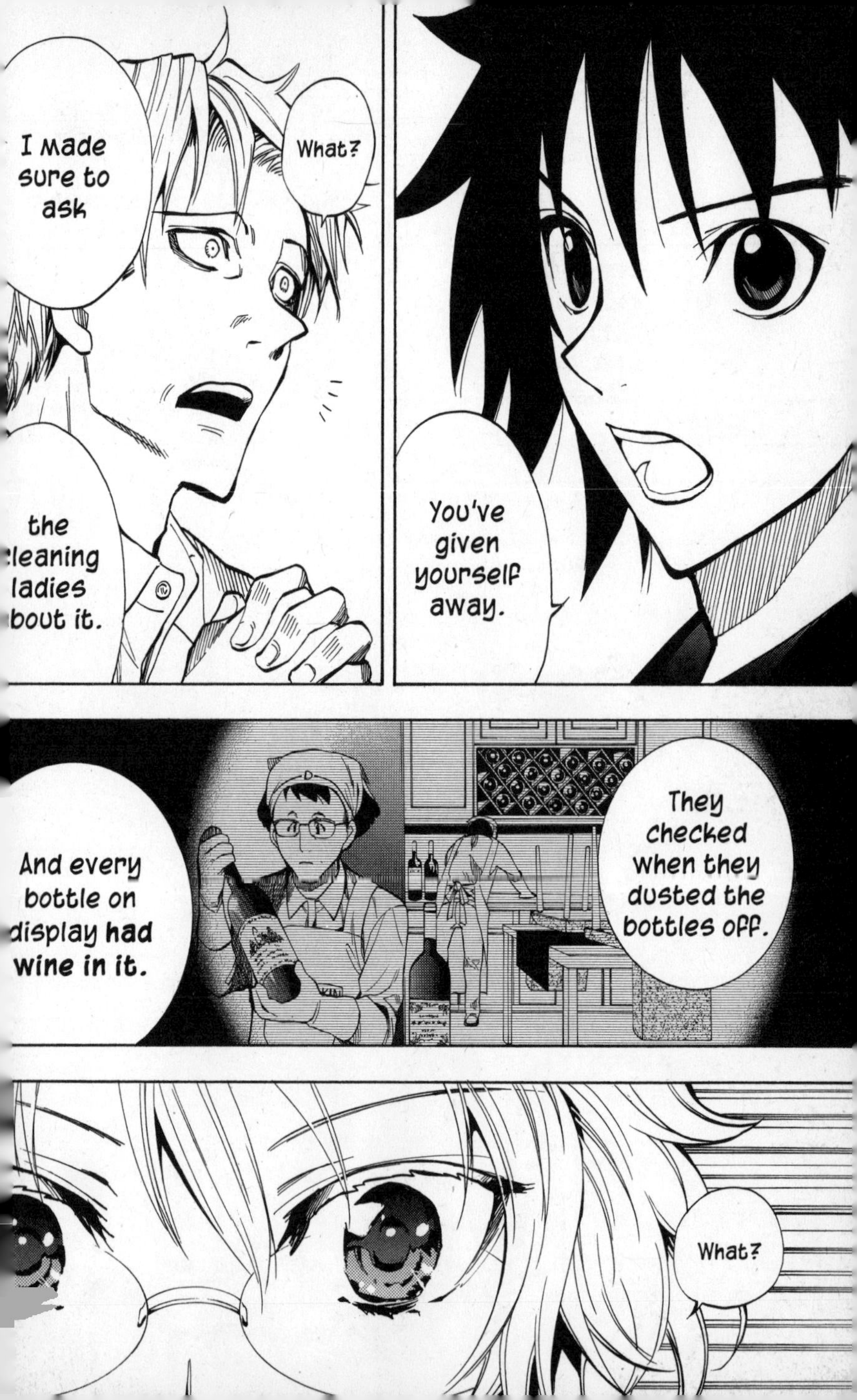

You've given yourself away.
What?
I made sure to ask
the leaning ladies bout it.
They checked when they dusted the bottles off.
And every bottle on display had wine in it.
What?

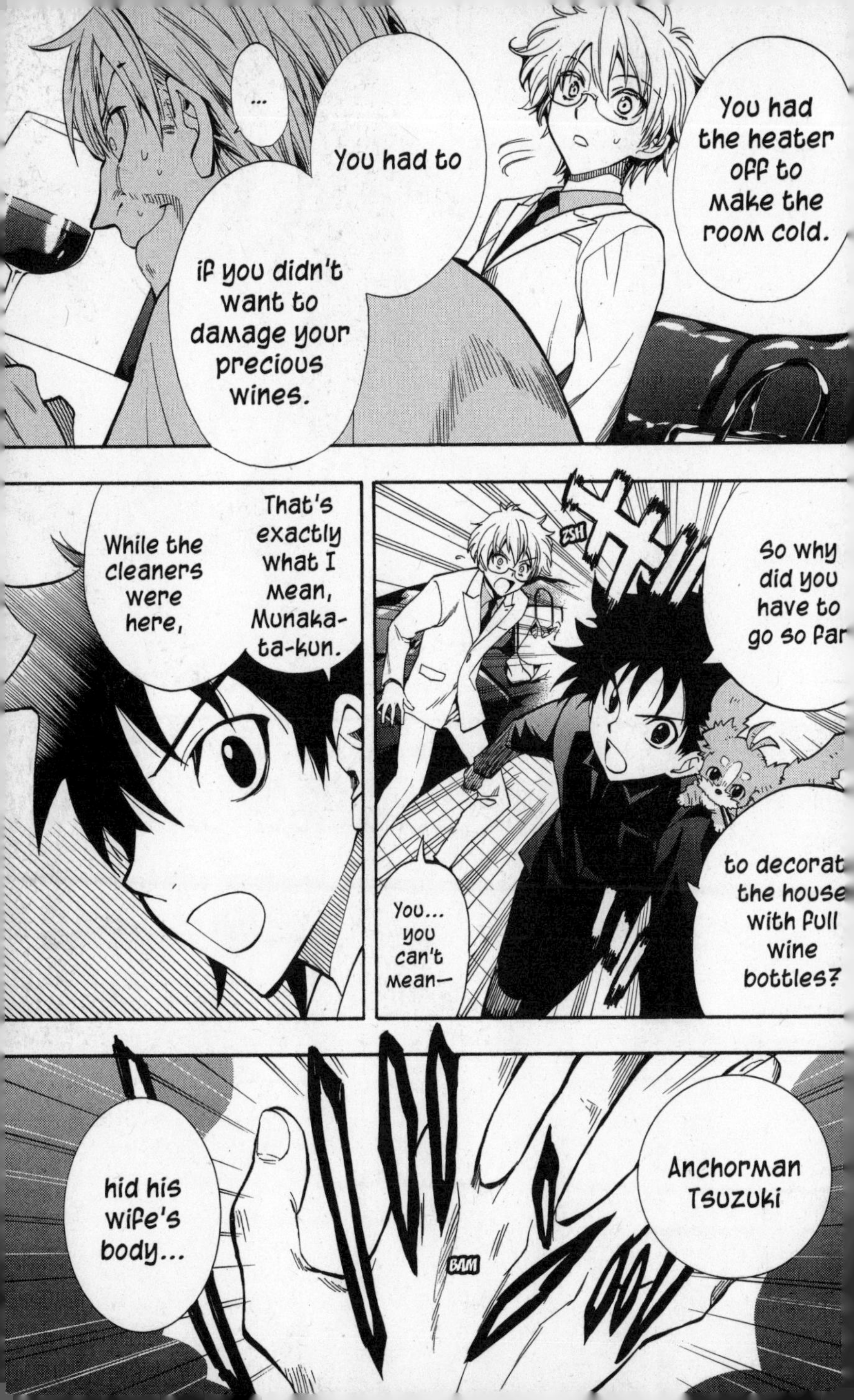
You had the heater off to make the room cold.
...
You had to
if you didn't want to damage your precious wines.
ZSH
So why did you have to go so far
to decorat the house with full wine bottles?
You... you can't mean—
That's exactly what I mean, Munakata-kun.
While the cleaners were here,
Anchorman Tsuzuki
BAM
hid his wife's body...

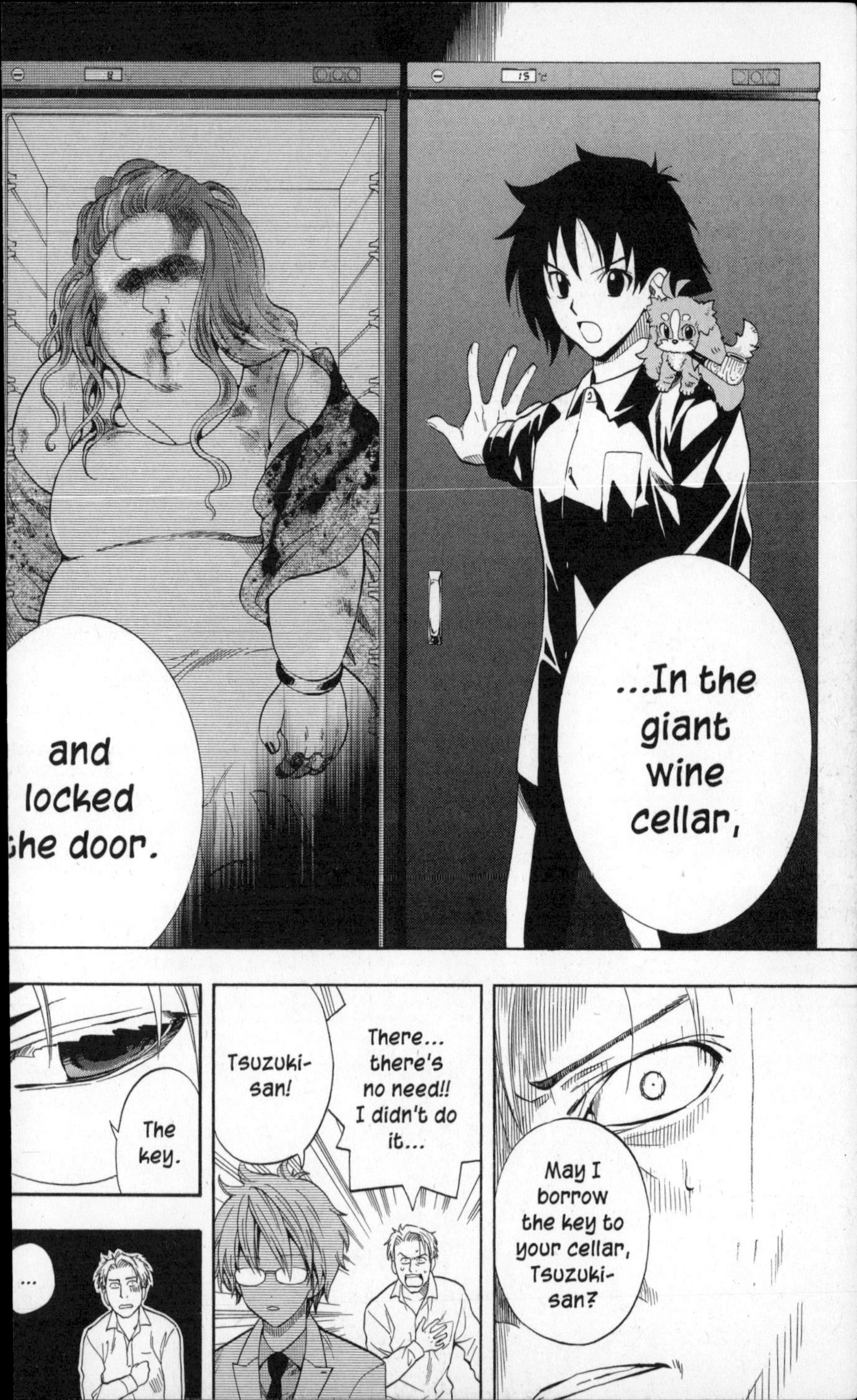
...In the giant wine cellar,
and locked the door.
May I borrow the key to your cellar, Tsuzuki-san?
There... there's no need!! I didn't do it...
Tsuzuki-san!
The key.
...

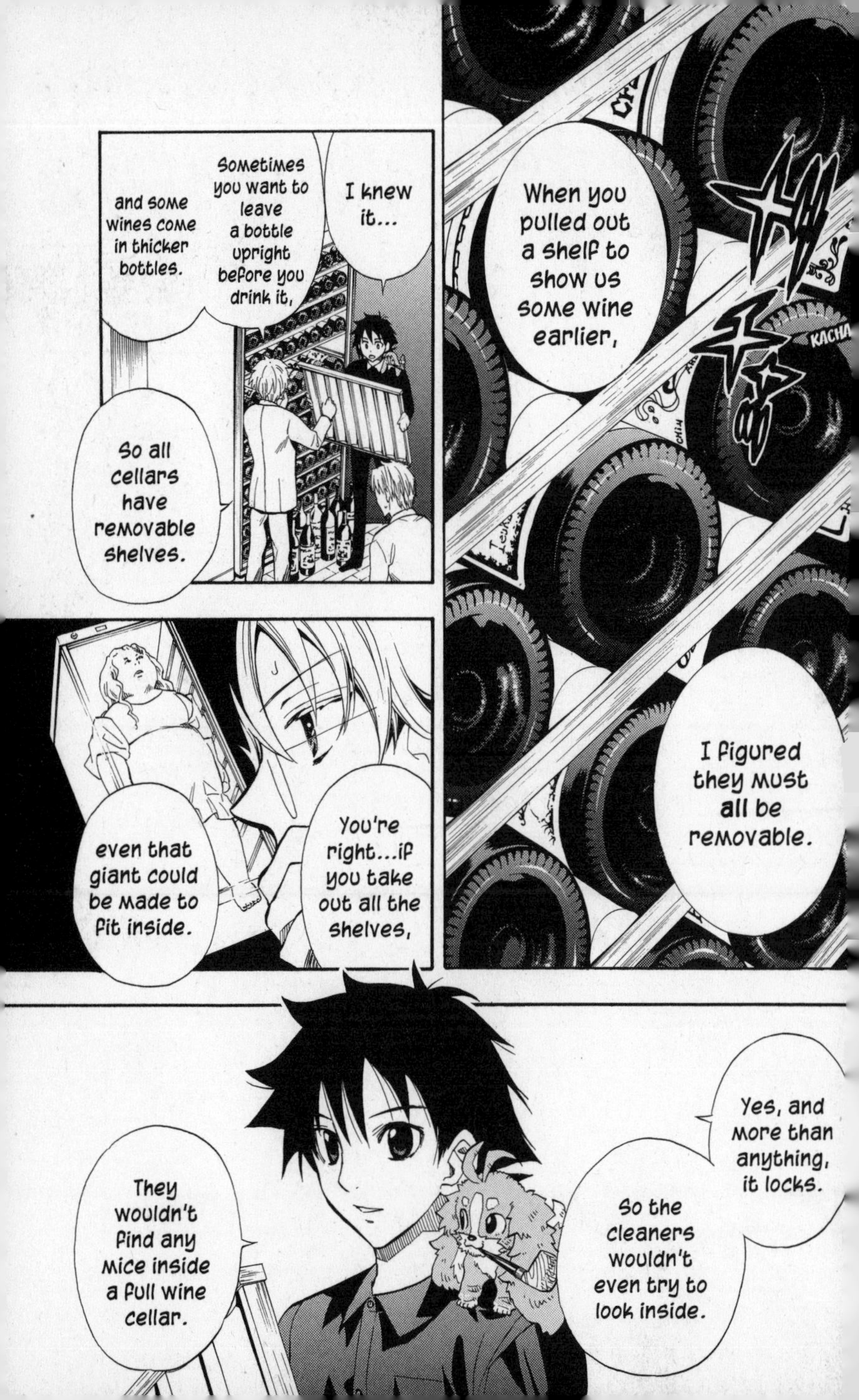
When you pulled out a shelf to show us some wine earlier,
KACHA
I figured they must all be removable.
I knew it...
Sometimes you want to leave a bottle upright before you drink it,
and some wines come in thicker bottles.
So all cellars have removable shelves.
You're right...if you take out all the shelves,
even that giant could be made to fit inside.
Yes, and more than anything, it locks.
So the cleaners wouldn't even try to look inside.
They wouldn't find any mice inside a full wine cellar.

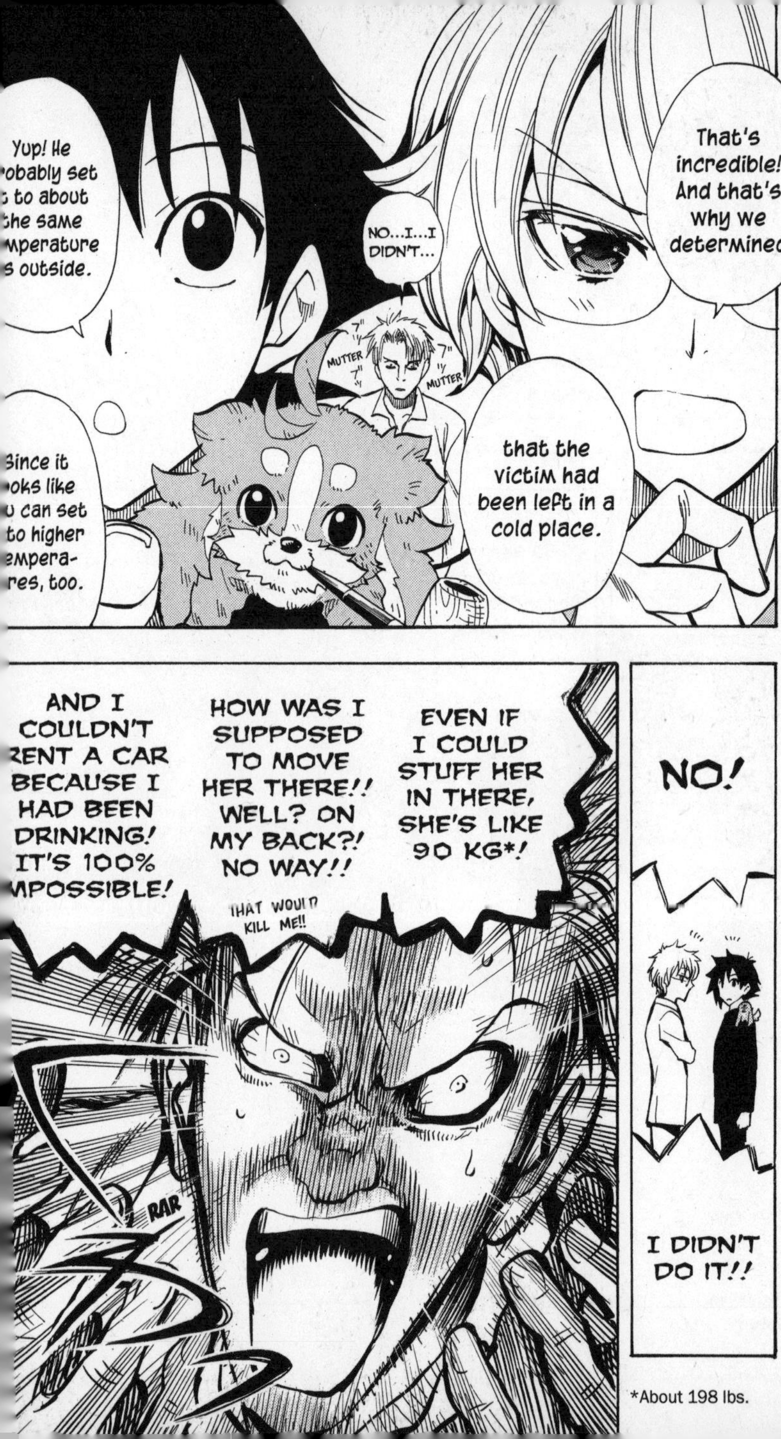
That's incredible! And that's why we determined
that the victim had been left in a cold place.
NO...I...I DIDN'T...
MUTTER
MUTTER
Yup! He obably set to about he same mperature s outside.
Since it oks like u can set to higher empera- res, too.
NO!
I DIDN'T DO IT!!
EVEN IF I COULD STUFF HER IN THERE, SHE'S LIKE 90 KG*!
HOW WAS I SUPPOSED TO MOVE HER THERE!! WELL? ON MY BACK?! NO WAY!!
AND I COULDN'T RENT A CAR BECAUSE I HAD BEEN DRINKING! IT'S 100% MPOSSIBLE!
THAT WOULD KILL ME!!
RAR

*About 198 lbs.

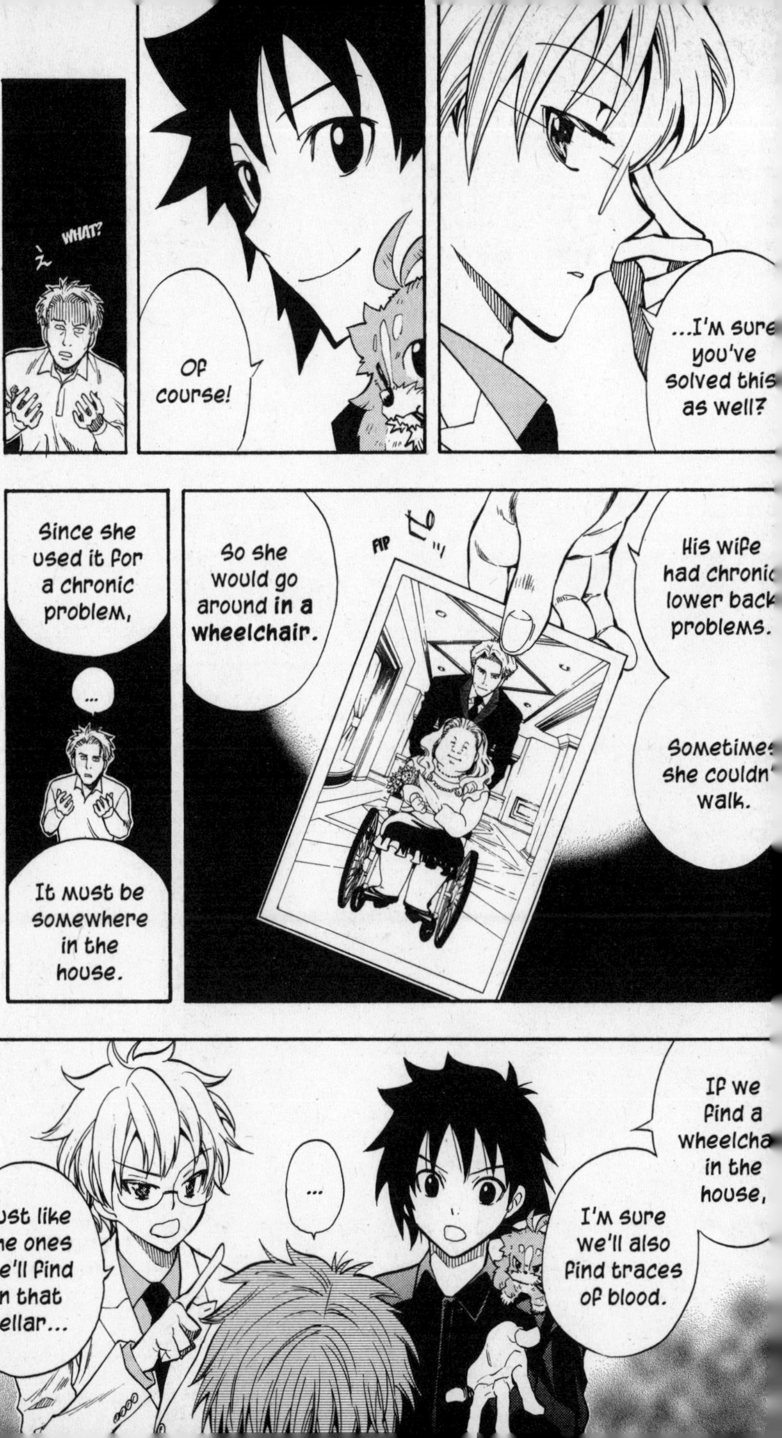
...I'm sure you've solved this as well?
Of course!
WHAT?
え
His wife had chronic lower back problems.
Sometimes she couldn't walk.
FIP
So she would go around in a wheelchair.
Since she used it for a chronic problem,
...
It must be somewhere in the house.
If we find a wheelcha in the house,
I'm sure we'll also find traces of blood.
...
Just like the ones we'll find in that cellar...

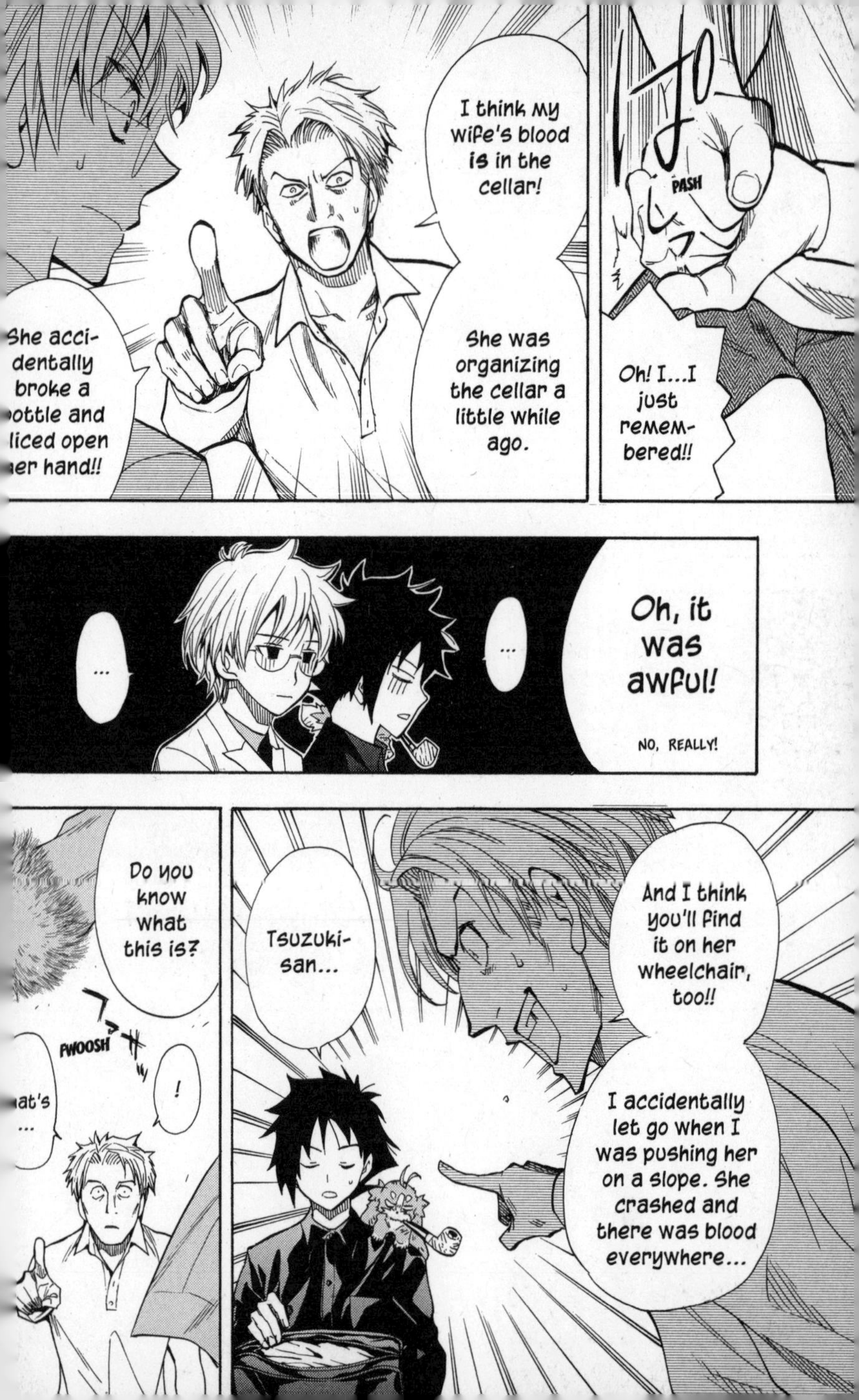
PASH
Oh! I...I just remembered!!
I think my wife's blood is in the cellar!
She was organizing the cellar a little while ago.
She accidentally broke a ottle and liced open er hand!!
Oh, it was awful!
NO, REALLY!
...
...
And I think you'll find it on her wheelchair, too!!
I accidentally let go when I was pushing her on a slope. She crashed and there was blood everywhere...
Tsuzuki-san...
Do you know what this is?
FWOOSH
!
at's ...

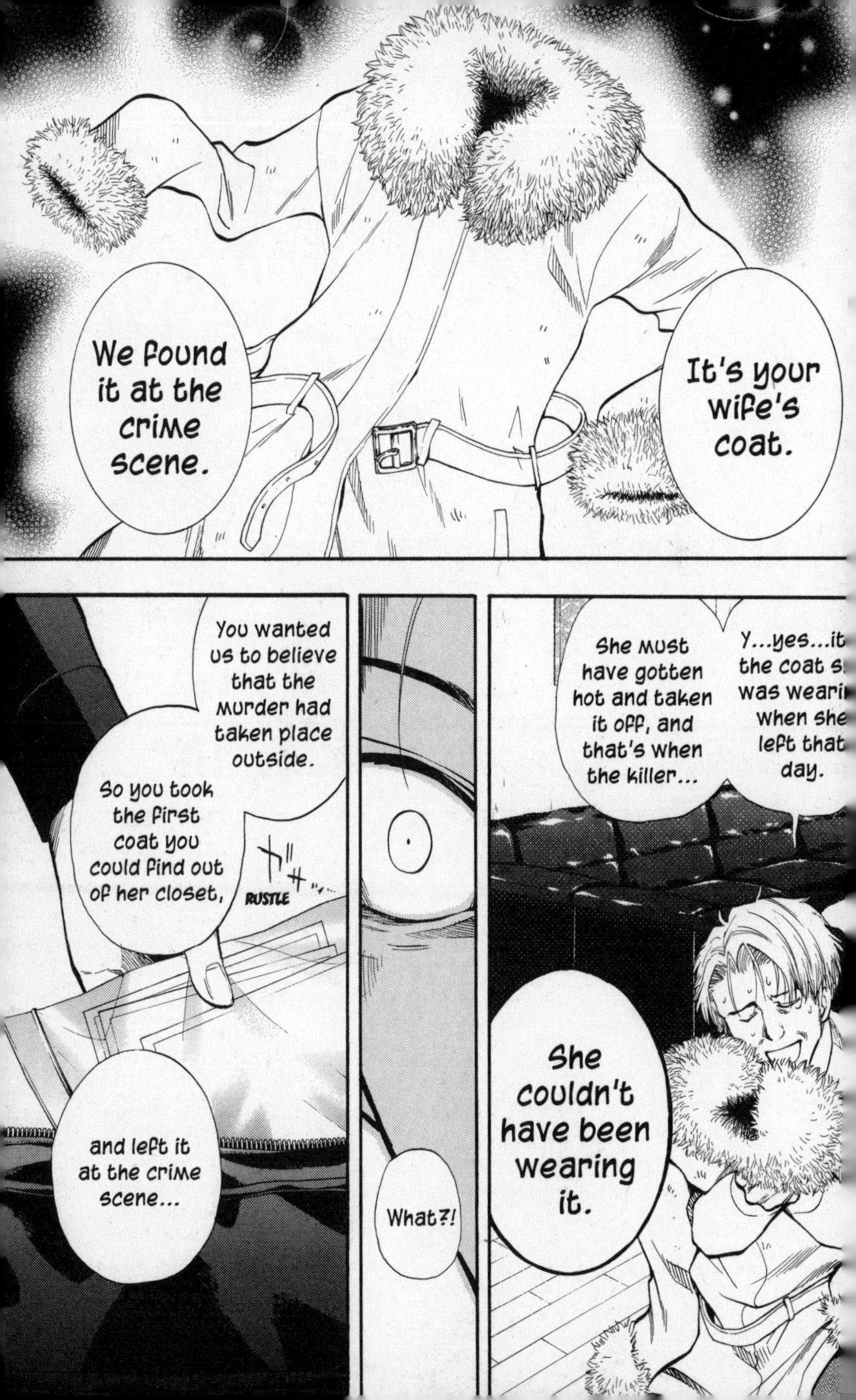
It's your wife's coat.
We found it at the crime scene.
Y...yes...it the coat s was weari when she left that day.
She must have gotten hot and taken it off, and that's when the killer...
She couldn't have been wearing it.
What?!
You wanted us to believe that the murder had taken place outside.
So you took the first coat you could find out of her closet,
RUSTLE
and left it at the crime scene...

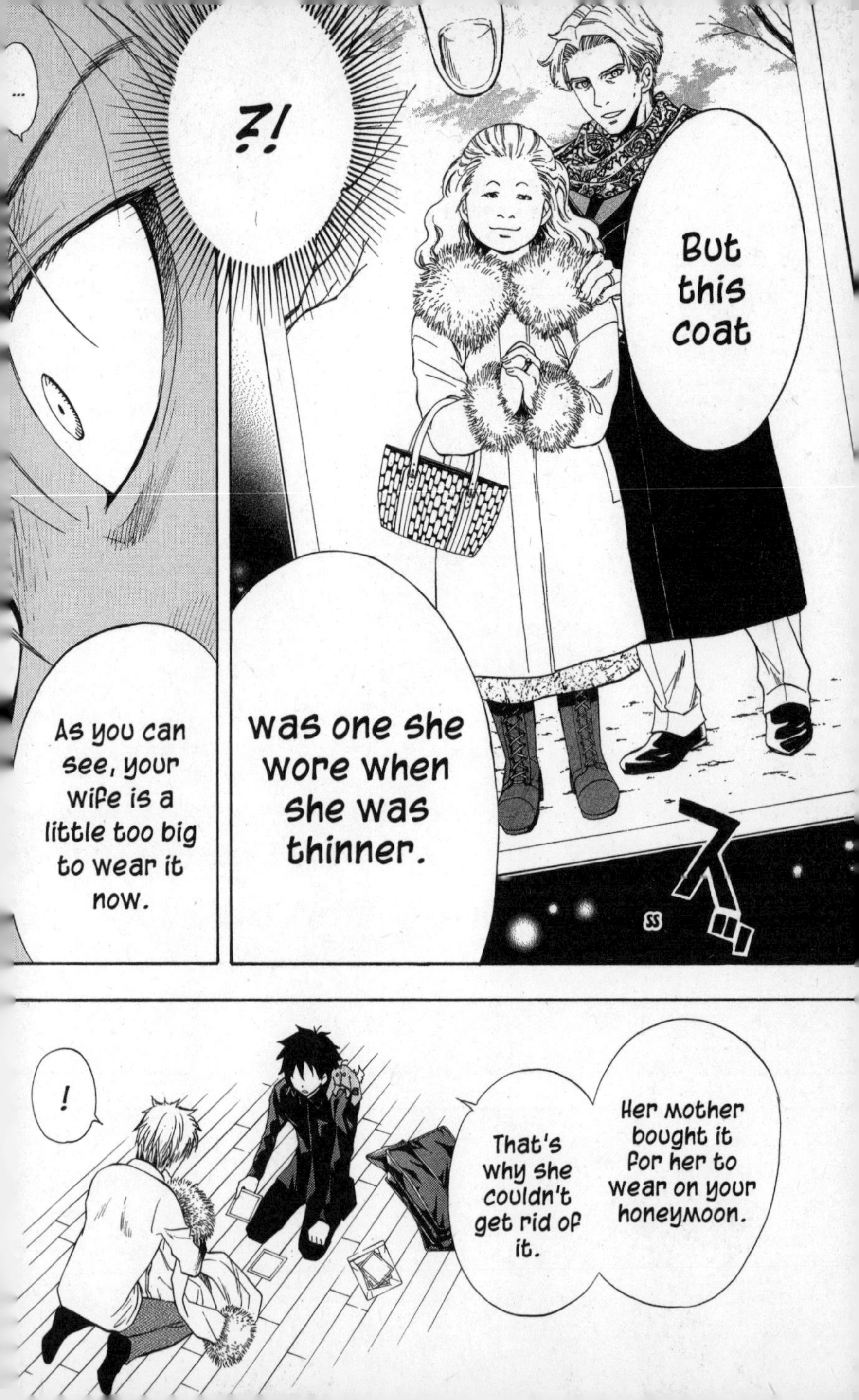
?!
But this coat
was one she wore when she was thinner.
SS
...
As you can see, your wife is a little too big to wear it now.
Her mother bought it for her to wear on your honeymoon.
That's why she couldn't get rid of it.
!

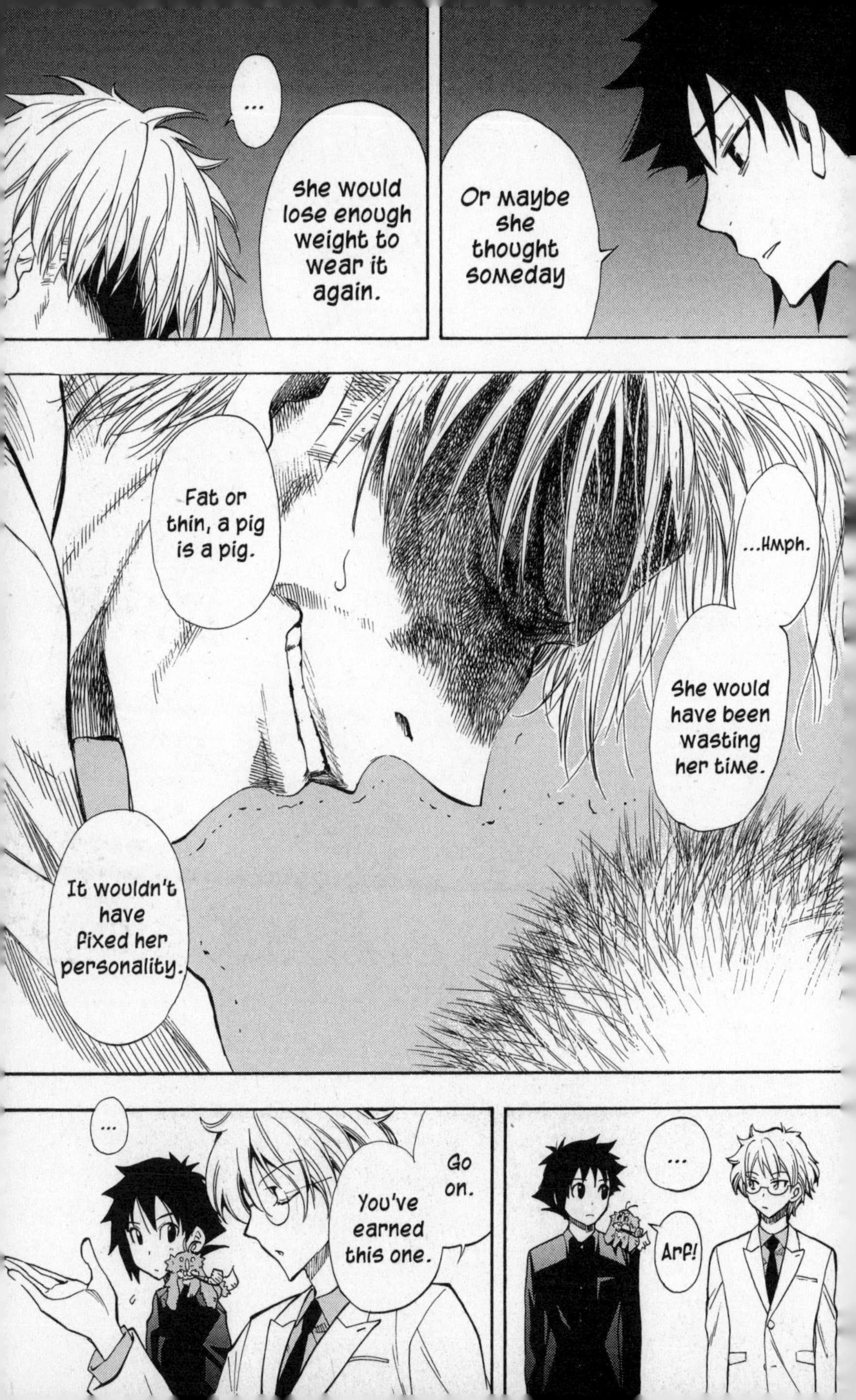
Or maybe she thought someday
She would lose enough weight to wear it again.
...
...Hmph.
She would have been wasting her time.
Fat or thin, a pig is a pig.
It wouldn't have fixed her personality.
...
Arf!
Go on.
You've earned this one.
...

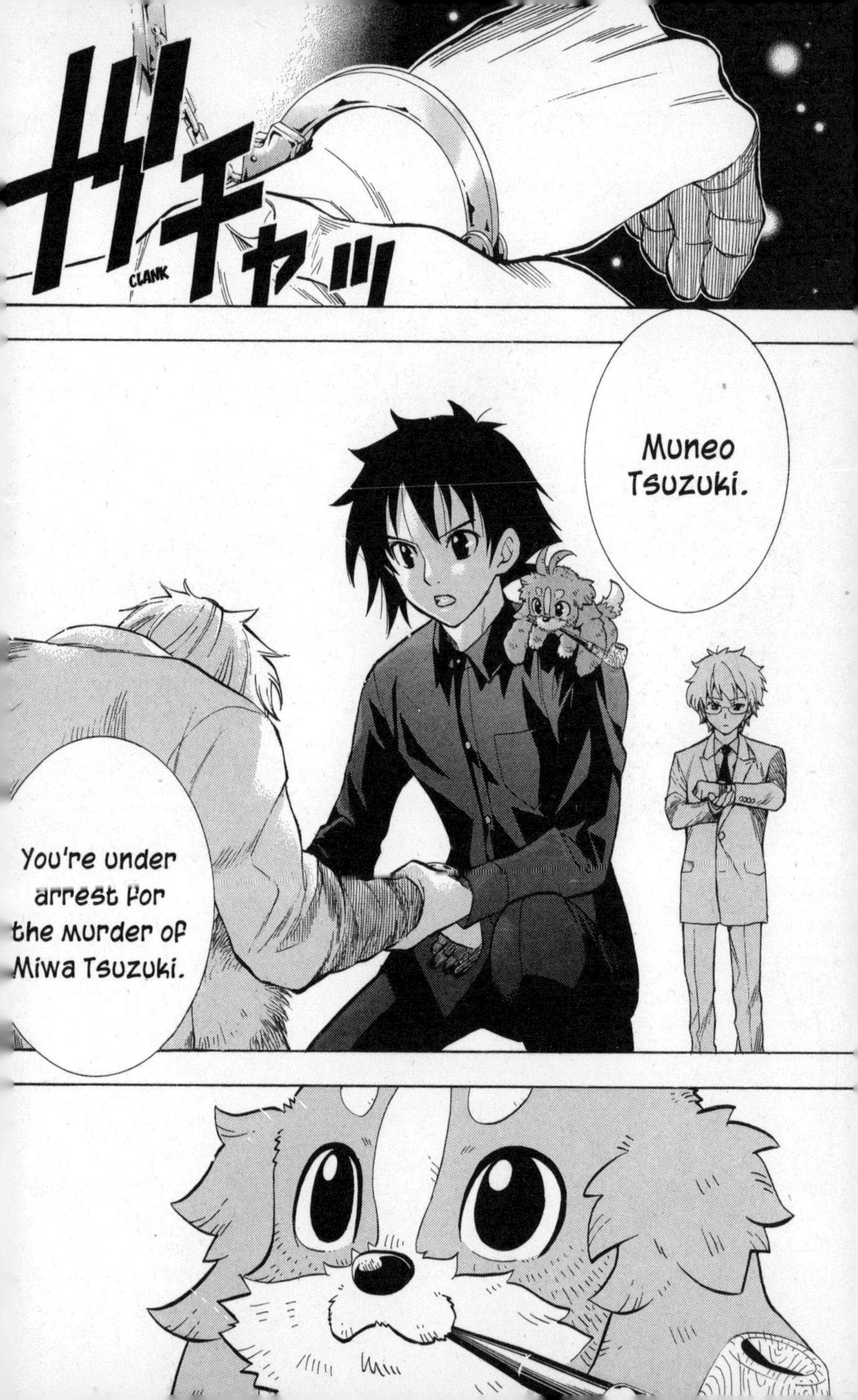
ガチャッ
CLANK
Muneo TSUZUKi.
You're under arrest for the murder of Miwa TSUZUKi.

Coffee Time 4 Reward for an Arrest

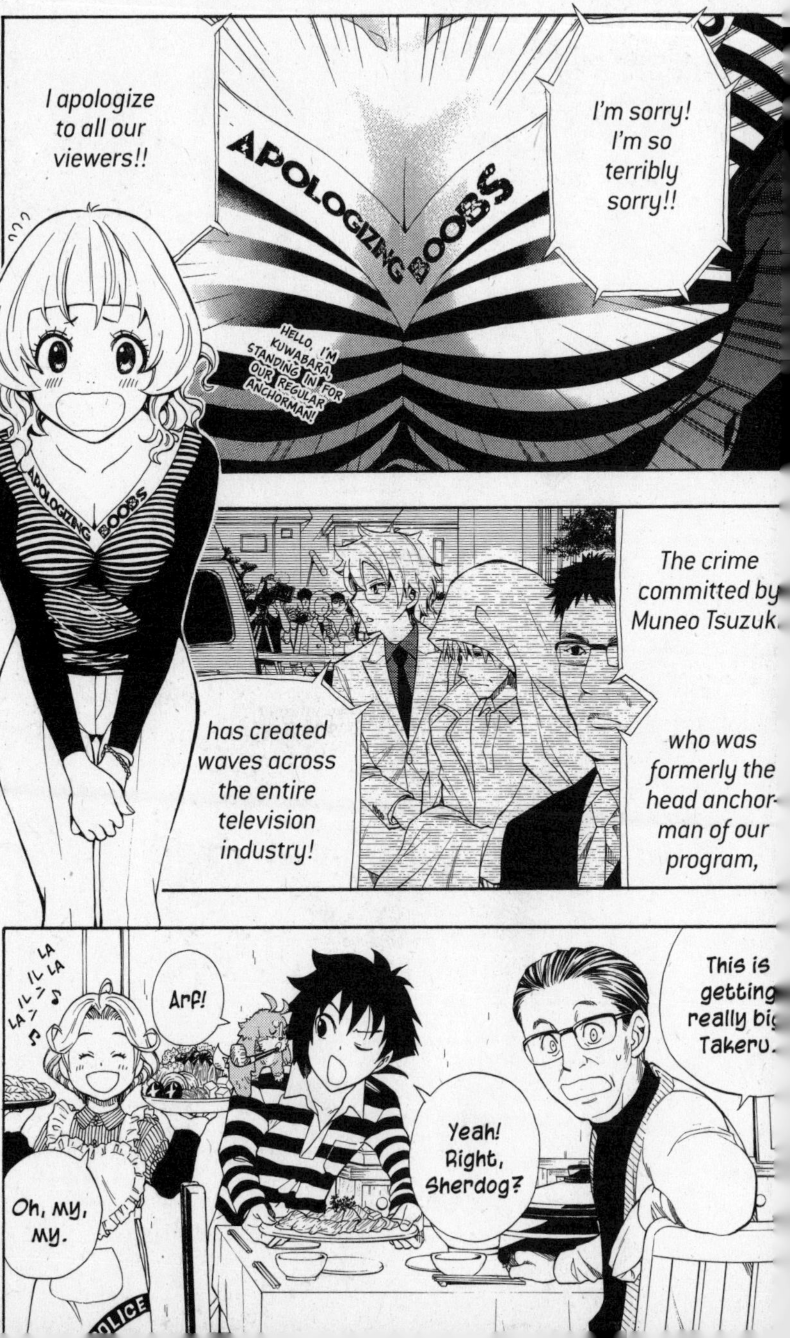
I'm sorry! I'm so terribly sorry!!
APOLOGIZING BOOBS
HELLO, I'M KUWABARA, STANDING IN FOR OUR REGULAR ANCHORMAN!
The crime committed by Muneo Tsuzuk
who was formerly the head anchor-man of our program,
has created waves across the entire television industry!
I apologize to all our viewers!!
APOLOGIZING BOOBS
This is getting really bi Takeru.
Yeah! Right, Sherdog?
Arf!
LA LA LA LA ♪
Oh, my, my.
POLICE

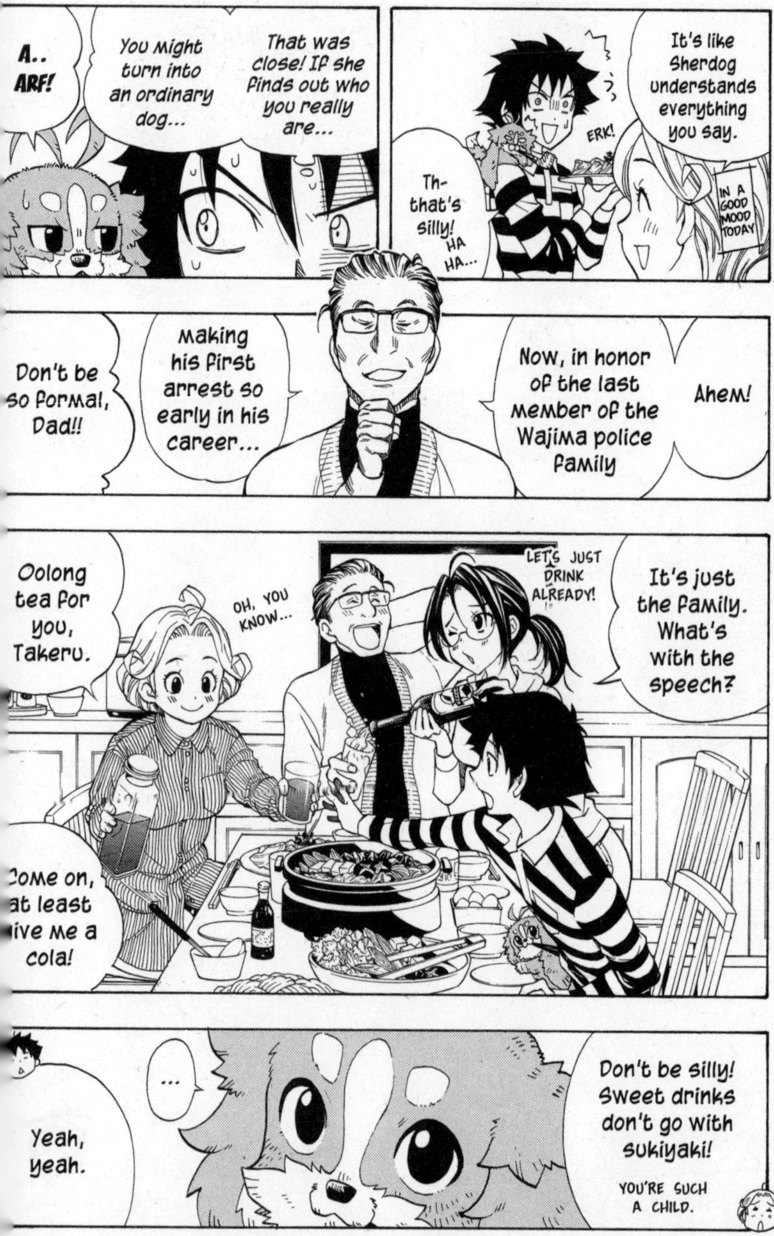
It's like Sherdog understands everything you say.
IN A GOOD MOOD TODAY
ERK!
Th-that's silly! HA HA...
That was close! If she finds out who you really are...
You might turn into an ordinary dog...
A.. ARF!
Ahem!
Now, in honor of the last member of the Wajima police family
Making his first arrest so early in his career...
Don't be so formal, Dad!!
It's just the family. What's with the speech?
LET'S JUST DRINK ALREADY!
OH, YOU KNOW...
Oolong tea for you, Takeru.
Come on, at least ive me a cola!
Don't be silly! Sweet drinks don't go with sukiyaki!
YOU'RE SUCH A CHILD.
...
Yeah, yeah.

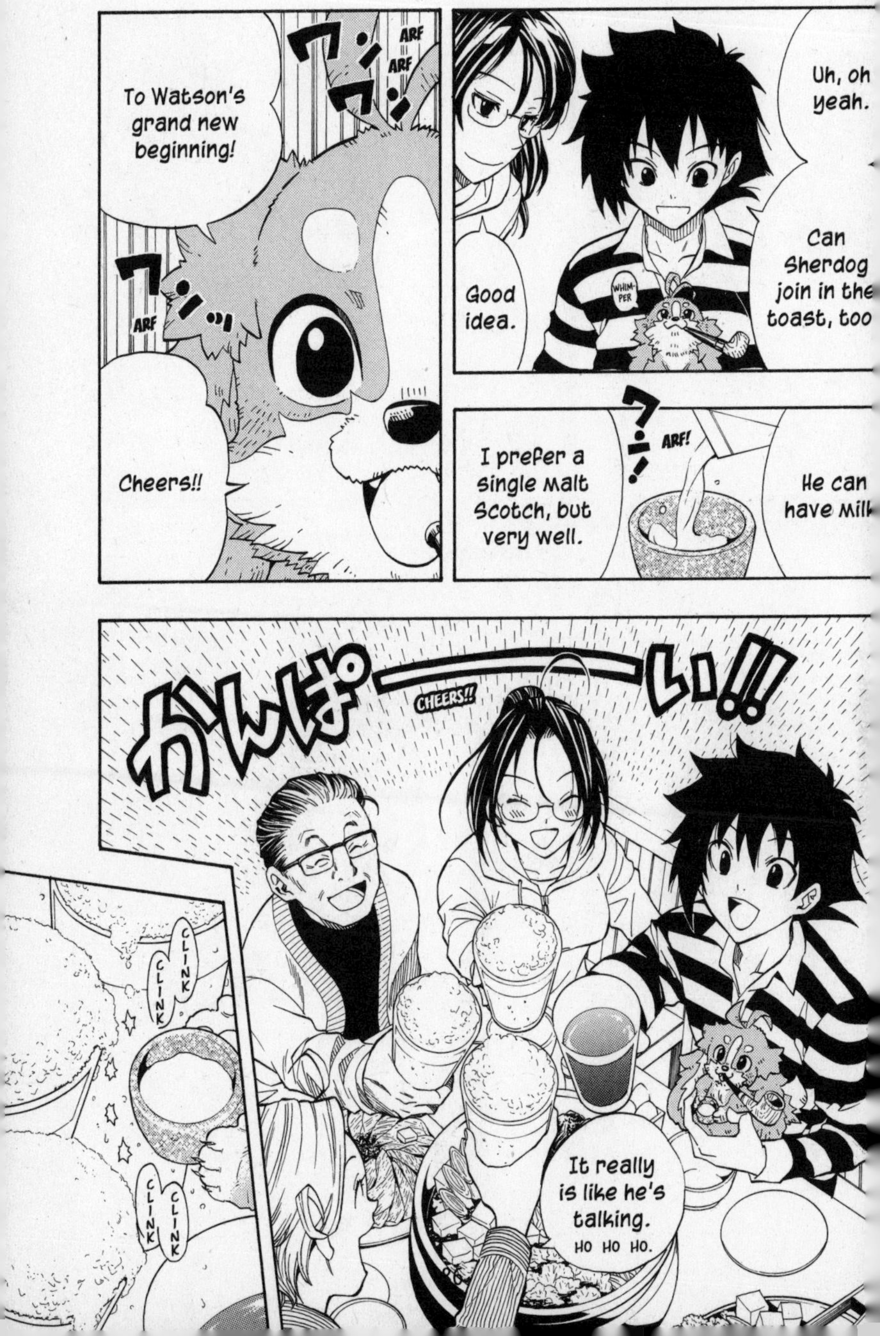
Uh, oh yeah.
Can Sherdog join in the toast, too
WHIMPER
Good idea.
He can have milk
ARF!
I prefer a single malt Scotch, but very well.
ARF
ARF
To Watson's grand new beginning!
ARF
Cheers!!
かんぱーーーい!!
CHEERS!!
It really is like he's talking.
HO HO HO.
CLINK
CLINK
CLINK
CLINK

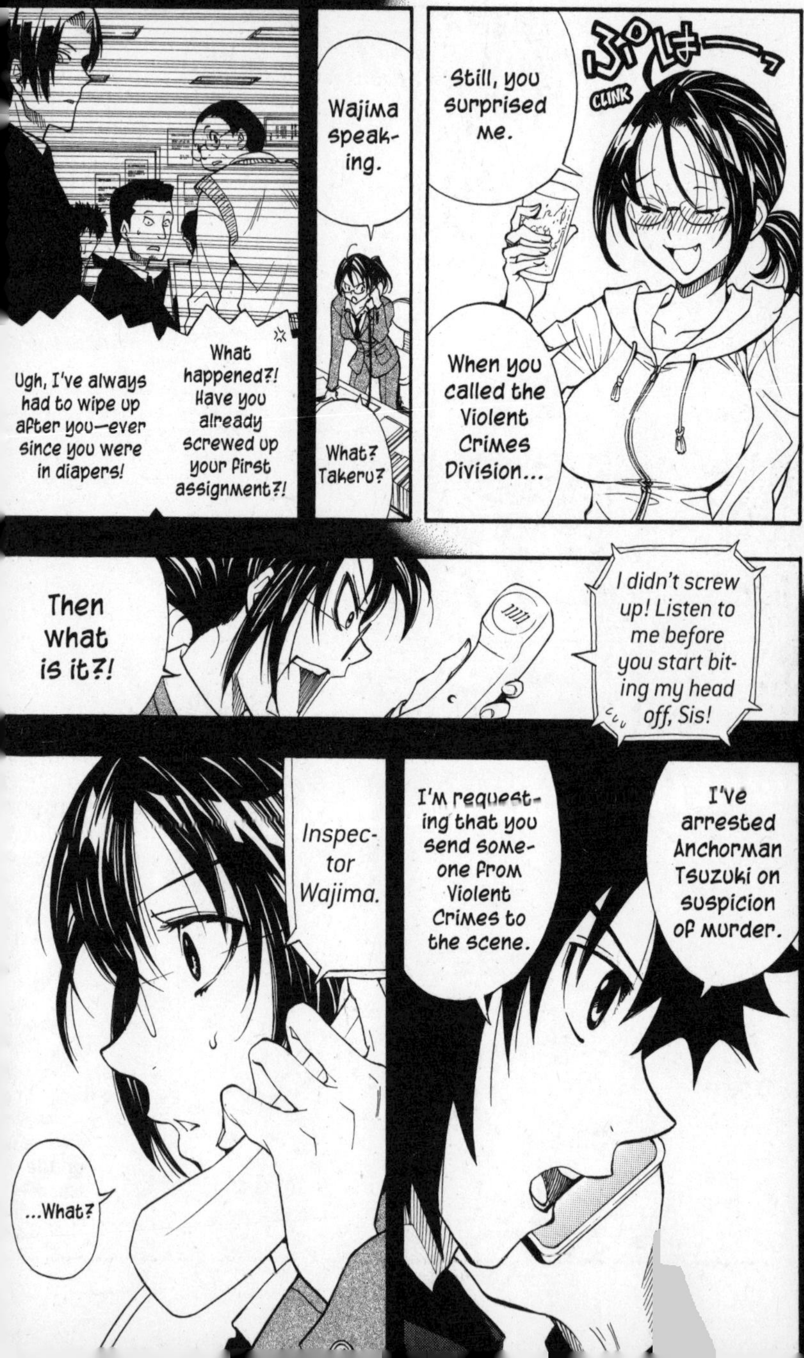
CLINK
Still, you surprised me.
When you called the Violent Crimes Division...
Wajima speaking.
What? Takeru?
What happened?! Have you already screwed up your first assignment?!
Ugh, I've always had to wipe up after you—ever since you were in diapers!
I didn't screw up! Listen to me before you start biting my head off, Sis!
Then what is it?!
I've arrested Anchorman Tsuzuki on suspicion of murder.
I'm requesting that you send someone from Violent Crimes to the scene.
Inspector Wajima.
...What?

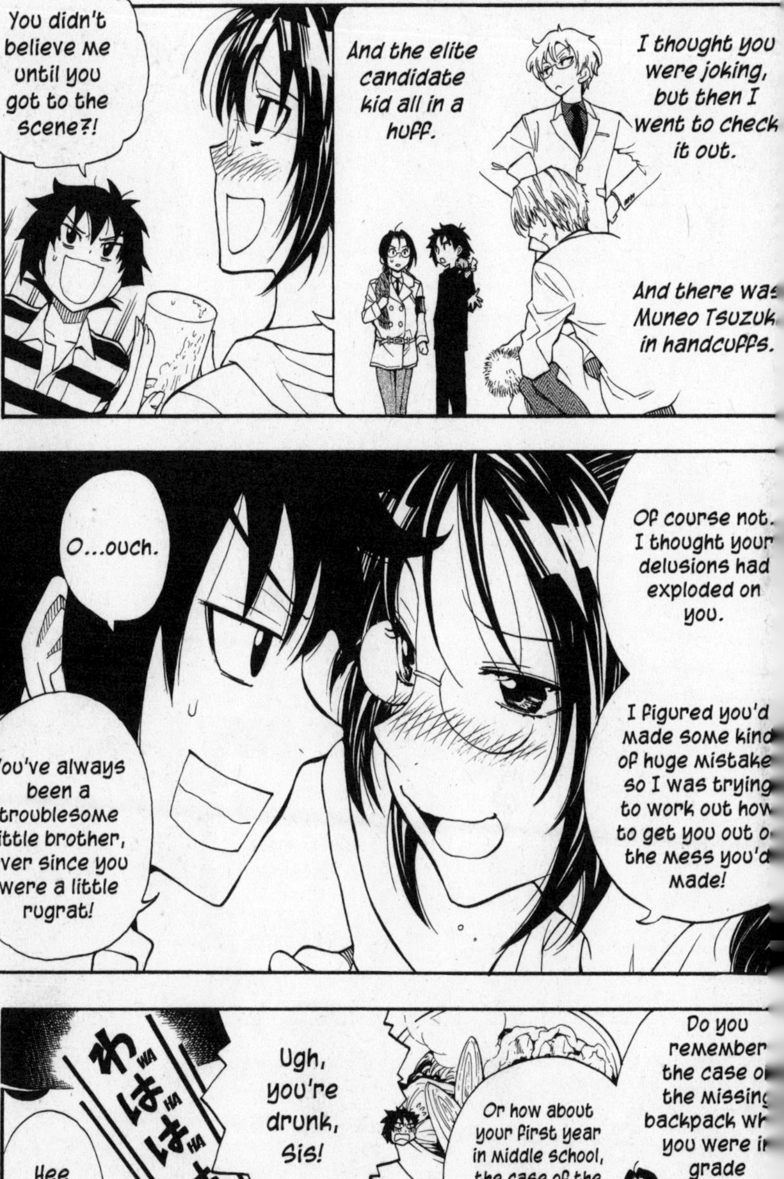
I thought you were joking, but then I went to check it out.
And the elite candidate kid all in a huff.
And there was Muneo Tsuzuk in handcuffs.
You didn't believe me until you got to the scene?!
Of course not. I thought your delusions had exploded on you.
I figured you'd made some kind of huge mistake so I was trying to work out how to get you out o the mess you'd made!
O...ouch.
You've always been a troublesome little brother, ever since you were a little rugrat!
Do you remember the case o the missing backpack wh you were i grade school?
Or how about your first year in middle school, the case of the robbery that never happened?
Ugh, you're drunk, Sis!
わWAはHAはHAはHAはHA
Hee hee hee...

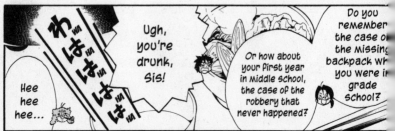

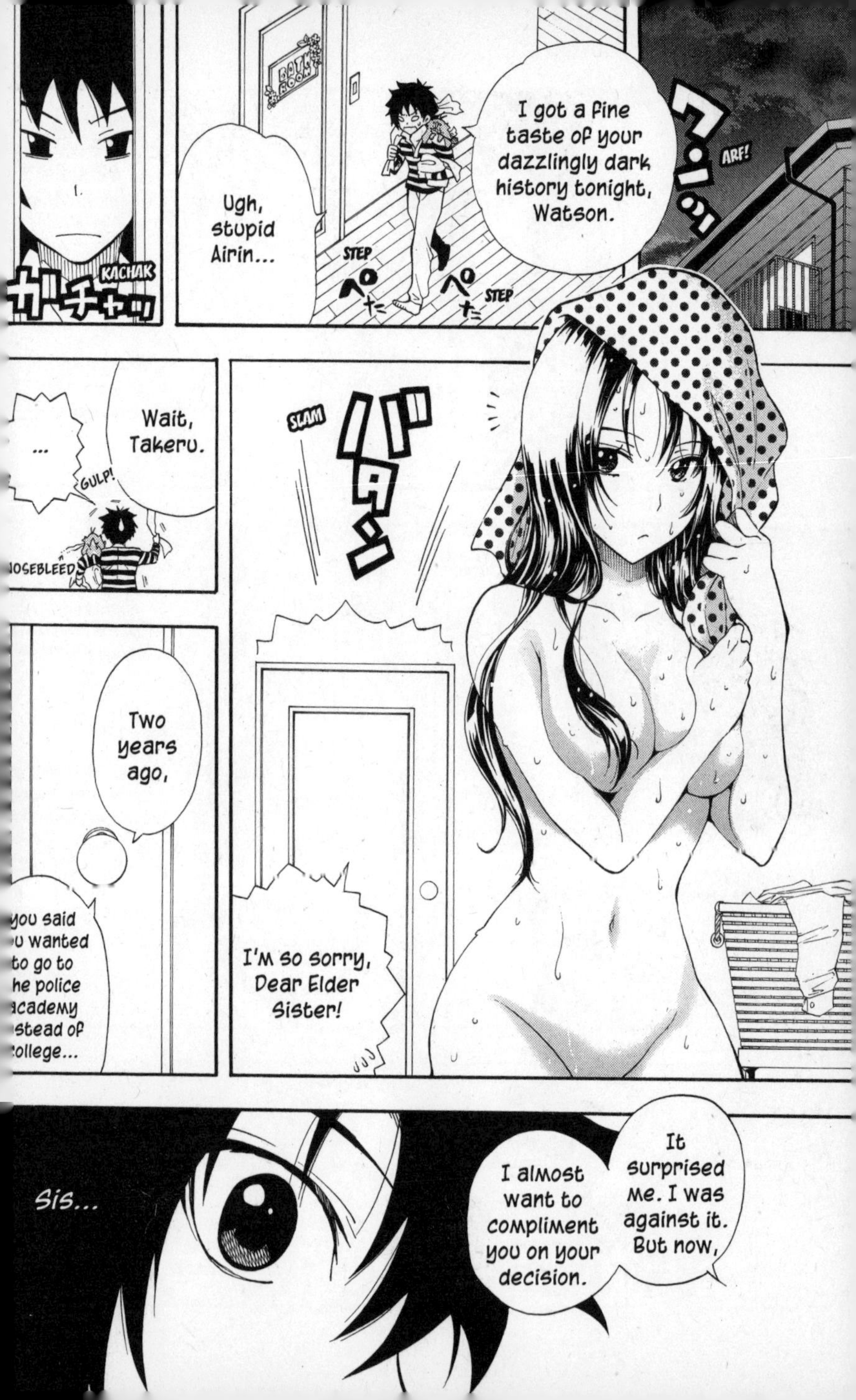
ARF!
I got a fine taste of your dazzlingly dark history tonight, Watson.
Ugh, stupid Airin...
STEP
STEP
KACHAK
SLAM
I'm so sorry, Dear Elder Sister!
Wait, Takeru.
...
GULP!
NOSEBLEED
Two years ago,
you said ou wanted to go to he police academy stead of college...
It surprised me. I was against it. But now,
I almost want to compliment you on your decision.
Sis...

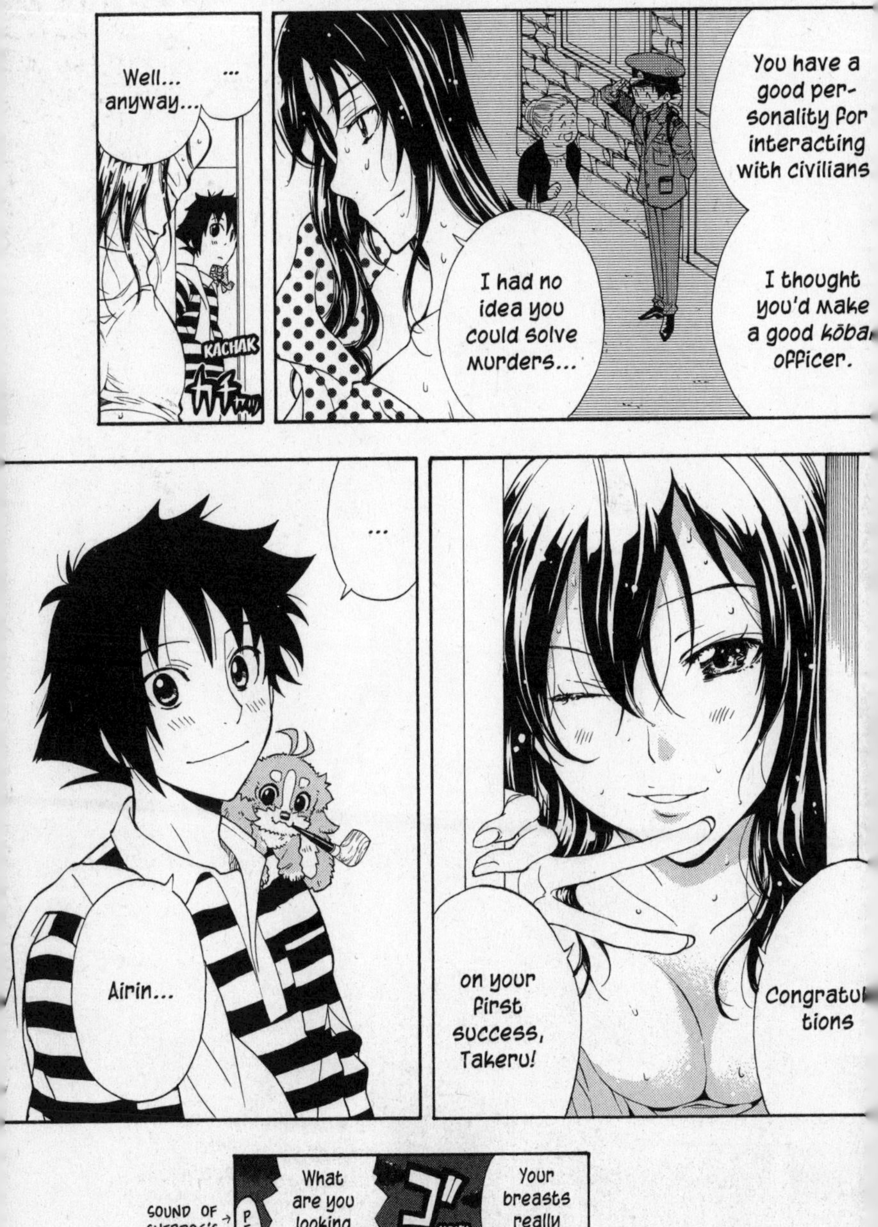
You have a good per-sonality for interacting with civilians
I thought you'd make a good kōba officer.
I had no idea you could solve murders...
...
Well... anyway...
KACHAK
カチャッ
Congratu tions
on your first success, Takeru!
...
Airin...
Your breasts really are big.
KONK
What are you looking at?!
PFFT
SOUND OF SHERDOG'S NOSEBLEED.

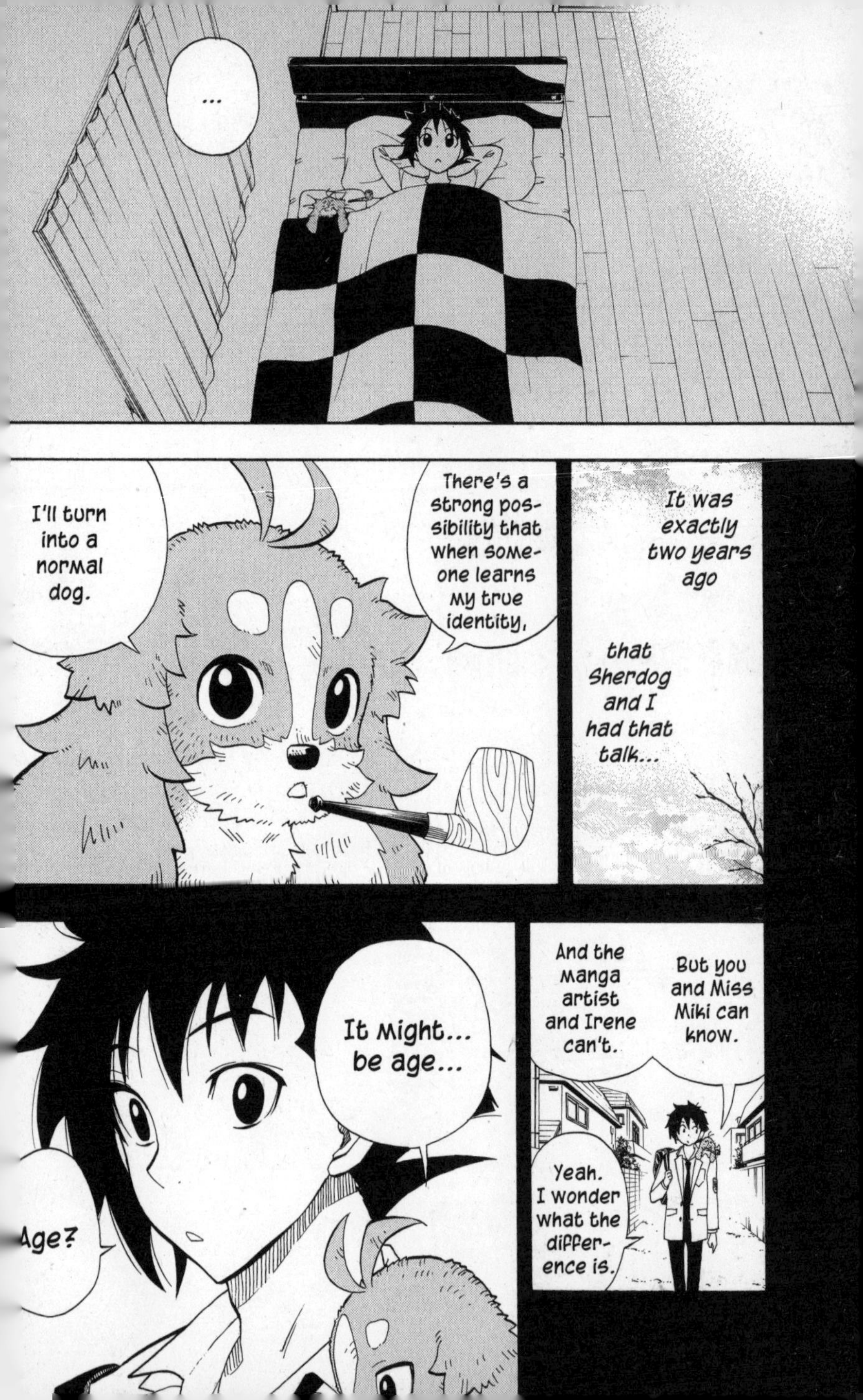
...
It was exactly two years ago
that Sherdog and I had that talk...
There's a strong possibility that when someone learns my true identity,
I'll turn into a normal dog.
But you and Miss Miki can know.
And the manga artist and Irene can't.
Yeah. I wonder what the difference is.
It might... be age...
Age?

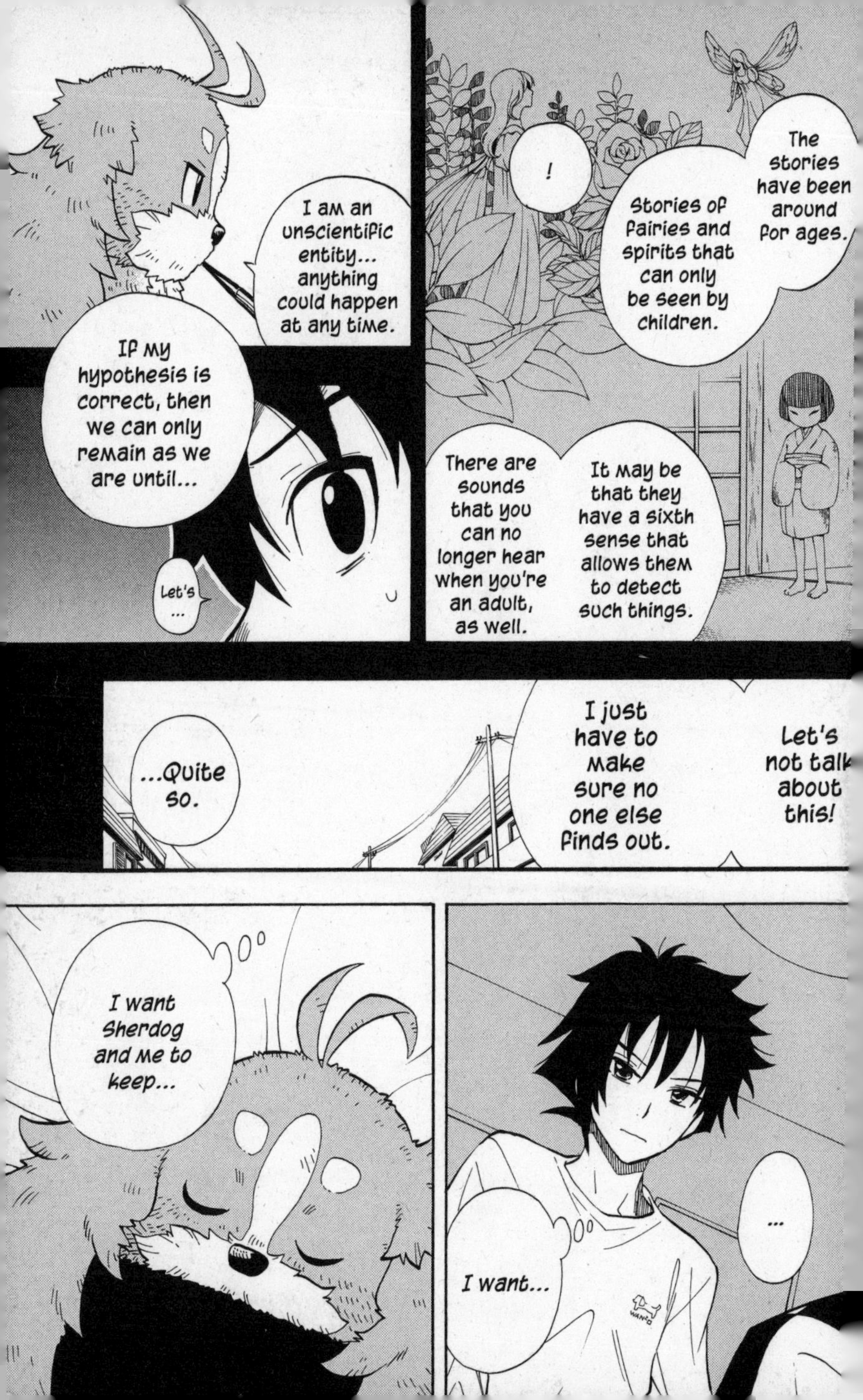
The stories have been around for ages.
Stories of fairies and spirits that can only be seen by children.
!
It may be that they have a sixth sense that allows them to detect such things.
There are sounds that you can no longer hear when you're an adult, as well.
I am an unscientific entity... anything could happen at any time.
If my hypothesis is correct, then we can only remain as we are until...
Let's ...
Let's not talk about this!
I just have to make sure no one else finds out.
...Quite so.
...
I want...
I want Sherdog and me to keep...

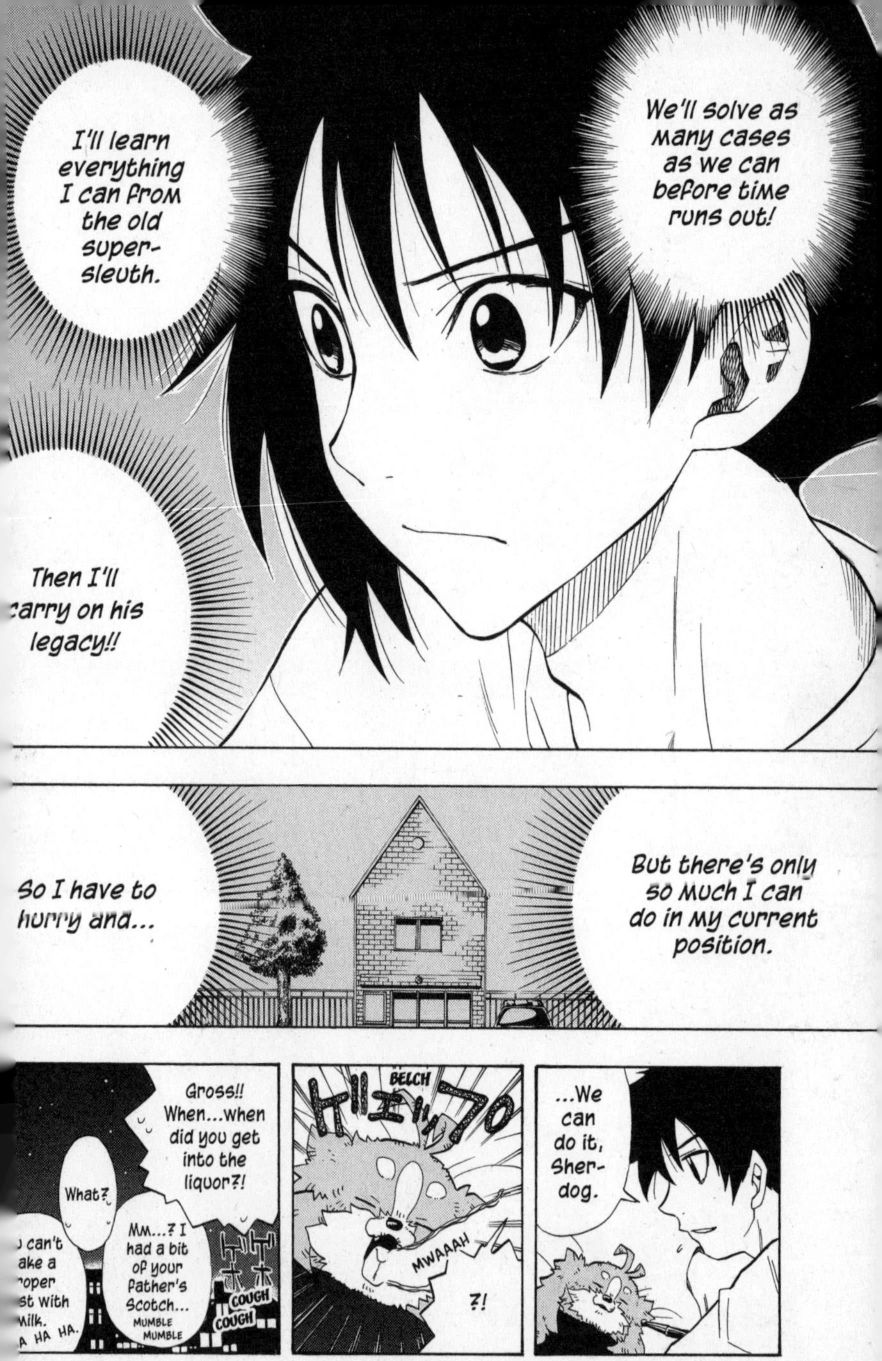
We'll solve as many cases as we can before time runs out!
I'll learn everything I can from the old super-sleuth.
Then I'll carry on his legacy!!
But there's only so much I can do in my current position.
So I have to hurry and...
...We can do it, Sher-dog.
BELCH
MWAAAH
?!
Gross!! When...when did you get into the liquor?!
What?
Mm...? I had a bit of your father's Scotch... MUMBLE MUMBLE
COUGH COUGH
can't ake a roper st with milk. A HA HA.

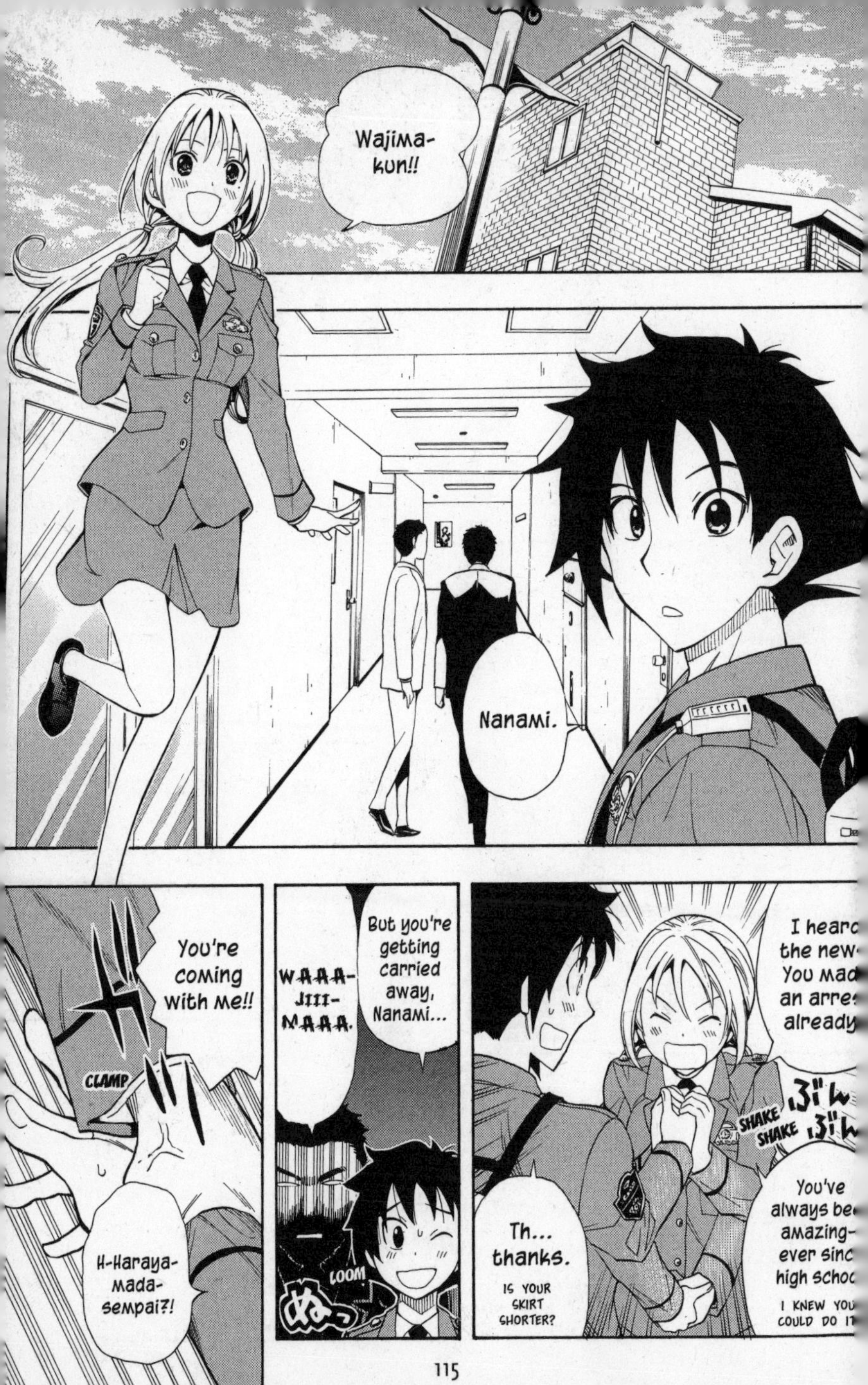
Wajima-kun!!
Nanami.
I hear
the new
You mad
an arres
already
SHAKE SHAKE
Th... thanks.
IS YOUR SKIRT SHORTER?
You've always bee amazing- ever sinc high schoo
I KNEW YOU COULD DO I
But you're getting carried away, Nanami...
WAAA-JIII-MAAA.
LOOM
ぬっ
You're coming with me!!
CLAMP
H-Haraya-Mada-sempai?!

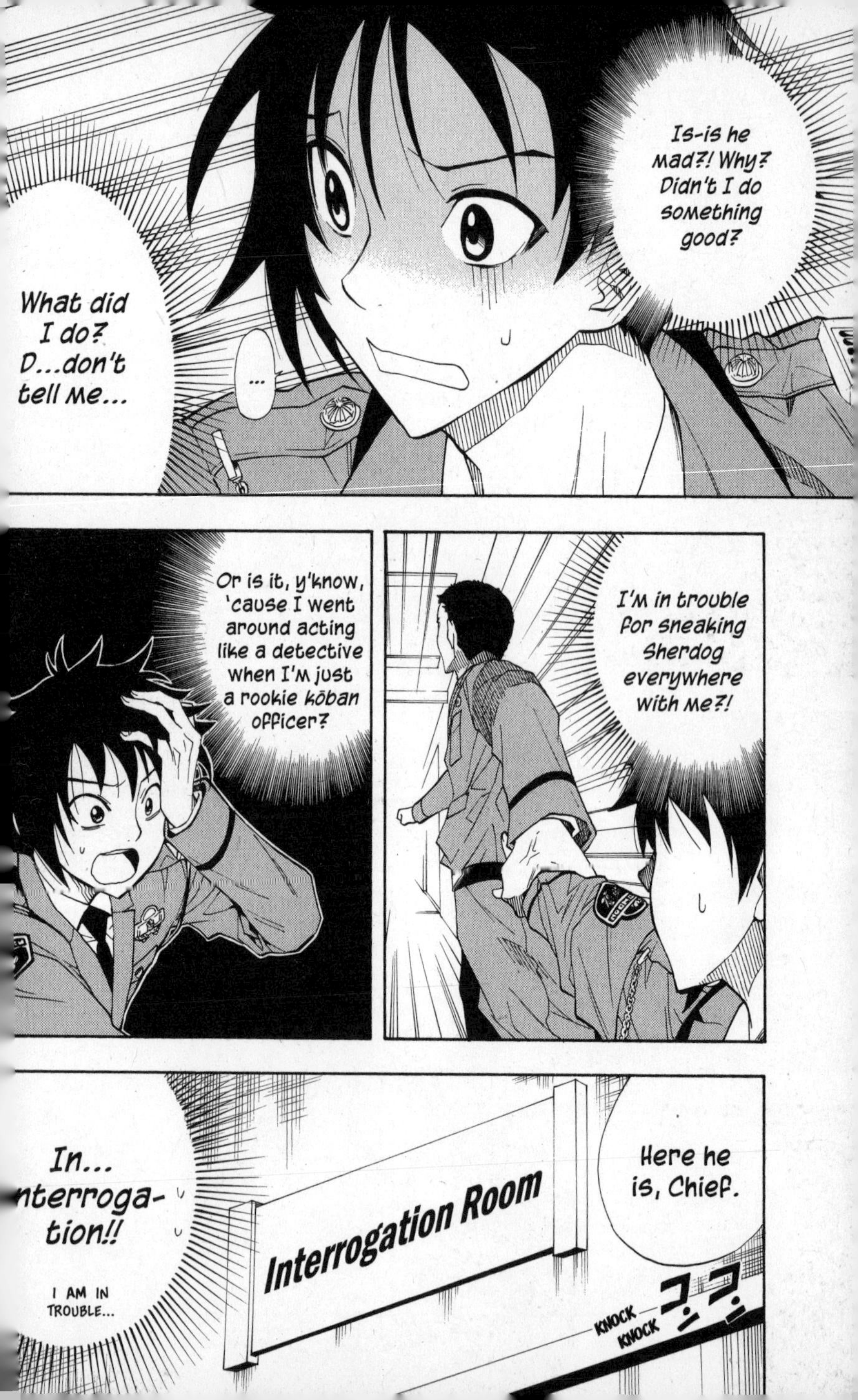
Is-is he mad?! Why? Didn't I do something good?
...
What did I do? D...don't tell me...
I'm in trouble for sneaking Sherdog everywhere with me?!
Or is it, y'know, 'cause I went around acting like a detective when I'm just a rookie kōban officer?
Here he is, Chief.
KNOCK KNOCK
Interrogation Room
In... nterroga-tion!!
I AM IN TROUBLE...

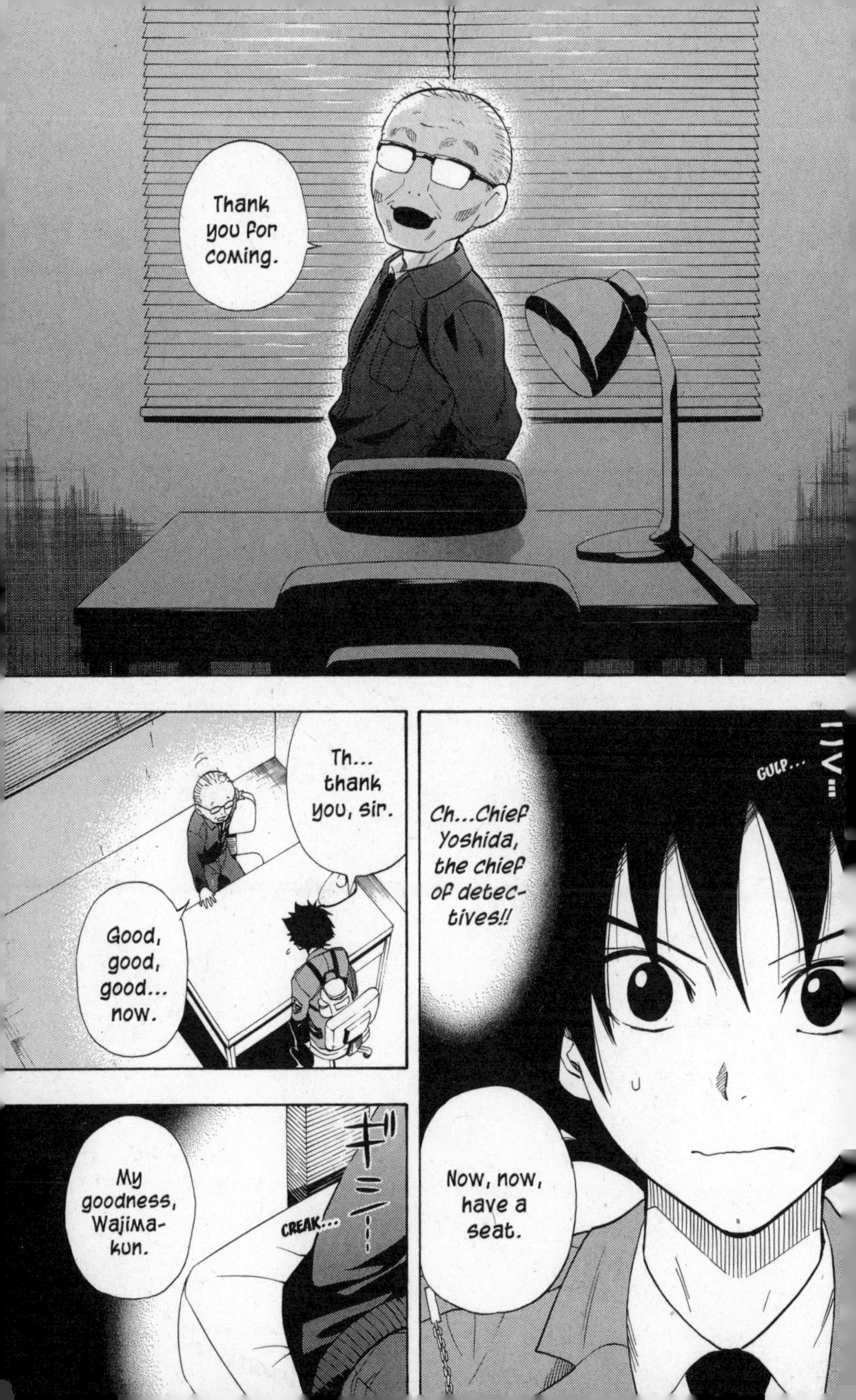
Thank you for coming.
GULP...
Ch...Chief Yoshida, the chief of detec-tives!!
Now, now, have a seat.
Th... thank you, sir.
Good, good, good... now.
My goodness, Wajima-kun.
CREAK...

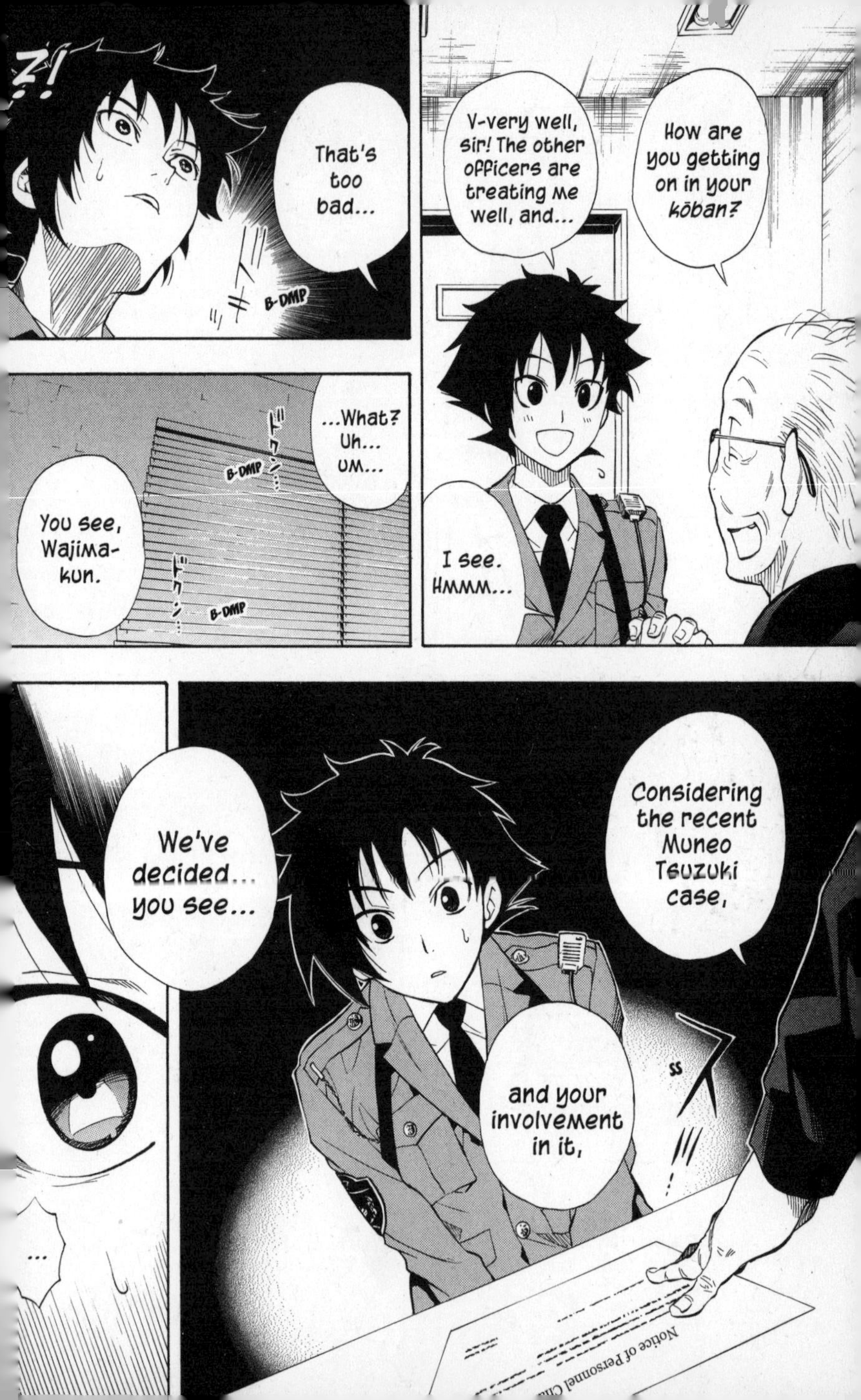
How are you getting on in your kōban?
V-very well, sir! The other officers are treating me well, and...
I see. HMMM...
Z!
That's too bad...
B-DMP
...What? Uh... um...
B-DMP
You see, Wajima-kun.
B-DMP
Considering the recent Muneo Tsuzuki case,
and your involvement in it,
SS
We've decided... you see...
...

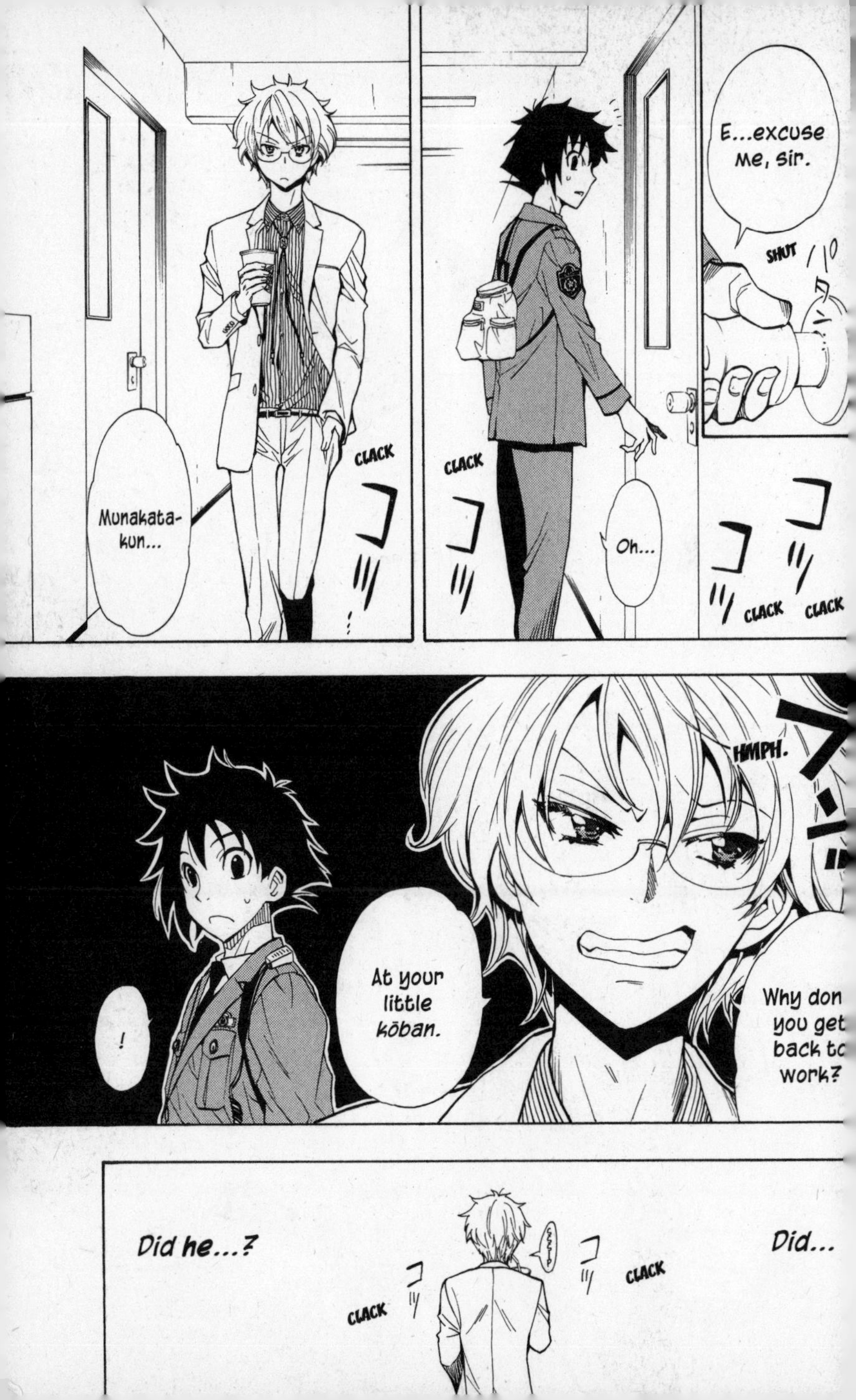
E...excuse me, sir.
SHUT
CLACK
CLACK
CLACK
Oh...
CLACK
Munakata-kun...
HMPH.
Why don you get back to work?
At your little kōban.
!
Did...
CLACK
CLACK
Did he...?

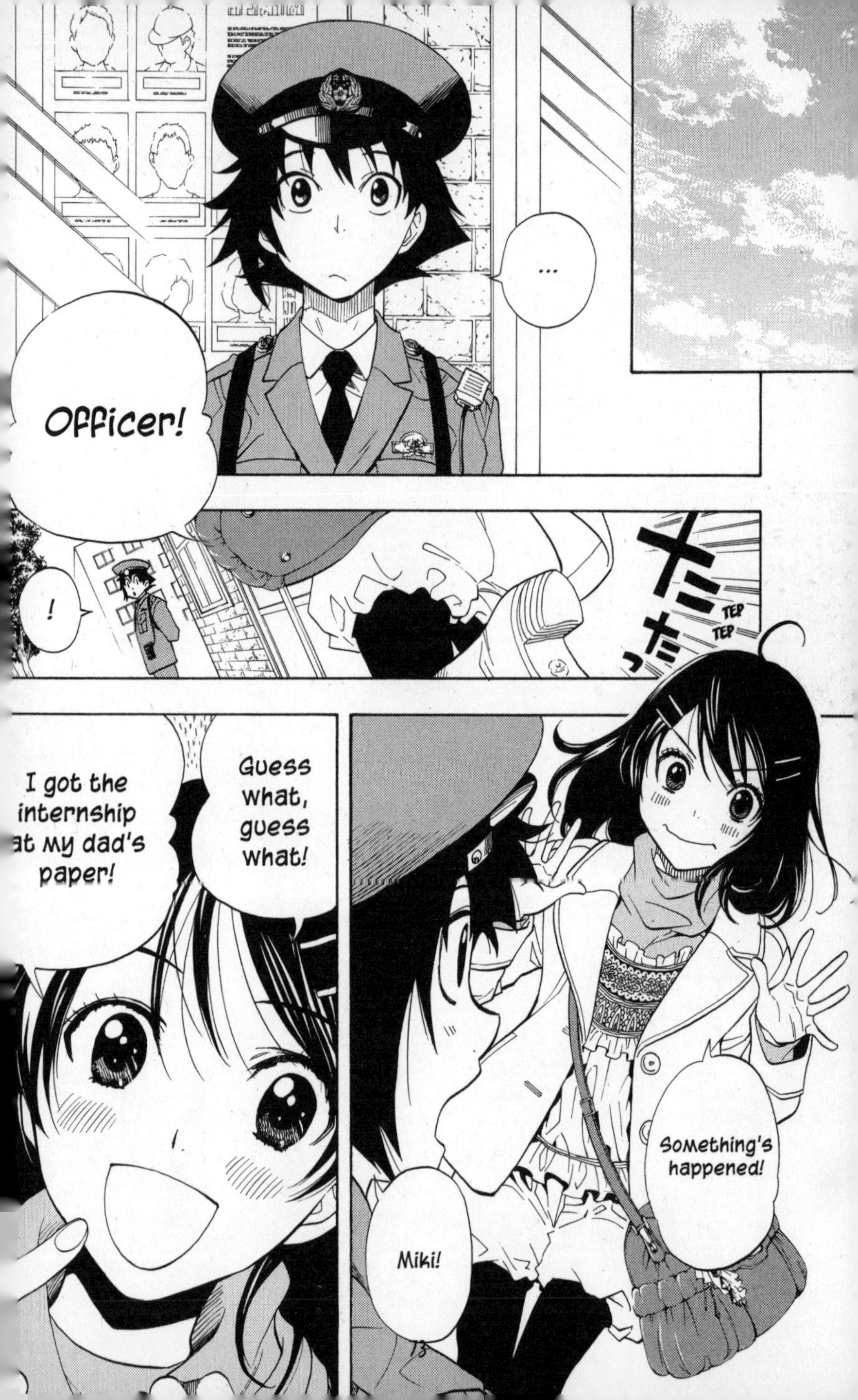
...
Officer!
たたっ
TEP TEP
!
Something's happened!
Miki!
Guess what, guess what!
I got the internship at my dad's paper!

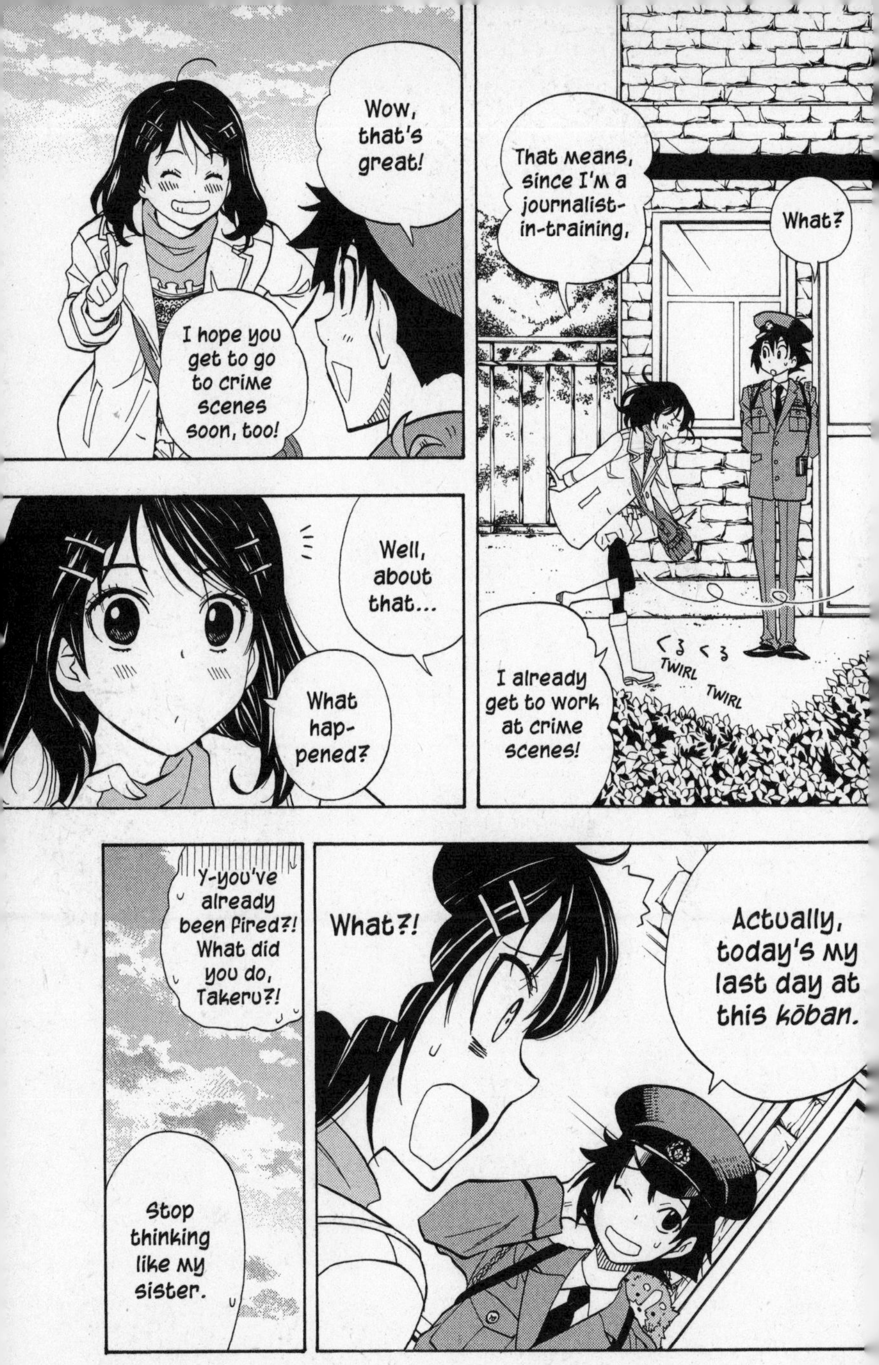
That means, since I'm a journalist-in-training,
What?
I already get to work at crime scenes!
くる くる
TWIRL TWIRL
Wow, that's great!
I hope you get to go to crime scenes soon, too!
Well, about that...
What hap-pened?
Actually, today's my last day at this *kōban*.
What?!
Y-you've already been fired?! What did you do, Takeru?!
Stop thinking like my sister.

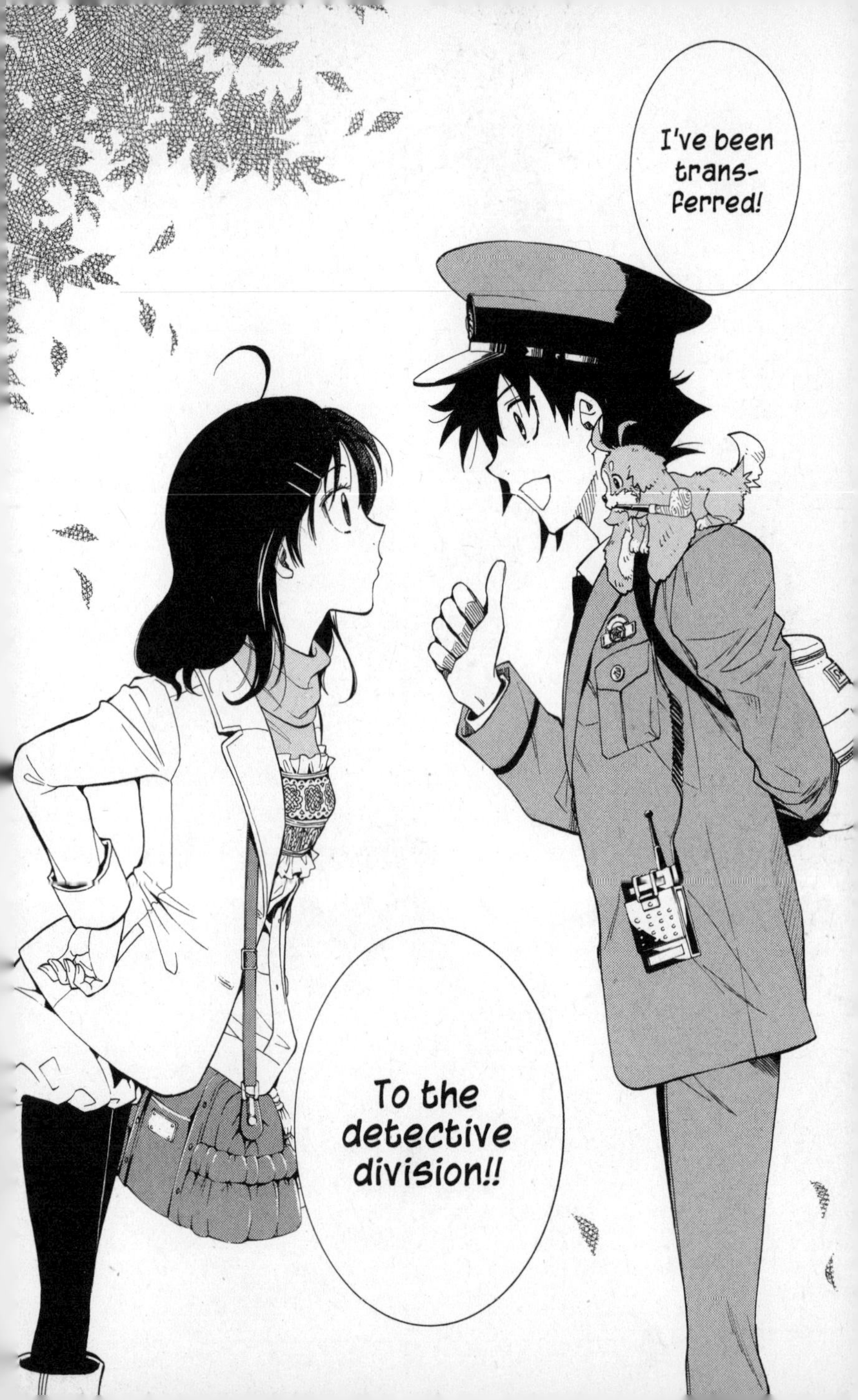
I've been trans-ferred!
To the detective division!!

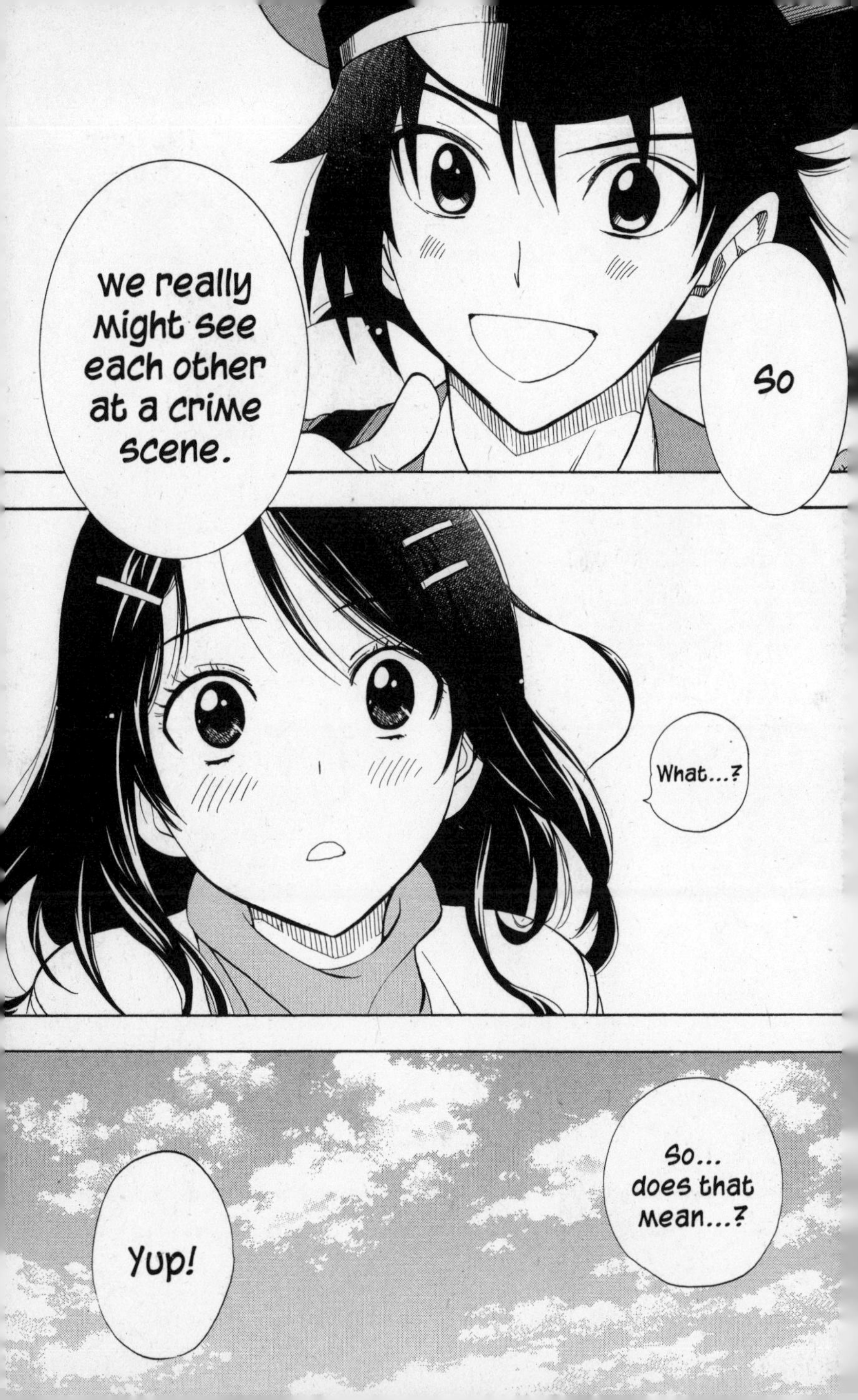
So
We really might see each other at a crime scene.
What...?
So... does that mean...?
Yup!

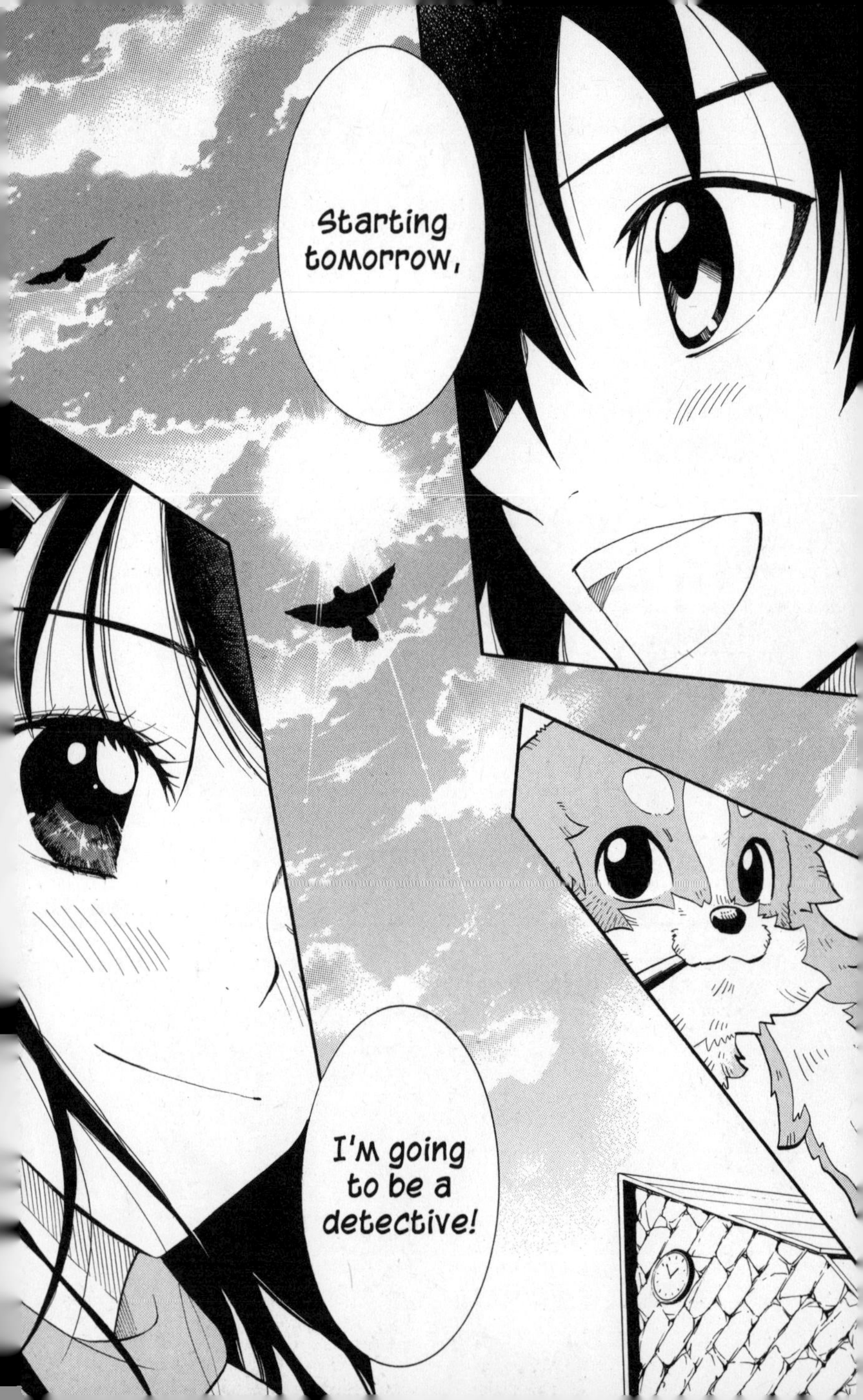
Starting tomorrow,
I'm going to be a detective!

Case 9: ⚜ The Stolen Face, Part 1

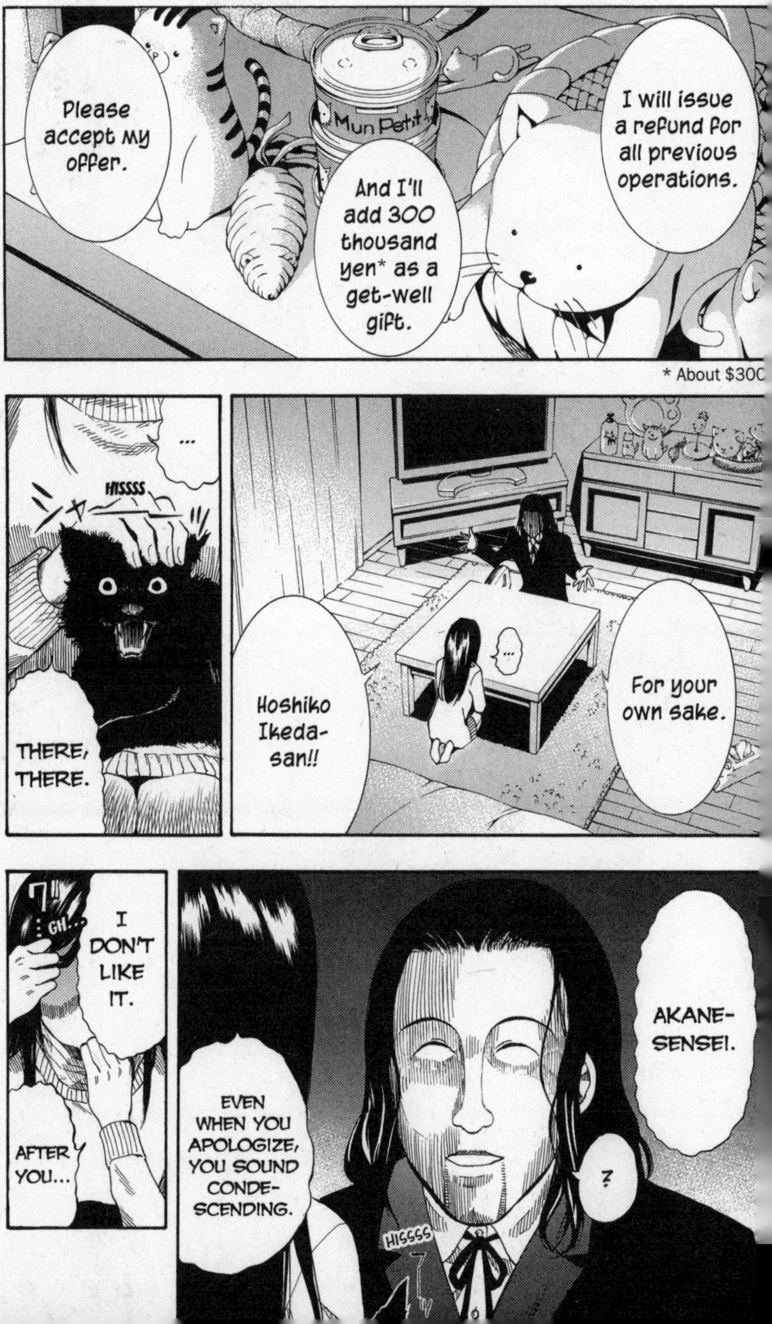
I will issue a refund for all previous operations.
Mun Petit
And I'll add 300 thousand yen* as a get-well gift.
Please accept my offer.
For your own sake.
...
Hoshiko Ikeda-san!!
...
HISSSS
THERE, THERE.
AKANE-SENSEI.
?
EVEN WHEN YOU APOLOGIZE, YOU SOUND CONDE-SCENDING.
HISSSS
GH...
I DON'T LIKE IT.
AFTER YOU...

* About $300

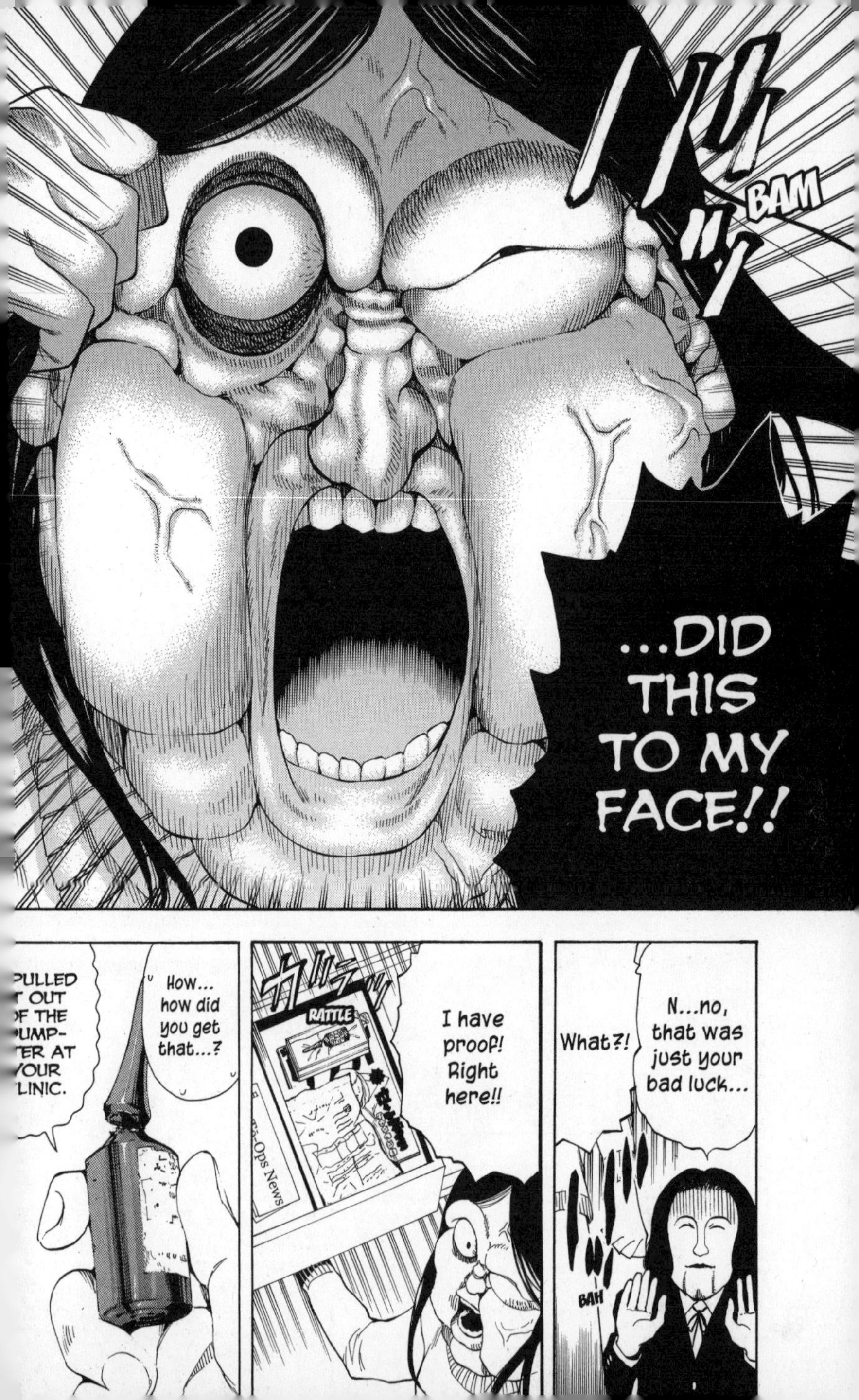
BAM
...DID THIS TO MY FACE!!
N...no, that was just your bad luck...
What?!
BAH
I have proof! Right here!!
RATTLE
-Ops News
How... how did you get that...?
PULLED
T OUT
OF THE
UMP-
TER AT
YOUR
LINIC.

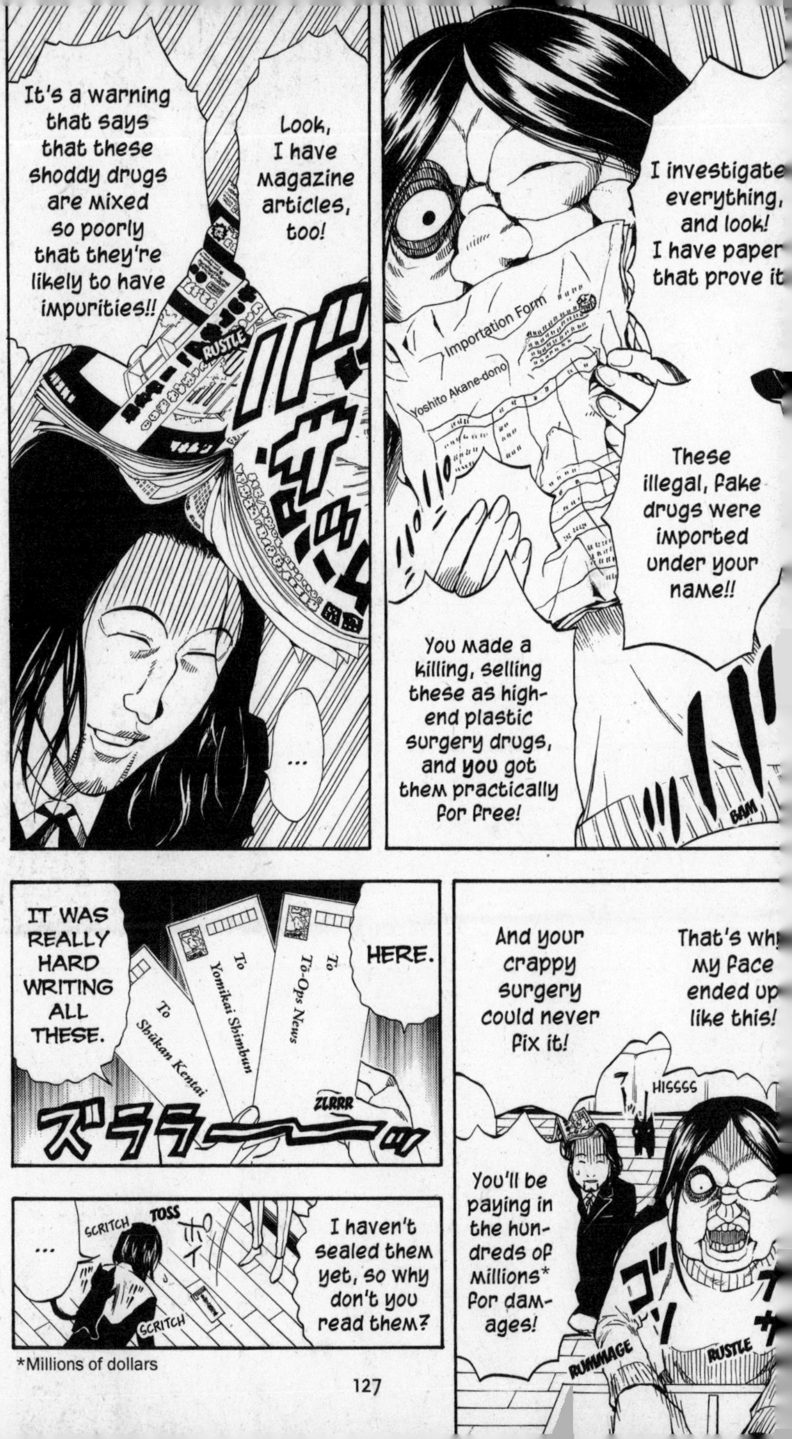
I investigate everything, and look! I have paper that prove it
Importation Form
Yoshito Akane-dono
These illegal, fake drugs were imported under your name!!
You made a killing, selling these as high-end plastic surgery drugs, and you got them practically for free!
BAM
Look, I have magazine articles, too!
It's a warning that says that these shoddy drugs are mixed so poorly that they're likely to have impurities!!
RUSTLE
...
That's wh my face ended up like this!
And your crappy surgery could never fix it!
HISSSS
You'll be paying in the hundreds of millions* for damages!
RUSTLE
RUMMAGE
HERE.
To Tō-Ops News
To Yomikai Shimbun
To Shūkan Kentai
IT WAS REALLY HARD WRITING ALL THESE.
ZLRRR
I haven't sealed them yet, so why don't you read them?
TOSS
SCRITCH
...
SCRITCH

*Millions of dollars

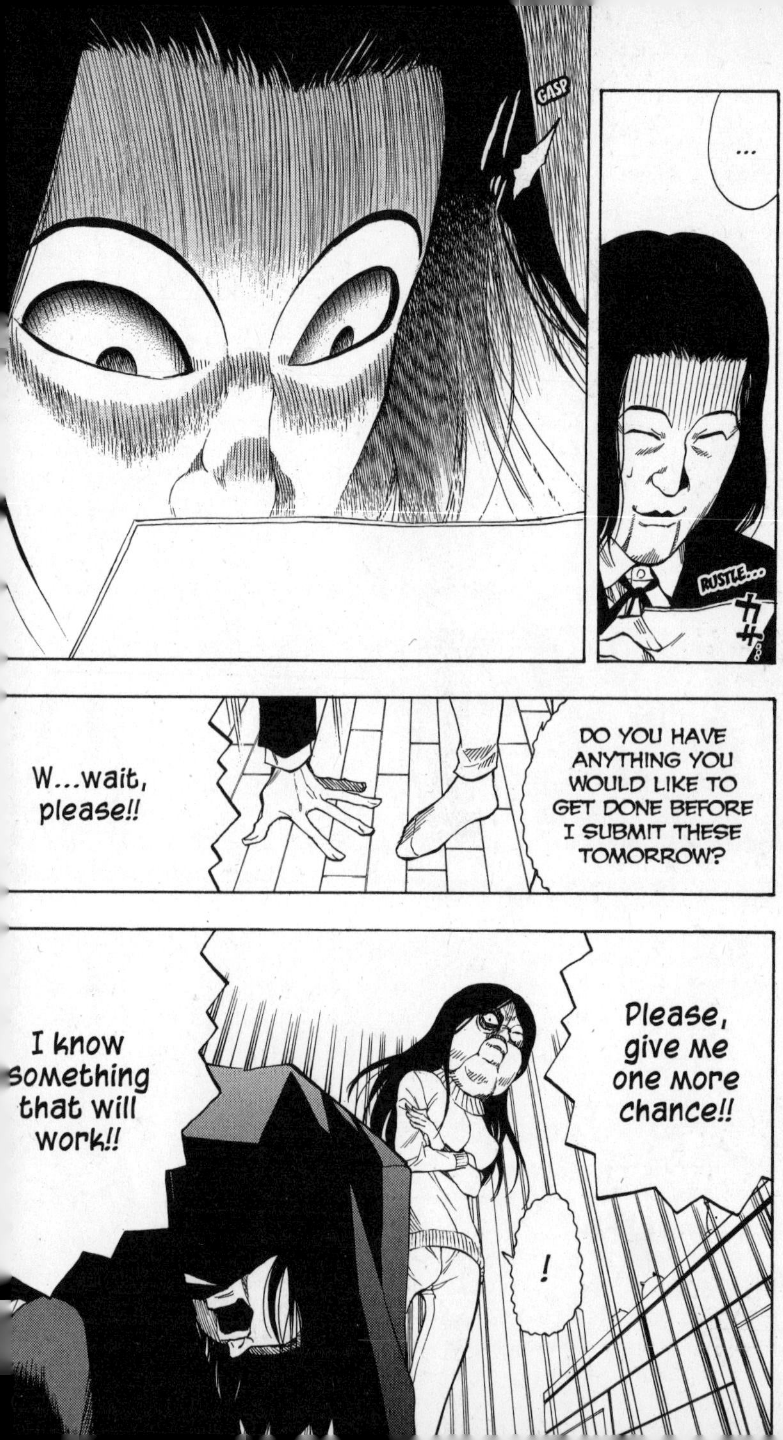
...
RUSTLE...
ｶｻ...
GASP
DO YOU HAVE ANYTHING YOU WOULD LIKE TO GET DONE BEFORE I SUBMIT THESE TOMORROW?
W...wait, please!!
Please, give me one more chance!!
!
I know something that will work!!

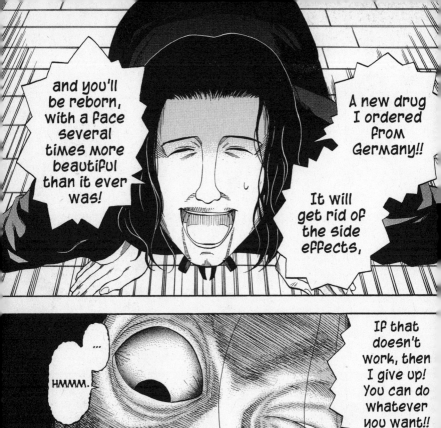

A new drug I ordered from Germany!!
It will get rid of the side effects,
and you'll be reborn, with a face several times more beautiful than it ever was!
If that doesn't work, then I give up! You can do whatever you want!!
...
HMMM.
...ALL RIGHT GIVE A TR
IN FOR A PENNY, IN FOR A POUND. YOU'VE ALREADY SCREWED UP THIS FAR, YOU MIGHT AS WELL GO ALL THE WAY.
すい
ZOOM
Th...tha you s much
Then I'll perform the surgery tomorrow night... How about...
You come to my clinic after hours...around 9p.m.?
THAT'S AWFULLY LATE. WHAT'S WRONG WITH COMING DURING YOUR CLINIC HOURS?
I'm booked solid with appointments tomorrow. But you'd rather have the surgery sooner than later, wouldn't you?
...

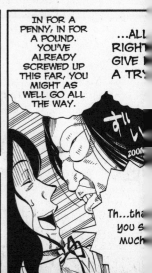

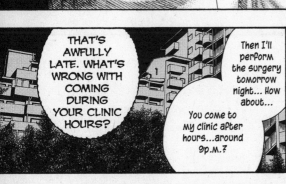

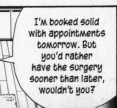

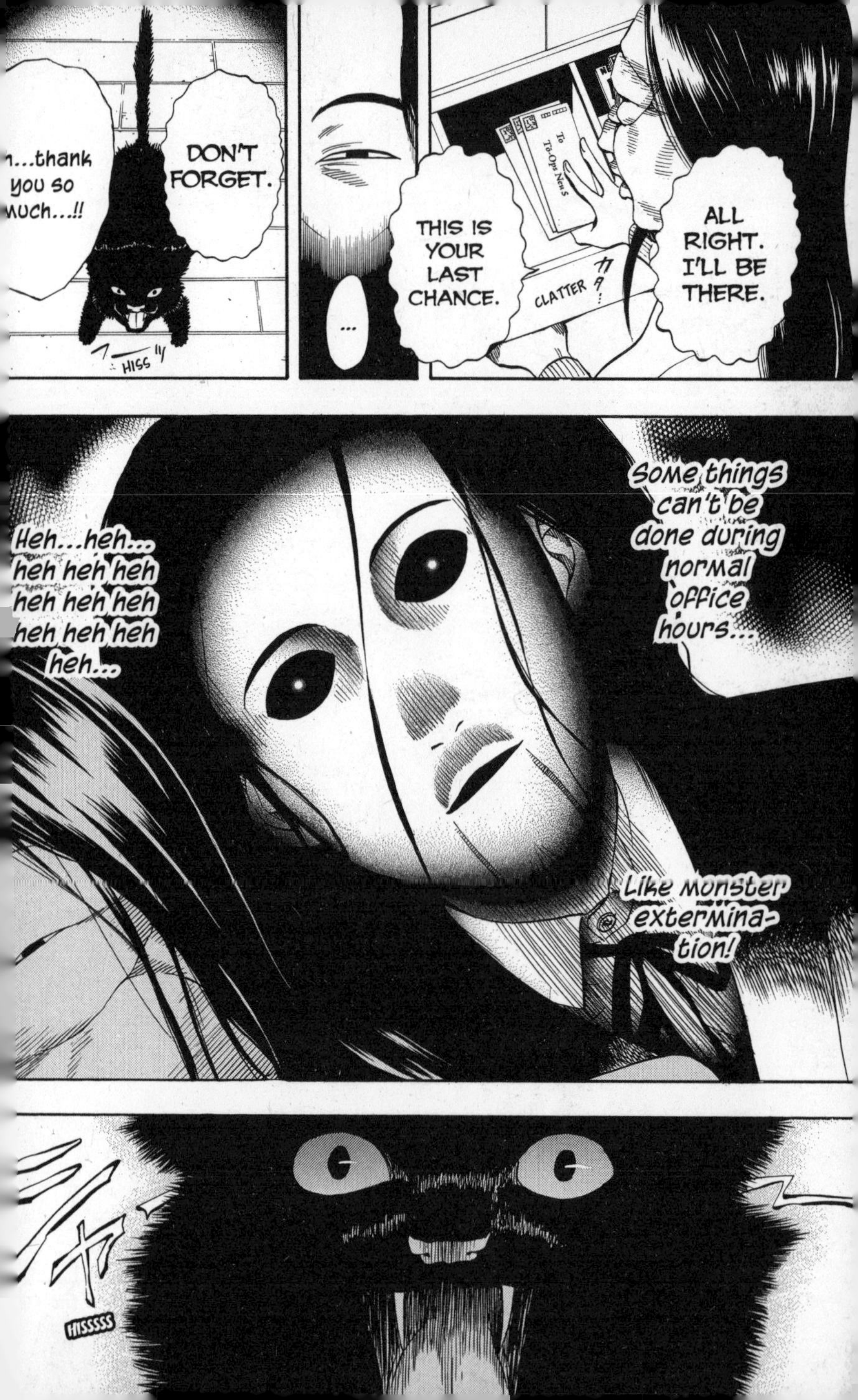
ALL RIGHT. I'LL BE THERE.
CLATTER
THIS IS YOUR LAST CHANCE.
...
DON'T FORGET.
...thank you so much...!!
HISS
Some things can't be done during normal office hours...
Heh...heh... heh heh heh heh heh heh heh heh heh heh...
Like monster extermina-tion!
HISSSSS

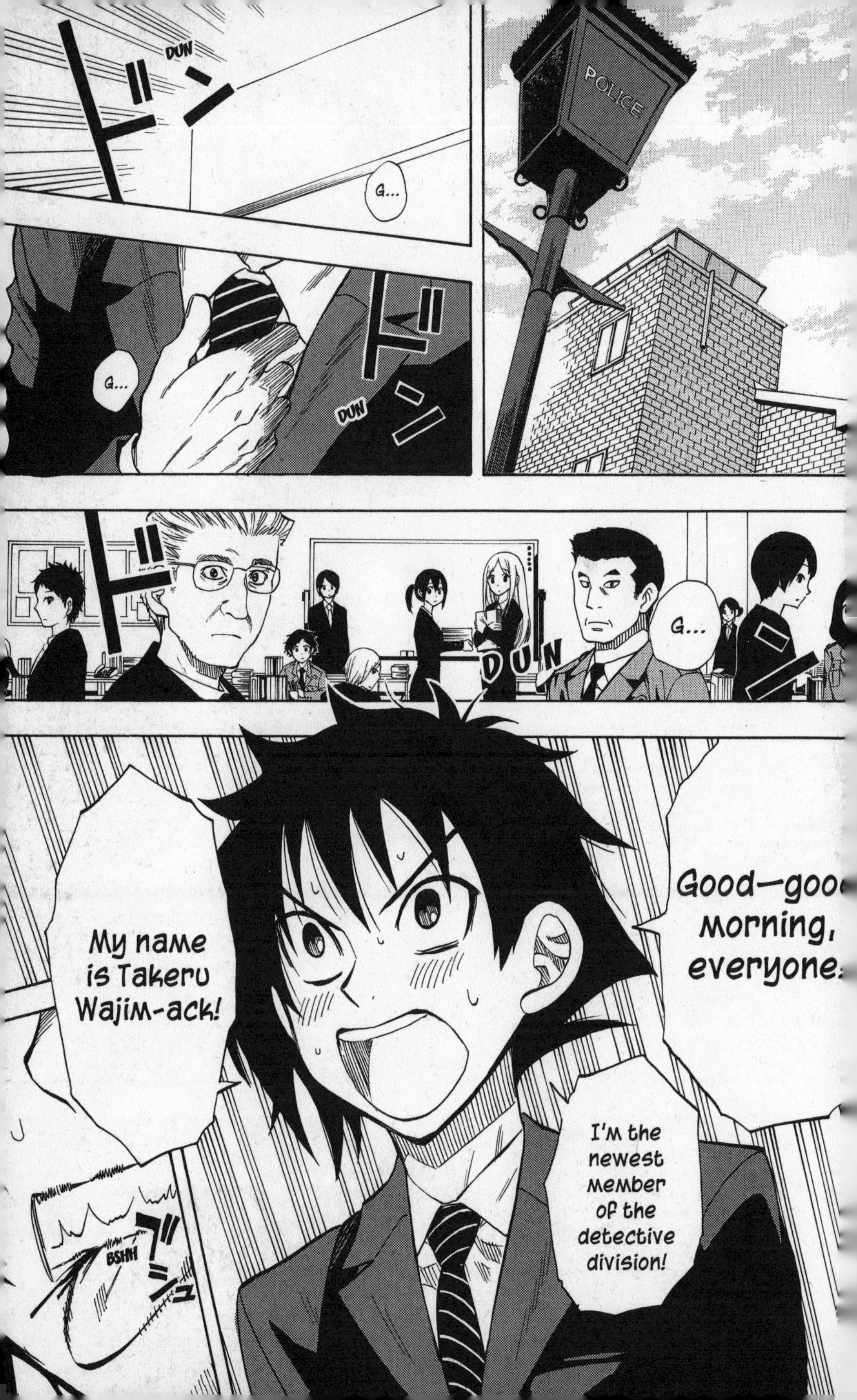
DUN
G...
G...
DUN
G...
DUN
Good—goo morning, everyone.
My name is Takeru Wajim-ack!
I'm the newest member of the detective division!
BSHH

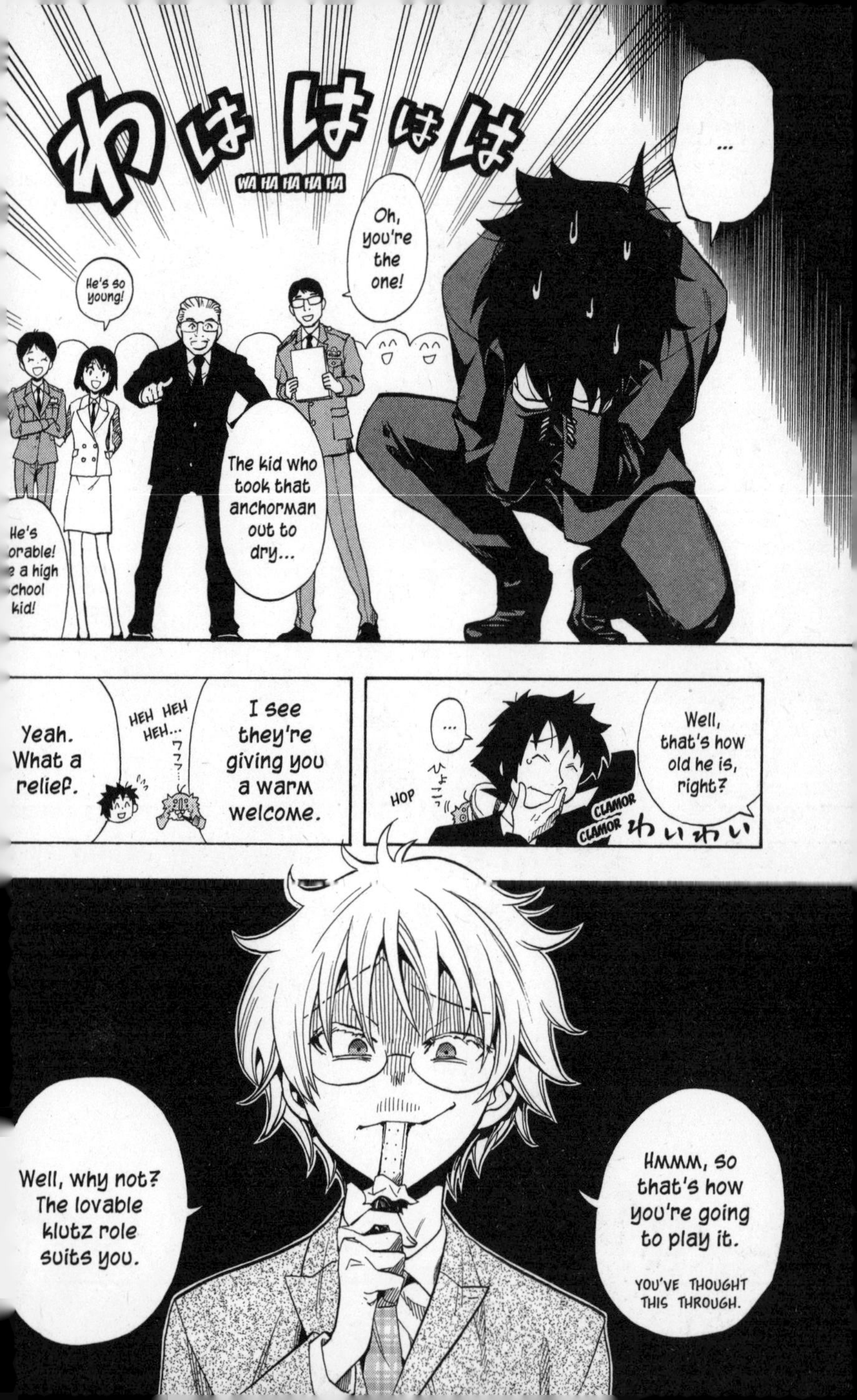
...
わははははは
WA HA HA HA HA
Oh, you're the one!
The kid who took that anchorman out to dry...
He's so young!
He's orable! e a high chool kid!
Well, that's how old he is, right?
CLAMOR CLAMOR わいわい
...
HOP ひょこっ
I see they're giving you a warm welcome.
HEH HEH HEH... ワフフ...
Yeah. What a relief.
Hmmm, so that's how you're going to play it.
YOU'VE THOUGHT THIS THROUGH.
Well, why not? The lovable klutz role suits you.

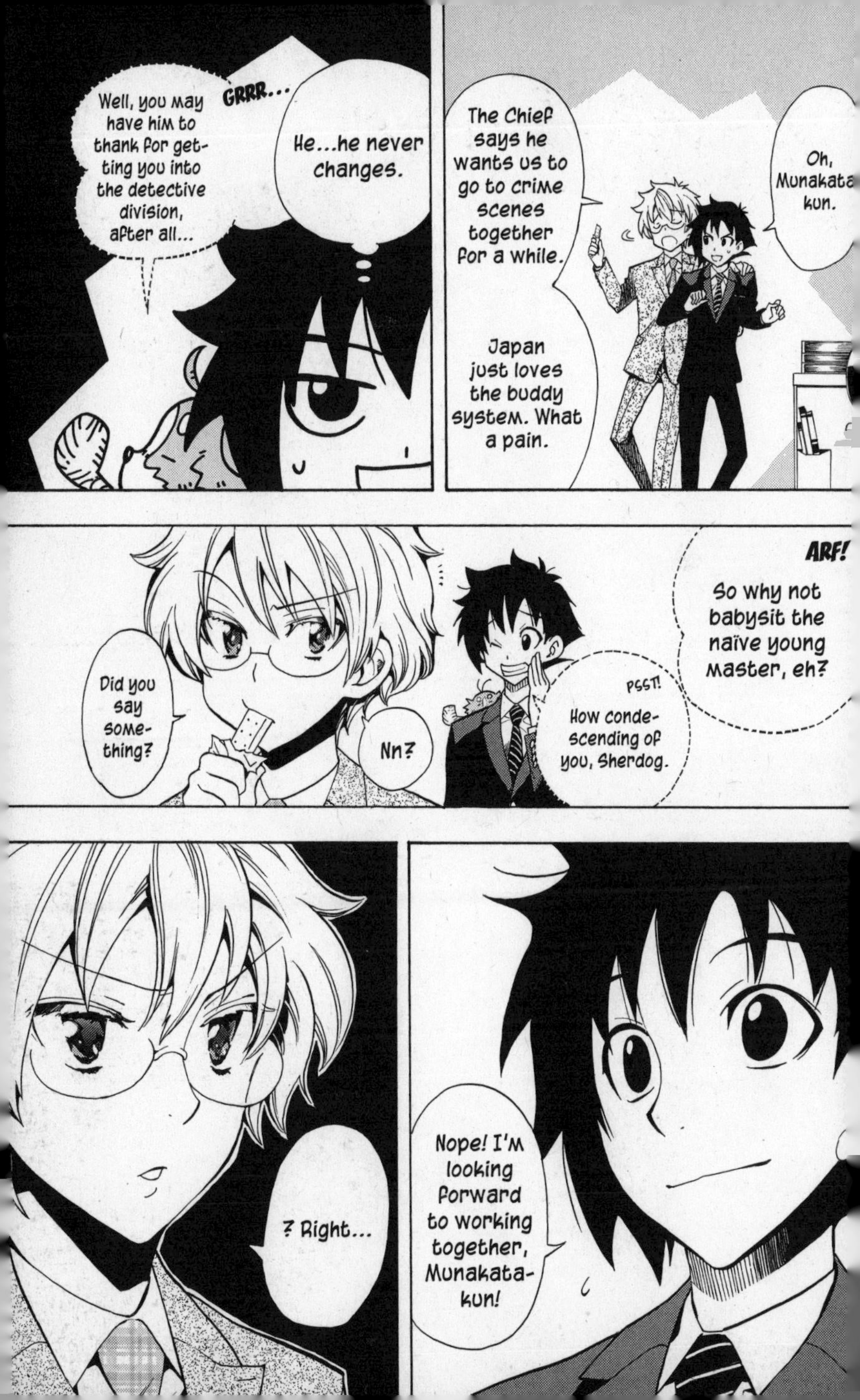
Oh, Munakata-kun.
The Chief says he wants us to go to crime scenes together for a while.
Japan just loves the buddy system. What a pain.
He...he never changes.
GRRR...
Well, you may have him to thank for getting you into the detective division, after all...
ARF!
So why not babysit the naïve young master, eh?
PSST!
How condescending of you, Sherdog.
Nn?
Did you say something?
Nope! I'm looking forward to working together, Munakata-kun!
? Right...

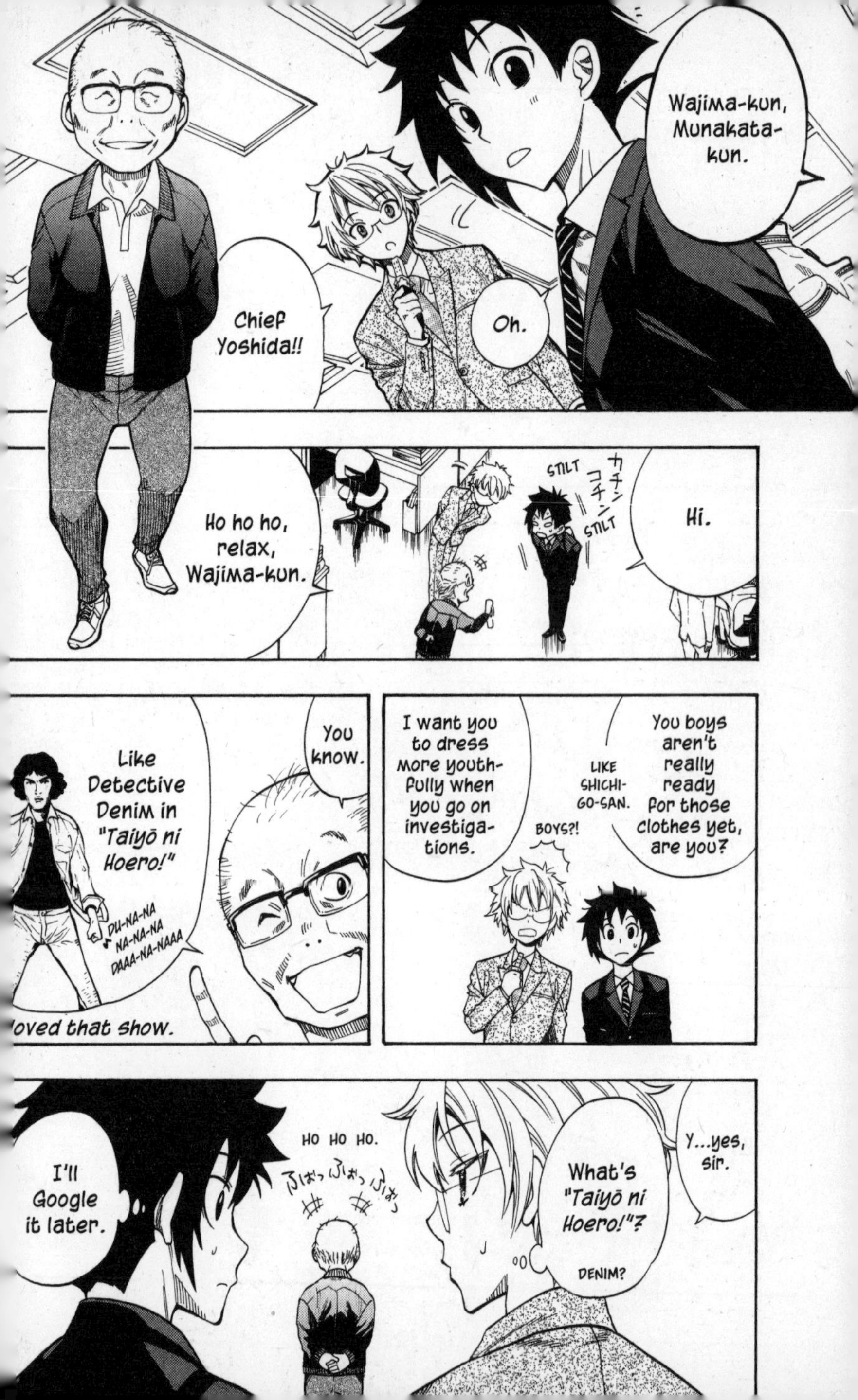

Wajima-kun, Munakata-kun.
Oh.
Chief Yoshida!!
Hi.
STILT
カチンコチン
STILT
Ho ho ho, relax, Wajima-kun.
You boys aren't really ready for those clothes yet, are you?
LIKE SHICHI-GO-SAN.
I want you to dress more youthfully when you go on investigations.
BOYS?!
You know.
Like Detective Denim in "Taiyō ni Hoero!"
DU-NA-NA NA-NA-NA DAAA-NA-NAAA
oved that show.
Y...yes, sir.
What's "Taiyō ni Hoero!"?
DENIM?
HO HO HO.
ふぉっふぉっふぉっ
I'll Google it later.

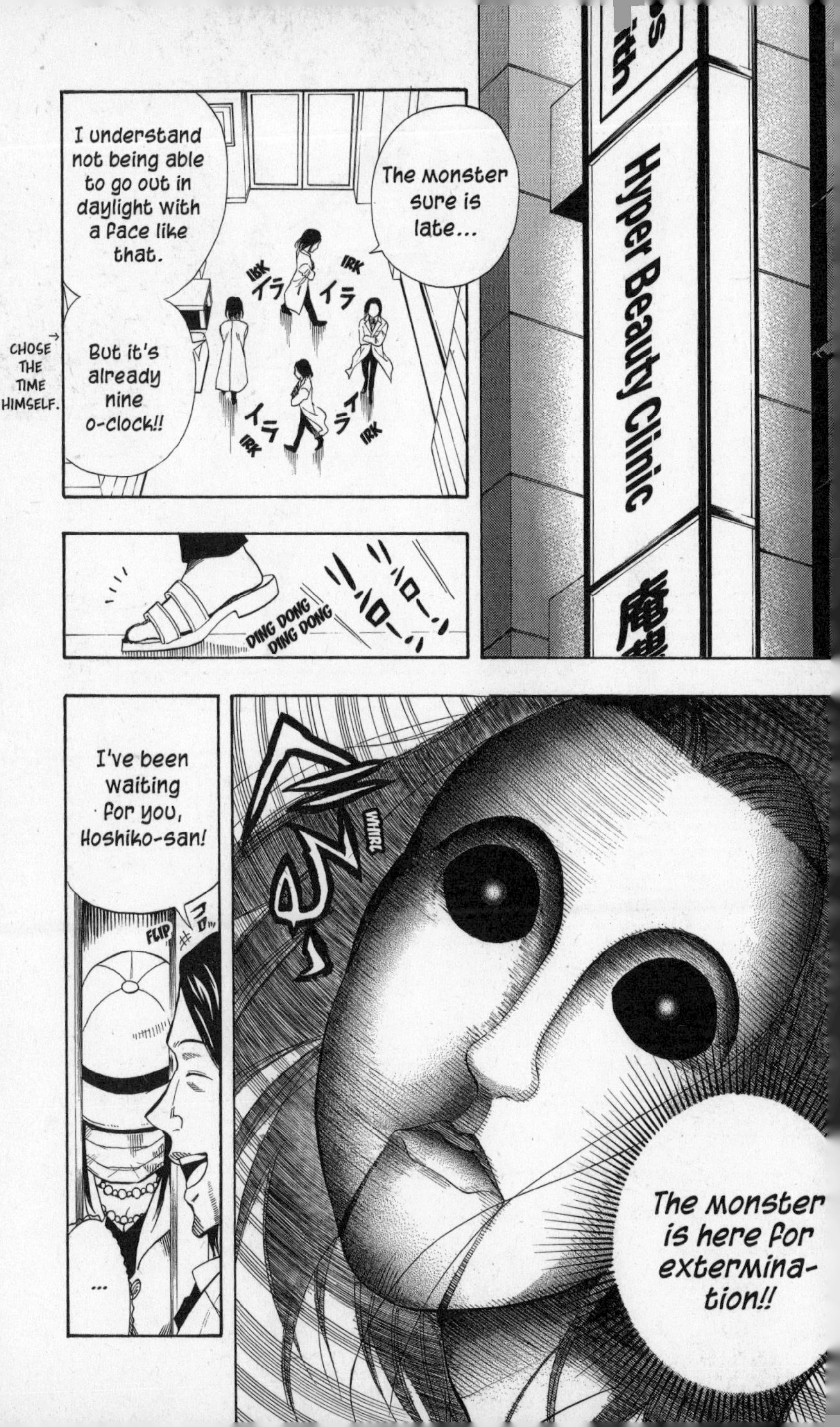
Hyper Beauty Clinic
The monster sure is late...
I understand not being able to go out in daylight with a face like that.
But it's already nine o-clock!!
CHOSE THE TIME HIMSELF.
IRK
イラ
IRK
イラ
イラ
IRK
イラ
IRK
DING DONG DING DONG
WHIRL
The monster is here for extermination!!
I've been waiting for you, Hoshiko-san!
FLIP
...

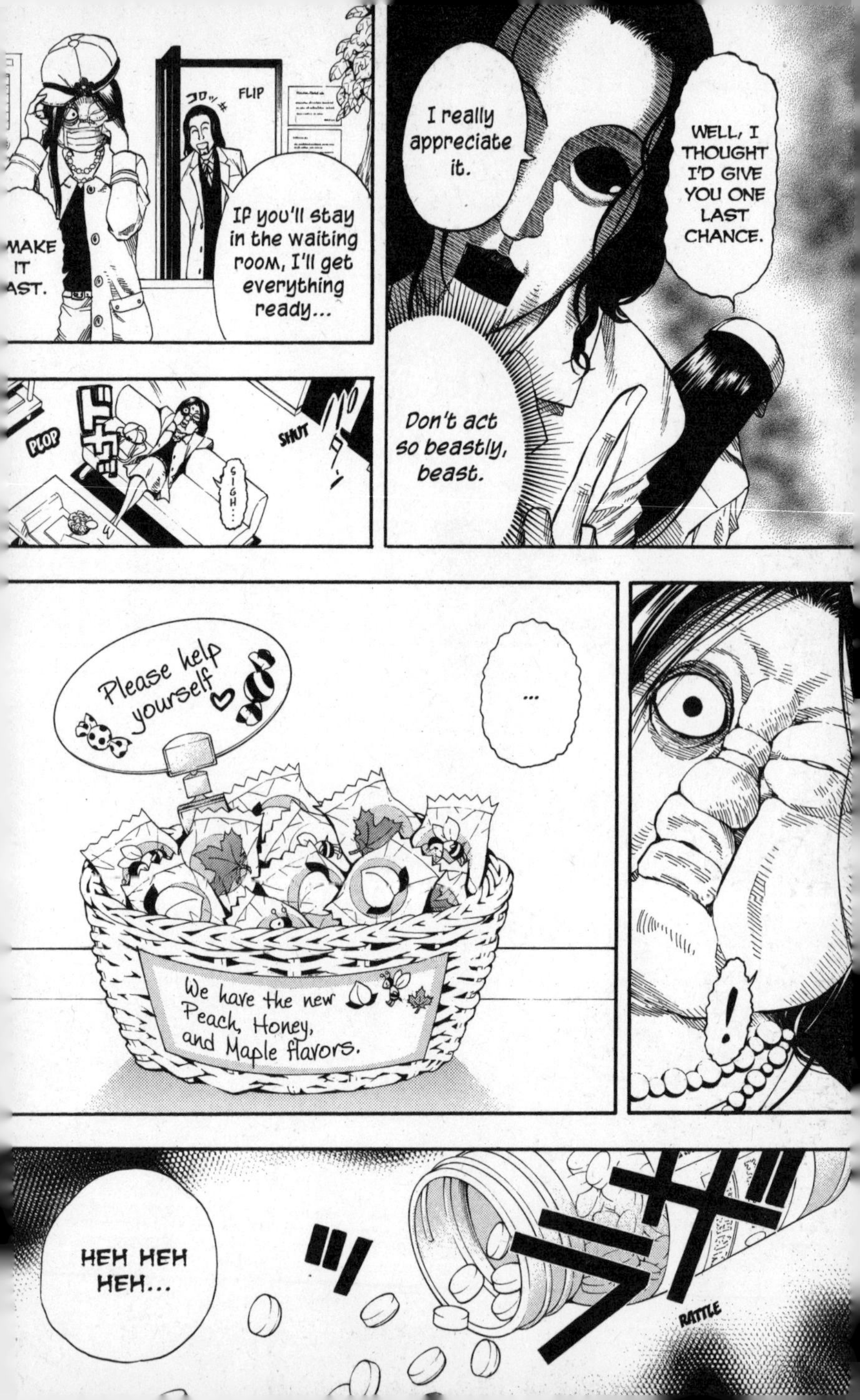
WELL, I THOUGHT I'D GIVE YOU ONE LAST CHANCE.
I really appreciate it.
Don't act so beastly, beast.
FLIP
If you'll stay in the waiting room, I'll get everything ready...
MAKE IT AST.
SHUT
SIGH...
PLOP
!
...
Please help yourself ♡
We have the new Peach, Honey, and Maple flavors.
RATTLE
HEH HEH HEH...

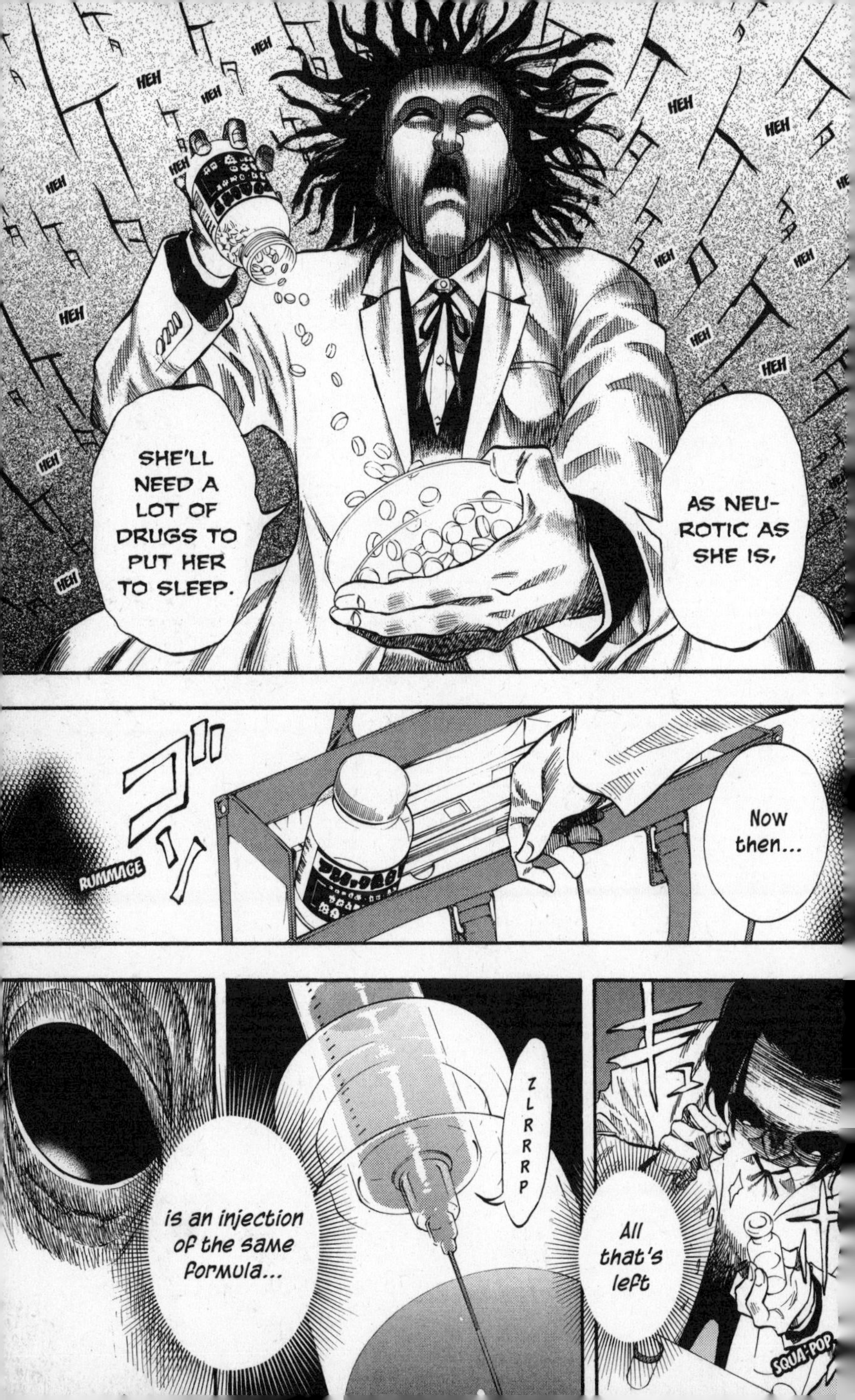
HEH
HEH
HEH
HEH
AS NEU-ROTIC AS SHE IS,
SHE'LL NEED A LOT OF DRUGS TO PUT HER TO SLEEP.
Now then...
RUMMAGE
All that's left
SQUA-POP
ZLRRRP
is an injection of the same formula...

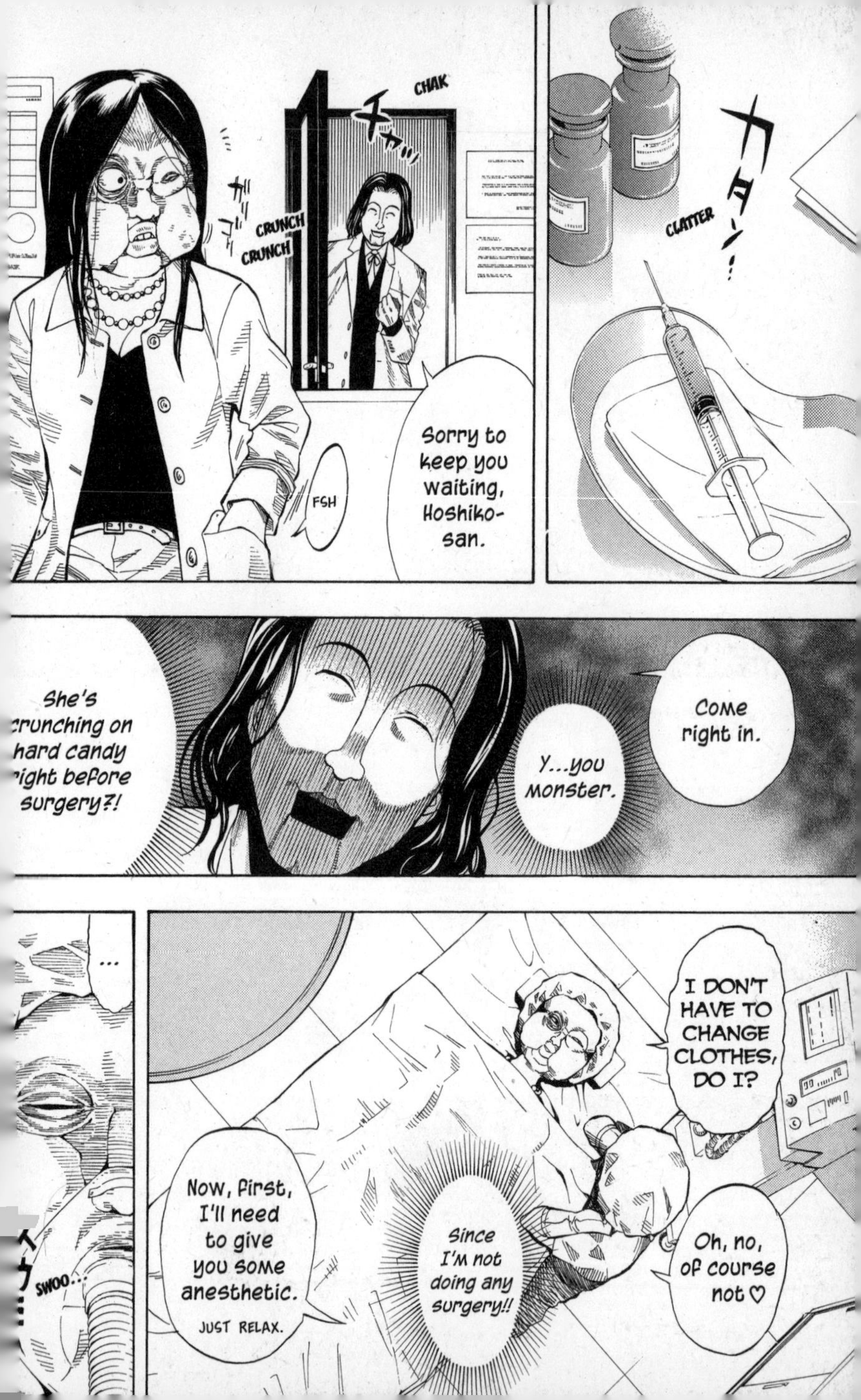

CLATTER
CHAK
Sorry to keep you waiting, Hoshiko-san.
CRUNCH CRUNCH
FSH
Come right in.
Y...you monster.
She's crunching on hard candy right before surgery?!
I DON'T HAVE TO CHANGE CLOTHES, DO I?
Oh, no, of course not ♡
Since I'm not doing any surgery!!
Now, first, I'll need to give you some anesthetic.
JUST RELAX.
...
SWOO...

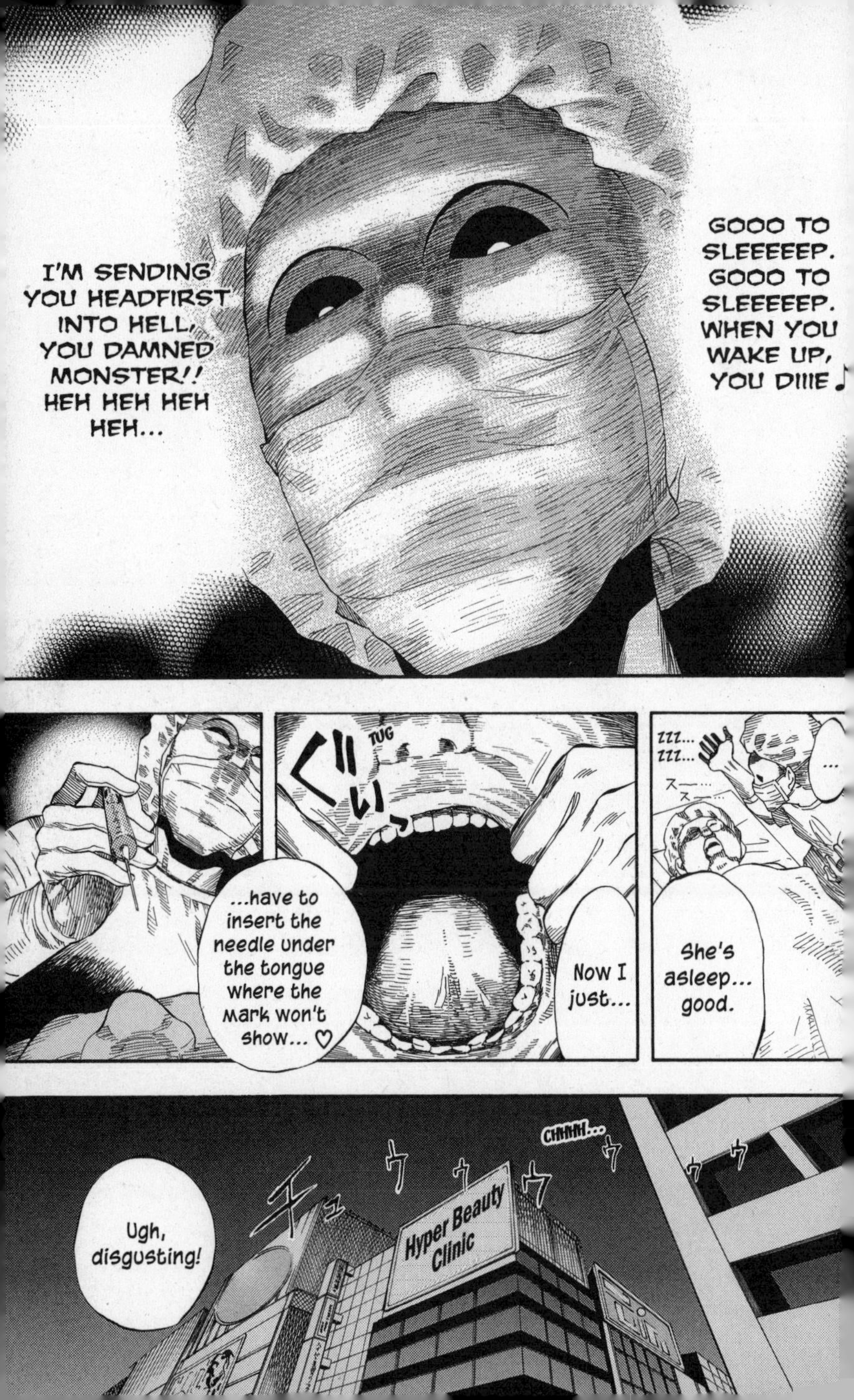
GOOO TO SLEEEEEP. GOOO TO SLEEEEEP. WHEN YOU WAKE UP, YOU DIIIE♪
I'M SENDING YOU HEADFIRST INTO HELL, YOU DAMNED MONSTER!! HEH HEH HEH HEH...
zzz... zzz...
スー... スー...
...
She's asleep... good.
TUG
ぐいっ
Now I just...
...have to insert the needle under the tongue where the mark won't show... ♡
CHHHH...
チュウウウウウウウ
Hyper Beauty Clinic
Ugh, disgusting!

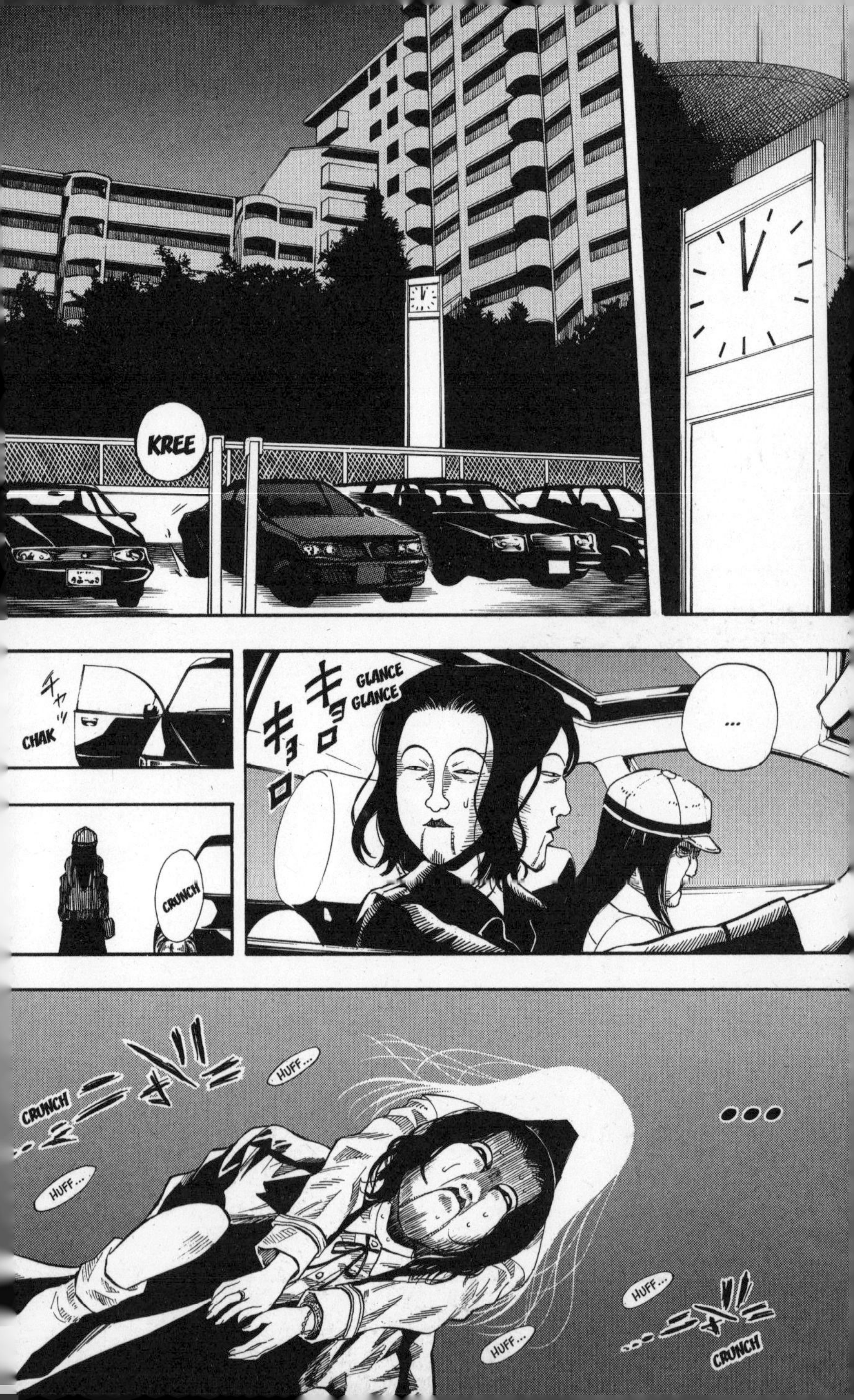
KREE
チャッ
CHAK
キョロ キョロ
GLANCE GLANCE
...
CRUNCH
CRUNCH
HUFF...
HUFF...
...
HUFF...
HUFF...
CRUNCH

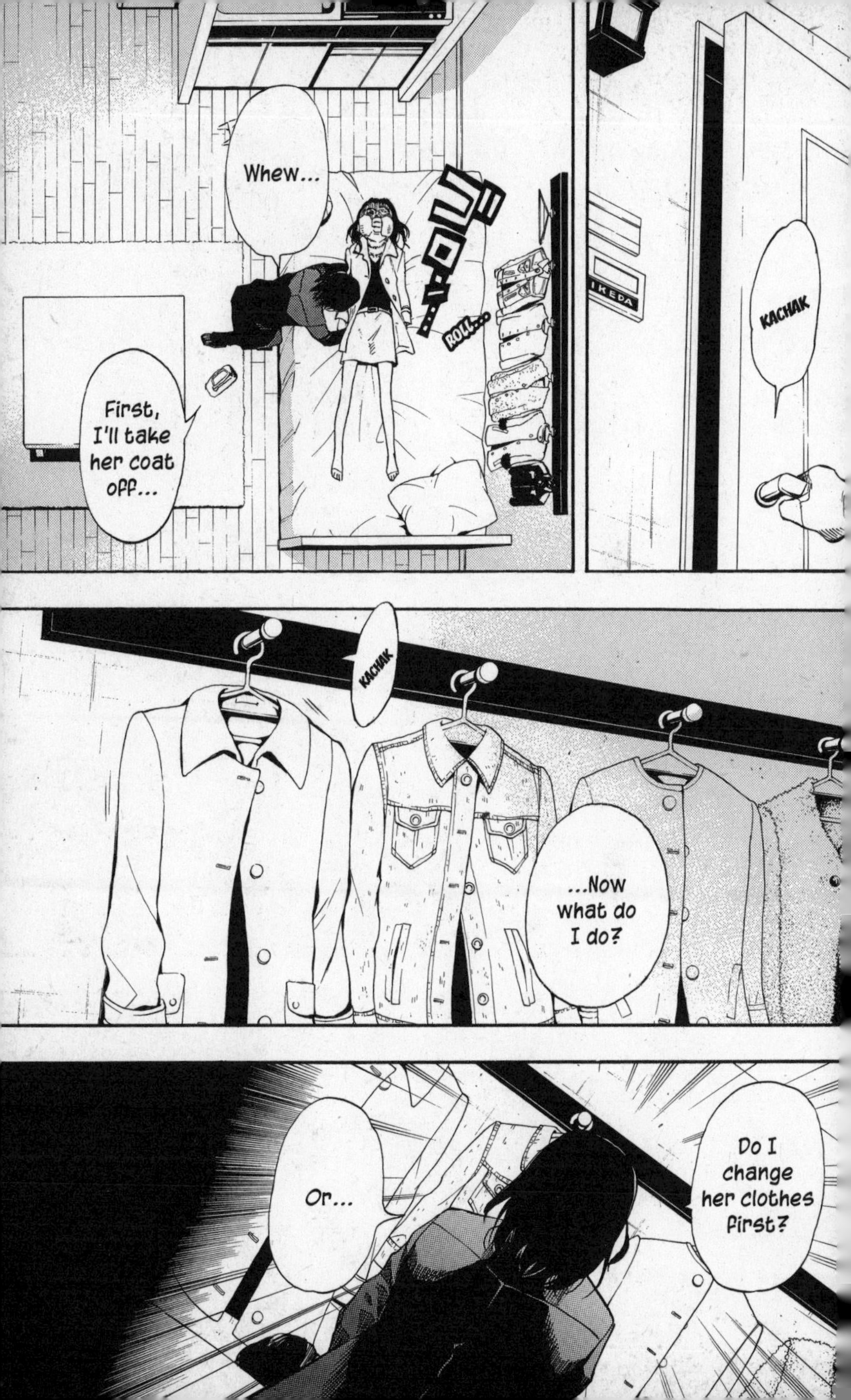
KACHAK
IKEDA
Whew...
ROLL...
First, I'll take her coat off...
KACHAK
...Now what do I do?
Do I change her clothes first?
Or...

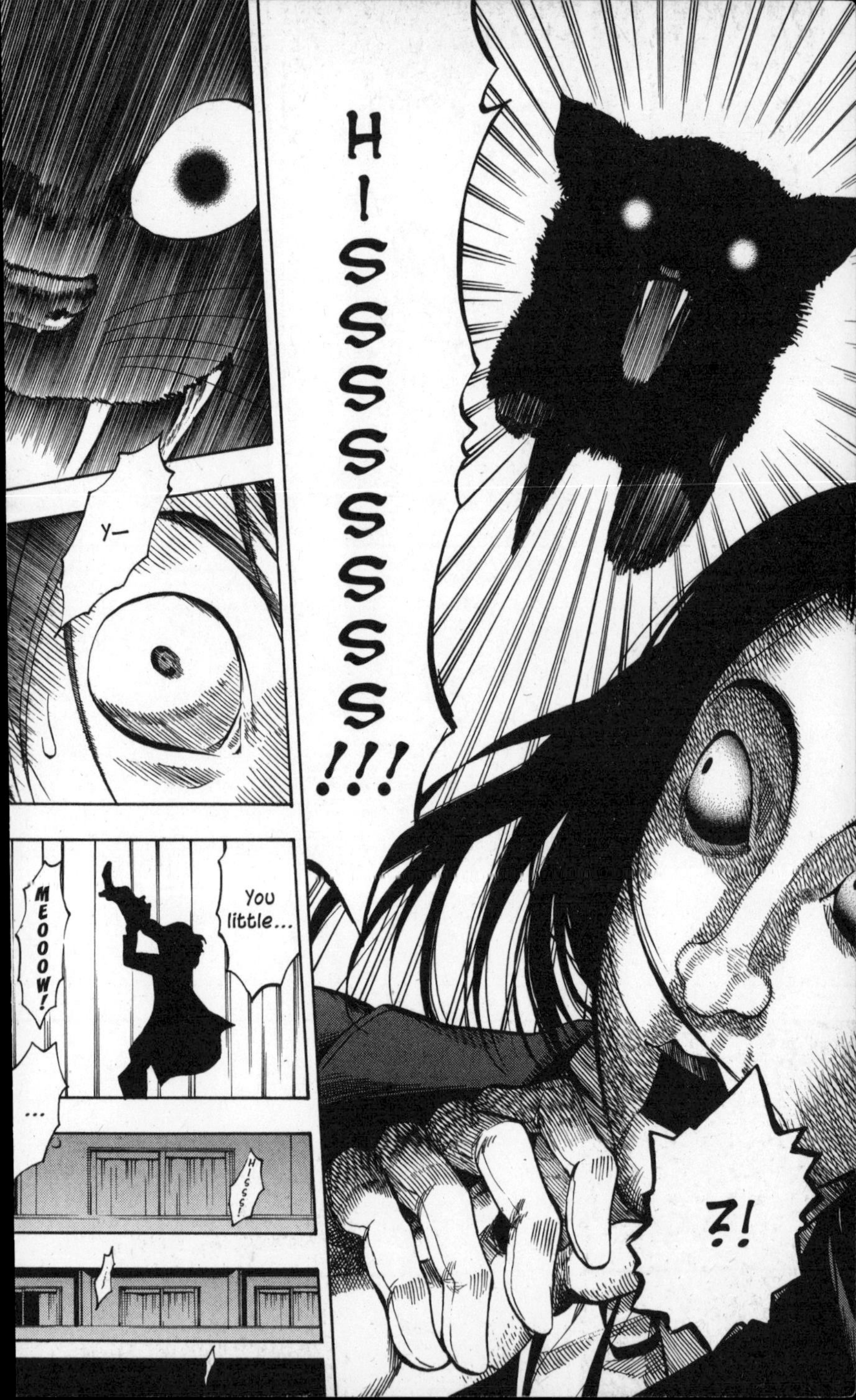
HISSSSSSSSS!!!
?!
Y—
You little...
MEOOOW!
...
HISSS!
!!

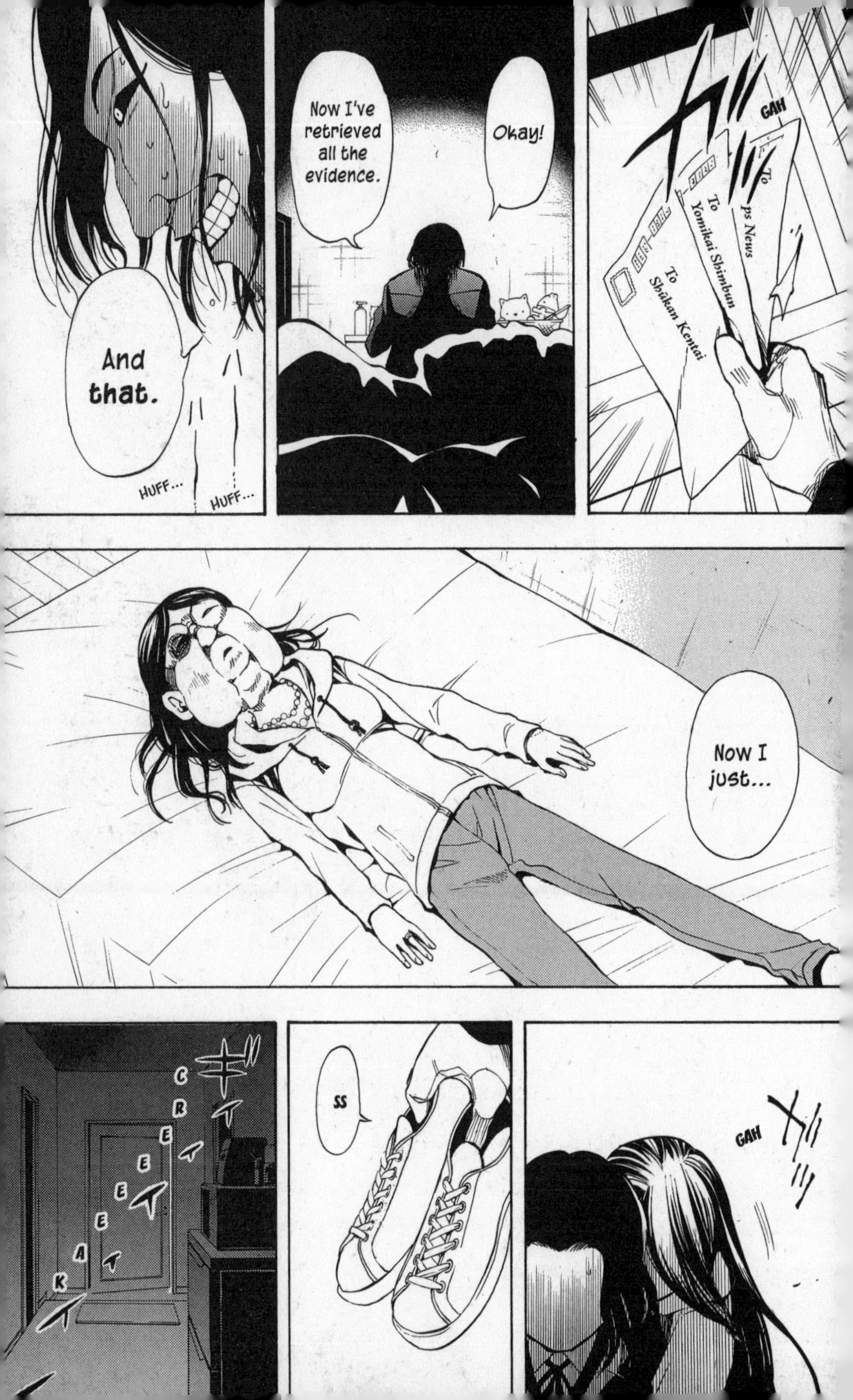
GAH
To
ps News
To
Yomikai Shimbun
To
Shikan Kentai
Okay!
Now I've retrieved all the evidence.
And that.
HUFF...
HUFF...
Now I just...
GAH
SS
CREEEEAK

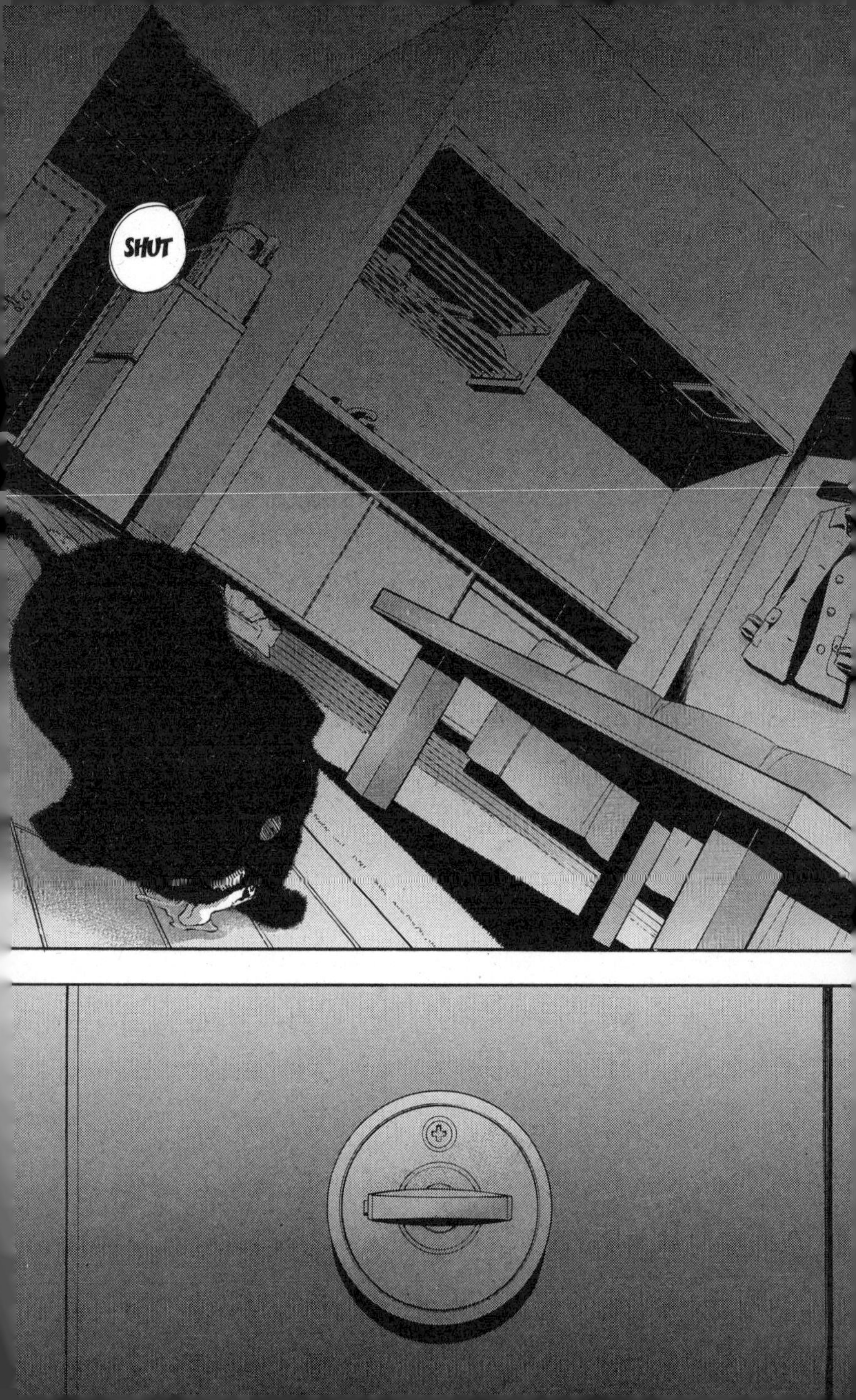
SHUT

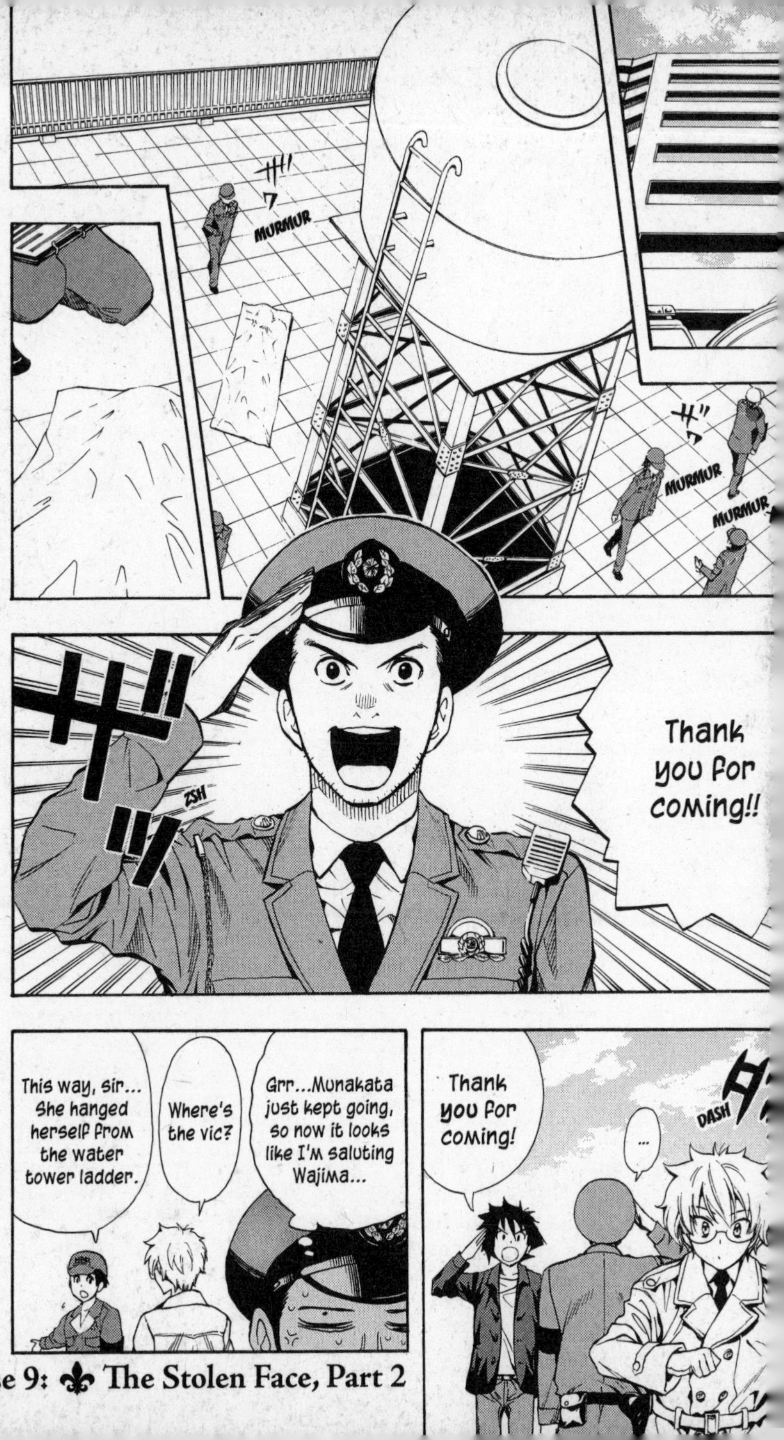

MURMUR
MURMUR
MURMUR
Thank you for coming!!
ZSH
DASH
Thank you for coming!
...
Grr...Munakata just kept going, so now it looks like I'm saluting Wajima...
Where's the vic?
This way, sir... She hanged herself from the water tower ladder.

Case 9: ⚜ The Stolen Face, Part 2

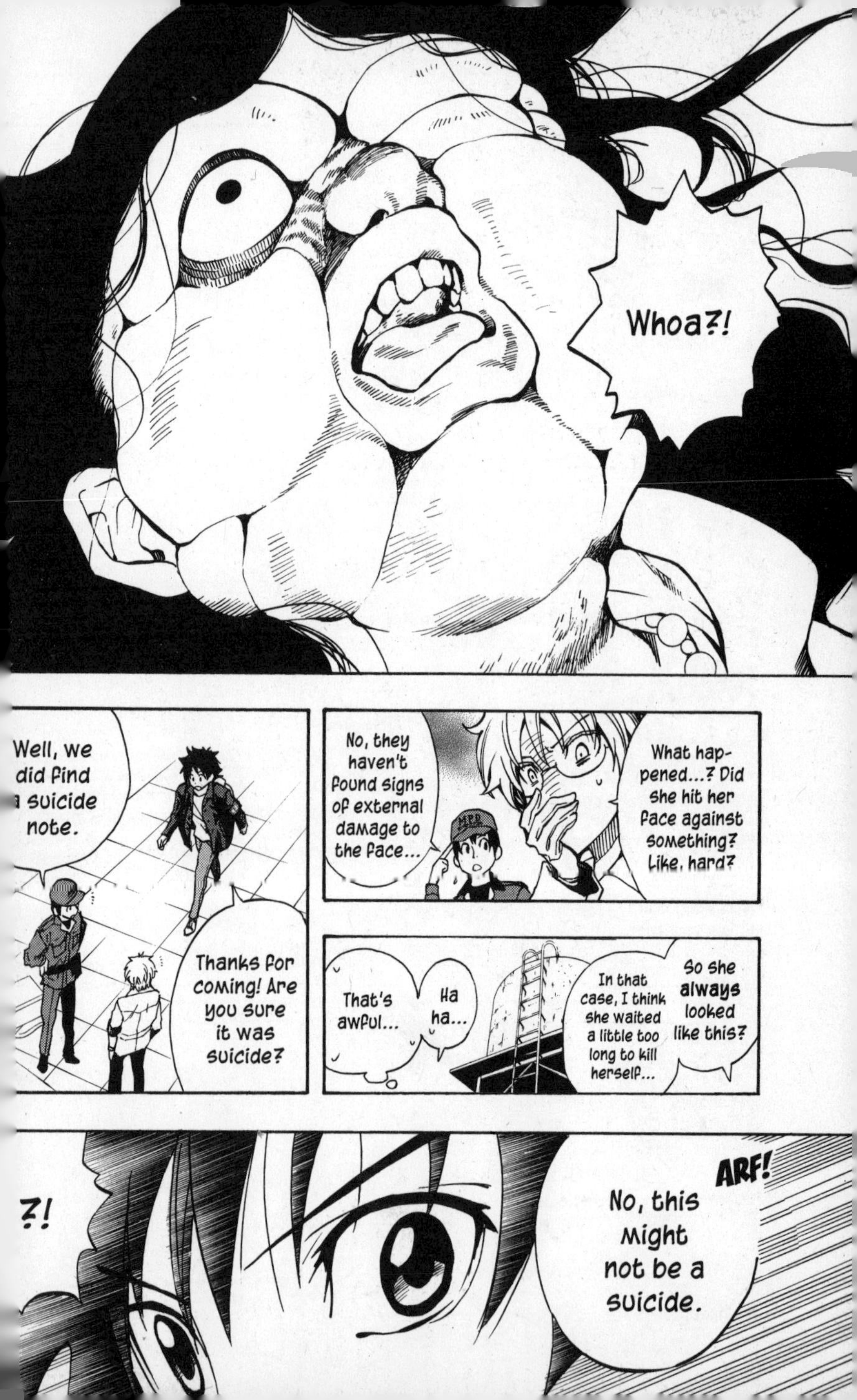
Whoa?!
What happened...? Did she hit her face against something? Like, hard?
No, they haven't found signs of external damage to the face...
So she always looked like this?
In that case, I think she waited a little too long to kill herself...
Ha ha...
That's awful...
Well, we did find a suicide note.
Thanks for coming! Are you sure it was suicide?
ARF!
No, this might not be a suicide.
?!

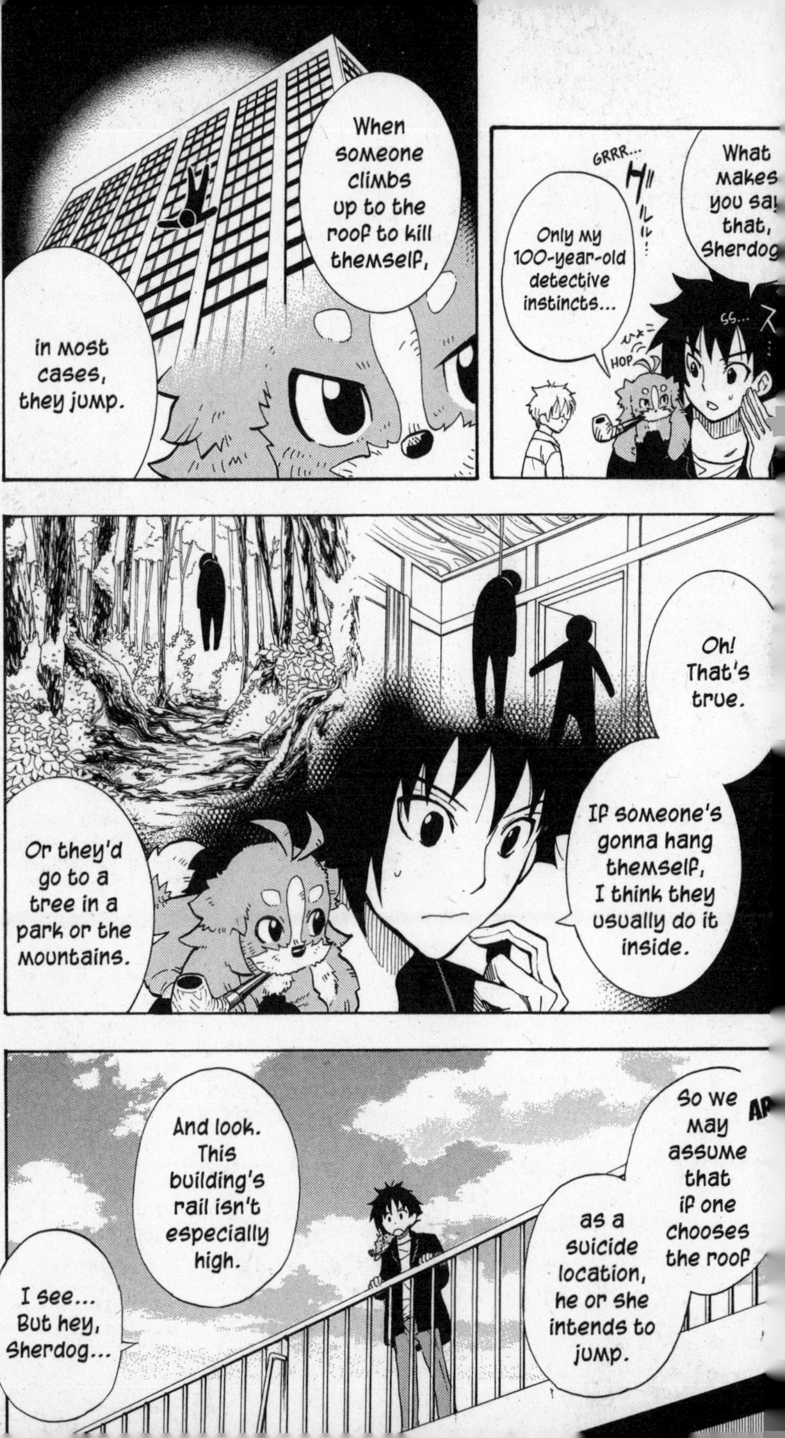
What makes you say that, Sherdog
GRRR...
Only my 100-year-old detective instincts...
HOP
SS...
When someone climbs up to the roof to kill themself,
in most cases, they jump.
Oh! That's true.
If someone's gonna hang themself, I think they usually do it inside.
Or they'd go to a tree in a park or the mountains.
So we may assume that if one chooses the roof
as a suicide location, he or she intends to jump.
And look. This building's rail isn't especially high.
I see... But hey, Sherdog...

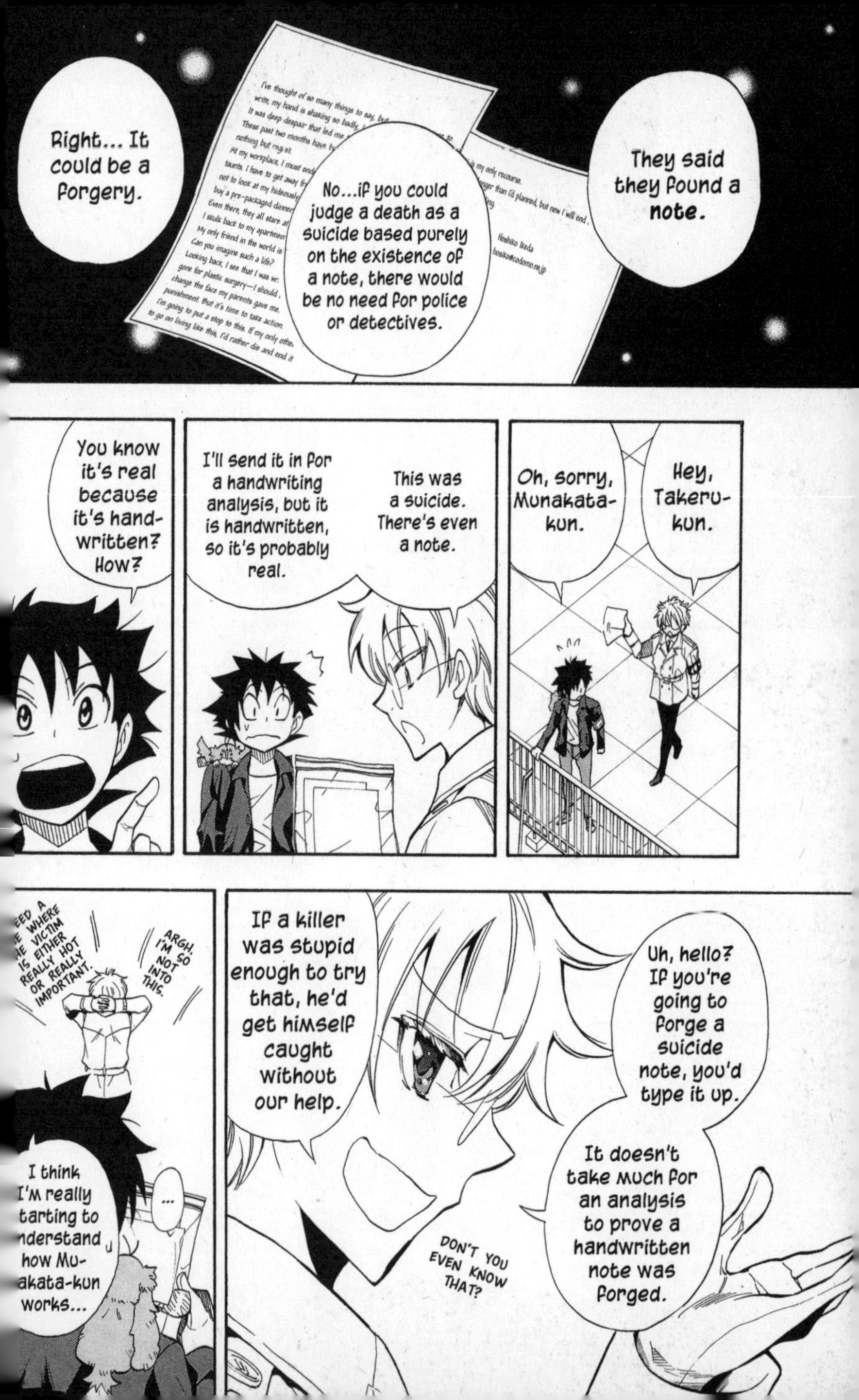
They said they found a **note.**
No...if you could judge a death as a suicide based purely on the existence of a note, there would be no need for police or detectives.
Right... It could be a forgery.
nothing but regret.
Can you imagine such a life?
Hoshiko Ikeda
hosiko@codomo.ne.jp
Hey, Takeru-kun.
Oh, sorry, Munakata-kun.
This was a suicide. There's even a note.
I'll send it in for a handwriting analysis, but it is handwritten, so it's probably real.
You know it's real because it's hand-written? How?
Uh, hello? If you're going to forge a suicide note, you'd type it up.
If a killer was stupid enough to try that, he'd get himself caught without our help.
It doesn't take much for an analysis to prove a handwritten note was forged.
DON'T YOU EVEN KNOW THAT?
ARGH. I'M SO NOT INTO THIS.
EED A
E WHERE
HE VICTIM
IS EITHER
REALLY HOT
OR REALLY
IMPORTANT.
...
I think I'm really tarting to nderstand how Mu- akata-kun works...

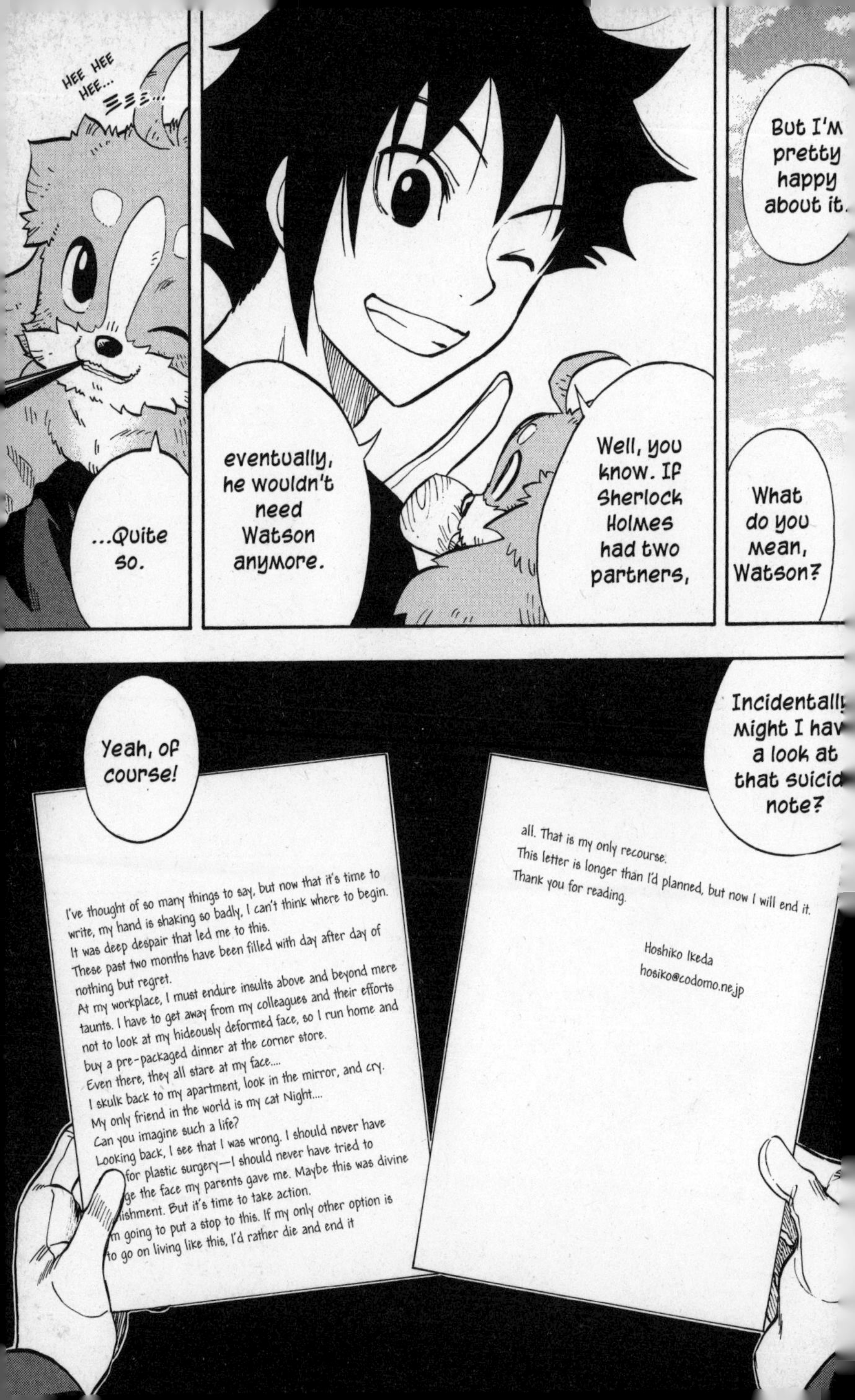

But I'm pretty happy about it.
What do you mean, Watson?
Well, you know. If Sherlock Holmes had two partners,
eventually, he wouldn't need Watson anymore.
HEE HEE HEE...
...Quite so.
Incidentall
Might I hav
a look at
that suicid
note?
Yeah, of course!
I've thought of so many things to say, but now that it's time to
write, my hand is shaking so badly, I can't think where to begin.
It was deep despair that led me to this.
These past two months have been filled with day after day of
nothing but regret.
At my workplace, I must endure insults above and beyond mere
taunts. I have to get away from my colleagues and their efforts
not to look at my hideously deformed face, so I run home and
buy a pre-packaged dinner at the corner store.
Even there, they all stare at my face....
I skulk back to my apartment, look in the mirror, and cry.
My only friend in the world is my cat Night....
Can you imagine such a life?
Looking back, I see that I was wrong. I should never have
for plastic surgery—I should never have tried to
ge the face my parents gave me. Maybe this was divine
ishment. But it's time to take action.
m going to put a stop to this. If my only other option is
to go on living like this, I'd rather die and end it
all. That is my only recourse.
This letter is longer than I'd planned, but now I will end it.
Thank you for reading.
Hoshiko Ikeda
hosiko@codomo.ne.jp

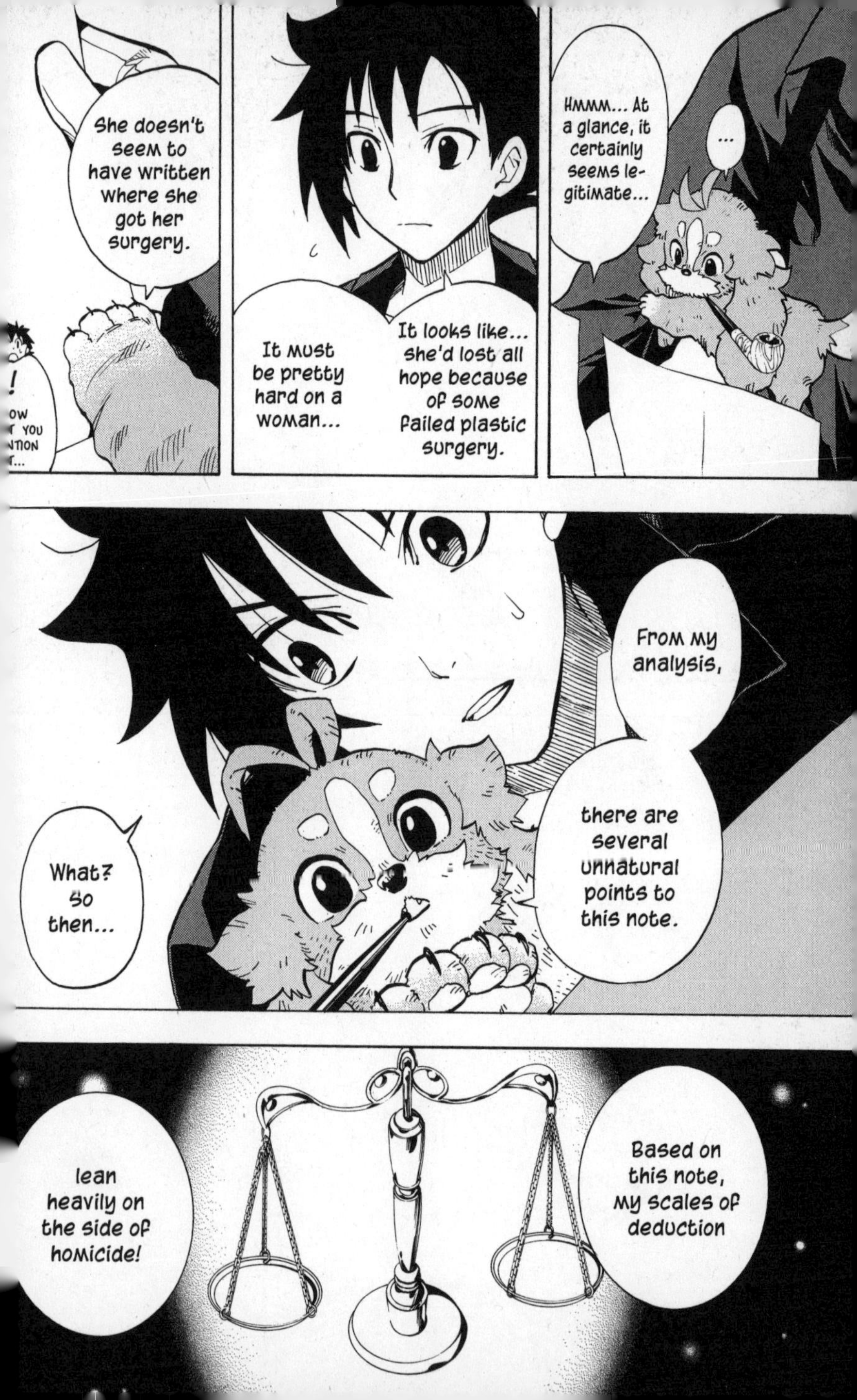
HMMM... At a glance, it certainly seems legitimate...
...
It looks like... she'd lost all hope because of some failed plastic surgery.
It must be pretty hard on a woman...
She doesn't seem to have written where she got her surgery.
From my analysis,
there are several unnatural points to this note.
What? So then...
Based on this note, my scales of deduction
lean heavily on the side of homicide!

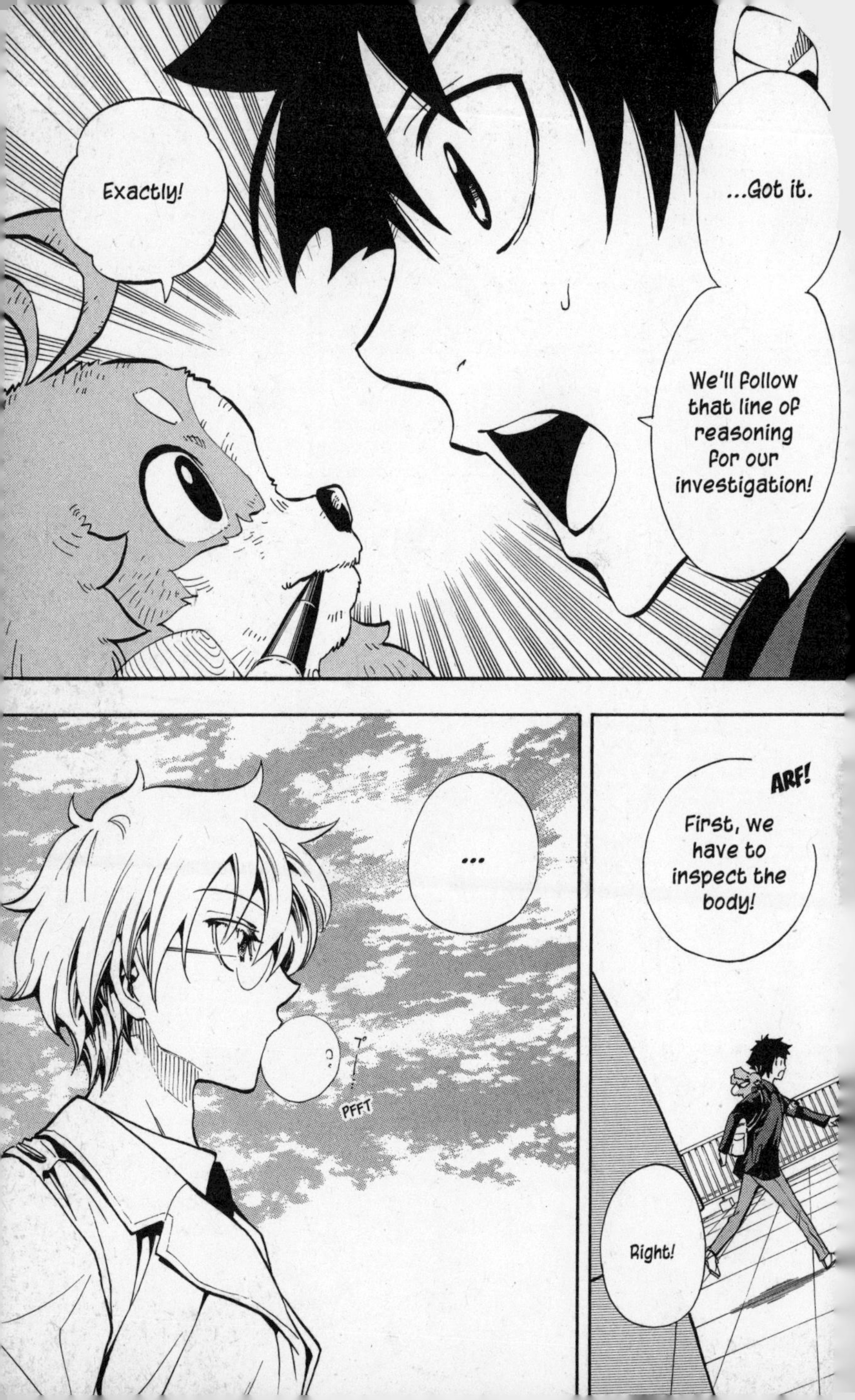
...Got it.
We'll follow that line of reasoning for our investigation!
Exactly!
ARF!
First, we have to inspect the body!
Right!
...
PFFT

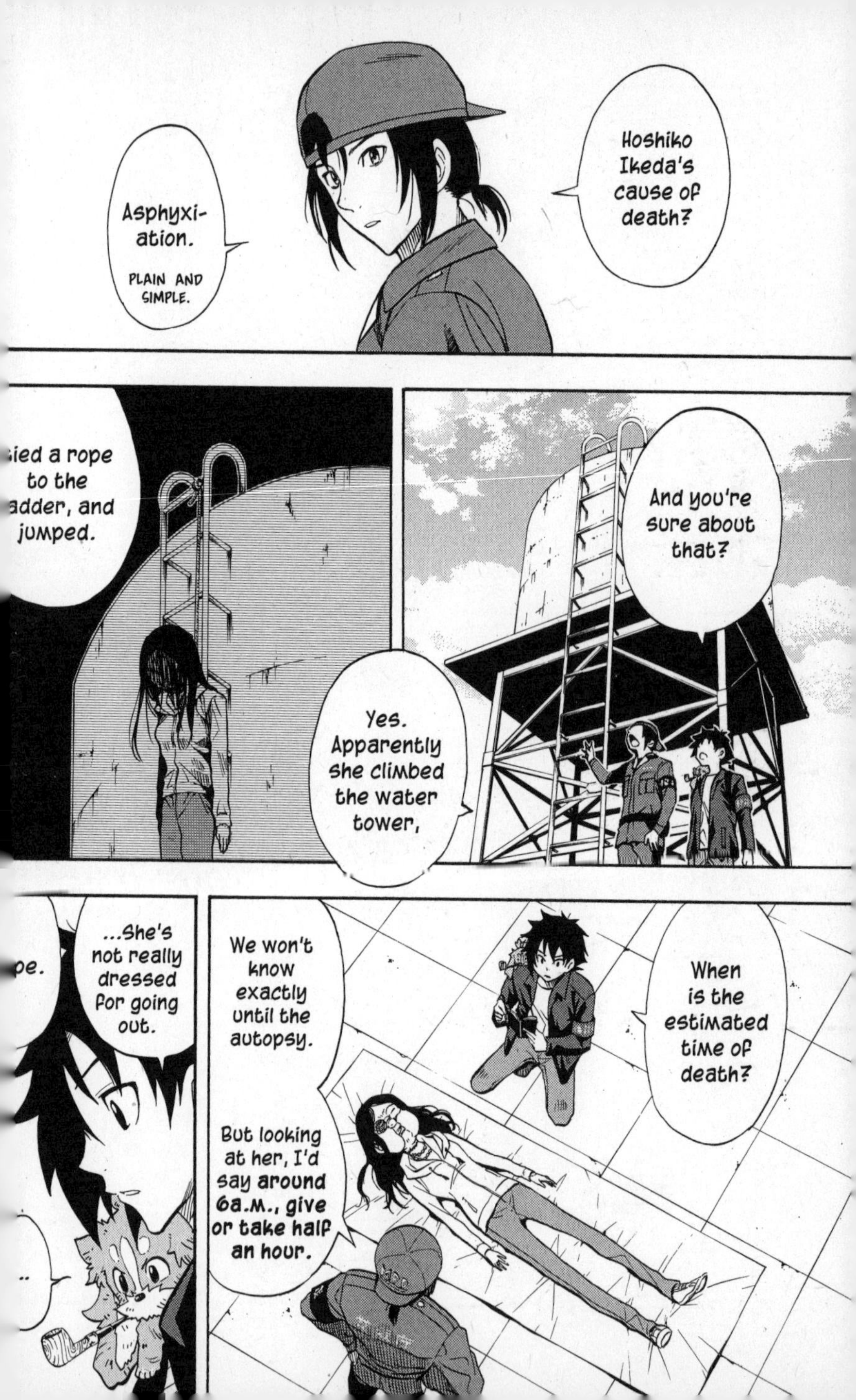

Hoshiko Ikeda's cause of death?
Asphyxiation.
PLAIN AND SIMPLE.
And you're sure about that?
Yes. Apparently she climbed the water tower,
ied a rope to the adder, and jumped.
When is the estimated time of death?
We won't know exactly until the autopsy.
But looking at her, I'd say around 6a.m., give or take half an hour.
...She's not really dressed for going out.
pe.
..

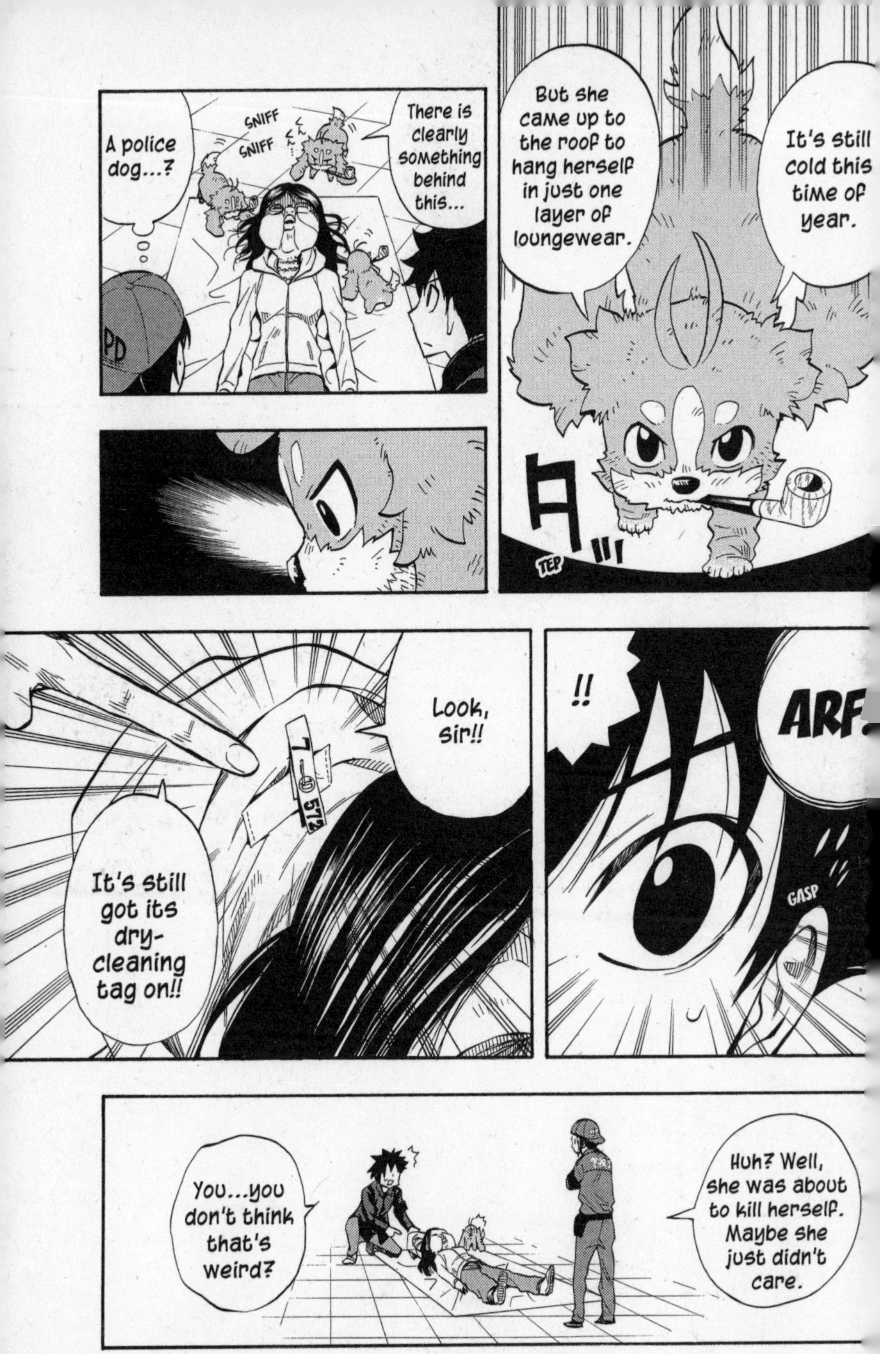
It's still cold this time of year.
But she came up to the roof to hang herself in just one layer of loungewear.
TEP
There is clearly something behind this...
SNIFF
SNIFF
A police dog...?
ARF.
!!
GASP
Look, sir!!
It's still got its dry-cleaning tag on!!
Huh? Well, she was about to kill herself. Maybe she just didn't care.
You...you don't think that's weird?

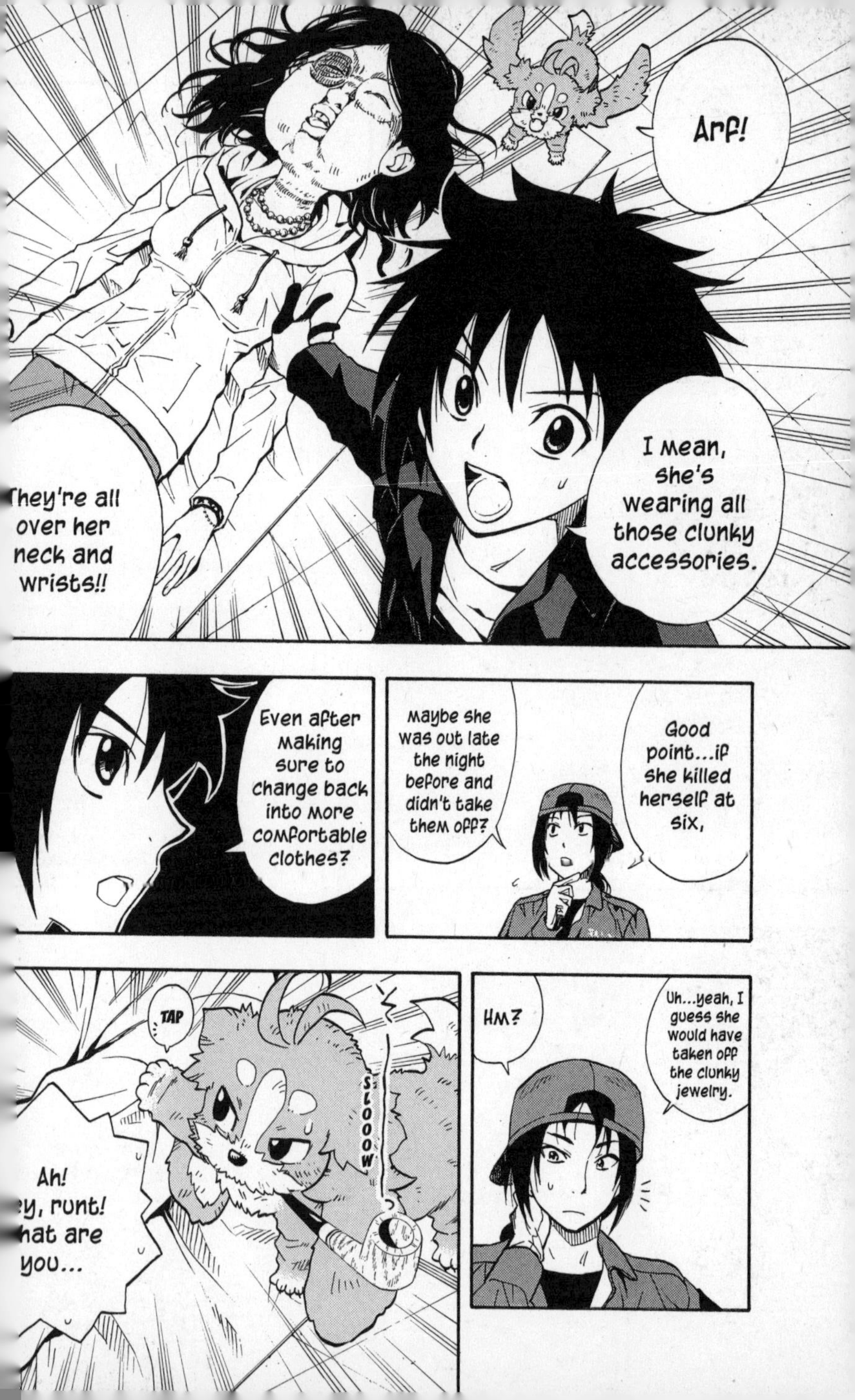
Arf!
I mean, she's wearing all those clunky accessories.
They're all over her neck and wrists!!
Good point...if she killed herself at six,
Maybe she was out late the night before and didn't take them off?
Even after making sure to change back into more comfortable clothes?
Uh...yeah, I guess she would have taken off the clunky jewelry.
HM?
TAP
SLOOOW
Ah! ey, runt! hat are you...

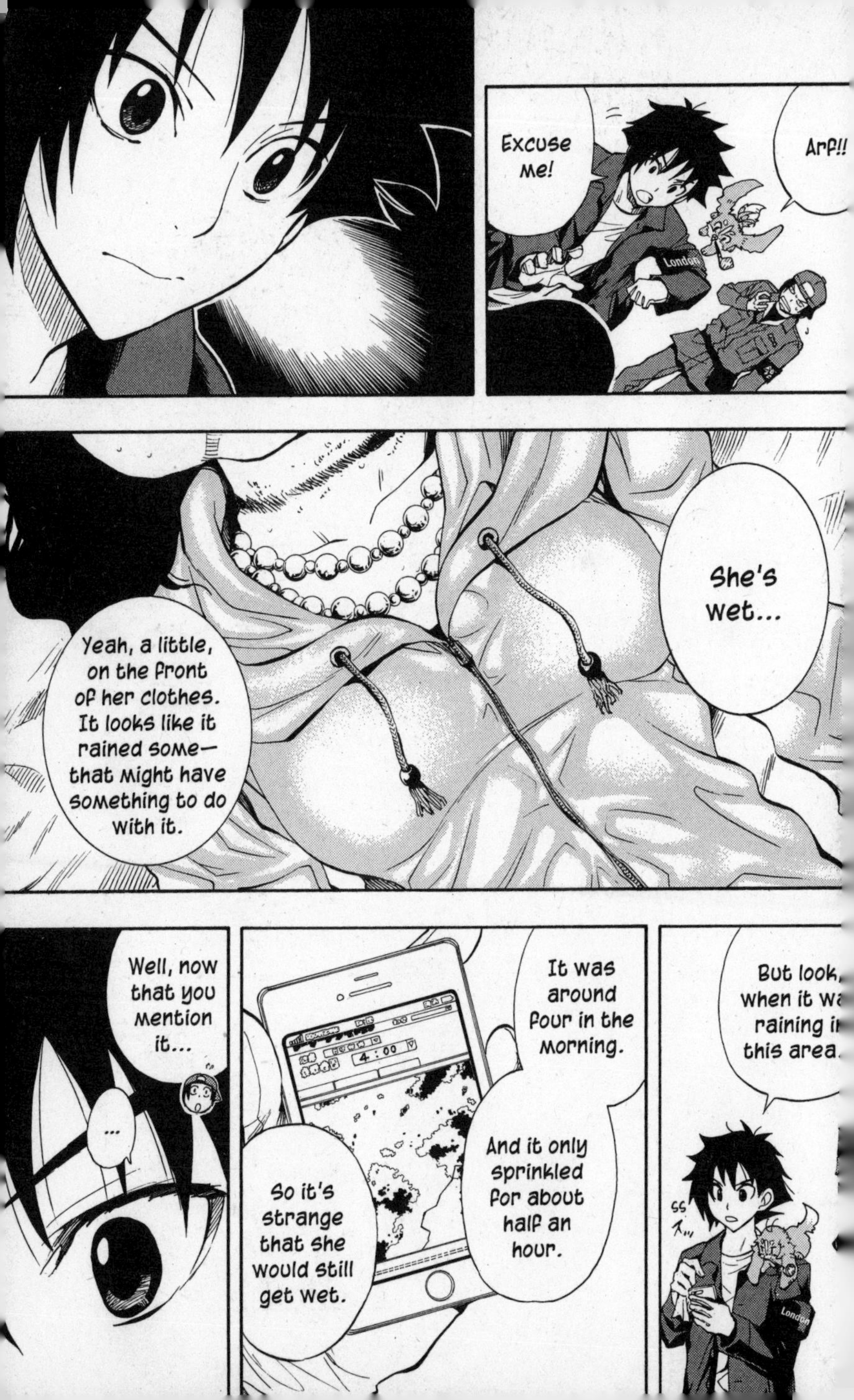
Arf!!
Excuse me!
She's wet...
Yeah, a little, on the front of her clothes. It looks like it rained some—that might have something to do with it.
But look, when it wa raining i this area.
It was around four in the morning.
And it only sprinkled for about half an hour.
So it's strange that she would still get wet.
Well, now that you mention it...
...

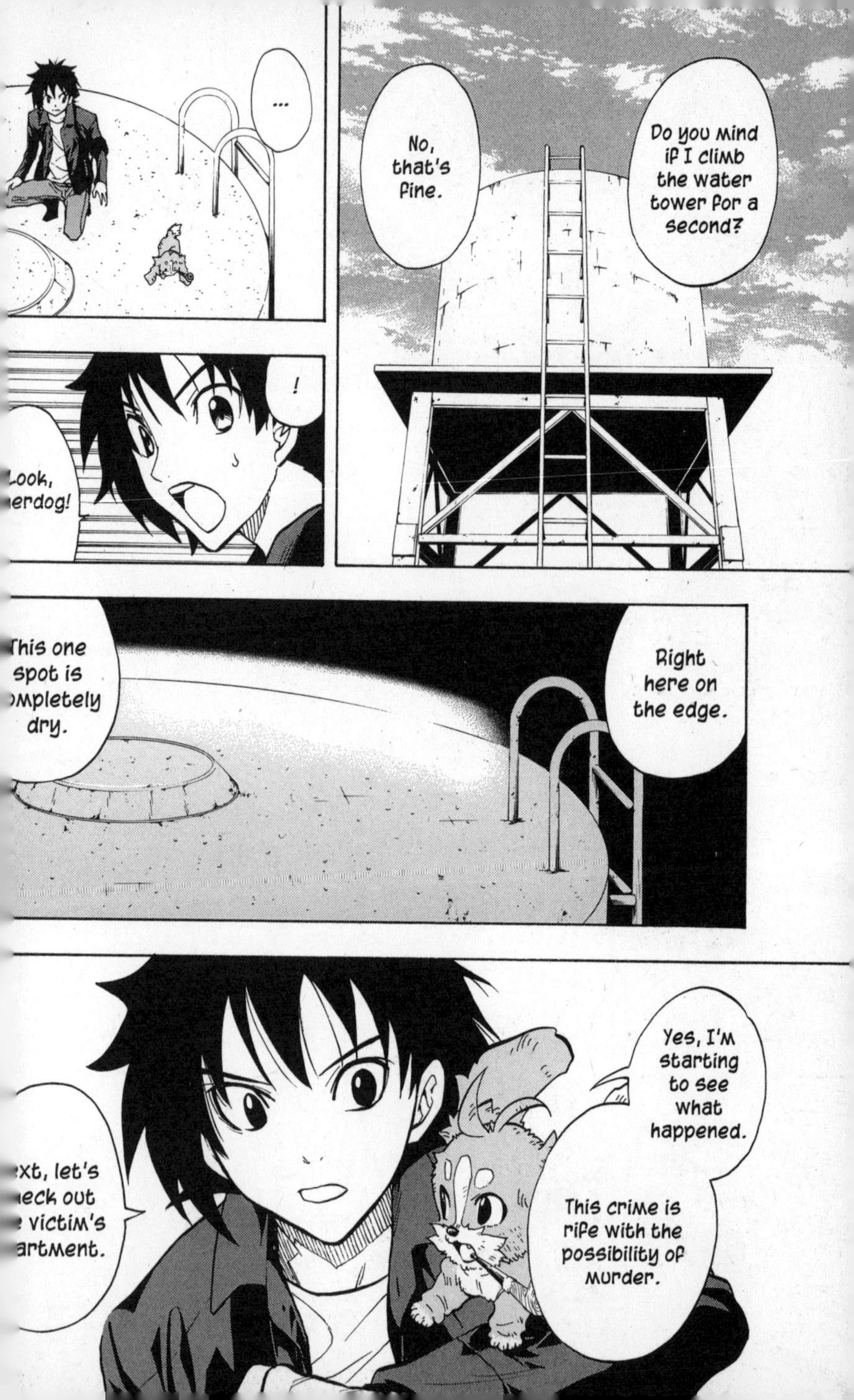
Do you mind if I climb the water tower for a second?
No, that's fine.
...
!
Look, erdog!
Right here on the edge.
This one spot is ompletely dry.
Yes, I'm starting to see what happened.
This crime is rife with the possibility of murder.
xt, let's eck out victim's artment.

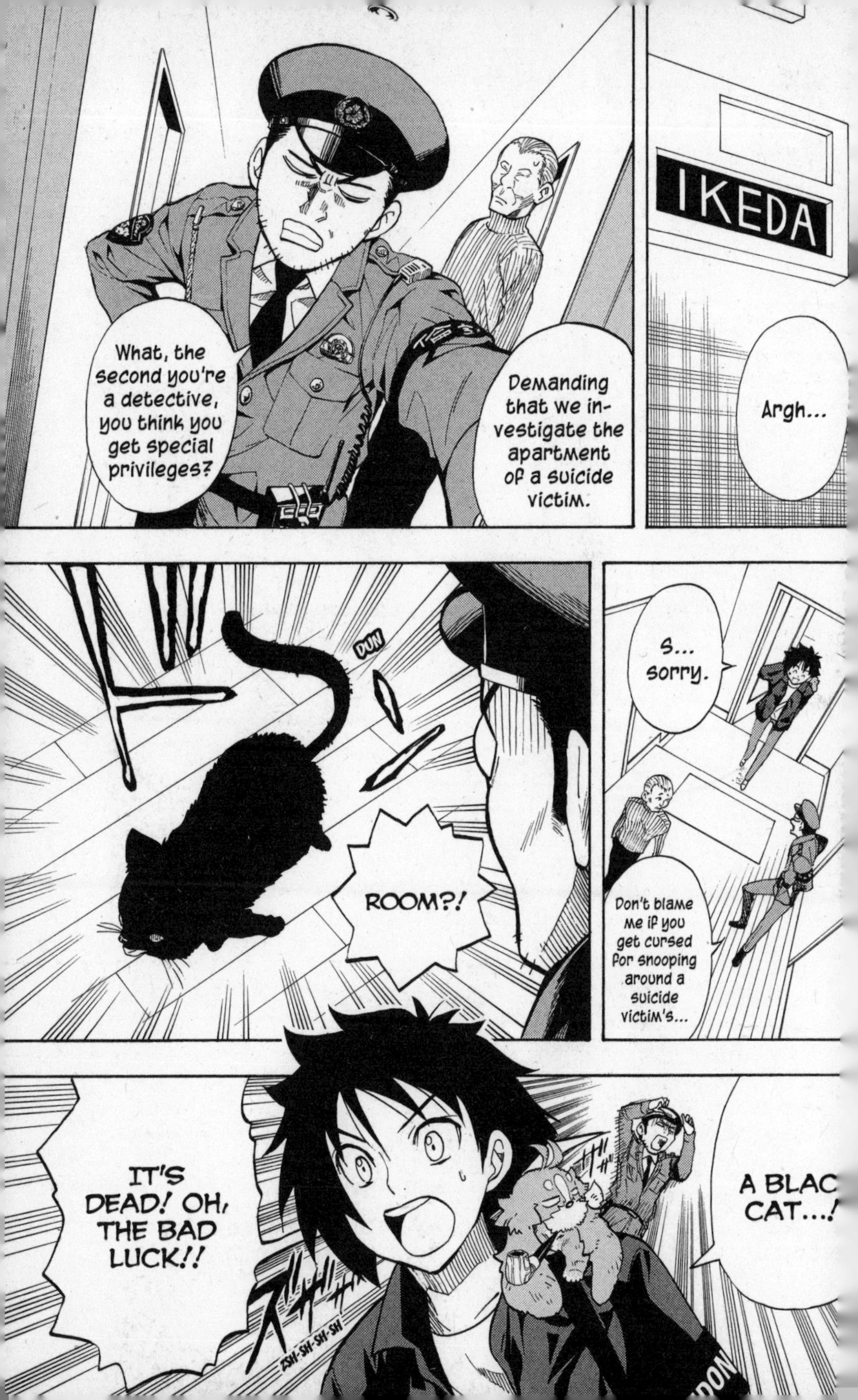
IKEDA
Argh...
Demanding that we investigate the apartment of a suicide victim.
What, the second you're a detective, you think you get special privileges?
S... sorry.
Don't blame me if you get cursed for snooping around a suicide victim's...
DUN
ROOM?!
A BLAC CAT...!
IT'S DEAD! OH, THE BAD LUCK!!
ZSH-SH-SH-SH

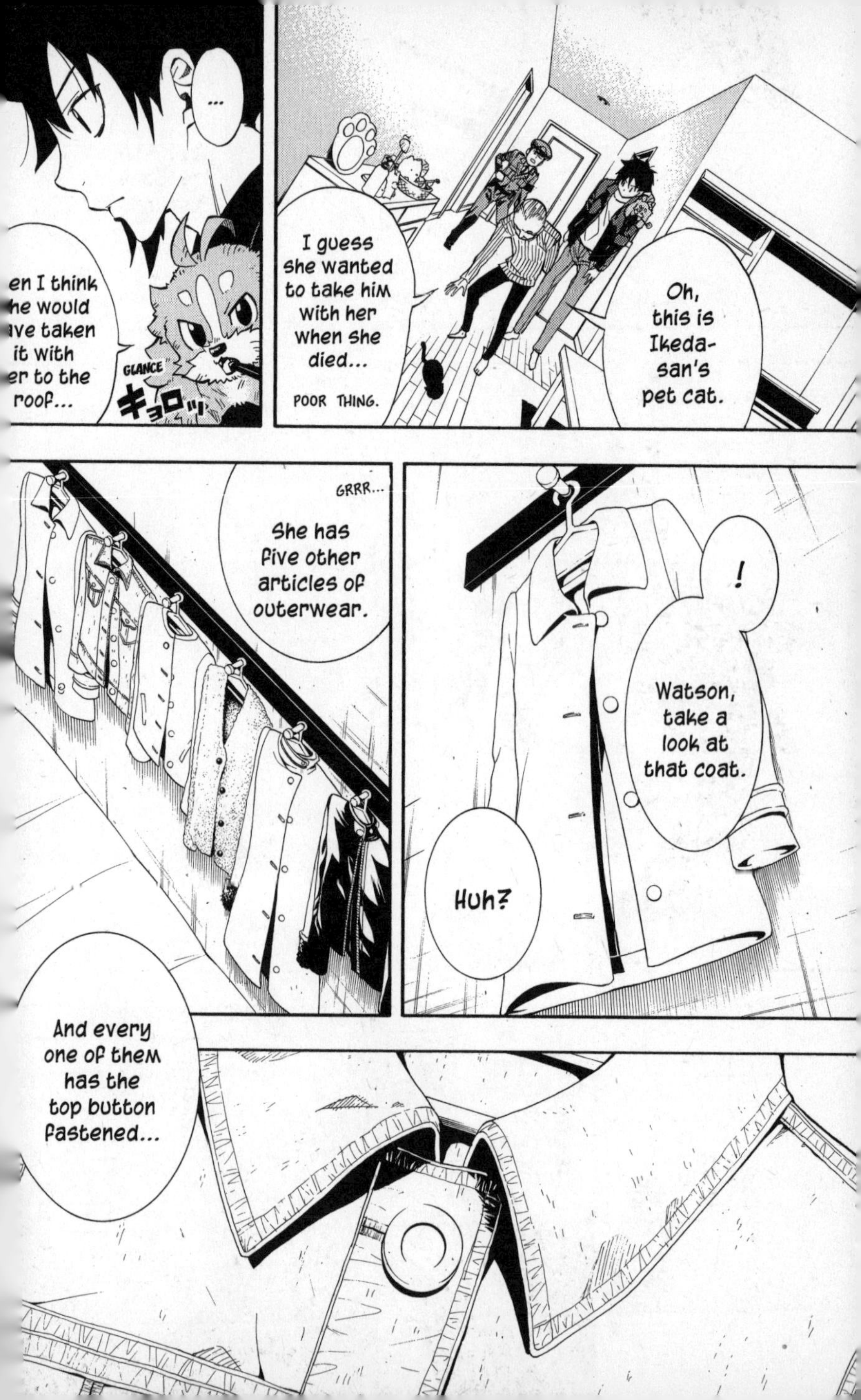
Oh, this is Ikeda-san's pet cat.
I guess she wanted to take him with her when she died...
POOR THING.
...
en I think he would ave taken it with er to the roof...
GLANCE
キョロッ
!
Watson, take a look at that coat.
Huh?
GRRR...
She has five other articles of outerwear.
And every one of them has the top button fastened...

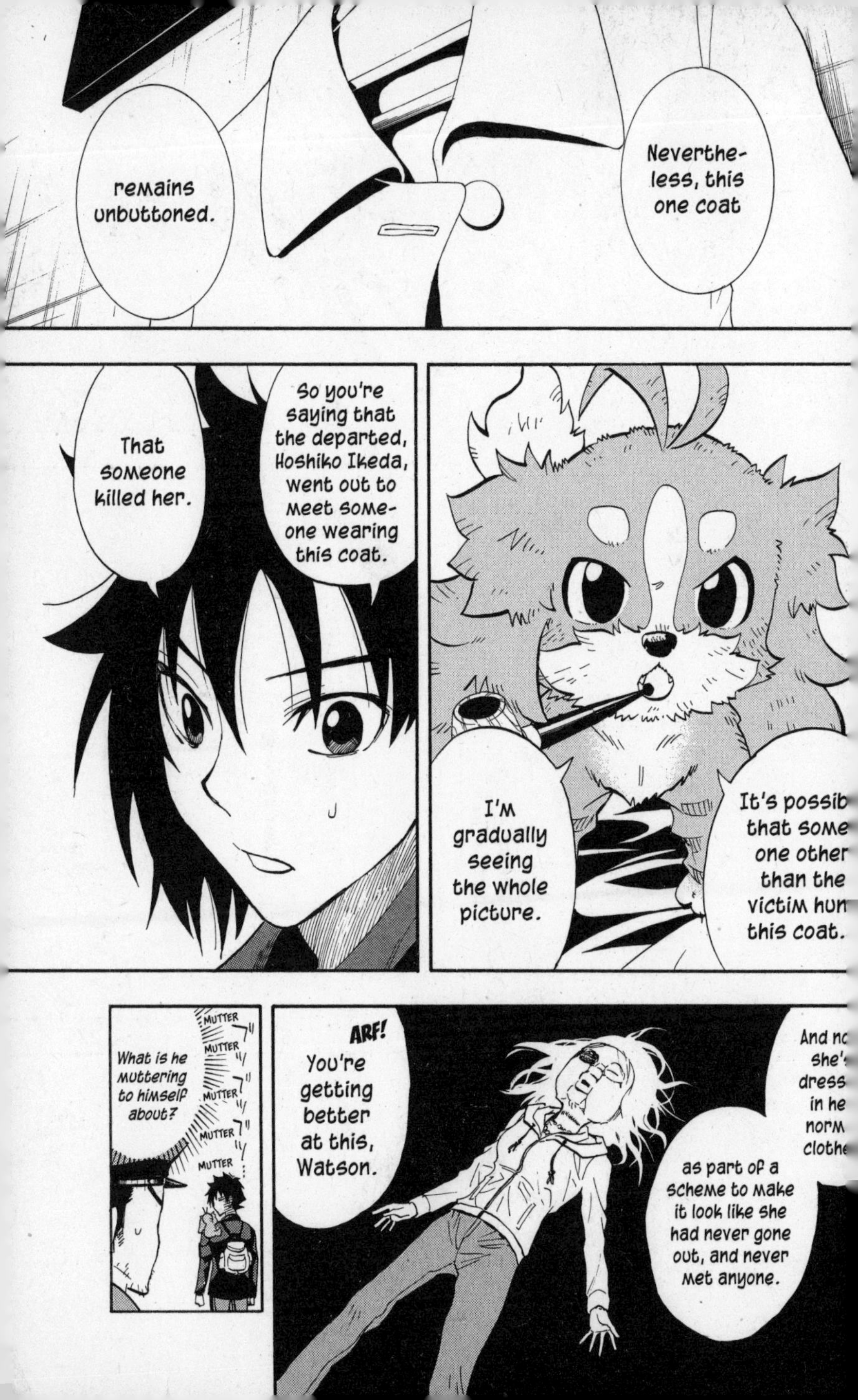

Neverthe-less, this one coat
remains unbuttoned.
It's possib that some one other than the victim hun this coat.
I'm gradually seeing the whole picture.
So you're saying that the departed, Hoshiko Ikeda, went out to meet some-one wearing this coat.
That someone killed her.
And no she's dress in he norm clothe
as part of a scheme to make it look like she had never gone out, and never met anyone.
ARF!
You're getting better at this, Watson.
MUTTER
MUTTER
MUTTER
MUTTER
MUTTER
What is he muttering to himself about?

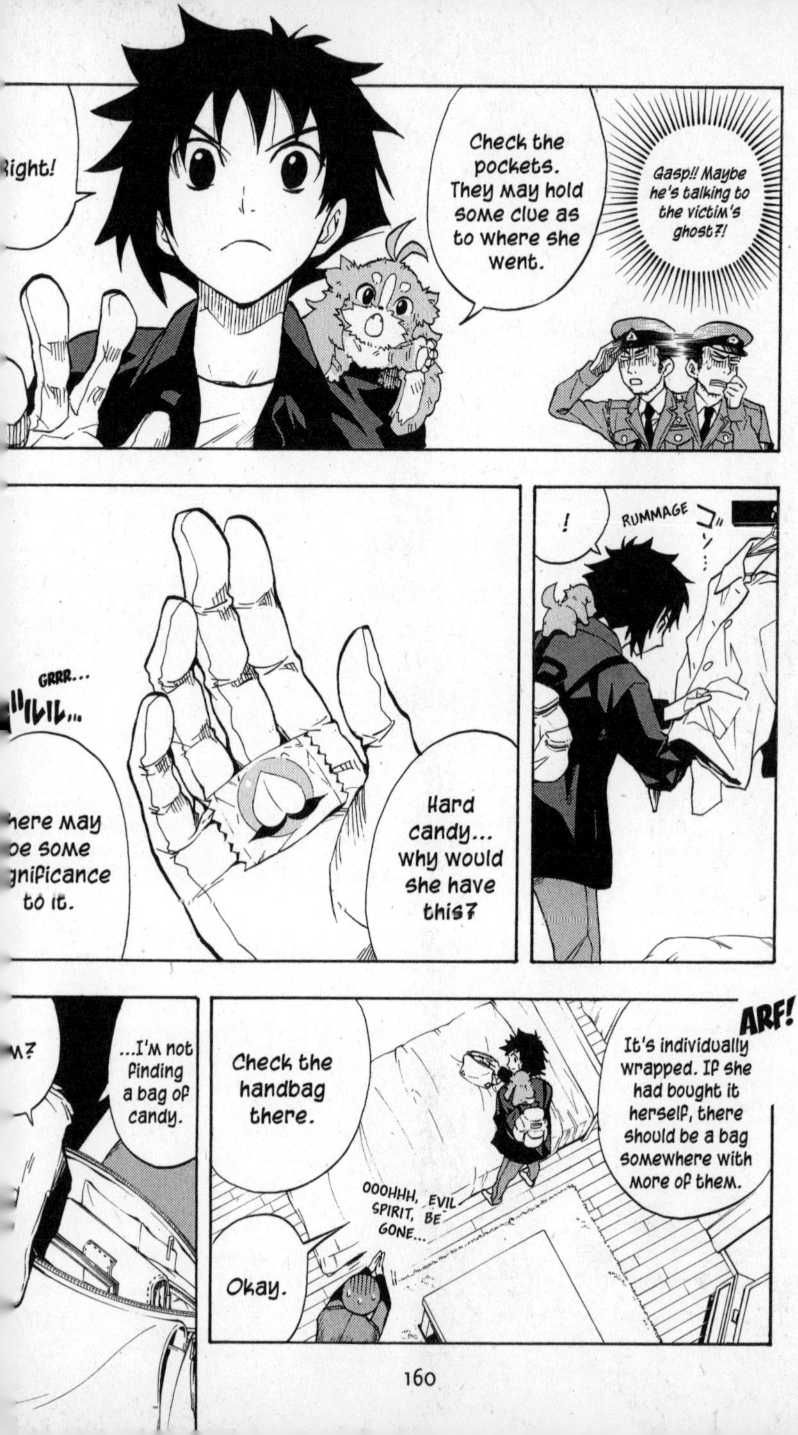
Gasp!! Maybe he's talking to the victim's ghost?!
Check the pockets. They may hold some clue as to where she went.
ight!
RUMMAGE
!
Hard candy... why would she have this?
GRRR...
here may oe some gnificance to it.
ARF!
It's individually wrapped. If she had bought it herself, there should be a bag somewhere with more of them.
Check the handbag there.
OOOHHH, EVIL SPIRIT, BE GONE...
Okay.
...I'm not finding a bag of candy.
m?

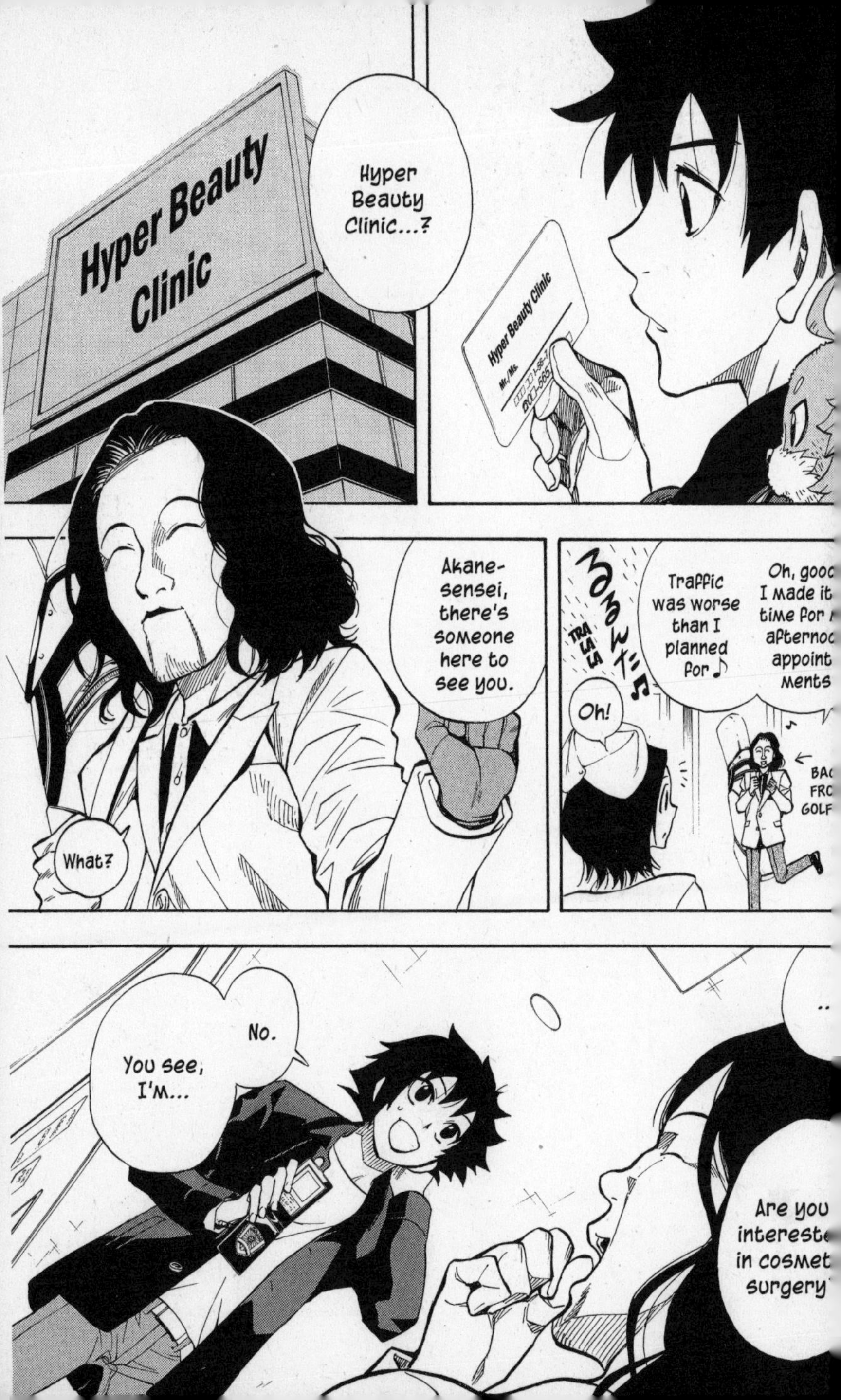
Hyper Beauty Clinic
Mr./Ms.
Hyper Beauty Clinic...?
Hyper Beauty Clinic
Oh, good I made it time for afternoo appoint ments
Traffic was worse than I planned for♪
TRA LA LA
Oh!
BAC FRO GOLF
Akane-sensei, there's someone here to see you.
What?
..
Are you intereste in cosmet surgery
No.
You see, I'm...

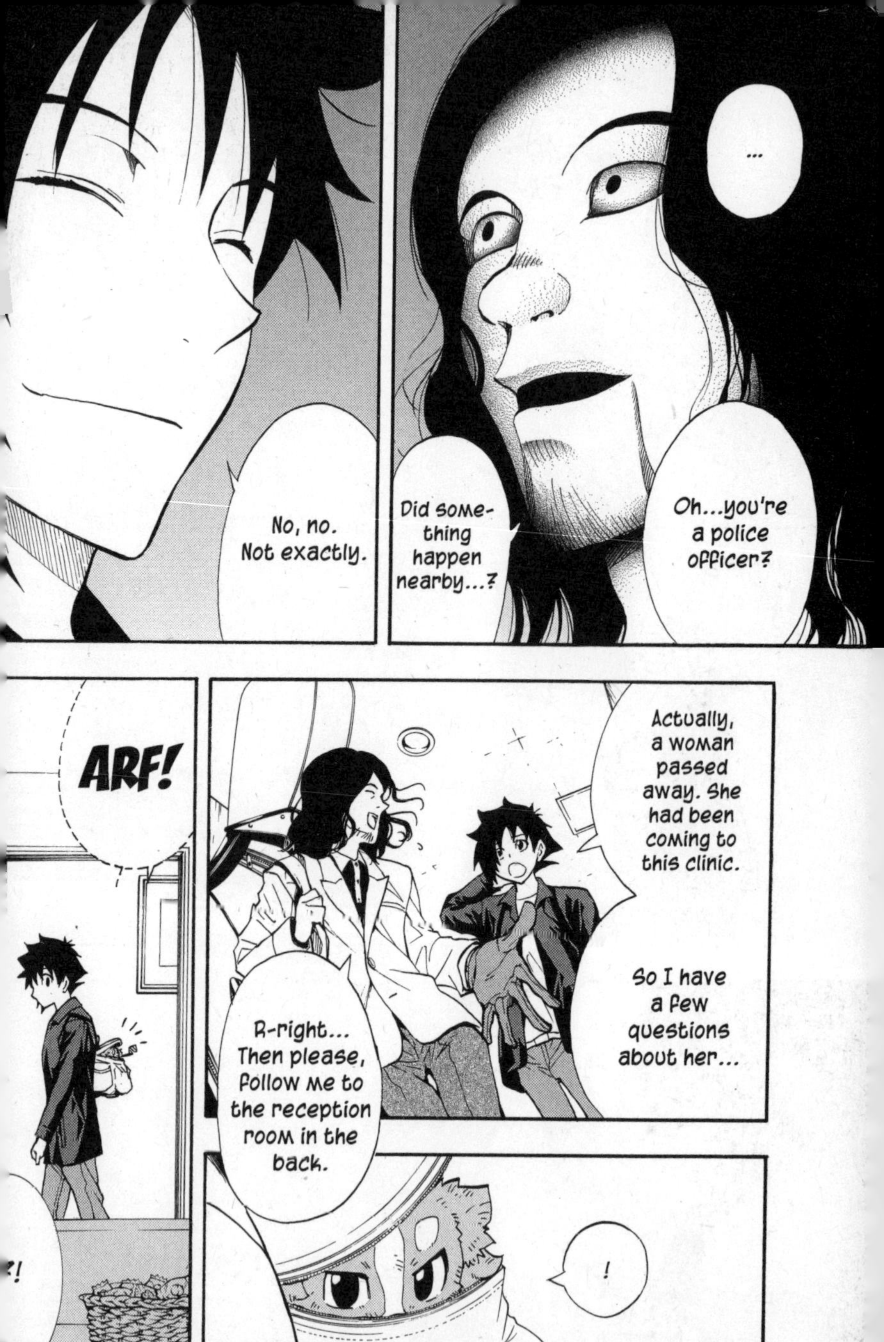

...
Oh...you're a police officer?
Did some-thing happen nearby...?
No, no. Not exactly.
Actually, a woman passed away. She had been coming to this clinic.
So I have a few questions about her...
R-right... Then please, follow me to the reception room in the back.
!
ARF!

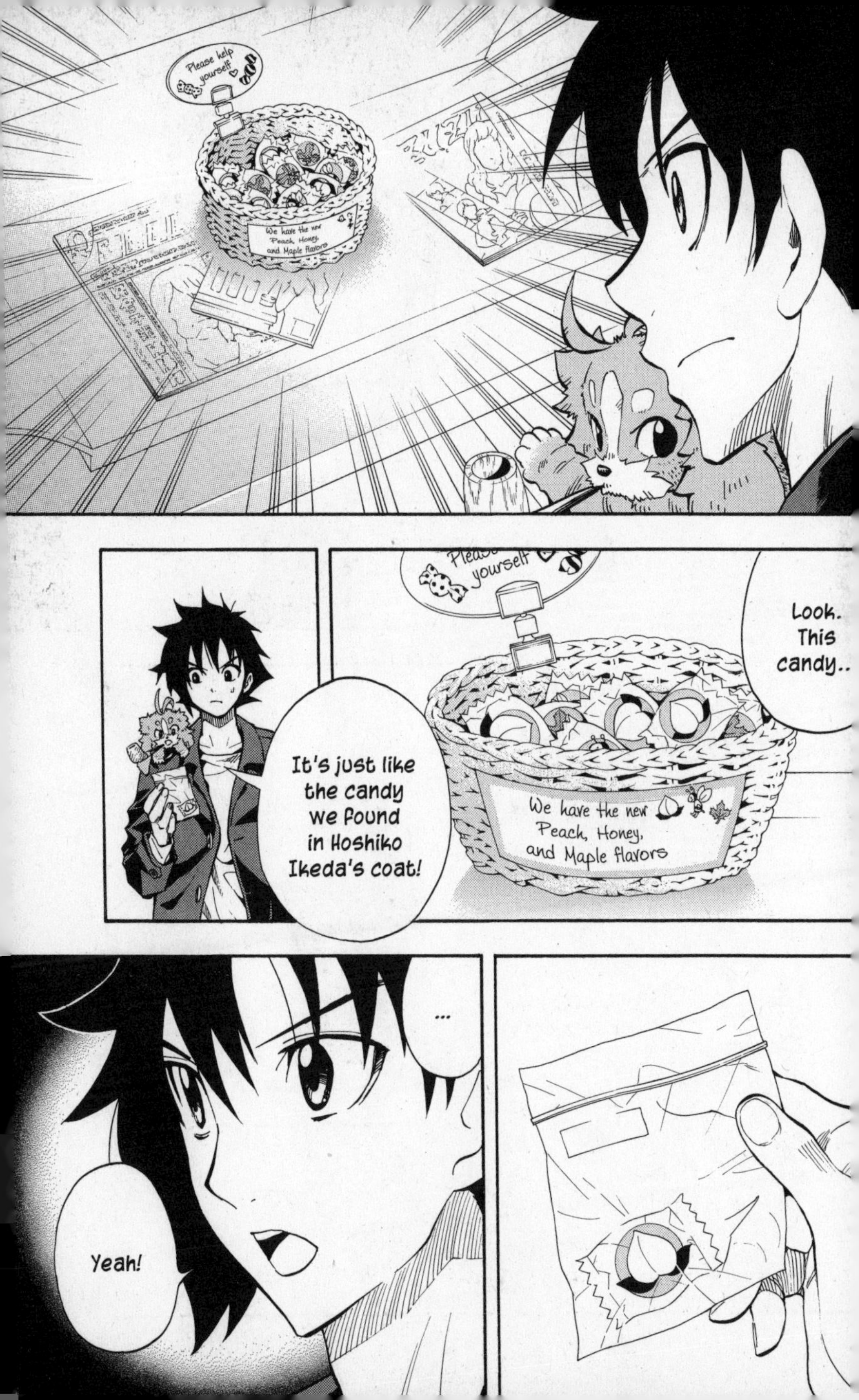
Please help yourself
We have the new Peach, Honey, and Maple flavors
Look. This candy..
yourself
We have the new Peach, Honey, and Maple flavors
It's just like the candy we found in Hoshiko Ikeda's coat!
...
Yeah!

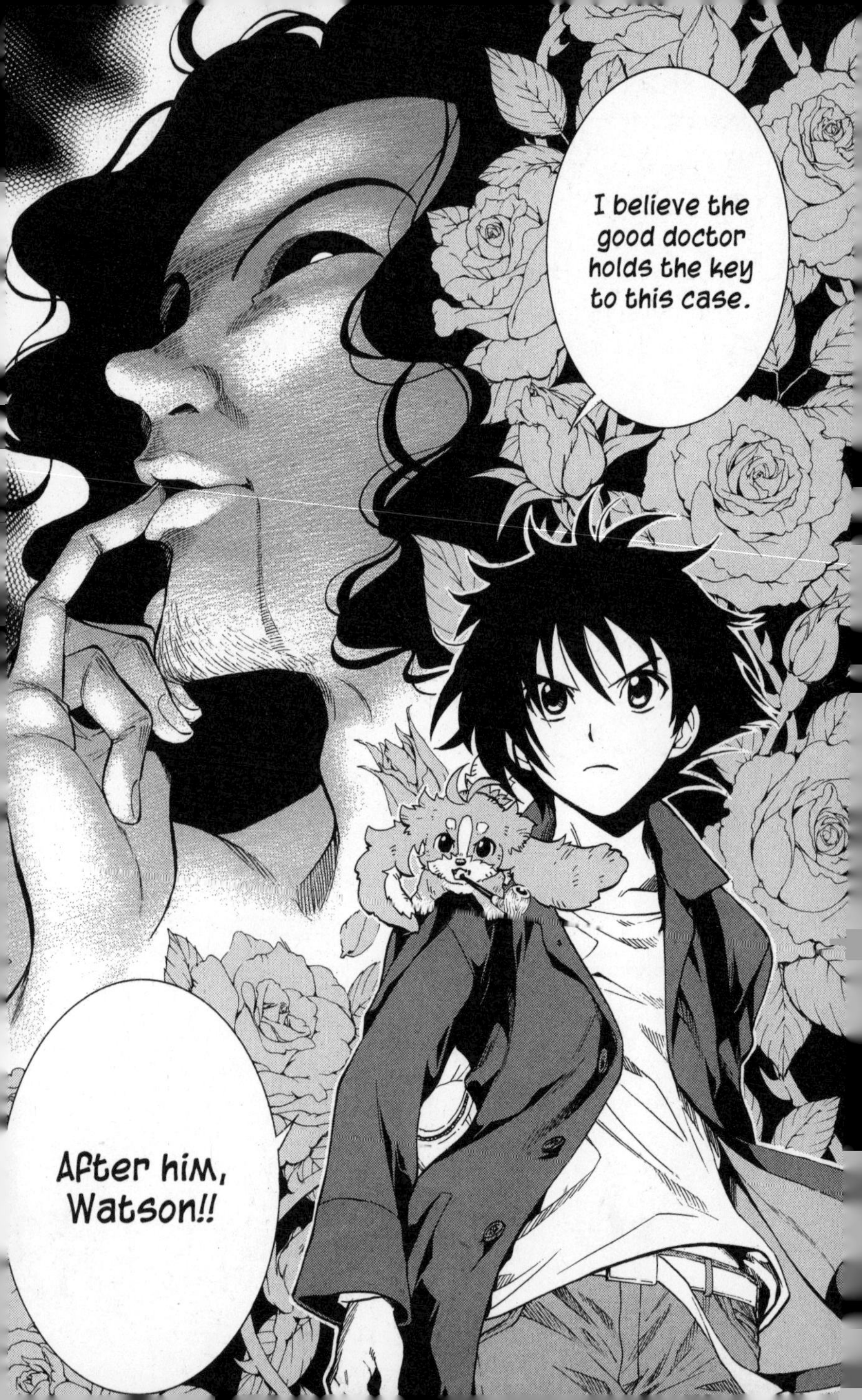
I believe the good doctor holds the key to this case.
After him, Watson!!

Case 9: ⚜ The Stolen Face, Part 3

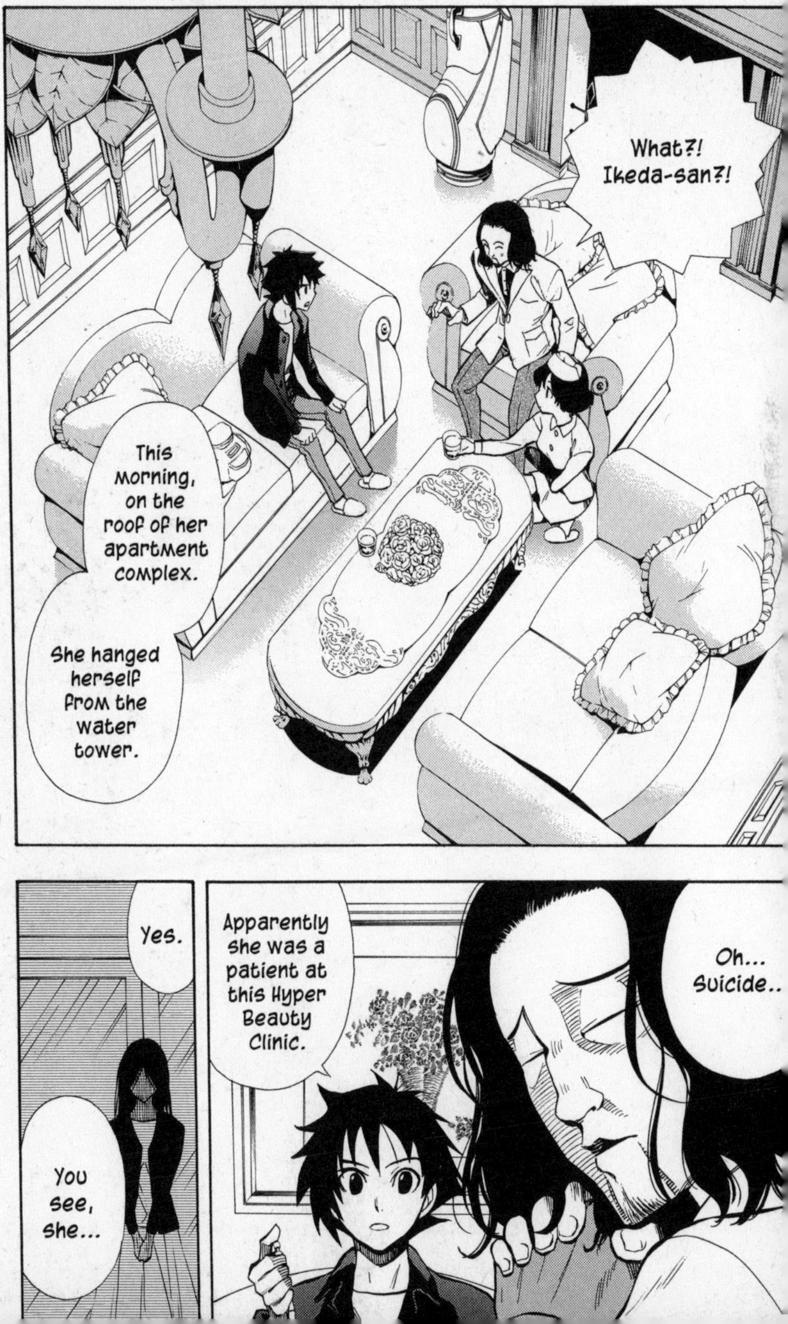
What?! Ikeda-san?!
This morning, on the roof of her apartment complex.
She hanged herself from the water tower.
Oh... Suicide...
Apparently she was a patient at this Hyper Beauty Clinic.
Yes.
You see, she...

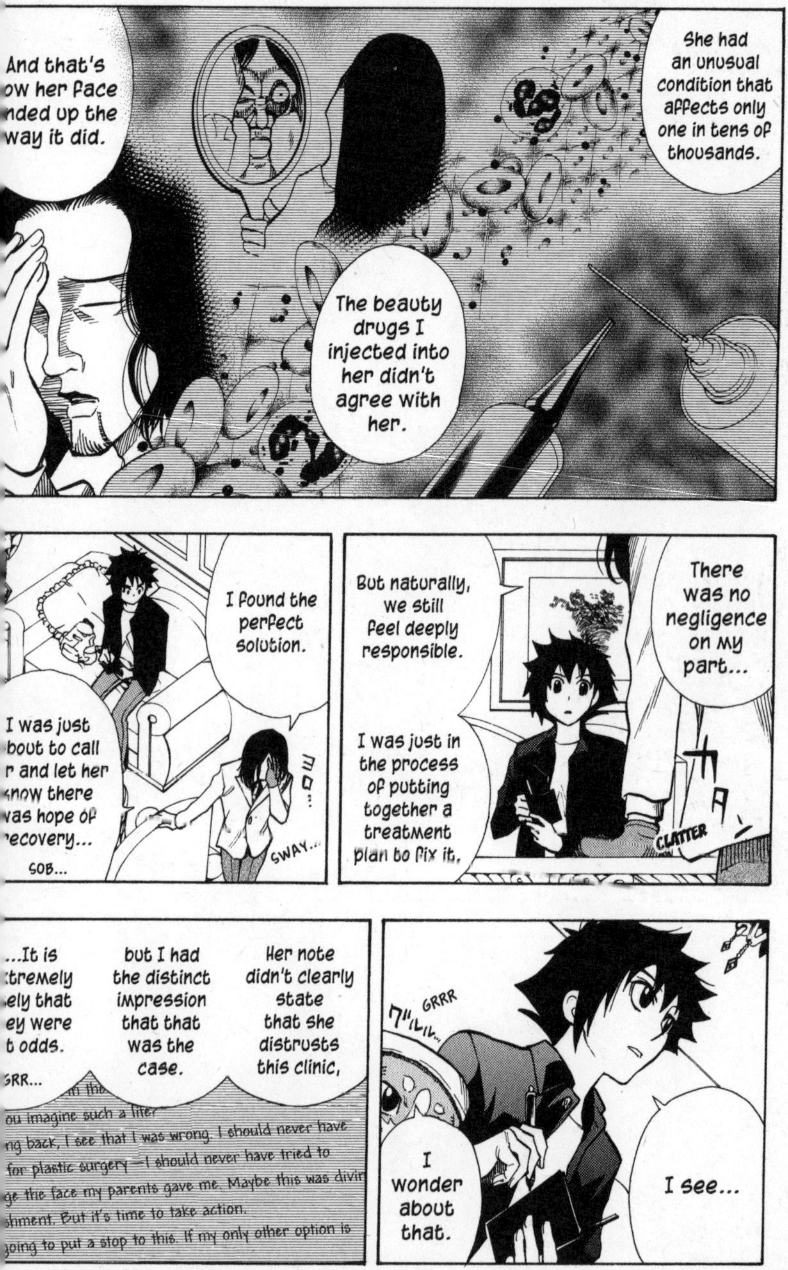

She had an unusual condition that affects only one in tens of thousands.
The beauty drugs I injected into her didn't agree with her.
And that's
ow her face
nded up the
way it did.
There was no negligence on my part...
CLATTER
But naturally, we still feel deeply responsible.
I was just in the process of putting together a treatment plan to fix it.
I found the perfect solution.
SWAY...
I was just
bout to call
r and let her
now there
vas hope of
ecovery...
SOB...
GRRR
I see...
I wonder about that.
Her note didn't clearly state that she distrusts this clinic,
but I had the distinct impression that that was the case.
...It is
tremely
ely that
ey were
t odds.
GRR...
ou imagine such a life?
ng back, I see that I was wrong. I should never have
for plastic surgery—I should never have tried to
ge the face my parents gave me. Maybe this was divir
shment. But it's time to take action.
going to put a stop to this. If my only other option is

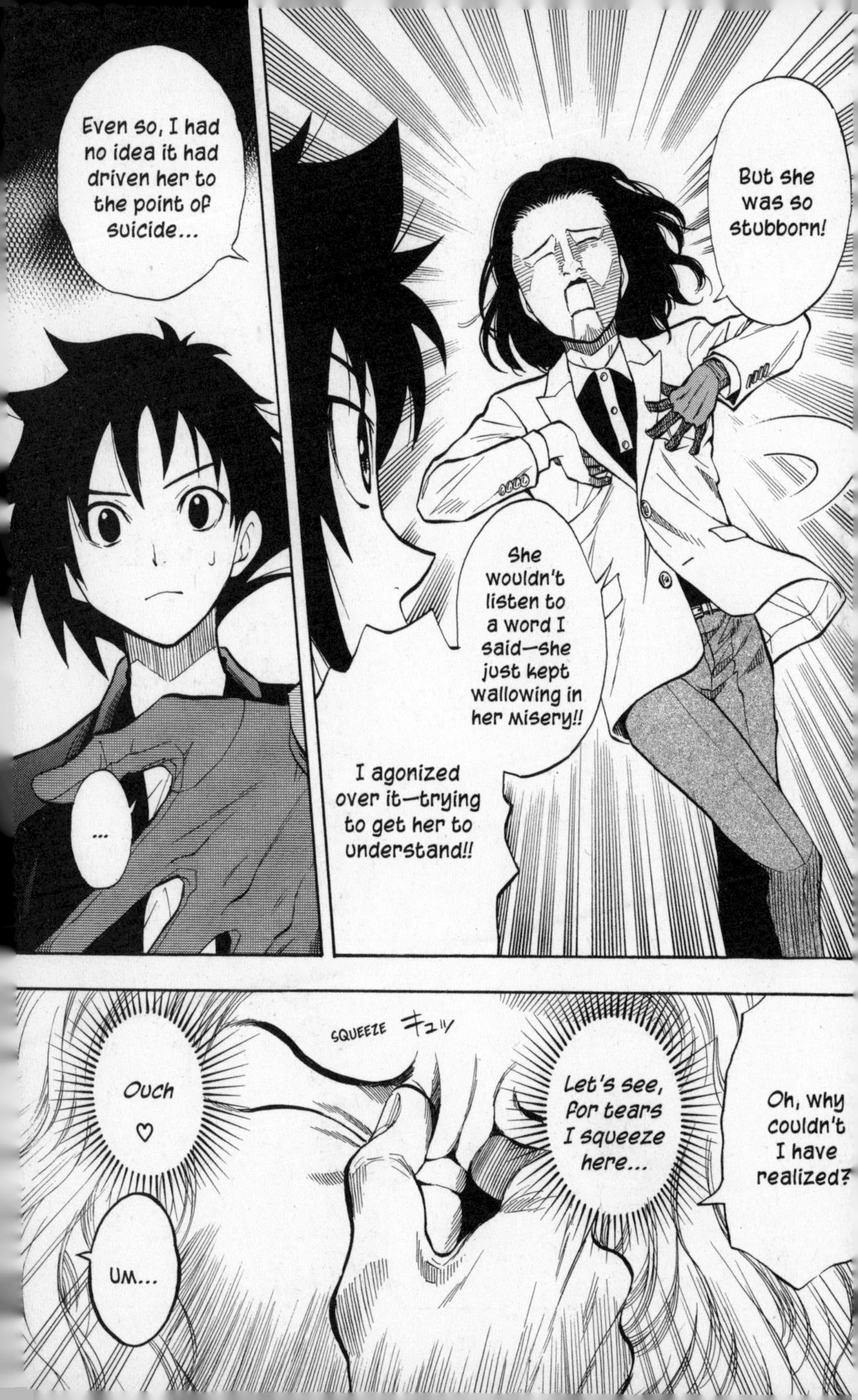
But she was so stubborn!
She wouldn't listen to a word I said—she just kept wallowing in her misery!!
I agonized over it—trying to get her to understand!!
Even so, I had no idea it had driven her to the point of suicide...
...
Oh, why couldn't I have realized?
Let's see, for tears I squeeze here...
SQUEEZE キュッ
Ouch ♡
Um...

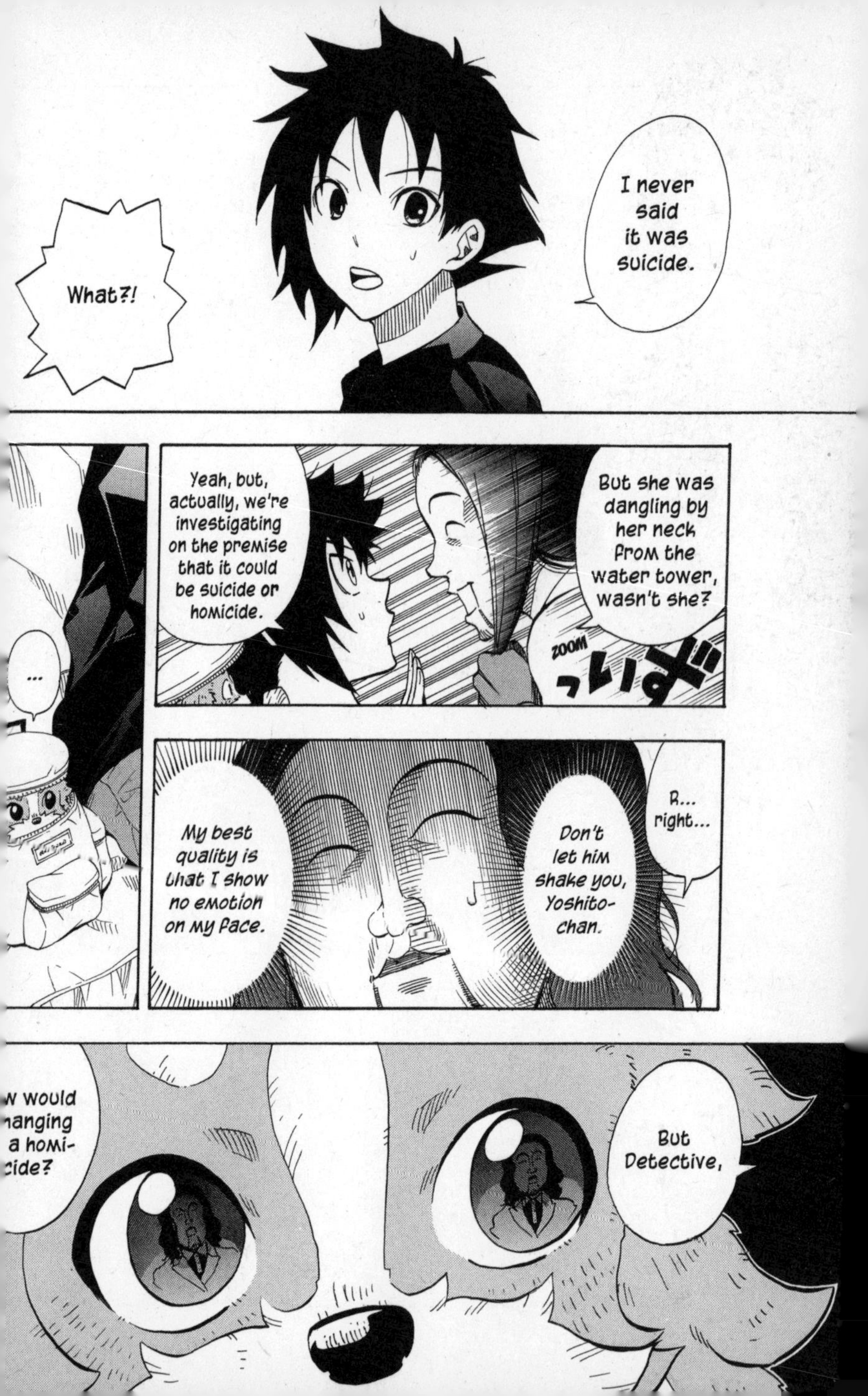
I never said it was suicide.
What?!
But she was dangling by her neck from the water tower, wasn't she?
ZOOM
Yeah, but, actually, we're investigating on the premise that it could be suicide or homicide.
R... right...
Don't let him shake you, Yoshito-chan.
My best quality is that I show no emotion on my face.
...
But Detective,
w would anging a homi- cide?

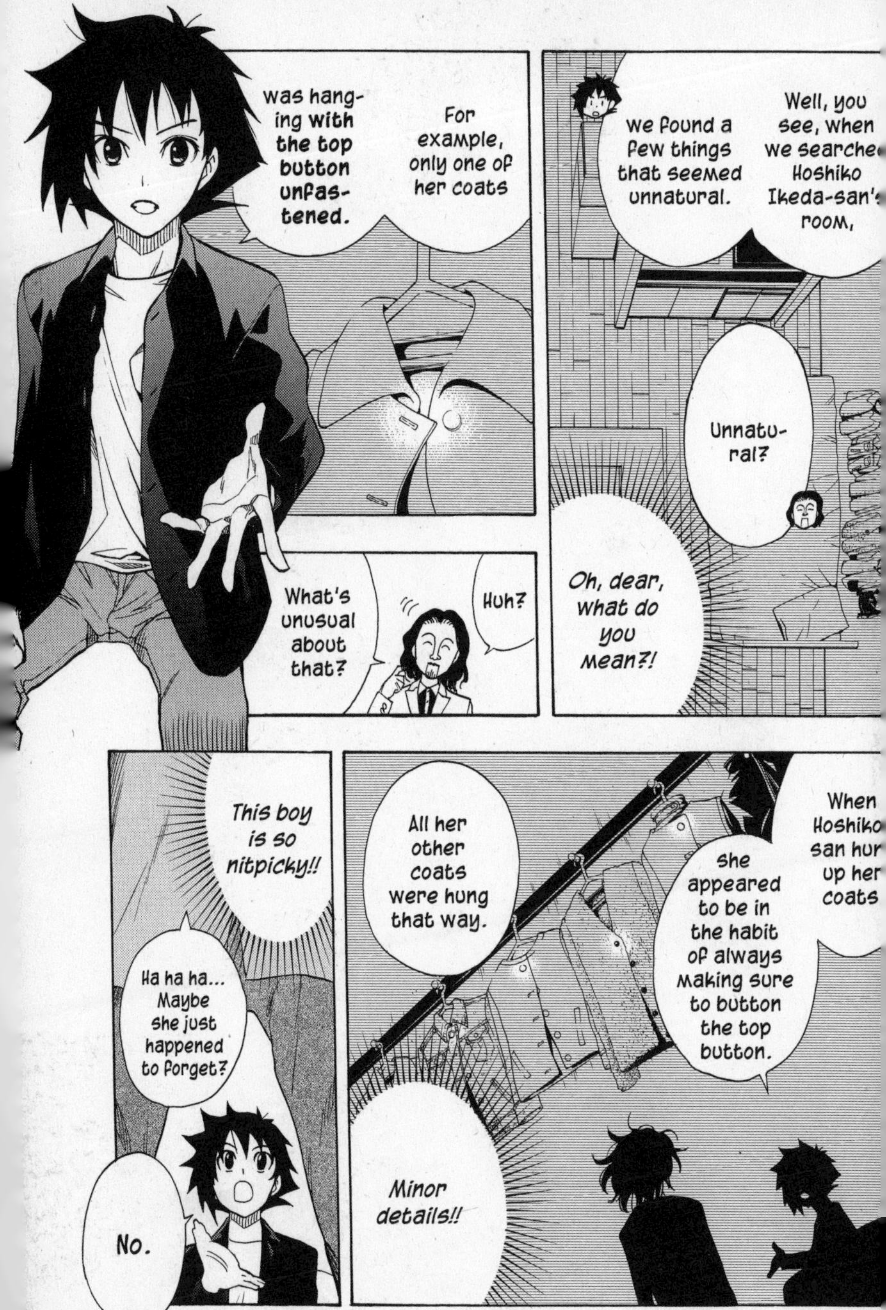

Well, you see, when we searche Hoshiko Ikeda-san's room,
we found a few things that seemed unnatural.
Unnatural?
Oh, dear, what do you mean?!
For example, only one of her coats
was hanging with the top button unfastened.
Huh?
What's unusual about that?
When Hoshiko san hun up her coats
she appeared to be in the habit of always making sure to button the top button.
All her other coats were hung that way.
Minor details!!
This boy is so nitpicky!!
Ha ha ha... Maybe she just happened to forget?
No.

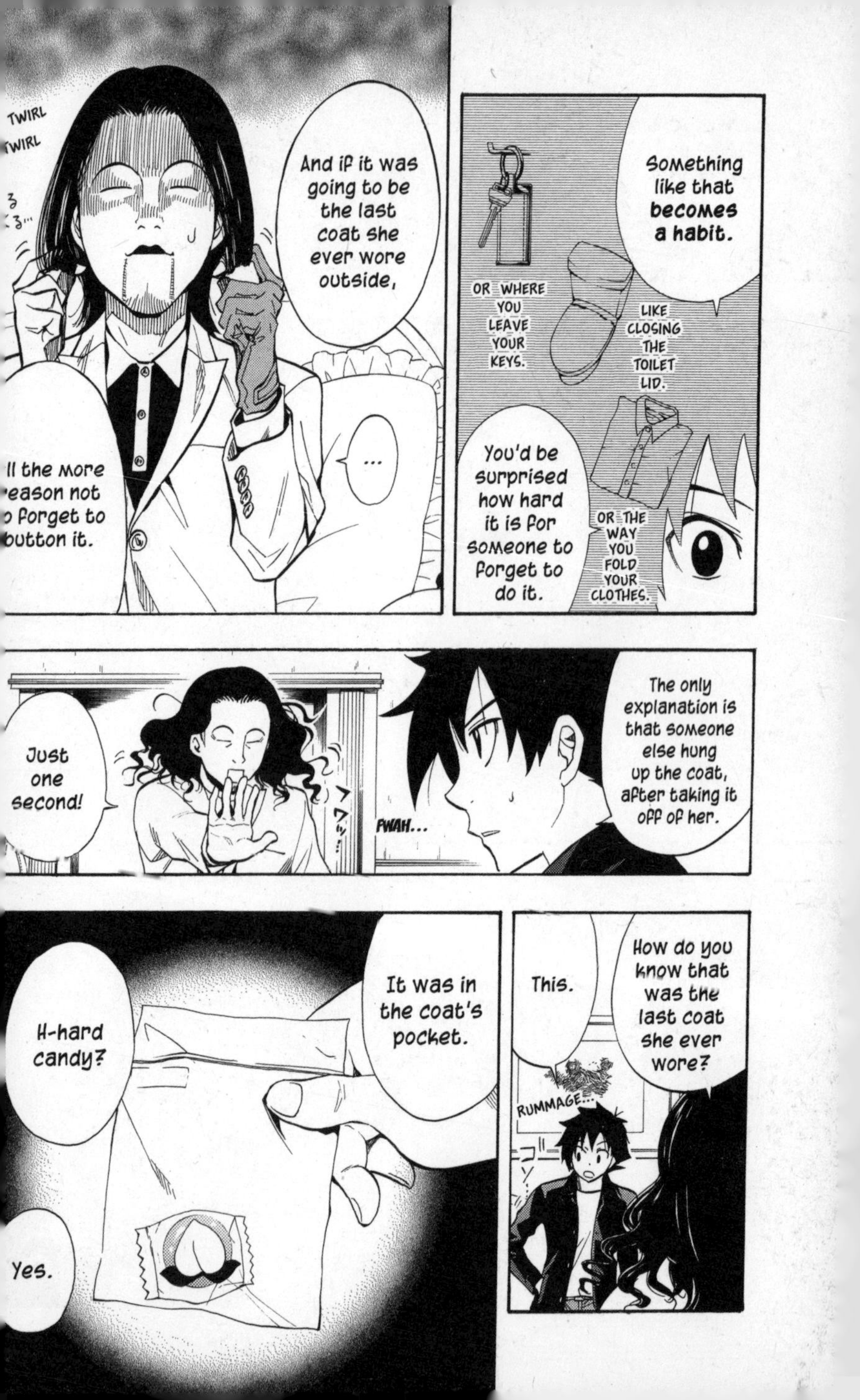
Something like that becomes a habit.
LIKE CLOSING THE TOILET LID.
OR WHERE YOU LEAVE YOUR KEYS.
You'd be surprised how hard it is for someone to forget to do it.
OR THE WAY YOU FOLD YOUR CLOTHES.
TWIRL
TWIRL
And if it was going to be the last coat she ever wore outside,
...
ll the more eason not o forget to button it.
The only explanation is that someone else hung up the coat, after taking it off of her.
FWAH...
Just one second!
How do you know that was the last coat she ever wore?
This.
RUMMAGE...
It was in the coat's pocket.
H-hard candy?
Yes.

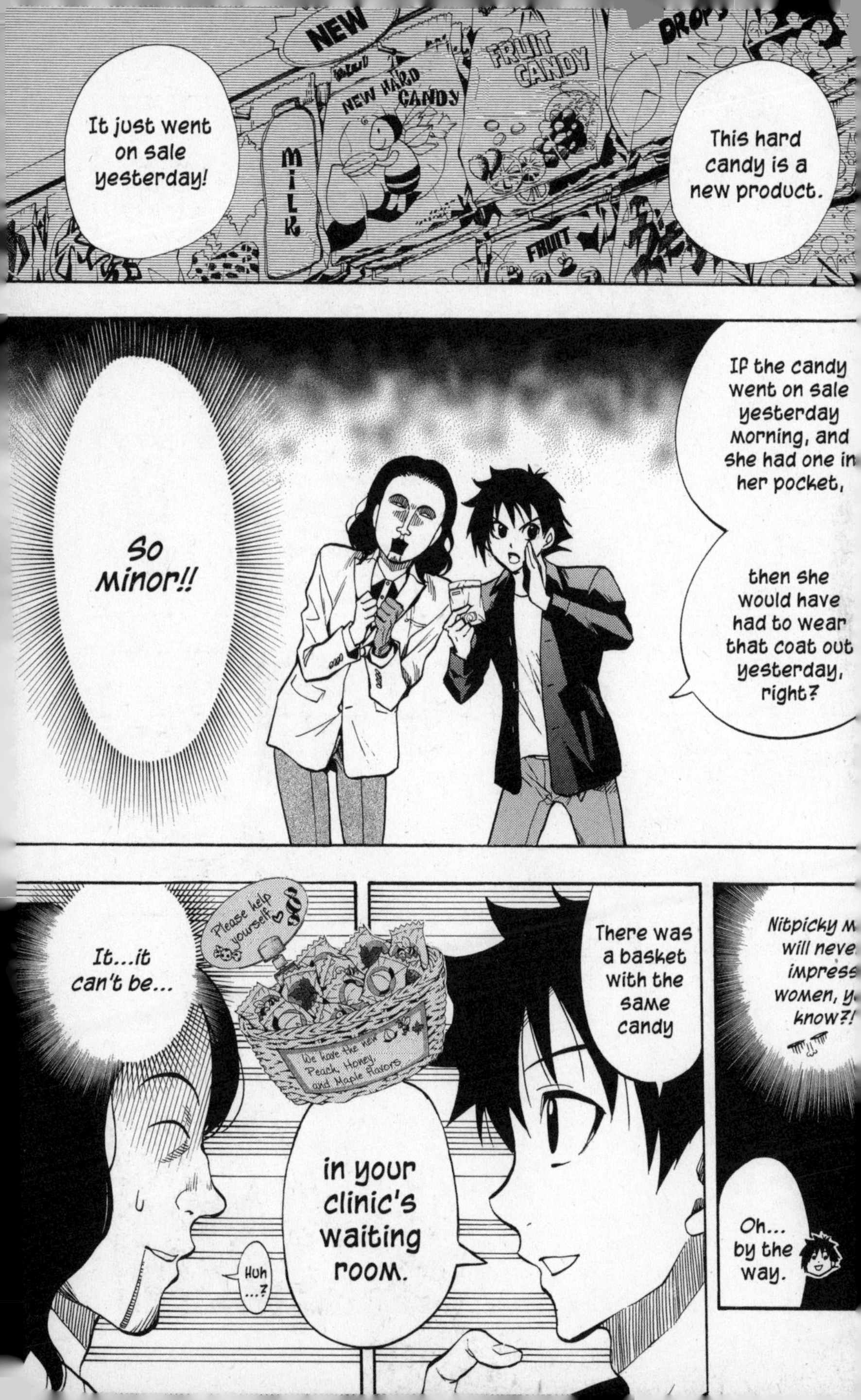
DROPS
FRUIT CANDY
NEW
NEW HARD CANDY
MILK
FRUIT
This hard candy is a new product.
It just went on sale yesterday!
If the candy went on sale yesterday morning, and she had one in her pocket,
then she would have had to wear that coat out yesterday, right?
So minor!!
Nitpicky m will neve impress women, y know?!
Oh... by the way.
There was a basket with the same candy
Please help yourself
We have the new Peach, Honey, and Maple flavors
in your clinic's waiting room.
Huh ...?
It...it can't be...

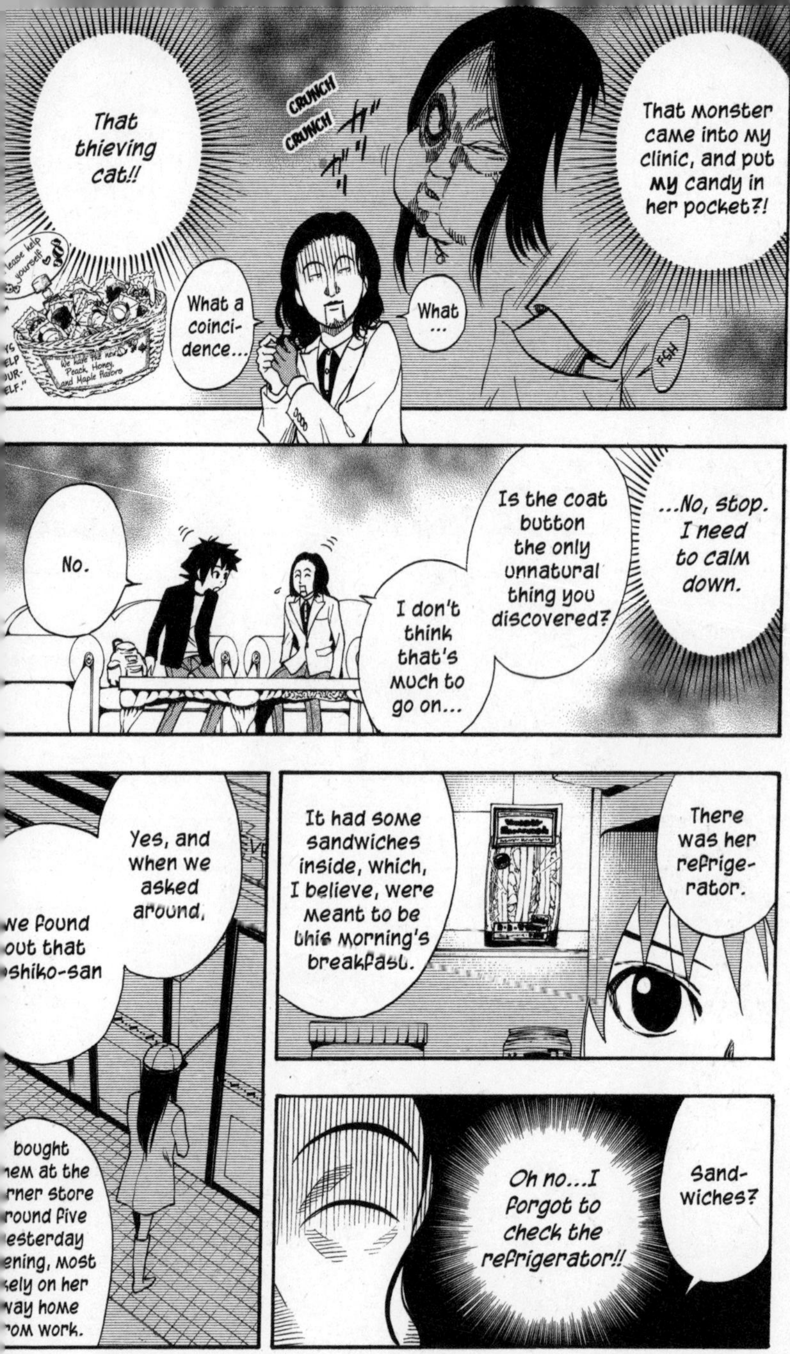
That monster came into my clinic, and put my candy in her pocket?!
CRUNCH
CRUNCH
That thieving cat!!
Please help yourself
We have the new Peach, Honey, and Maple flavors
PSH
What...
What a coincidence...
...No, stop. I need to calm down.
Is the coat button the only unnatural thing you discovered?
I don't think that's much to go on...
No.
There was her refrigerator.
It had some sandwiches inside, which, I believe, were meant to be this morning's breakfast.
Sandwiches?
Oh no...I forgot to check the refrigerator!!
Yes, and when we asked around,
we found out that
shiko-san
bought
nem at the
rner store
round five
esterday
ening, most
ely on her
vay home
om work.

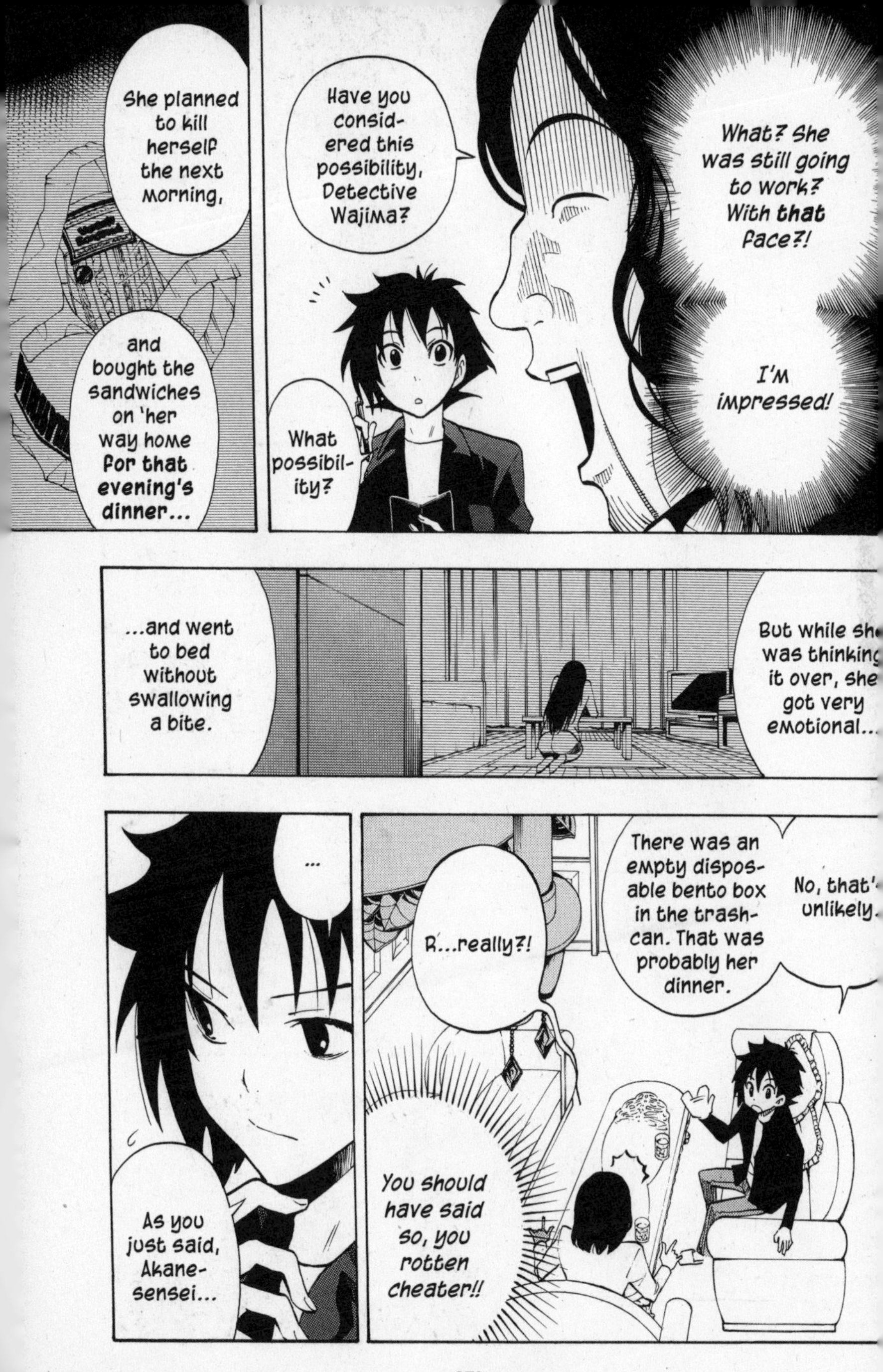
What? She was still going to work? With that face?!
I'M impressed!
Have you consid-ered this possibility, Detective Wajima?
What possibil-ity?
She planned to kill herself the next morning,
and bought the sandwiches on 'her way home for that evening's dinner...
But while sh was thinkin it over, she got very emotional...
...and went to bed without swallowing a bite.
No, that' unlikely.
There was an empty dispos-able bento box in the trash-can. That was probably her dinner.
R...really?!
You should have said so, you rotten cheater!!
...
As you just said, Akane-sensei...

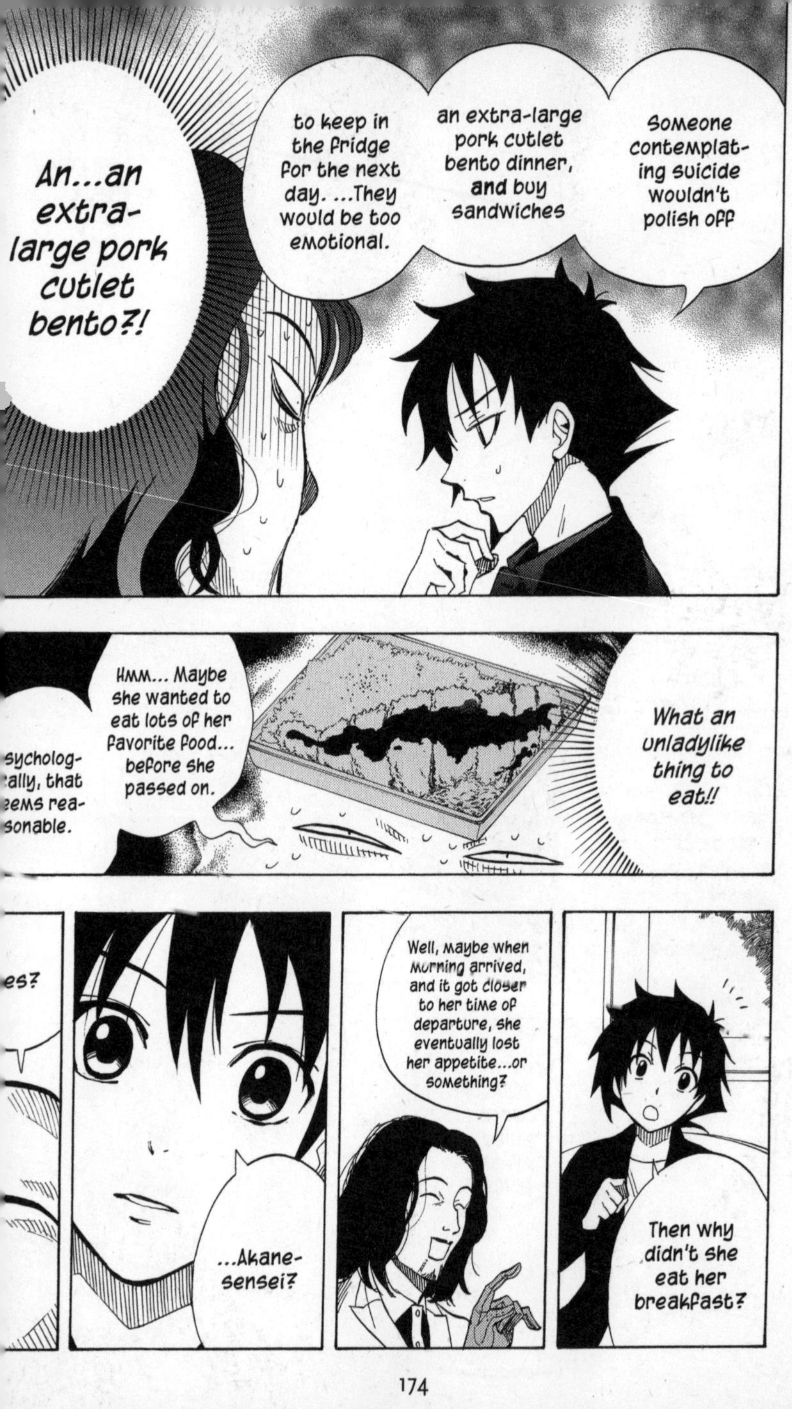

Someone contemplating suicide wouldn't polish off
an extra-large pork cutlet bento dinner, and buy sandwiches
to keep in the fridge for the next day. ...They would be too emotional.
An...an extra-large pork cutlet bento?!
What an unladylike thing to eat!!
Hmm... Maybe she wanted to eat lots of her favorite food... before she passed on.
sycholog- ally, that eems rea- sonable.
Then why didn't she eat her breakfast?
Well, maybe when morning arrived, and it got closer to her time of departure, she eventually lost her appetite...or something?
...Akane-sensei?
es?

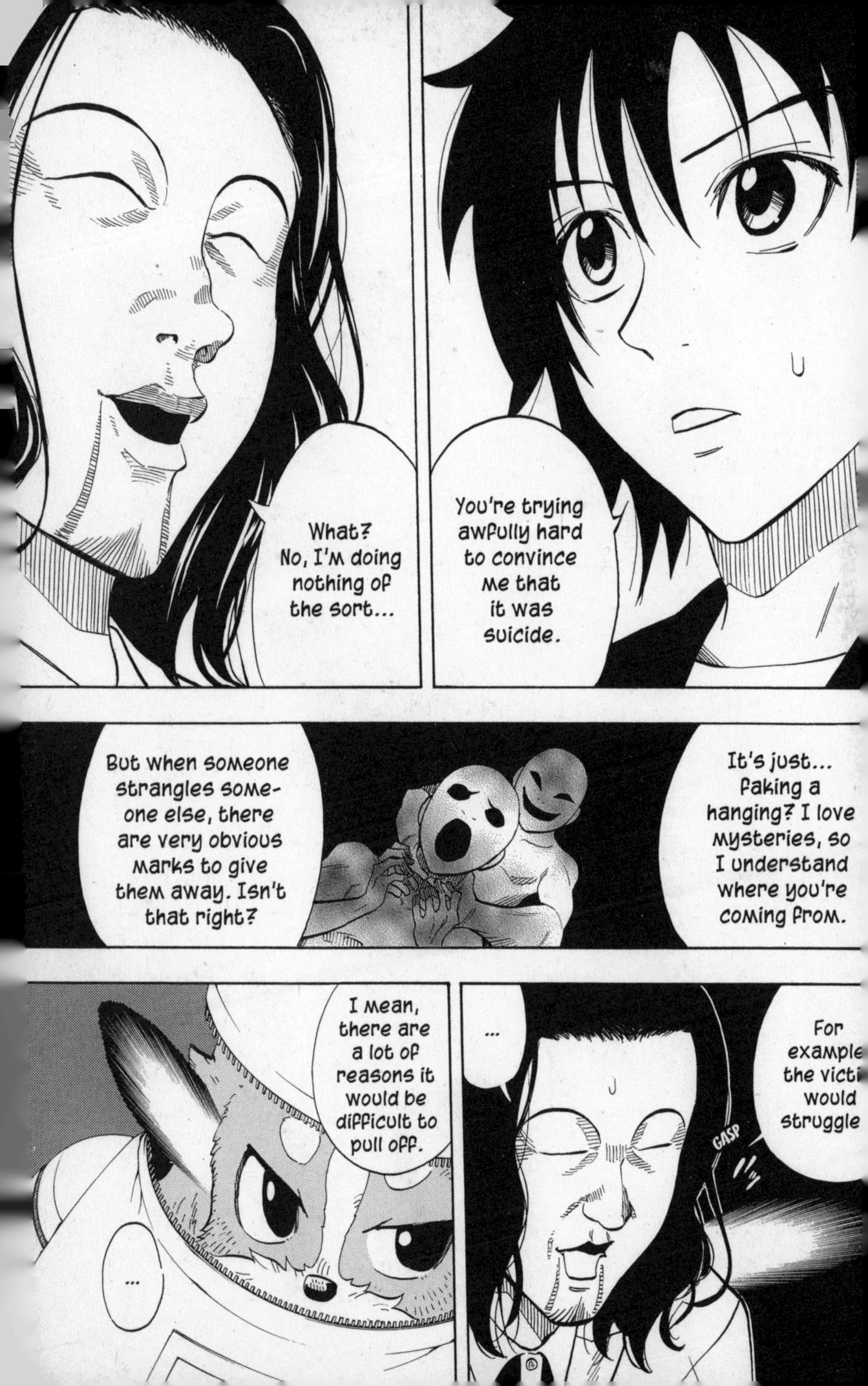
You're trying awfully hard to convince me that it was suicide.
What? No, I'm doing nothing of the sort...
It's just... faking a hanging? I love mysteries, so I understand where you're coming from.
But when someone strangles some-one else, there are very obvious marks to give them away. Isn't that right?
For example the victi would struggle
GASP
...
I mean, there are a lot of reasons it would be difficult to pull off.
...

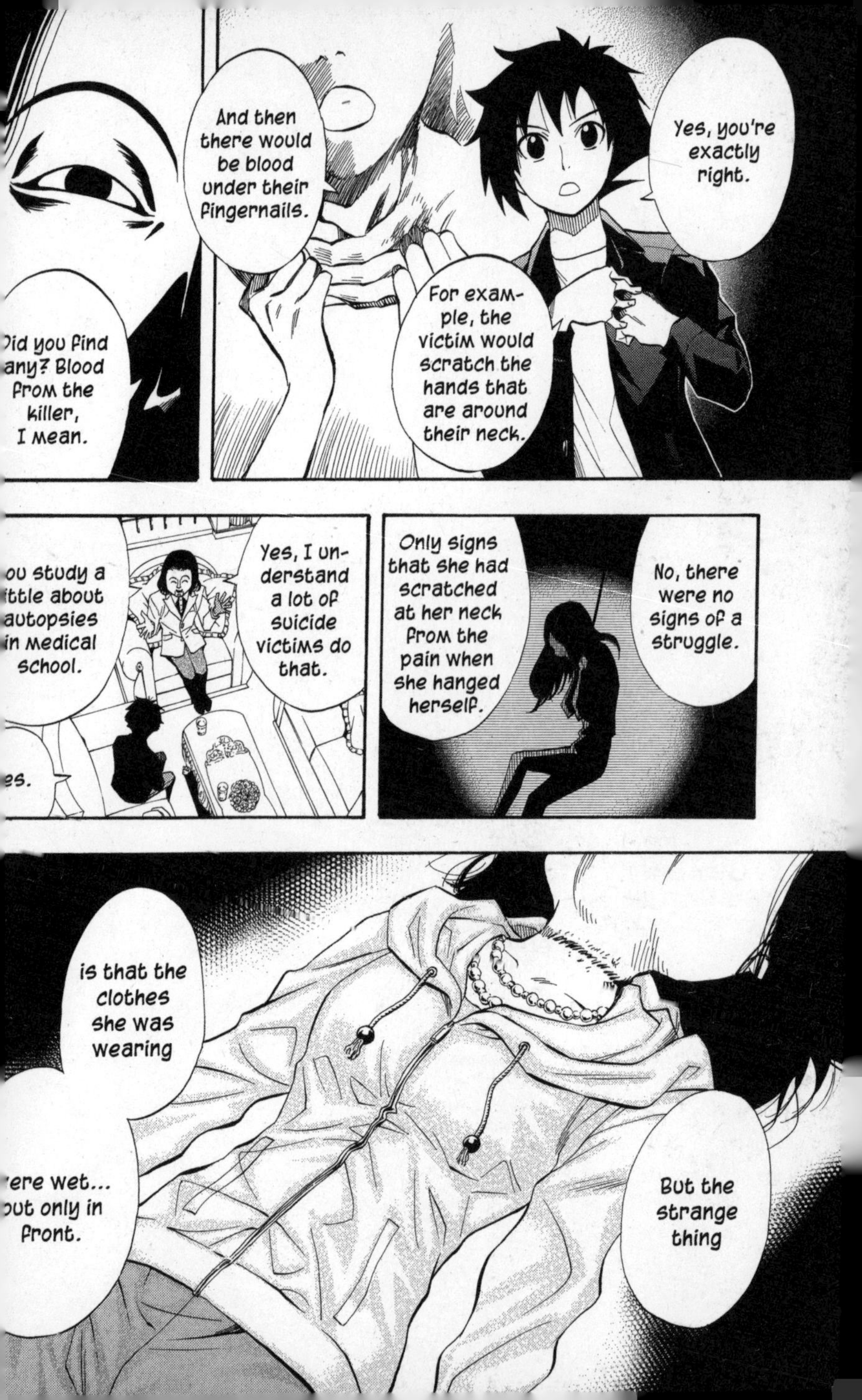
Yes, you're exactly right.
For example, the victim would scratch the hands that are around their neck.
And then there would be blood under their fingernails.
id you find any? Blood from the killer, I mean.
No, there were no signs of a struggle.
Only signs that she had scratched at her neck from the pain when she hanged herself.
Yes, I understand a lot of suicide victims do that.
ou study a ittle about autopsies in medical school.
es.
But the strange thing
is that the clothes she was wearing
ere wet... out only in front.

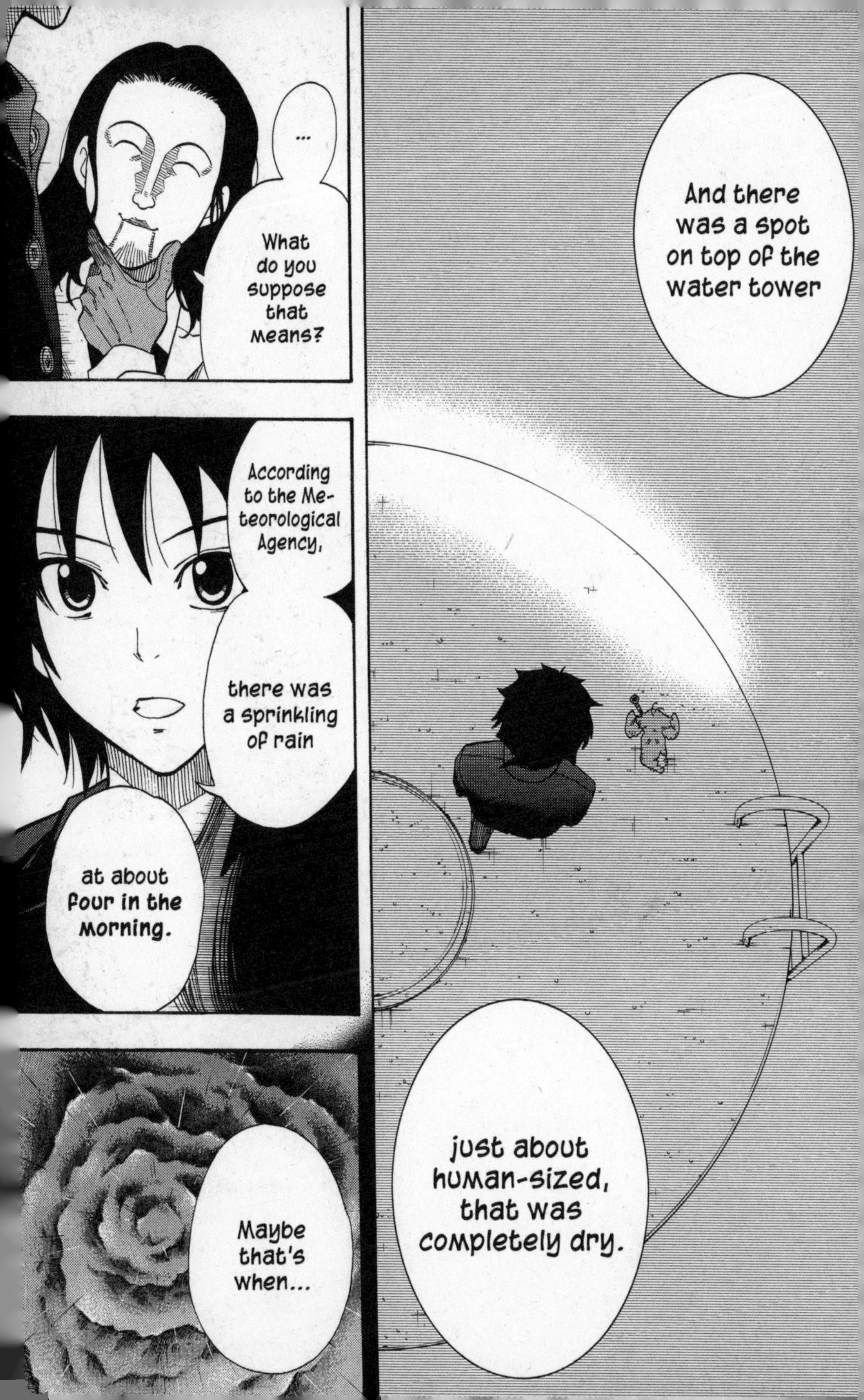
And there was a spot on top of the water tower
just about human-sized, that was completely dry.
...
What do you suppose that means?
According to the Meteorological Agency,
there was a sprinkling of rain
at about four in the morning.
Maybe that's when...

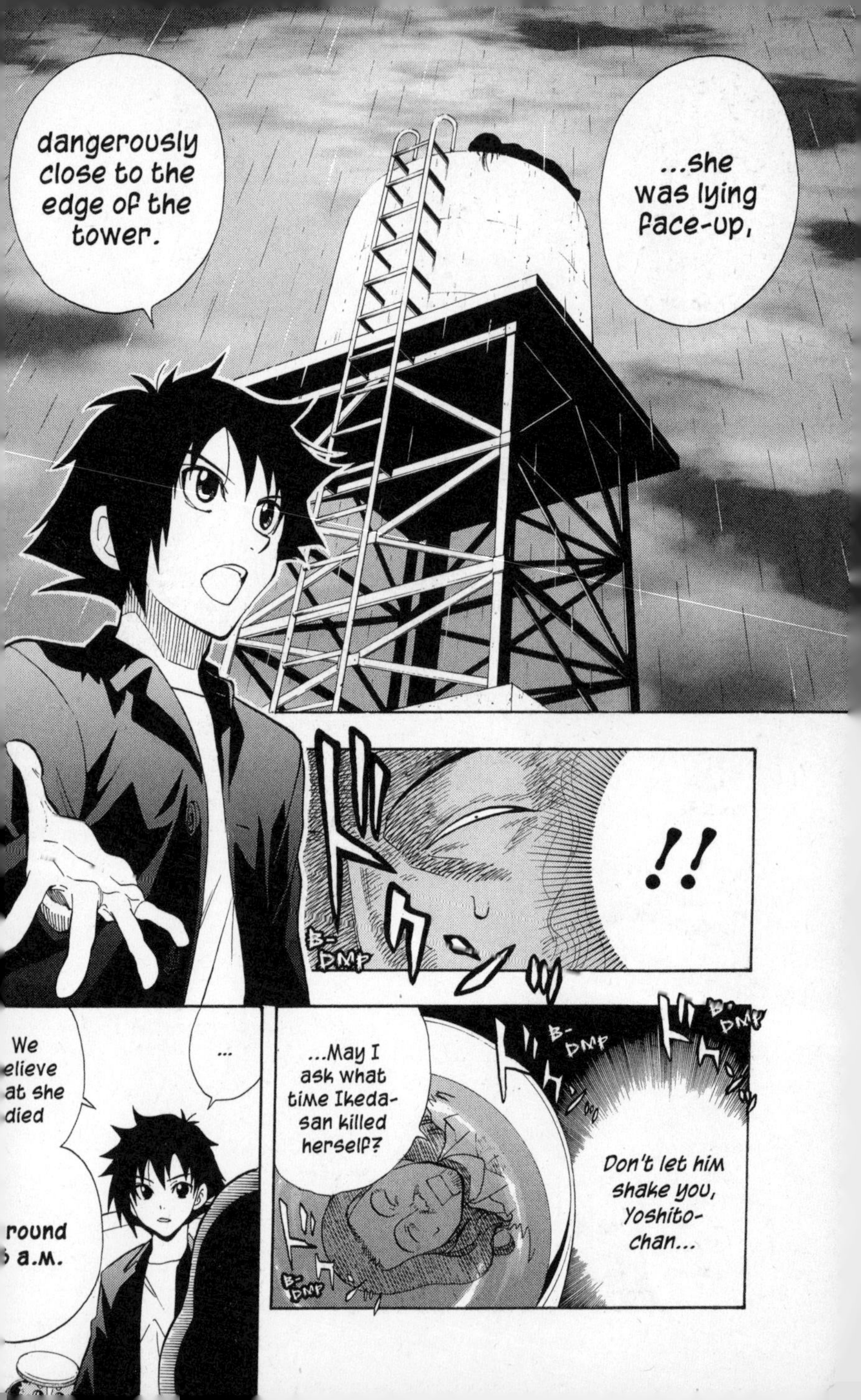
...she was lying face-up,
dangerously close to the edge of the tower.
!!
B-DMP
B-DMP
B-DMP
...May I ask what time Ikeda-san killed herself?
Don't let him shake you, Yoshito-chan...
B-DMP
...
We elieve at she died
round a.m.

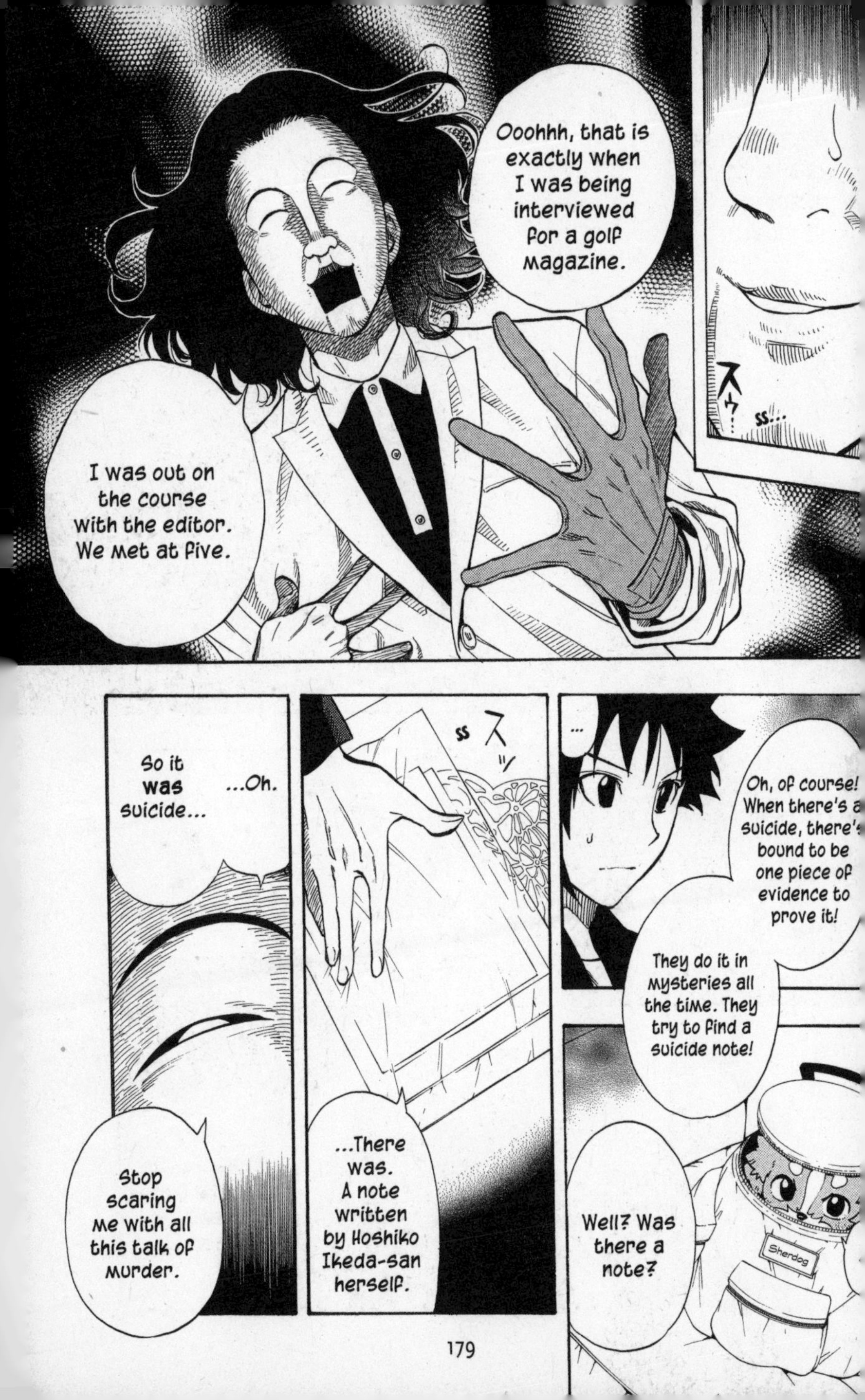
ss...
Ooohhh, that is exactly when I was being interviewed for a golf magazine.
I was out on the course with the editor. We met at five.
...
Oh, of course! When there's a suicide, there's bound to be one piece of evidence to prove it!
They do it in mysteries all the time. They try to find a suicide note!
Well? Was there a note?
Sherdog
ss
...There was. A note written by Hoshiko Ikeda-san herself.
So it was suicide...
...Oh.
Stop scaring me with all this talk of murder.

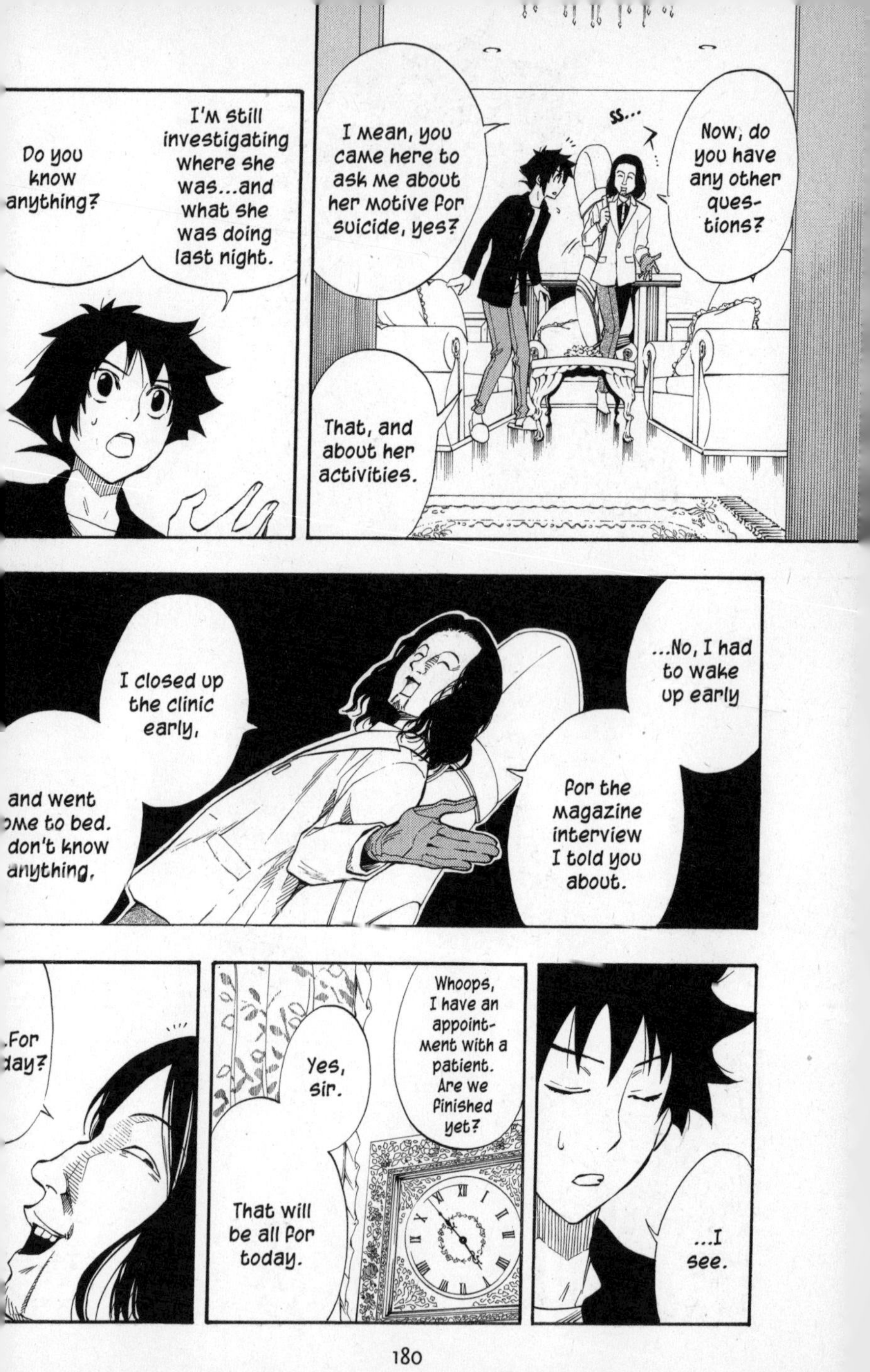
Now, do you have any other questions?
SS...
I mean, you came here to ask me about her motive for suicide, yes?
That, and about her activities.
I'm still investigating where she was...and what she was doing last night.
Do you know anything?
...No, I had to wake up early
for the magazine interview I told you about.
I closed up the clinic early,
and went
ome to bed.
don't know
anything.
...I see.
Whoops, I have an appointment with a patient. Are we finished yet?
Yes, sir.
That will be all for today.
.For
day?

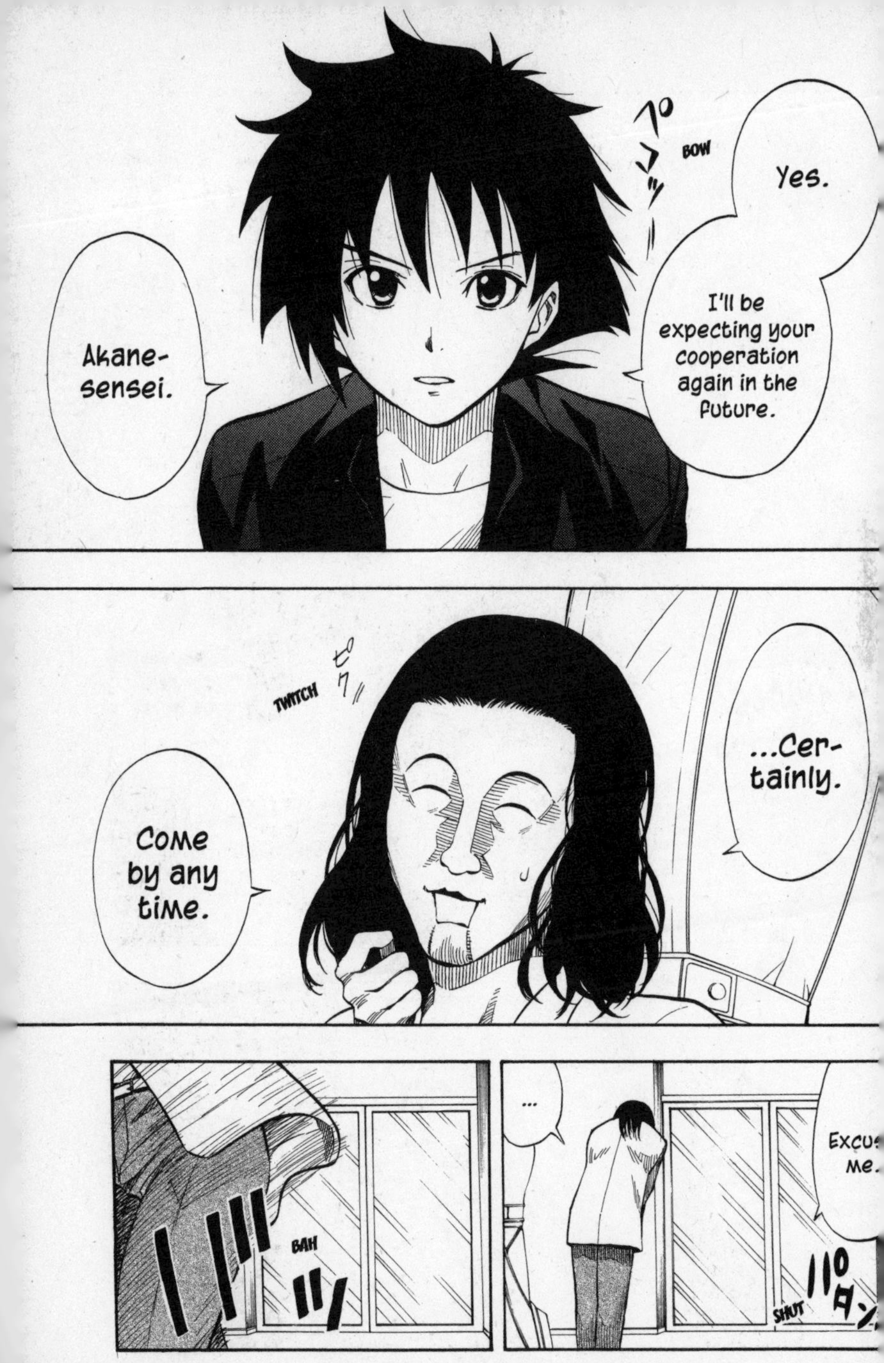
Yes.
BOW
I'll be expecting your cooperation again in the future.
Akane-sensei.
...Cer-tainly.
TWITCH
Come by any time.
Excu me.
SHUT
...
BAH

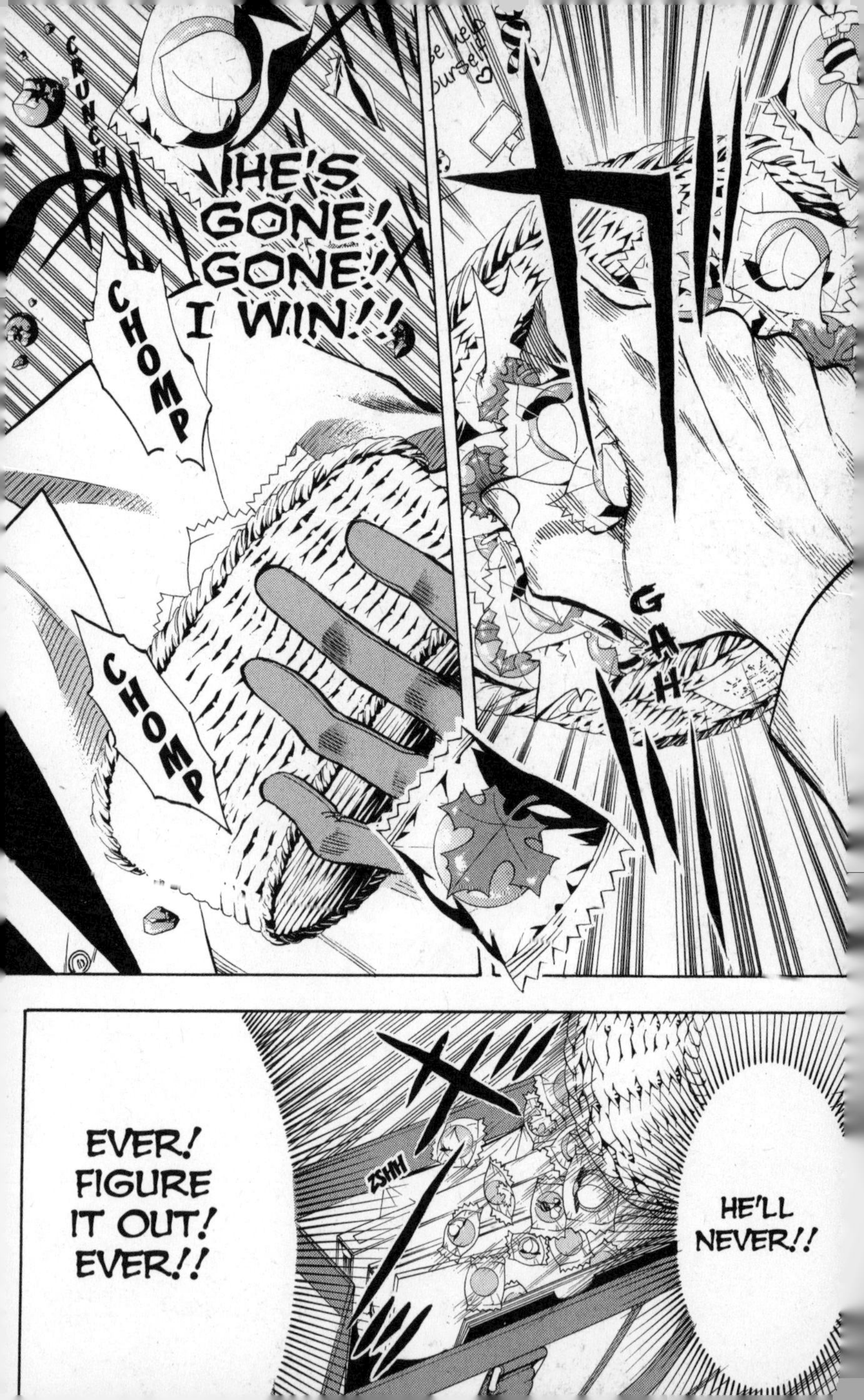
HE'S GONE! GONE! I WIN!!
CRUNCH
CHOMP
GAH
CHOMP
HE'LL NEVER!!
ZSHH
EVER! FIGURE IT OUT! EVER!!

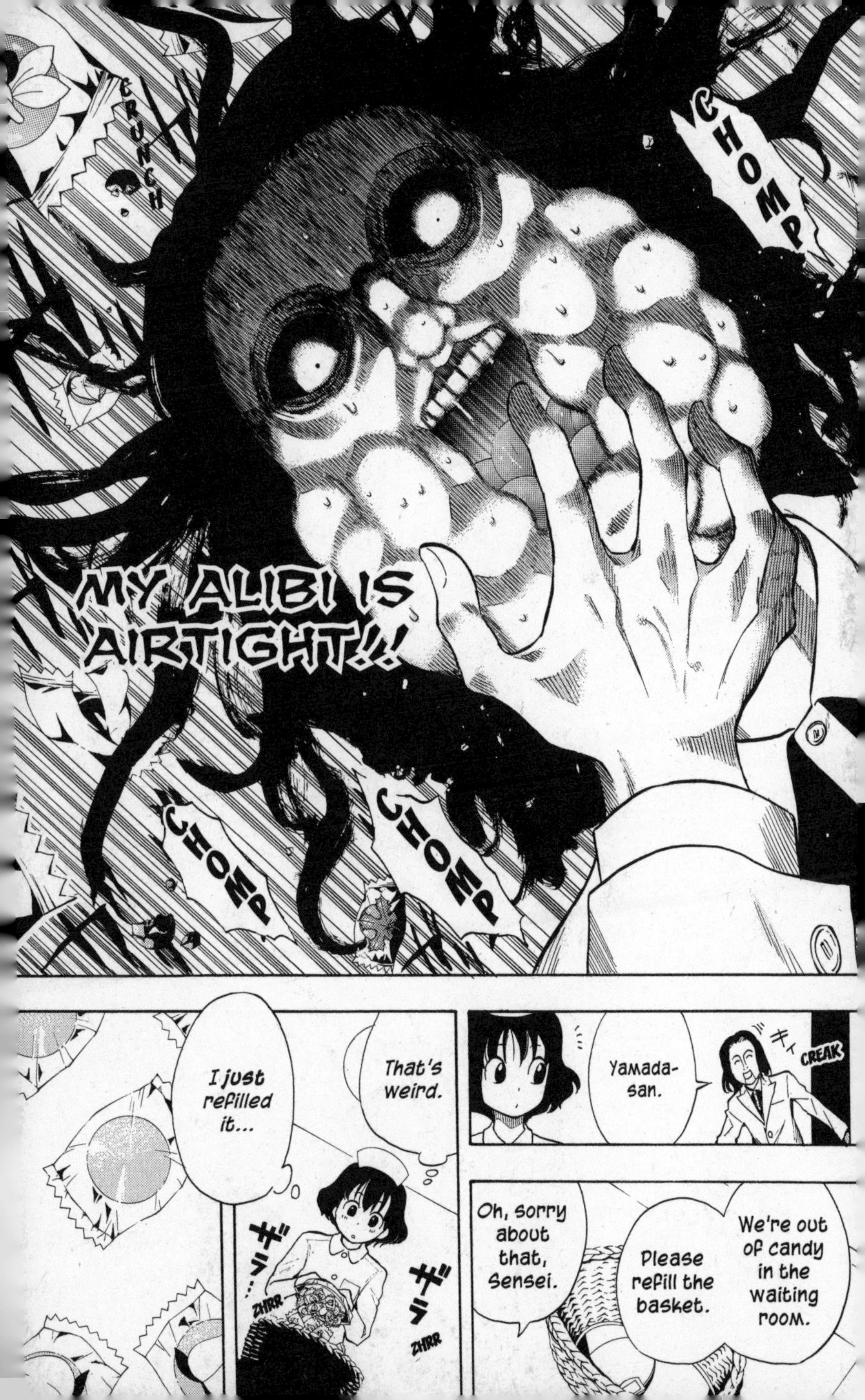
CHOMP
CRUNCH
MY ALIBI IS AIRTIGHT!!
CHOMP
CHOMP
キィ
CREAK
Yamada-san.
We're out of candy in the waiting room.
Please refill the basket.
Oh, sorry about that, Sensei.
That's weird.
I just refilled it...
ザラ
ZHRR
ザラ…
ZHRR

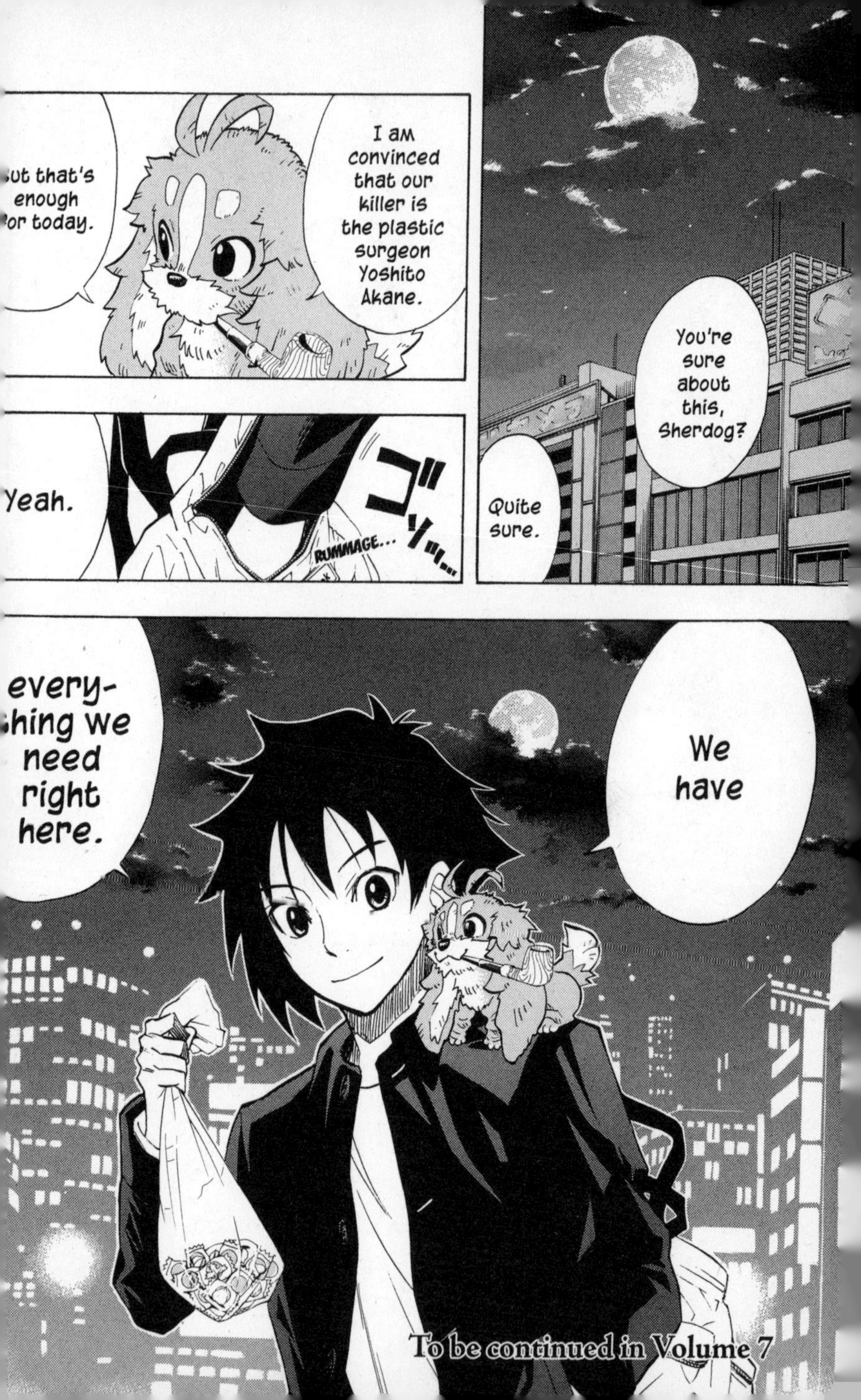
You're sure about this, Sherdog?
Quite sure.
I am convinced that our killer is the plastic surgeon Yoshito Akane.
ut that's enough or today.
Yeah.
ゴソ…
RUMMAGE…
We have
every- hing we need right here.
To be continued in Volume 7

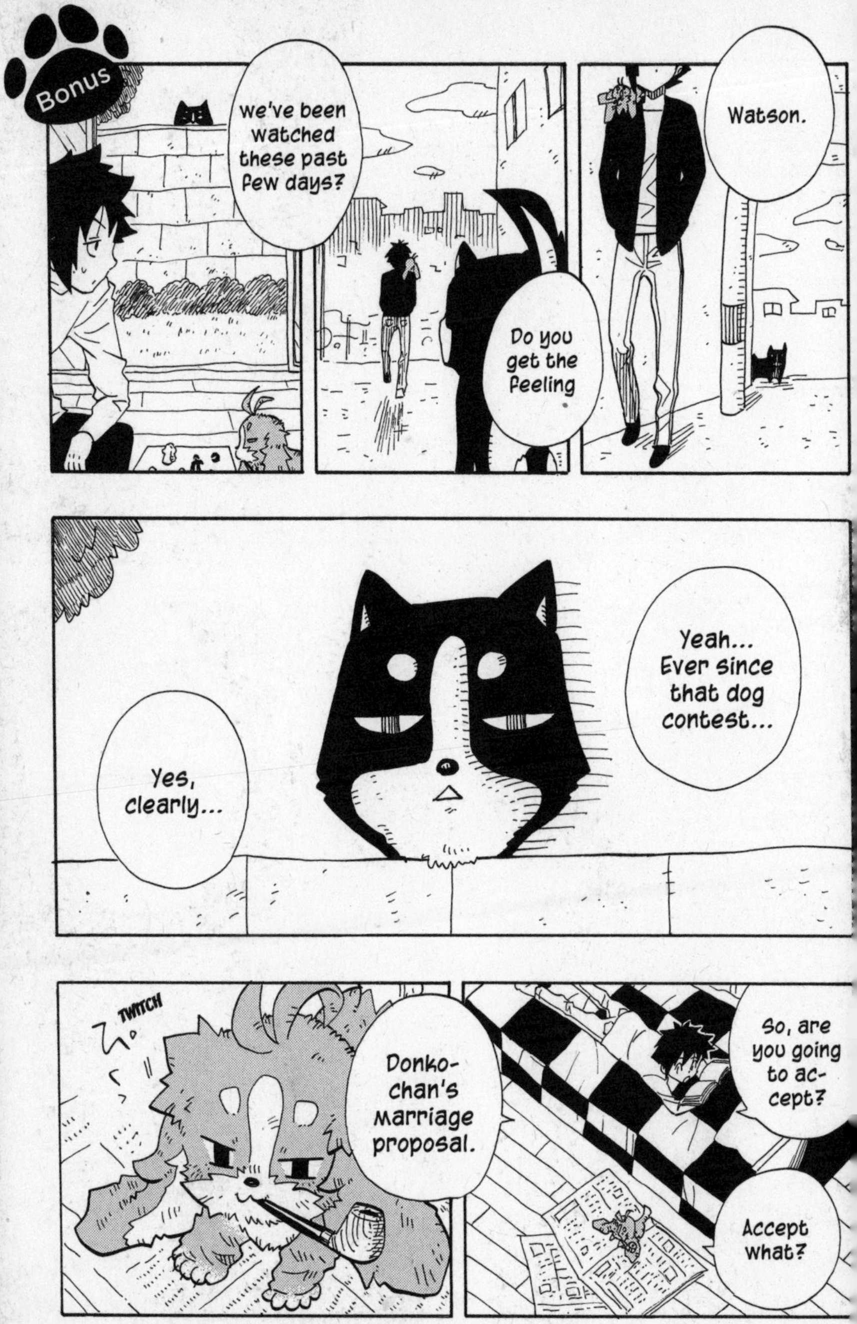
Bonus
Watson.
Do you get the feeling
we've been watched these past few days?
Yeah... Ever since that dog contest...
Yes, clearly...
So, are you going to ac-cept?
Accept what?
Donko-chan's marriage proposal.
TWITCH

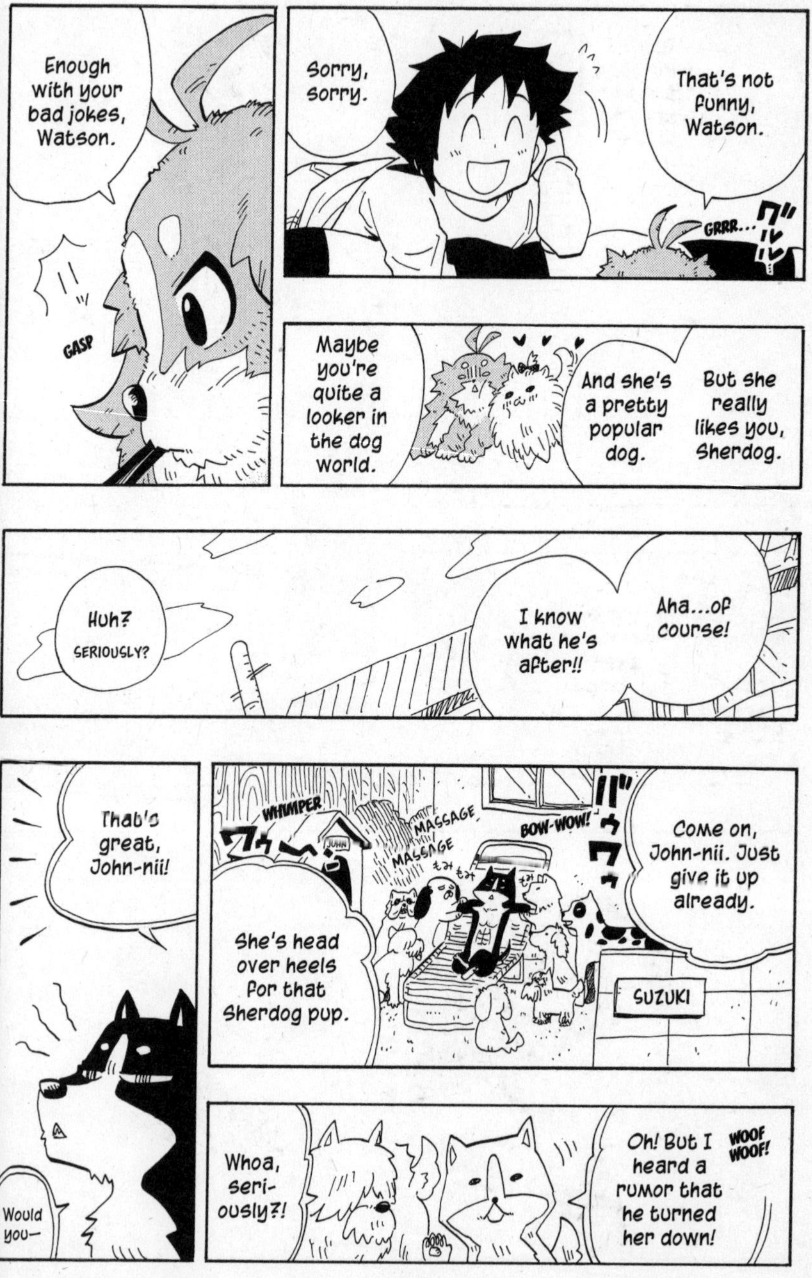
That's not funny, Watson.
Sorry, sorry.
GRRR...
But she really likes you, Sherdog.
And she's a pretty popular dog.
Maybe you're quite a looker in the dog world.
Enough with your bad jokes, Watson.
GASP
Aha...of course!
I know what he's after!!
Huh?
SERIOUSLY?
Come on, John-nii. Just give it up already.
BOW-WOW!
MASSAGE
MASSAGE
WHIMPER
JOHN
SUZUKI
She's head over heels for that Sherdog pup.
WOOF WOOF!
Oh! But I heard a rumor that he turned her down!
Whoa, seri-ously?!
That's great, John-nii!
Would you—

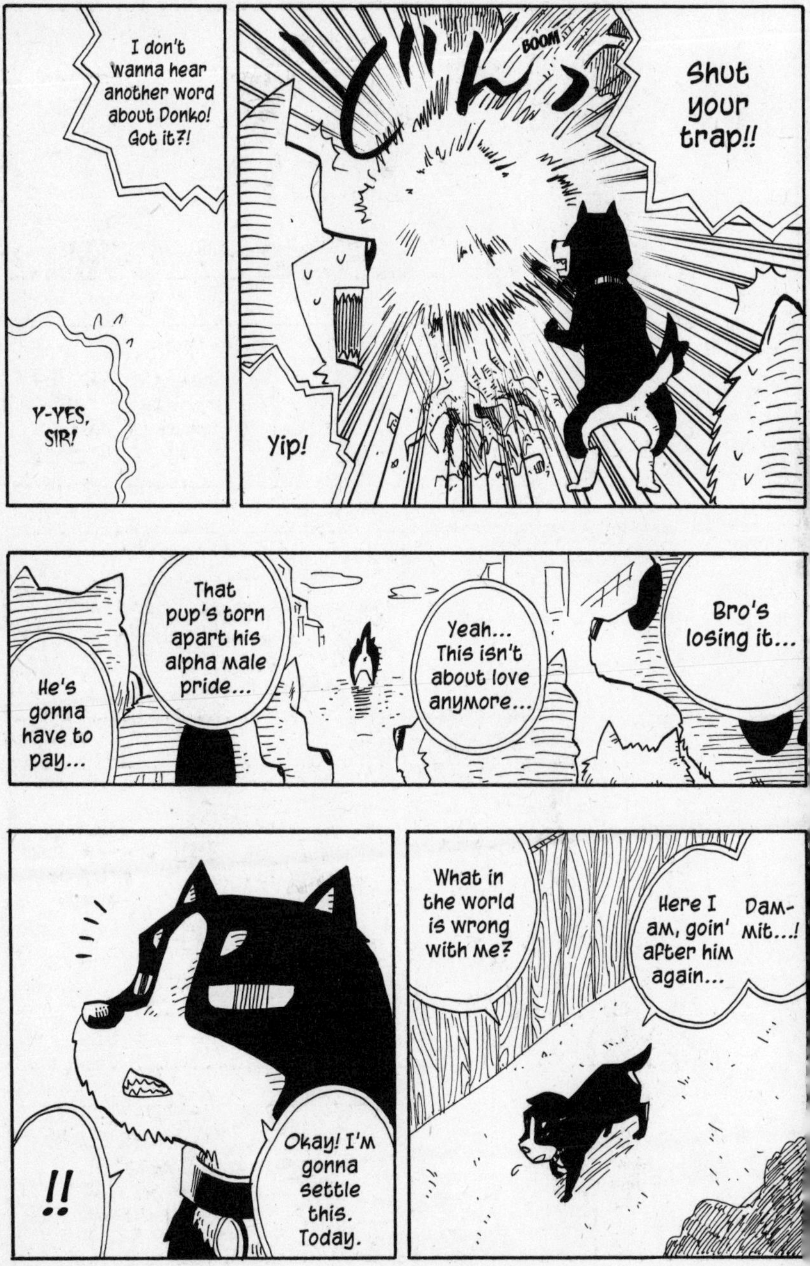
BOOM
Shut your trap!!
Yip!
I don't wanna hear another word about Donko! Got it?!
Y-YES, SIR!
Bro's losing it...
Yeah... This isn't about love anymore...
That pup's torn apart his alpha male pride...
He's gonna have to pay...
Dam-mit...!
Here I am, goin' after him again...
What in the world is wrong with me?
Okay! I'm gonna settle this. Today.
!!

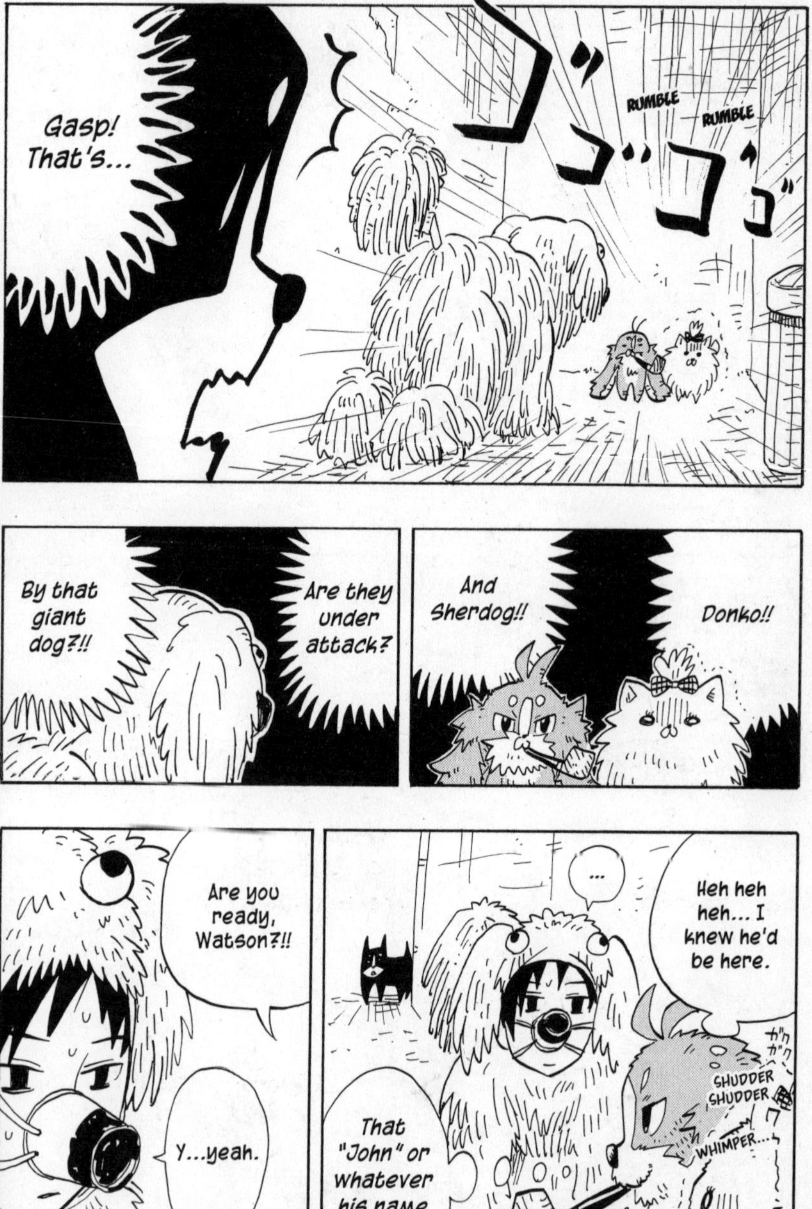
RUMBLE
RUMBLE
Gasp! That's...
Donko!!
And Sherdog!!
Are they under attack?
By that giant dog?!!
Heh heh heh... I knew he'd be here.
...
SHUDDER SHUDDER
WHIMPER...
That "John" or whatever his name is...
SHIVER SHIVER
Are you ready, Watson?!!
Y...yeah.

ANDO-SENSEI, EDITOR S-SAN, DESIGNER-SAN, PUBLISHING COMPANY-SAN, EVERYONE IN SALES, MY STAFF, MY MENTOR, MY FRIENDS

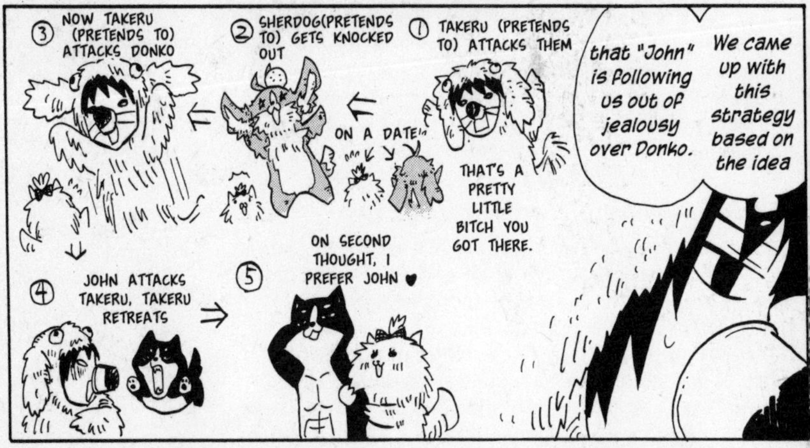

We came up with this strategy based on the idea
that "John" is following us out of jealousy over Donko.
① TAKERU (PRETENDS TO) ATTACKS THEM
ON A DATE
THAT'S A PRETTY LITTLE BITCH YOU GOT THERE.
② SHERDOG(PRETENDS TO) GETS KNOCKED OUT
③ NOW TAKERU (PRETENDS TO) ATTACKS DONKO
④ JOHN ATTACKS TAKERU, TAKERU RETREATS
⑤ ON SECOND THOUGHT, I PREFER JOHN ♥

MY FAMILY, AND ALL MY READERS, THANK YOU SO MUCH! I'LL KEEP WORKING HARD. (^^)

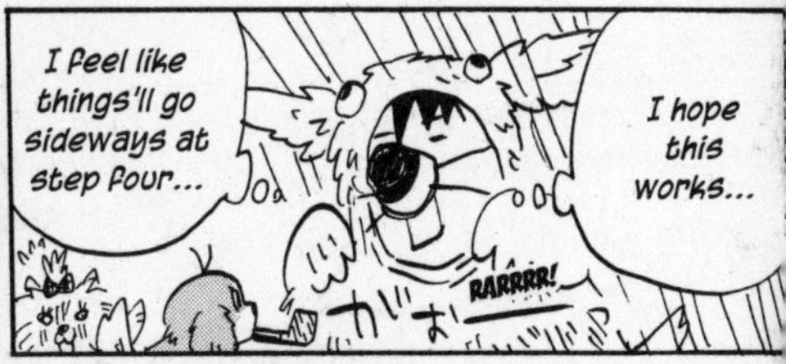

I hope this works...
I feel like things'll go sideways at step four...
RARRRR!

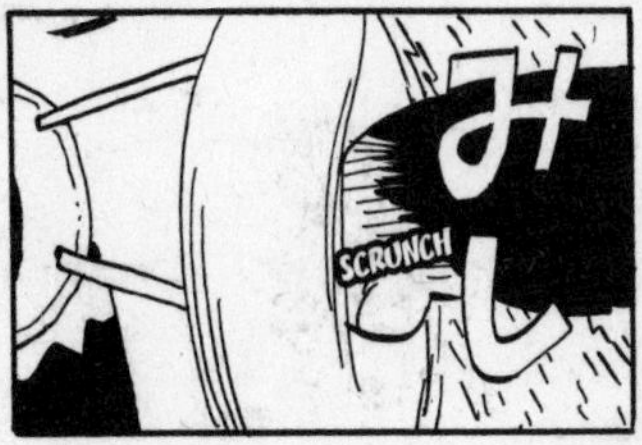

SCRUNCH

YUKI

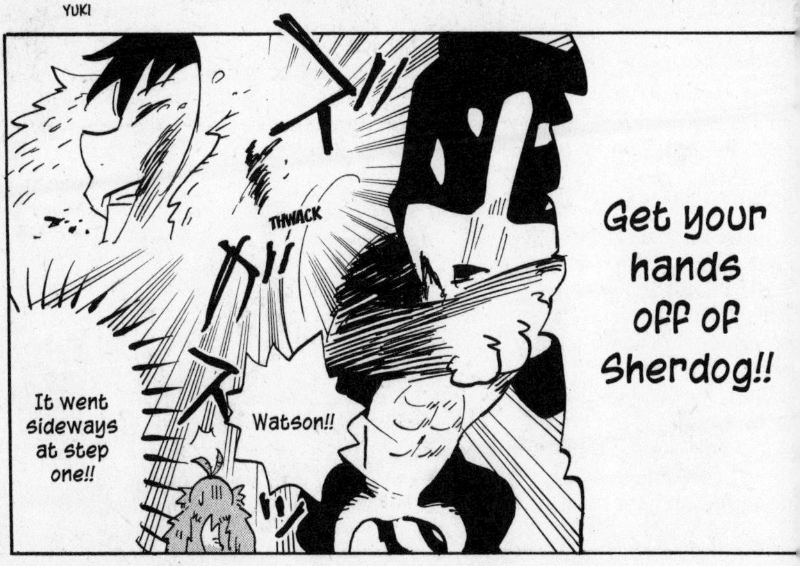

Get your hands off of Sherdog!!
THWACK
Watson!!
It went sideways at step one!!

OOPS! IT'S A CLIFFHANGER!!

Translation Notes

Japanese is a tricky language for most Westerners, and translation is often more art than science. For your edification and reading pleasure, here are notes on some of the places where we could have gone in a different direction with our translation of the work, or where a Japanese cultural reference is used.

Munakata-kun and Takeru-kun, page 13

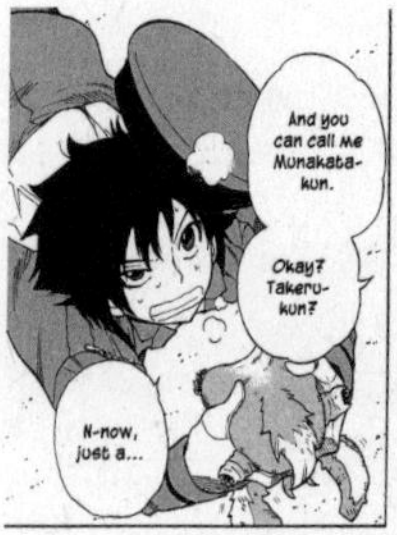

And you can call me Munakata-kun.
Okay? Takeru-kun?
N-now, just a...

A discerning reader will notice that Detective Munakata, while graciously insisting that he and Takeru are on good enough terms to use the more familiar name honorific of -kun, he still tells Takeru to call him by his family name—a more respectful form of address—while at the same time being presumptuous enough to call Takeru by his given name. In other words, he is asserting that he is above Takeru in his own personal hierarchy.

Yuuhi beer, page 20

The Sherlock Bones universe's version of the real-world Asahi beer. "Asahi" means "morning sun," while "Yuuhi" means "setting sun."

Rohto and Sante de U, page 26

Rohto is a Japanese pharmaceutical company known for its eye drops. Sante de U is a specific brand of eye drops, manufactured by Santen Pharmaceutical Co.

Gindaichi, page 46

There is a famous fictional Japanese detective named Kindaichi, of which this is a parody. Incidentally, Yuma Ando, the writer of Sherlock Bones, wrote another series under a different pen name about Kindaichi's grandson.

Gakitsuka No Laughing Special, page 65

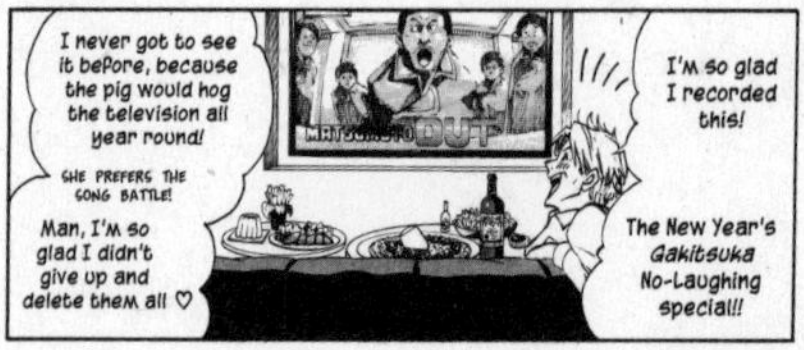

I'm so glad I recorded this!
The New Year's Gakitsuka No-Laughing special!!
I never got to see it before, because the pig would hog the television all year round!
SHE PREFERS THE SONG BATTLE!
Man, I'm so glad I didn't give up and delete them all ♡

Gakitsuka is short for Downtown no Gaki no Tsukai ya Arahende! (Downtown, This is No Task for Kids!), a popular Japanese variety show. On New Year's they have a "no-laughing" special, in which cast members are put in ridiculous situations and challenged not to laugh. Tsuzuki would not have been able to watch these throughout the years, because his wife preferred another big New Year's television event—the Kōhaku Utagassen

(Red and White Song Battle), in which teams of popular musical artists take part in a singing competition.

Capsule Monster, page 86

This is a reference to the Japanese action series, Ultra Seven. The hero has capsules containing monsters, much like Pokémon, that he will send to fight in his place when he is unable to fight himself.

Tō-Ops News, Yomikai Shimbun, and Shūkan Kentai, page 127

These are all parodies of existing Japanese newspapers. Namely, Tokyo Sports (To-Spo for short), Yomiuri Shimbun, and Shūkan Gendai, respectively.

Shichi-Go-San, page 13

Meaning "seven-five-three," Shichi-Go-San is a Japanese festival that celebrates children, specifically three- and seven-year-old girls, and three- and five-year-old boys. Parents dress their children in more formal attire and they visit shrines. In other words, Chief Yoshida is saying that in their suits and ties, Takeru and Kento look like very small children celebrating Shichi-Go-San.

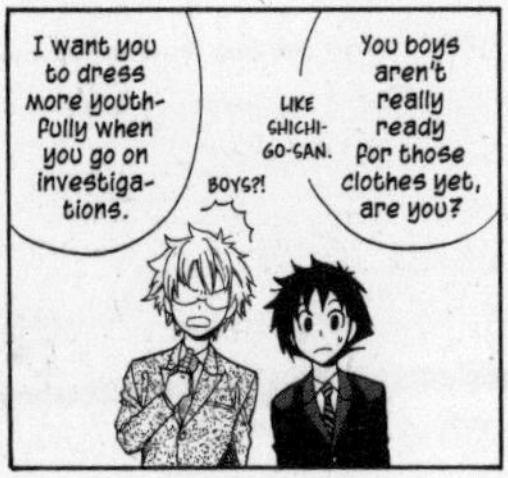
You boys aren't really ready for those clothes yet, are you?
LIKE SHICHI-GO-SAN.
BOYS?!
I want you to dress more youthfully when you go on investigations.

Taiyō ni Hoero!, page 134

"Taiyō ni Hoero!", or "Howl at the Sun!", is the title of a Japanese crime drama from the 70's and 80's. Detective Denim, or Jii-pan Keiji, is a nickname for one of the main characters, Jun Shibata.

Sherlock Bones volume 6 is a work of fiction. Names, characters, places, and incidents are the products of the author's imagination or are used fictitiously. Any resemblance to actual events, locales, or persons, living or dead, is entirely coincidental.

A Kodansha Comics Trade Paperback Original.

Sherlock Bones volume 6 copyright © 2012 Yuma Ando & Yuki Sato
English translation copyright © 2014 Yuma Ando & Yuki Sato

Published in the United States by Kodansha Comics,
an imprint of Kodansha USA Publishing, LLC, New York.

Publication rights for this English edition arranged through Kodansha Ltd., Tokyo.

First published in Japan in 2012 by Kodansha Ltd., Tokyo, as *Tanteiken Sherdock* volume 6.

ISBN 978-1-61262-555-3

Printed in the United States of America.

www.kodanshacomics.com

9 8 7 6 5 4 3 2 1

Translator: Alethea Nibley and Athena Nibley
Lettering: Kiyoko Shiromasa
Kodansha Comics edition cover design: Phil Balsman